R:E:D:

Rescue Endangered by Design

Rescue Endangered
by Design

Why is the most intellectual creature to ever walk Earth destroying its only home?

Up to 1 million plant and animal species are at risk of extinction and many will disappear within decades. Over the last 100 years chimpanzee numbers have decreased to less than 1/6th of their population, and many live in fragmented patches of forest, isolated from each other, with little chance of long- term survival.

Their forests are being destroyed as a result of logging, mining and agriculture, they are being hunted for the illegal bushmeat trade and hundreds of chimp mothers are shot to steal their infants for the live animal trade. Moreover, as people move deeper into the forest the chimpanzees may be infected by diseases, to which they have not built up resistance. Orang-utans and gibbons are also losing their forest habitats especially as a result of the proliferation of oil palm plantations.

The recent UN report on biodiversity provides a stark warning, we humans are threatening all life on Planet Earth with extinction. Every species has a role to play in the tapestry of life and if we do not protect this biodiversity, if we continue over-consuming and wasting natural resources, the tapestry will fall apart. This, of course, is what scientists have been predicting for years and what I have been speaking about in lectures all around the world.

So is there hope?
I believe there is a window of time during which, if we all get together and use our extraordinary intellects, we should be able to start to heal the harm we have inflicted on Mother Earth and at least slow down the climate crisis. But we need everyone – from all walks of life. From politicians to shop keepers, from lawyers, teachers, parents and children.

Together we must:

- Make changes in our typically unsustainable lifestyles. We must ask how our daily actions may harm the environment and future generations. We must minimise our consumption, stop wasting food and water and other commodities, eat less meat (or become vegetarian or vegan) and move towards renewable energy.
- Alleviate poverty, for the rural poor will cut down the last trees to get more land in their desperation to grow food for themselves or make charcoal to get money in a desperate effort to survive. And the urban poor will buy the very cheapest things – they cannot afford to ask how it was produced and whether this harmed the environment.

- And we must tackle the problem of human overpopulation and the astounding proliferation of our livestock. How can we expect continued economic development on a planet with finite natural resources – resources on which we rely for clean air and water and on which millions depend for their livelihood. Indeed in some places, natural resources are being consumed more rapidly than nature can restore them.

Fortunately nature is amazingly resilient: places we have destroyed, given time and help, can once again support life, and endangered species can be given a second chance. And a growing number of people, especially young people, are aware of the problems and are fighting for the survival of our only home, Planet Earth.

Every one of us makes some difference – every day.
And we can choose what kind of difference we make.

This wonderful book highlights some of the planets endangered animal species that are in danger of extinction. Through raising awareness of their plight, and having conversations, the book may encourage people to do their bit to create a better world for future generations, and have fun knitting. The book has cleverly highlighted for every species the reasons why each animal is endangered and what YOU can do to help.

I wish Dorte, Lisa and Polly great success with this book and thank them for raising awareness as well as funds, for the chimpanzee and the work the Institute undertakes in Africa with the communities to protect wildlife and nature.

Jane Goodall, PhD, DBE
Founder – the Jane Goodall Institute
& UN Messenger of Peace

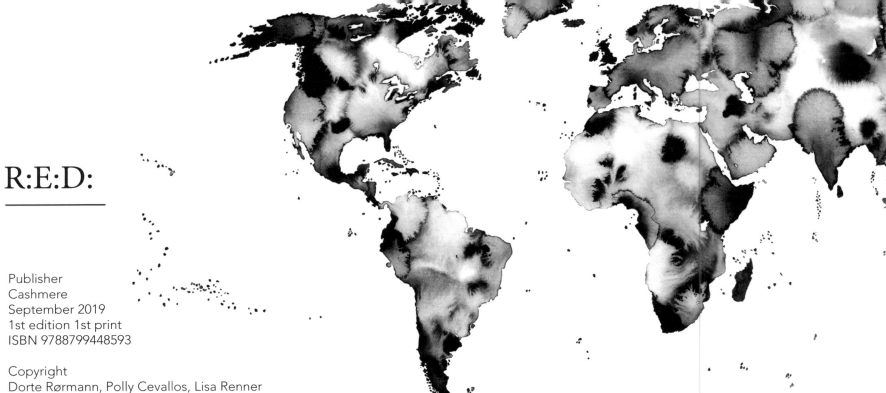

R:E:D:

Publisher
Cashmere
September 2019
1st edition 1st print
ISBN 9788799448593

Copyright
Dorte Rørmann, Polly Cevallos, Lisa Renner

Designers
Mea Andresen
Laura Locher
Bruno Kleist
Emalie Dam
Charlotte Kaae
Lisa Renner

Illustrations
Lea Hoffmann

Fashion photography
Asger Mortensen

Make-up and Styling
Norma Denmark
Luupe
Mos Mosh
Gabba

Layout consulting
CO/PLUS
Gaute Høgh, Thomas B Nielsen

Proofreading
ML Text Mette Lindquist
Proofreading, patterns
Chrissie Day

Print
Frederiksberg Bogtrykkeri

www.rescueendangeredbydesign.com

Looking forward

To enrich your lives through knitting
To inspire you through the animal stories
To live a compassionate, sustainable, joyful life

One dark and dull day in November, two friends stepped into a little yarn shop in southern Denmark. And what was meant to be a cosy yarn shopping, turned out to become the first step of a very long and fiery journey, which has created the book that is now, finally, in your hands.
A vague idea from Lisa, ignited by the fire from Polly, grabbed by the sharp attention of Dorte turned into a book project, which we have been involved in for nearly two years and which we hope will inspire you all.

It is a troubled world. The climate crisis, loss of biodiversity and the mass extinction of animals are well known. Experts and activists have predicted this for decades. Now, finally the world community is listening. And this creates a vital but fragile window of opportunity.

With this book we want to move from anxiety to action. We want to raise awareness for endangered species all over the world. We want to speak out for those who cannot speak for themselves. We aim to show that there are things we can change in our everyday lives to avoid mass extinction of animal species.
We want to show that there is still hope. However, the time to act is now.

We hope you will learn a lot about the 17 animals portrayed in this book. We hope that through knitting these jumpers you will not only find the joy of knitting and of giving, but also be inspired by all the animals to share their stories and to help the Planet in your way. It is by sharing our stories and listening to the stories of others we become compassionate beings.

Rescue Endangered by Design

Dorte Rørmann, Polly Cevallos and Lisa Renner
September 2019

R:E:D: maps

—————————————————

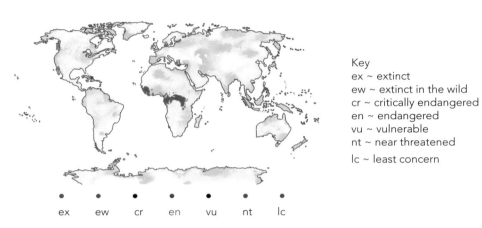

Key
ex ~ extinct
ew ~ extinct in the wild
cr ~ critically endangered
en ~ endangered
vu ~ vulnerable
nt ~ near threatened

lc ~ least concern

ex   ew   cr   en   vu   nt   lc

This book is called R:E:D: Rescue Endangered by Design.
The word 'red' is a powerful word, and it means so many things on so many different levels. It's the colour of alarm, passion, action and vital energy.
In many cultures, it is a colour used to signal the need to stop and pay attention. It is also the name of the global list of threatened animals, created by the International Union for Conservation of Nature (IUCN) started in 1964, and updated regularly. It is an indispensable tool for scientists working with species at risk and is called the Red List of Threatened Species.

Maps have been created for every animal that is featured in this book, showing where it lives. The different symbols used, highlighted in red, shows the Red List categories and criteria, used by scientists and conservationists to identify the population status for each animal. It ranges from the far left of Extinct which are species no longer seen on this Earth, like the Dodo bird, through to Endangered Species to animals of Least Concern.

Choosing Animals
From the Red List we chosen 16 endangered non iconic species and one vulnerable animal species, representing all the continents and different habitats of Planet Earth.
We chose these animals to highlight all the different family types of the animal kingdom, ranging from corals through to birds, reptiles, marsupials to great apes.
The animals featured in this book are also flagship species for their kind. Like the chimpanzee represents all other great apes and primates worldwide.

We also chose our different animals to show the different kinds of threats that put them in danger of extinction. The polar bear is a great example of how a species is being affected by the changes we have created in the Earth's climate patterns. And with all the animals, we have highlighted some of the organisations that are supporting each species. And if you would like to help, we have listed what you can do to help.

IUCN and the RED list

Humanity's actions are compromising our food and water supplies, our climate and, increasingly, our political stability. The growing scarcity of natural resources is contributing to insecurity, conflicts and forced migration flows. Climate change and population growth are exacerbating these pressures. Meanwhile, species are disappearing up to 1,000 times faster than before humans got involved and many ecosystems are on the brink of collapse. Unless we take action together, the degradation of nature could threaten the very survival of our own species.

But there is no need to succumb to this dark picture of our future. Because we have a very powerful anecdote, conservation. Conservation can help turn this pessimistic vision around, if we take action now.

For over 70 years, IUCN has been proving that conservation works. And these seven cumulative decades of experience have provided the world with the knowledge needed to take action. So, the problem is not a technical one, it is one of will. As a global society, we have a singular opportunity to design a new future, one where humans and nature thrive together.

To achieve this vision, we need to get the next decade right. With the Sustainable Development Goals giving us a clear and beautiful picture of what our Planet and those that inhabit it could look like.

This book called R:E:D: shows a similar optimism and provides a model for how individuals can do something to make this a better Planet.
Knitting like nature has known values for us all.

I thank the three authors for utilising the IUCN Red List of Threatened Species for choosing their endangered animals, and also the animal texts which are derived from the work of the thousands of scientists and experts that work cooperatively, through the IUCN Red List, to build on the conservation stories of hope and what we can do to help.

Grethel Aguilar Rojas
IUCN Acting Director General

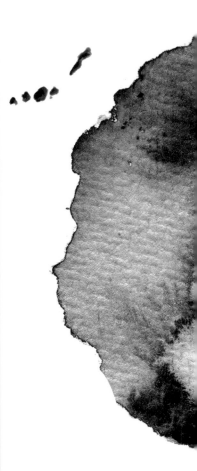

Africa

African Wild Dog

Chimpanzee

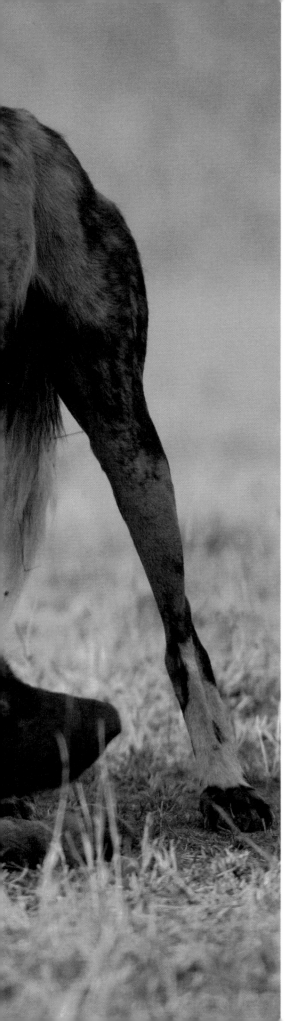

African Wild Dog

African wild dogs have enormous home ranges and are constantly on the move.

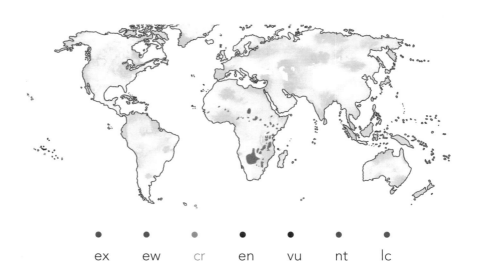

● ● ● ● ● ● ●
ex ew cr en vu nt lc

latin name: Lycaon pictus
status: Critically endangered
threats: habitat fragmentation, human-wildlife conflict, diseases

African Wild Dog

Did you know that the dog family, called Canids, has 34 different kinds of dogs in it? They all have elongated legs, an amazing sense of smell, using their noses to find not only their food but also to find each other and find out where their predators may be.

All Canids lack sweat glands, so instead of sweating to regulate their body temperature, like we do, they will open their mouths and pant to regulate their temperature.

Canids are native to every continent except Antarctica and Australia, as the people that arrived into Australia brought their dogs with them, now commonly called dingoes.

The largest wild Canid is the gray wolf that weighs up to 43 kilos, with the smallest being the Fennec fox weighing only 6 kilos.

They eat only meat and are all very social and live in groups.

The African wild dog is one of the world's most social and distinctive members of the dog family. Their short wiry coat is distinctly coloured, and highly variable combinations of black, yellow-brown and white is seen, each with its own distinctive pattern.

Also known as Cape hunting dog or painted dog, the African wild dog is in its own group, in the Canidae family, which also includes wolves, jackals, coyotes, dogs and foxes.

African wild dogs are very effective predators. They use extraordinary cooperation and teamwork to pursue and bring down their prey. As a result, possibly 70% of their hunts are successful, comparing it to the success rate of lions which may only be 10%.

They have an extremely powerful bite with specialised molars for shearing meat and breaking bone and they have good vision and hearing. Large rounded ears lined with numerous muscles allow the dogs to swivel them like two radar dishes, picking up the minutest of sounds. Long legs, a lean build and rapid muscle recovery all assist in making this animal a formidable endurance hunter.

It was only recently discovered, that they use sneezing to 'vote' on their hunting decisions. It is thought they communicate when hunting, using calls and body language to signal each other. They weigh 20-30 kilos and hunt mainly medium-sized antelope, but they are capable of bringing down a 250 kilos wildebeest.

This cooperation extends also to their social structure; they have complex hierarchies that are tight and highly organised. The African wild dog lives in packs of up to 30 members all answering to an alpha pair who sire most of the offspring in a mature pack.

Wild dogs are obligate social breeders, with the pack rather than the individual considered the breeding unit. Packs typically form when a group of same-sex litter mates leave their natal pack and join a subgroup of the opposite sex.

The pack regurgitates food for the young and this is also extended to adults, to the point of being the bedrock of their social life. On the whole, they are surprisingly non-aggressive, for example they do not fight over food instead beg to indicate their wish to eat.

They breed at the coldest time of the year and after approximately 70 days, the alpha female gives birth to 10 -11 pups, who are taken care of by the whole pack. Pups are allowed to eat first whilst adults wait their turn. They are known to share food and assist ill and weak pack members, never abandoning their old or sick.

The African wild dog ranges particularly widely and needs larger areas than almost any other terrestrial carnivore species in the world. Wild dogs are nomadic animals and can traverse 50 km in a single day. As a result, their territories are typically between 400 and 600 square km, with ranges as large as 2,500 recorded in the Serengeti. They only remain in one area when they have very young pups.

African wild dogs are generalist predators, occupying a range of habitats in Sub-Saharan Africa. Early studies in the Serengeti National Park, Tanzania, led to a belief that African wild dogs were primarily an open plains species, more recent data indicate they reach their highest densities in thicker bush.
African wild dogs are rarely seen, even where they are relatively common, and it appears that populations have always existed at very low densities. They occupy very discrete areas of resident range, and at present there are 39 distinct sub-populations estimated to range in size from two to 276 mature individuals.

The principal threat to African wild dogs is human-wildlife conflict caused by habitat fragmentation, where their homes are broken up by human land use, which increases their contact with people and domestic animals, resulting in increased human-wildlife conflict and transmission of infectious diseases.
Even in large, well-protected reserves or in stable populations, African wild dogs live at low population densities. Predation by lions, and perhaps competition with spotted hyaenas, contribute to keeping African wild dog numbers below the level that their prey base could support. Such low population density brings its own problems.

"Catastrophic" events such as outbreaks of disease may threaten small populations, when larger populations have a greater probability of recovery – such an event seems to have led to the local extinction of the African wild dog population in the Serengeti ecosystem on the Kenya-Tanzania border.
All of these causes are associated with human encroachment on African wild dog habitat and, as such, have not ceased and are unlikely to be reversible across the majority of the species' historical range.

The hope

Regional conservation strategies have been developed for the species, and many range states have used these strategies as templates for their own national action plans.
They all encourage land use planning to maintain and expand wild dog populations, outreach to improve public perceptions of wild dogs at all levels of society.

Established in Australia, the Painted Dog Conservation works specifically with dog populations in Zimbabwe, at Hwange National Park. Their mission is to create an environment where painted dogs can thrive. There are 700 painted dogs in Zimbabwe.
They are achieving their goals by designing a conservation model that works in the long term, to make a significant difference in the dog population in Zimbabwe. They employ more than 60 people from the local villages to run their conservation programs and run the education and outreach programs.

These programs include their Anti-poaching Unit, which patrols local areas daily to provide protection for the dogs. They also manage a rehabilitation facility where they treat injured and orphaned dogs before releasing them back where they were found.

Some organisations helping this species
IUCN Canid Specialist Group |
Rangewide Conservation Programme for Cheetah and African wild dog |
Botswana Predator Conservation | Zambia Carnivore Project | Serengeti Wild Dog Conservation Fund.

What you can do to help
Learn more about these dogs through the organisations that are saving them, volunteer or donate to their cause.

Peek a boo

BY
Mea Andresen

Yarn Isager Alpaca 1

Pattern P. 268

Unseen

BY
Mea Andresen

Yarn Madelinetosh, Light and Prairie

Pattern P. 271

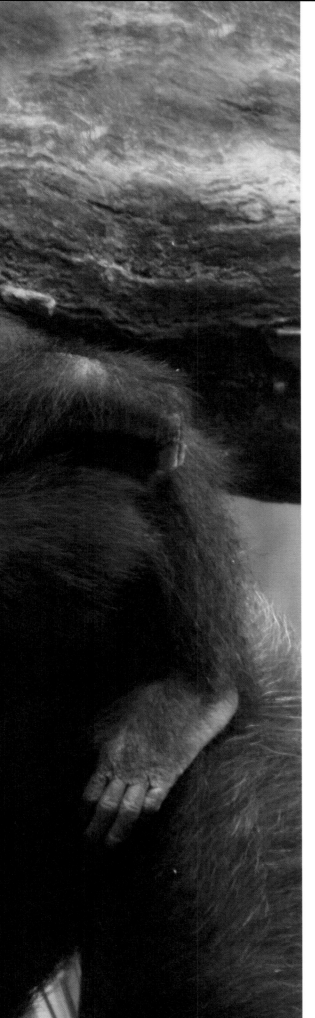

Chimpanzee

Just like us, Chimpanzees have an opposable thumb, which is not aligned to the other 4 fingers on our hands.

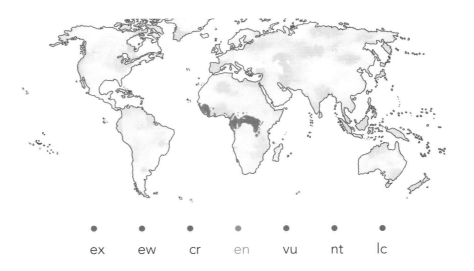

●   ●   ●   ●   ●   ●   ●

ex   ew   cr   en   vu   nt   lc

latin name: Pan troglodytes
status: Endangered
threats: pet and bush meat trade, habitat loss, diseases

Chimpanzee

Chimpanzees are part of the grouping called primates, which has over 300 different species and includes monkeys, apes and prosimians and lemurs. Humans are primates, too.

Some primate species serve as indicator species for the health of their habitats, others disperse seeds helping their forests maintain their cover and, in many places, primates help draw tourists to them, which is a great source of community revenue where you can also see iconic species face to face.

The biggest living primate is the African eastern lowland gorilla weighing almost 200 kilos and standing just over 1,70 metres, and the smallest is Berthe's mouse lemur being only 9.2 cm long and weighing 30 grams, found only on the island of Madagascar.

Apes are a grouping of primates that includes great apes: chimpanzee, bonobo, gorillas and orang-utan and the lesser apes, called gibbons.

Chimpanzees and bonobos are more closely related to humans than to any other great ape, they share at least 98.6% of human DNA. They have black hair covering almost their entire body, short legs and long arms that extend below the knees, which help them to climb trees. Their faces are flat with big eyes, small nose and wide mouth. When born, chimpanzees' skins are pink and gradually as they grow older, become darker, often going completely black. Chimpanzee and the bonobo are genetically almost identical; however they show very different behaviour. Chimpanzees males are dominant, whilst bonobo females are dominant. The chimpanzee has four known subspecies, with little physical differences between them.

Chimpanzees live in communities; they can be as small as 20 and as large as 140 individuals. Males will stay in the community of their birth, while females may migrate to neighbouring communities when they are sexually mature.
Females reach puberty around 7-8 years and have their first offspring at around 10-12 years, whilst boys reach puberty a bit later. Females usually have a baby every 4-5 years, when the last offspring is weaned. Mothers look after their young for many years and will have lifelong bonds with their offspring.

The chimpanzees' community is called a fission-fusion group, which means they come and go in different sub-groups, constantly changing. They may not see members of their community for days or weeks, but when they do, they recognise them as belonging to their community and greet them. Towards other communities they are aggressive and they protect their territory.

They groom themselves and each other, not only just for hygiene, but also for creating strong social bonds with their community, especially individuals that are important.

Chimpanzees lack a tail, making them great apes and not monkeys, and their opposable thumbs and toes help them grasp objects easily and climb up trees with ease.
Chimpanzees live in tropical forests and woodlands to the savannahs of West and Central Africa in over twenty countries. They can be found from Tanzania to Mali, yet occupy only a fraction of their former territory. The largest populations are found in the Congo Basin in countries like Gabon, Democratic Republic of Congo and Cameroon.

There are three main reasons why chimpanzees are endangered.
Firstly, they are hunted by humans for live animal trade (pets, entertainment and zoos) or because of conflict and competition with farmers, and sometimes affected by the bushmeat trade.

Secondly, their habitat, is being destroyed by humans. The rainforest of equatorial Africa is being destroyed, humans need timber for cooking or building their homes or they need to clear the land for roads, mining, farming or towns.

Chimpanzees are vulnerable to diseases that also affect humans. Diseases like the flu, Ebola, measles and polio can kill them. When human populations have outbreaks of these diseases, they can also contract these diseases.

As the human population grows, there is more need for land, and there needs to be a coordinated and effective land-use planning across the chimpanzee range to avoid land clearing. This effective planning would support not only the chimpanzees but also all other species which live in that habitat. Chimpanzees do not know country borders and these cross-boundary areas are becoming most important to protect regionally.

Maintaining large, well-protected areas of forest will be key to maintaining chimpanzee populations in the long term and this can only be done by a combination of the actions detailed above.

The hope

Dr Jane Goodall began her research in 1960 on the chimpanzees in Gombe, Tanzania and that work continues to this day, being the longest uninterrupted study on one animal in the world. Through her ground-breaking research, man was redefined, as up until then only man could make and use tools. Dr Goodall was the first to see a chimpanzee strip the leaves of a branch and use this primitive tool to 'fish' for termites. She was also the first to observe primitive warfare between different groups of chimpanzees fighting over the same land for food.
Jane entered the forests of Gombe as a keen observer, became a scientist and then left her forest home to become an advocate for the chimpanzee, as she realised that if she did not raise awareness globally, chimpanzees would certainly become extinct, in her lifetime.
She started the Jane Goodall Institute in 1977 primarily to continue her research in Gombe and to conserve the species. In the 80's she revolutionised conservation by commencing the community-based conservation programs, TACARE which looks at problems and the solutions in a totally holistic way. Primarily looking at the needs of the communities, the people that live close to chimpanzees and working their needs first. These include education, health and family planning, water sanitation, land use planning and forestry.
By solving the communities' needs, they become conservation champions for the chimpanzee and all the wildlife that shares their forest.
Giving people, animals, and their forest hope for their continued future.

Dr Goodall also launched a youth led environmental program called Roots & Shoots. This program also started in Tanzania, February 1991 and has been active in over 100 countries with youth undertaking projects on Animals, People and the Environment.
If you would like to know more about this program have a look at www.rootsandshoots.global

Some of the NGO's working to save chimpanzees
The Jane Goodall Institute – found in over 30 countries and working in eight countries in Africa and running two chimpanzee sanctuaries. www.janegoodall.global | WWF | WCS | PASA | Taronga Conservation Society | Lincoln Park Zoo | Lwiro | Greater Mahale Chimpanzee | Liberia Chimpanzee Rescue Project | Ngamba Island chimpanzee sanctuary.

What you can do to help
Share this information with family and friends and support, volunteer or donate to organisations helping chimpanzees.
Visit chimpanzees in the wild in Africa and share that experience with all your friends.
Avoid visiting places that use chimpanzees and any other wildlife for entertainment.
Never buy bushmeat and always buy sustainable palm oil.

photo Abeselom Zerit

Thumbs Up

BY
Mea Andresen

Yarn Zealana Air

Pattern P. 261

David Greybeard

BY
Mea Andresen

Yarn Ônling no 1

Pattern P. 264

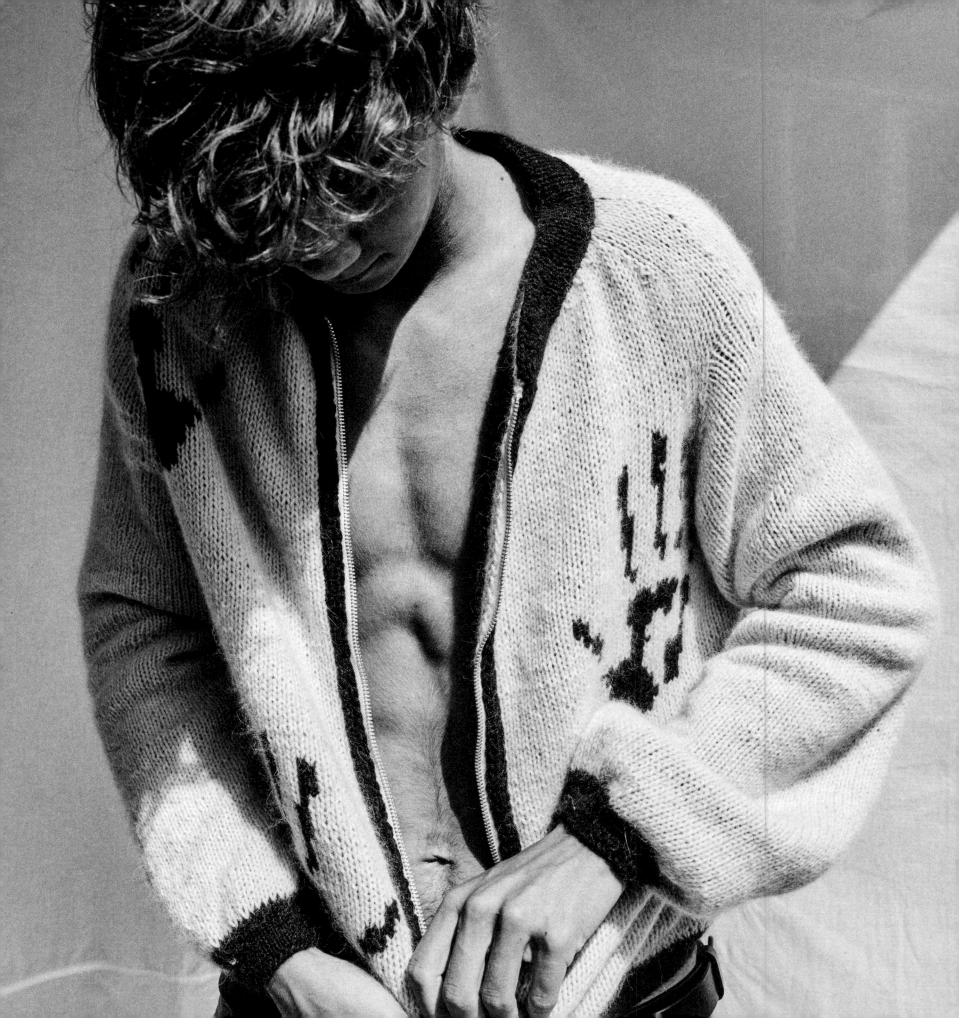

David Greybeard

BY
Mea Andresen

Reversable

Pattern P. 264

Asia

Chinese Pangolin

Javan Rhino

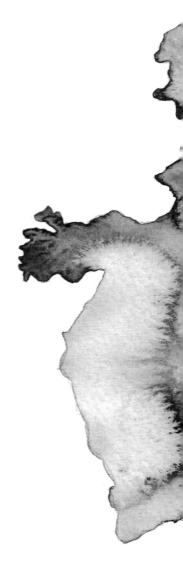

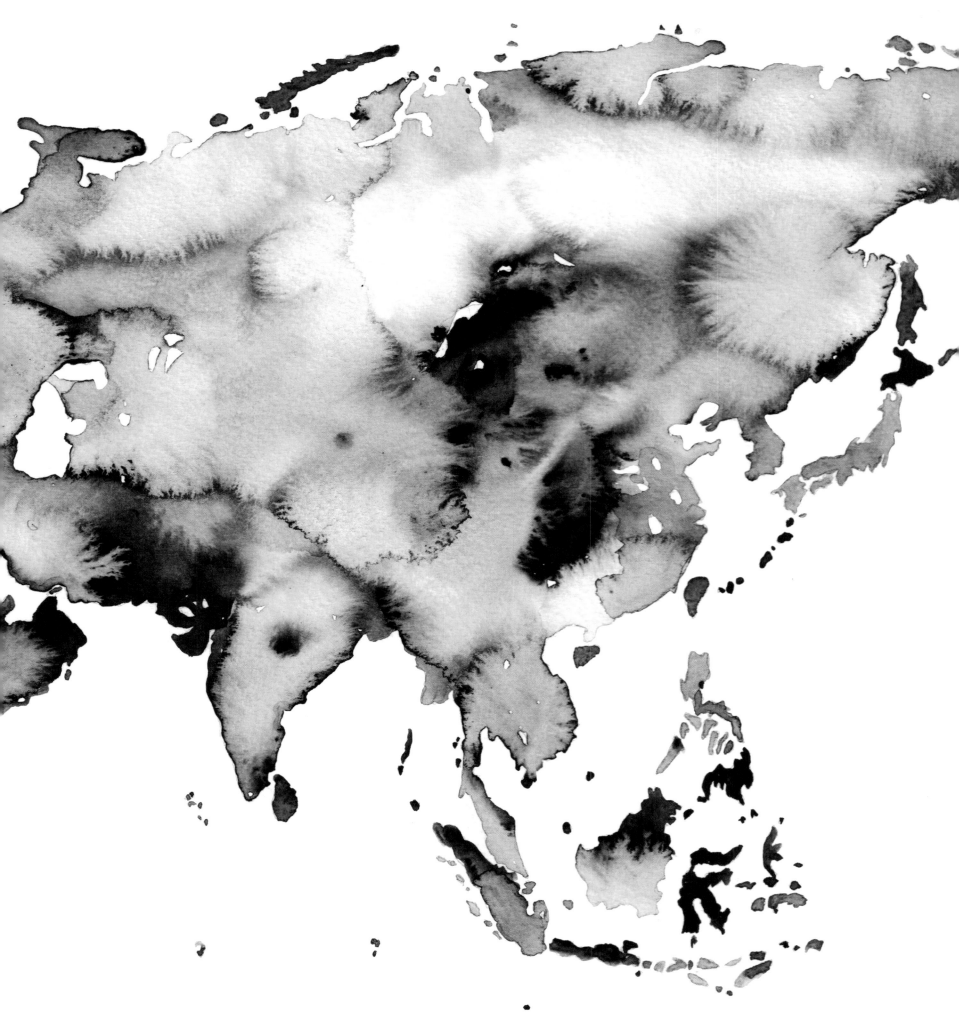

Chinese Pangolin

The most trafficked mammal in the world . The four Asian species are commercially extinct, so the animal trade now pressures the 4 African pangolin species.

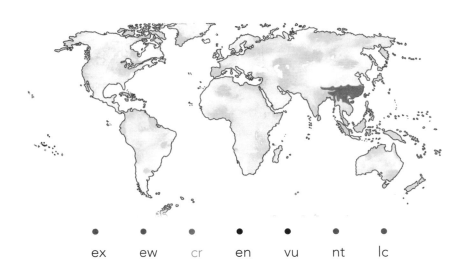

●   ●   ●   ●   ●   ●   ●
ex   ew   cr   en   vu   nt   lc

latin name: Manis pentadactyla
status: Critically endangered
threats: illegal and commercial hunting for scales and meat

photo Ben Mc Rae

Chinese Pangolin

Pangolins are the only animals in the world that are covered from head to toe in scales. Like hair, these scales continue growing throughout the pangolins' lifetime and accounts for 20% of their total weight.
Some pangolins live up in trees and others burrow underground. They are mostly found in tropical forests, dry woodlands and the savannah. They can all use their tails as weapons, and those that live in trees can actually hang from them; also, females use their tails to carry their young.
Like skunks, pangolins secrete a very noxious fluid that can deter predators, but also this fluid is used to mark their territories.

In some pangolin species, the male can be up to 90% heavier than females, with the largest pangolin, the African giant ground pangolin reaching up to 1.8 metres long, and smallest, the African black-bellied pangolin, measuring 80 cm long including its tail.

The most heavily-trafficked wild mammal in the world, pangolins are all either vulnerable, endangered or critically endangered.

The Chinese pangolin is the size of a domestic cat. It has claws to excavate the nests of their prey and for pulling off bark to find insects. They may have poor vision and hearing, yet have an excellent sense of smell and they are good swimmers.
The Chinese pangolin has no teeth; however, its long sticky tongue can extend 40 cm longer than its own body which is the perfect tool for catching insects. It eats 70 million insects every year.
The Chinese pangolin is mostly secretive, solitary, primarily nocturnal, and terrestrial, and according to the IUCN there is no available information on any Asian pangolin's population levels. The pangolin numbers began to decline in 1990's and their numbers have halved in the last 15 years.

The biggest threat to the Chinese pangolin is the illegal and commercial hunting of this species, for human meat consumption and scales for Chinese traditional medicine (CTM).
It is believed that keratin reduces swelling, promotes blood circulation and stimulates milk production in lactating women; however, scientific studies show that animal keratin has no medicinal or curative properties.

Scales of pangolin were worth $10 a kilo in early 90's, $175 a kilo in 2009 and $200 in 2011. The demand has not stopped and the over-exploitation increases its steep decline across most of its range.
Reports in China suggest pangolins, the Chinese, Javan and the Indian pangolin, were commercially extinct by 1995, with Chinese demand for pangolin products subsequently being met through imports, largely from Southeast Asia, and now being met by the African pangolin species.

The Chinese pangolin is found in a wide range of habitats, and indications are that home ranges are relatively large, although concrete data is lacking.

The primary threat to this species is hunting and poaching for local, i.e. national level use, as well as international trade which is now driven largely by the Chinese market.
This species has been hunted at a local level historically, both for the consumption of its meat as a protein source and for its scales for use in traditional medicines among other spiritual and ritualistic uses.

This trade has continued to date, despite the introduction of zero export quotas for wild-caught specimens for commercial purposes. Although local use of pangolins continues today, evidence suggests that this is often forgone in favour of selling the animals into trade, which is primarily destined to China.
In China and Vietnam, pangolin meat is consumed conspicuously as a luxury wild meat dish for which affluent consumers are willing to pay very high prices.
Pangolin scales continue to be prescribed for ailments, including cancer, through designated outlets such as hospitals, but also through traditional medicine retailers, as in Vietnam.

Based on reported seizures between 2011 and 2013, an estimated 116,990-233,980 pangolins were killed which represents only the tip of the trade, maybe as little as 10% of actual volume.

Protected area designation alone is insufficient to protect this and all pangolin species. Greater enforcement and management within protected areas to prevent poaching is needed as is strict enforcement along national and international trade routes, the identification and verification of strongholds, areas of major impact, where conservation efforts should be focused as well as efforts to reduce consumer demand in key markets could greatly assist the conservation of all pangolin species.

Roots and Shoots China is presently involved in a campaign, where students work in groups to visit maternity hospitals and inform the mother-to-be that pangolins are also lovely mothers and that they take care of their offspring just like humans do with much love and protect their babies fiercely, and that pangolins should be loved and protected instead of being consumed.

Some organisations helping this species
IUCN Specialist Pangolin group | WildAid | TRAFFIC | WWF | CBCGDF.
"CBCGDF is a Chinese NGO dedicated to biodiversity conservation since 1985 which has been working on pangolin conservation since 2015. They investigate illegal trade, sources of scales, big data analysis, challenging China's official confiscated wildlife rescue system for pangolins, filing environmental public interest litigations, establishing Community Conservation Areas and advising wildlife protection rules of law."

The hope

WildAid is a global not for profit organisation leading the fight to end the illegal wildlife trade of many species. They have been working since 2016 to save pangolins by reducing consumption and eliminating demand for their meat and scales in China and Vietnam – the two largest consuming nations.

"When the buying stops, the killing can too" This strong statement from WildAid nails the problem. It has been more than two years since the ban on global trade in all pangolin species went into effect. Roughly two million pangolins have since been poached.

Traditional medicine practitioners must find sustainable substitutes that maintain the efficacy of traditional medicines but adapt to the changing environment. We know it can be done. At a recent conference in Hong Kong, TCM experts stated that there are over 100 viable alternatives to the uses of pangolin scales already prescribed in traditional medicines." (WildAid)

What can you do to combat the illegal wildlife trade and help pangolins
As this is a global crisis, we must strengthen the collaboration and compliance within, and between countries, prosecuting wildlife trafficking as a serious organized crime.
"In our communities, we can raise awareness through education, promoting positive actions and livelihoods and address poverty so that people stop buying and supplying endangered wildlife" (WildAid)

You can also get involved with any of the NGO's combating the illegal wildlife trade listed above, and/or donate or volunteer your time.
Do not buy Chinese medicines that have pangolin scales or eat pangolin.
Be conscious of what souvenirs you buy when travelling as it could be contraband.

Celebrate World Pangolin Day – third Saturday in February. Get a group of your friends together, register your group as a Roots & Shoots group at www.roots&shoots.org and you will get help on how to run your group.

photo Johan van Zyl

Scale Up

BY
Lisa Renner

**Yarn Purl Soho Alpaca pure
Madelinetosh Prairie**

Pattern P. 308

All About the Scales

BY
Lisa Renner

Yarn Madelinetosh Tosh Merino Light

Pattern P. 304

Javan Rhino

This rhinoceros is the second most threatened rhinoceros and the least studied of all the rhino species, due to its rarity. It has no predators other than humans and there are approximately only 68 individuals left in the world with none in captivity.

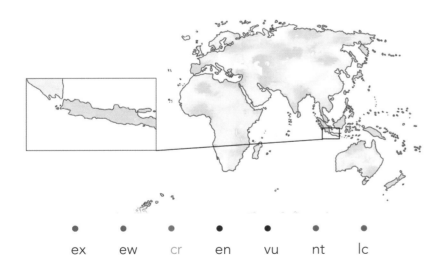

ex   ew   cr   en   vu   nt   lc

latin name: Rhinoceros sondaicus
status: Critically endangered
threats: traditional chinese medicine, habitat fragmentation

Javan Rhino

There are five species of rhinoceros, two in Africa – the black and white species – and three in South East Asia, the Indian, Sumatran and Javan.
Interestingly enough they do not all eat the same things.

The black, Javan and Sumatran are called browsers, because of their upper lip which is quite flexible, allowing them to reach bushes and so wrap their upper lip around leaves and twigs. Whilst the remaining two species the white and Indian are considered grazers and eat mainly grass from the ground.

All rhinos have fantastic hearing and a great sense of smell; however, they have terrible eyesight and cannot see much past 30 metres.
Rhinos love to wallow in mud. This is very useful as it allows the rhinos to cool down as well as protect them from parasites and as this mud dries it also protects them from the hot sun. Much like us putting on sunscreen to prevent us from getting sunburnt.

The largest rhino is the African southern white rhino weighing 1,800 kilos to 2,700 kilos and standing 1.5 to 1.8 metres tall. Whilst the smallest the South East Asian Sumatran rhino can still weigh up to 1,000 kilos and measure 1.45 metres in hight.

The Javan rhinoceros is the second most threatened rhinoceros and the least studied of all the rhino species, due to its rarity. It has no predators other than humans and there are approximately only 68 individuals left in the world with none in captivity.
Rhinos are mammals, in an order called Ungulates, which means they have hoofs and have an odd number of toes, which include the tapir, zebra and horses. They are part of the rhinoceros family found only in Asia and Africa.
This unique rhinoceros is also known as Sunda (a biographical region in Sumatra) or the lesser one-horned rhino.

It is smaller than its Indian cousin, in fact more the size of the African black rhino at over 3 metres long and 1.8 metres high weighing over 1,500 kilos.
They have a greyish-brown hairless skin, with the skin folding like armour plates.
Longevity is unknown but they probably live 30-40 years. Gestation is also unknown, however, presumed to be 15-16 months as in other rhinos.
Age at sexual maturity is estimated at 5-7 years for females and 10 years for males.
The Javan Rhinoceros has a single horn, growing to about 25 cm and females do not appear to have a prominent horn.

This rhino, with its armour-like covering, is an herbivore and its diet is based on leaves, young shoots, twigs and fruit.

The species is generally solitary and rarely seen, except for mating pairs and mothers with young. Females bear only one offspring which remain with their mothers from 1 to 3 years.

The Javan rhinoceros currently occurs in lowland tropical rainforest areas, especially in the vicinity of water. The species formerly occurred in more open mixed forest and grassland and on high mountains.
Due to its rarity, little is known about the species' biology and home range requirements.

The species was declared extinct in Vietnam in 2010 and is now found only in Ujung Kulon National Park (UKNP), on the peninsula of western Java in Indonesia. In 1967, there were only 25 rhinos and by the 1980's it doubled to 50 and now numbers 68 individuals.

The cause of the Javan rhino's initial population decline is mainly attributable to the excessive demand for rhino horn and other products for Chinese and allied medicine. Over-hunting for its horn has driven this formerly widespread species to the brink of extinction.

With such a small population another major threat is disease.

In addition, such a small population faces a continual threat from poachers, although no poaching has occurred in Ujung Kulon National Park in more than 20 years.

There is also a need to survey parts of its historical range for the very remote possibility that small populations may exist, especially in parts of Lao.

For 28 years, the International Rhino Foundation (IRF) has championed the conservation of rhinos world-wide. In Java, in partnership with the Rhino Foundation of Indonesia (YABI) and the Ujung Kulon National Park management authority, IRF funds and operates five rhino protection units (RPU) in UKNP. They are highly trained, four-person anti-poaching teams that intensely patrol key areas within the national parks. Their goal is to prevent the extinction of Javan Rhinos and other threatened species and to protect critical habitats in Java through the proactive prevention of poaching and habitat destruction.

Although the RPUs in the park have been very successful, protection itself is not going to be enough to save the species from extinction. Over the long-term, the population needs to expand, with a second viable population established somewhere else within the species' historic range.

The hope

The Rhino Foundation Indonesia (YABI) has also built a 5,000-hectare Javan Rhino Study and Conservation area in Gunung Honje along the eastern boundary of UKNP. The work includes habitat management, with the removal of more than 100 hectares of Arenga palm which inhibits the growth of rhino food plants.
More than 150 local people have been hired to work on the project over the past few years, including constructing an 8 km perimeter fence and building three guard posts and a base camp.

Some organisations helping this species
The International Rhino Foundation | WWF | And many zoo's globally.

What you can do to help
Learn more about rhinos and share the news with your family and friends
Never buy any rhino horn and avoid medicines that include rhino horn.

Primary forests, the most diverse of forests and the most at risk
Primary forests are pristine forests that exist in their original condition, relatively unaffected by human activities. Often characterised by a full ceiling canopy and usually several layers of understorey, it is the most biologically diverse forest type.
They store unrivalled amounts of carbon; they provide the necessities of life to more species than anywhere else on land. They replenish the air, are a source of water, and enrich the soil.
Primary forests are vital ecosystems of many forest types and are found around the world. They are found in areas of the Amazon, the Boreal area of the northern hemisphere, the Congo basin and Indonesia.

Primary forests represent about 1/3 of all remaining forested land and are irreplaceable and invaluable global assets in terms of biodiversity, carbon sequestration and storage, regulating climate, providing crucial ecological and environmental services, supporting livelihoods and life paths for indigenous peoples and in aiding human health.
All forest types are generally treated with equal standing; however, this underlines the importance and priority required for these primary forests. Neglecting to recognise and prioritise primary forests and their conservation value, we will end up irreparably reducing the full potential of the world's forested areas.
Although 12-22% of primary forests are protected areas, the remainder is vulnerable to exploitation.

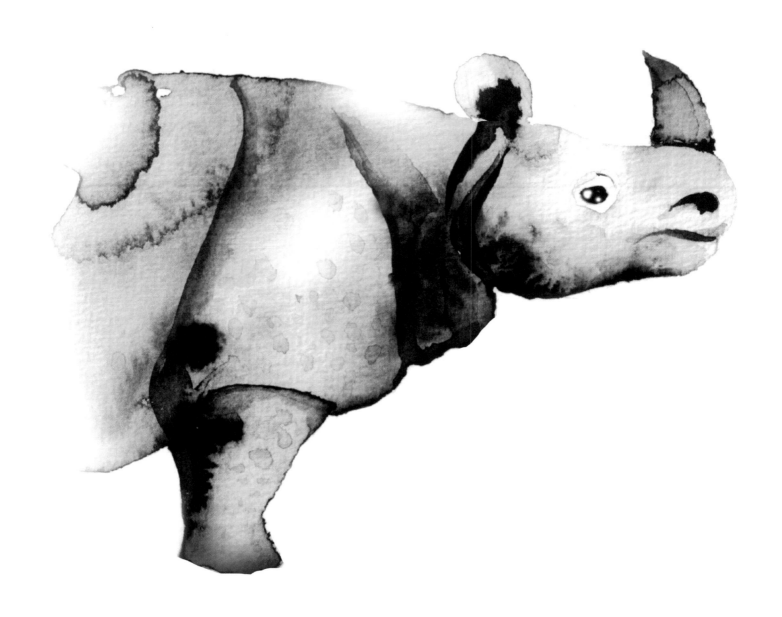

Javan rhinos are so rare, photos are unavailable, so we used this illustration.

Gold Within

BY
Mea Andresen

Yarn Madelinetosh, ASAP. Purl Soho, Spun Silk.

Pattern P. 255

Simply Surviving

BY
Mea Andresen

Yarn Purl Soho, Spun Silk.

Pattern P. 258

North and Central America

Polar Bear

Pygmy Three Toed Sloth

Variable Harlequin Frog

Polar Bear

The vulnerable polar bear is one of the flagship species that clearly demonstrates the effects of climate change.

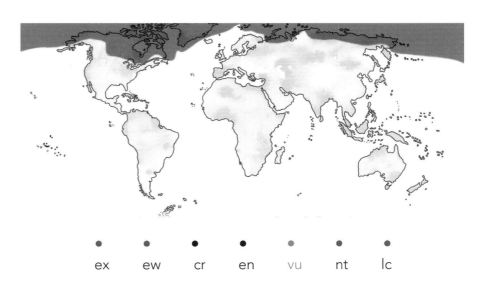

ex   ew   cr   en   vu   nt   lc

latin name: Ursus maritimus
status: Vulnerable
threats: climate change, pollution

Polar Bear

Did you know this bear is the only bear that depends totally on the ocean for its food and it is therefore known as a marine mammal?
They spend most of their lives on the sea ice of only the Arctic Ocean.

They are really strong swimmers reaching up to 10 kilometers an hour and swim long distances, sometimes days, to get to another piece of sea ice. They have large paws especially adapted for swimming, which they use as paddles to get through the water, and their flattened hind legs are used more like a rudder.

They spend about half of their waking time searching for food; however, they are not very successful hunters.
Polar bears have specific adaptations to their marine environment, having a thick layer of fat, ranging from 5-10 cm, which insulates them from freezing temperatures and ice-cold water. It also allows them to float, and during summer when their food supply is limited, this fat is an energy reserve.

The bear family has 8 species, which includes the brown/grizzly, Asiatic black, American black, sun, sloth, spectacled and the giant panda. Polar bears are the most carnivorous bears, however it's the energy-rich blubber of seals rather than meat that makes the Arctic lifestyle of polar bears possible.

They are the largest of the bears and reach up to 800 kilos, which is the weight of 10 men and measure up to 2.5 metres long, making them the largest land carnivore in the world.

They appear a white/yellowish colour, however their hair is hollow and transparent and their skin is black, so their pale colouring is caused by the reflection and scattering of light on their see-through hair.

They have a very powerful sense of smell for hunting seals, their main food source. In ideal conditions, the bear will only eat the blubber and leave the rest for scavengers, however, they will eat almost anything from walrus, belugas, narwhal, birds, eggs, carrion, kelp and berries as well as human garbage.

Female polar bears are half the size of males and live up to 28 years; males live to 25 years. Females are sexually mature at 4 years and produce their first cubs at 5 years. While males are capable of reproducing at 4 years of age, mating success peaks in the mid-teens when males reach top condition and are able to succeed in competitions for mating opportunities.

Only pregnant females enter a dormant state akin to a shallow hibernation similar to other bears. After mating in spring, the females will eat vast quantities of food and prepare a den, usually for 2 cubs but sometimes single and triplets also occur.

The cubs grow rapidly, fed on rich milk (36% fat) from their mother, and when they emerge from the den, they weigh 10 - 12 kilos. In some regions, after emerging from the den, the female may not have fed for up to 8 months, which may be the longest period of food deprivation for any mammal. The mother may have lost up to 55% of their body mass over winter and slimmed by up to 225 kilos while rearing her cubs.

Polar bears are found only where northern sea ice persists for most of the year. There are 19 populations of polar bear, recognized by the Polar bear Specialist Group of the IUCN.

Global warming is the primary long-term threat to polar bear, with the melting ice limiting access to seals, extending the on land fasting period, increasing conflicts with humans and changing ecosystem structure.

Environmental pollution originating from industrial and agricultural activities are an ongoing threat to polar bears. Pollution is known to affect polar bear hormone regulation, growth, tissue development and immune system. An impaired immune system poses new challenges for increased deaths due to disease.

Arctic sea ice loss has thus far progressed faster than most climate models have predicted but the loss varies widely across the Arctic.

The US, Canada and Greenland governments allow and manage a subsistence harvest of polar bears; harvest is prohibited in Norway and Russia with the exception of subsistence hunting in eastern Russia.

The International Agreement on the Conservation of Polar bears signed in 1973 by Canada, Denmark (Greenland), Norway, Soviet Union (Russian Federation) and USA, provides some guidance. Due to the growing concern over polar bear conservation in relation to climate change, they have agreed to initiate a coordinated approach to conservation and management strategies for polar bear. Nonetheless, without action to reduce greenhouse gases, options for polar bear conservation are limited.

The hope

One major success story comes from the "Polar bear Capital of the World" in Churchill, Canada. It's home to less than 1000 people, and nearby a similar number of polar bears spend the ice-free summer on land. Mostly, the bears are spread far and wide waiting for autumn and the ice to reform to resume hunting seals. The challenge for the human-bear relationship is the town sits directly on the north migration path of bears where the ice forms earlier. Decades ago, the bears regularly got into trouble in town and commonly the outcome was a dead bear. The situation was unsustainable for both bears and the people that were increasingly reliant on tourists to view the bears. The solution was simple: reduce things that attract the bears, deter bears away from town, and for the real trouble makers, put them in jail.
The Polar bear Alert Program has become the model for human-polar bear co-existence. A polar bear jail made from repurposed military building housed the bears, called the Polar bear Holding Facility, which serves as a temporary home for bears until they can either be moved further north by helicopter if the jail gets too full or released onto the ice. The bears are not fed, reducing their desire to return and matches their fasting on land in the wild. They are provided fresh snow or water to drink. The program has saved hundreds of bears over the years. It is harder to know how many humans it has protected and the community of Churchill are aware that they live in bear country and know that help is only a phone call away.
Written by Andrew Derocher

Some organisations helping this species
IUCN Polar bear Specialist Group | Polar bears International | WWF.

What you can do to help
Reduce your, and your families, carbon footprint by choosing CO2-friendly transport.
Buy energy saving appliances and support research and development of green technology and investments. Buy locally produced products and recycle.

photo 64 + 67 Daisy Gilardini

Global Sunrise

BY
Lisa Renner

Yarn Madelinetosh, Tosh Merino Light

Pattern P. 294

Sunset Getaway

BY
Lisa Renner

Yarn Önling no. 2

Pattern P. 290

Pygmy Three Toed Sloth

Sloths are possibly the slowest moving mammal in the world.

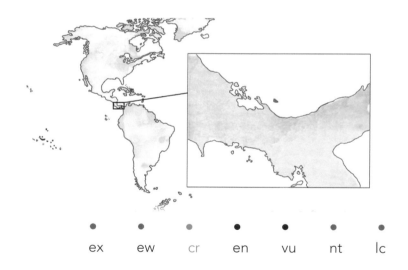

●	●	●	●	●	●	●
ex	ew	cr	en	vu	nt	lc

latin name: Bradypus pygmaeus
status: Critically endangered
threats: habitat destruction, tourism

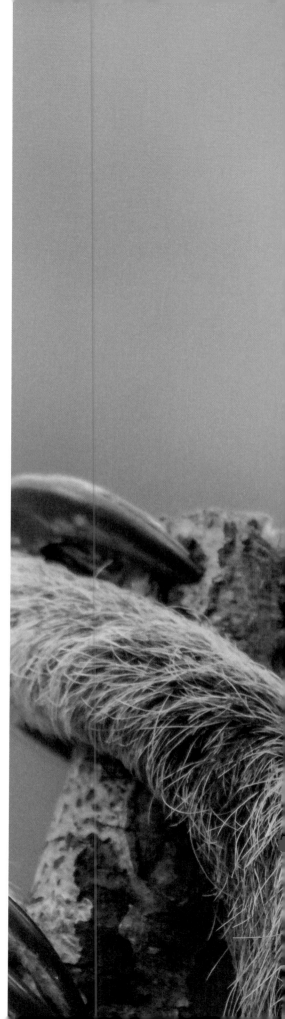

photo Abeselom Zerit

Pygmy Three Toed Sloth

There are two different types of sloths. Those that have two toes and those that have three toes – and there are six different species.
The really confusing thing is that all sloths actually have three toes, but the two-toed sloths actually have only two fingers.

The other main difference between the sloths is that the two-toed are most active at night while the three-toed are mostly active during the day.
All sloths live in the trees and are only found in the forests of central and south America, they are usually solitary and only come together to mate.

All sloths have a four-part stomach, which slowly digests the tough leaves they usually eat; it can take them up to a month to digest a single meal. This means that the sloth does have very little energy and so it is very slow moving.
Sloths spend 90 % of their time hanging upside down from tree branches. It's an amazing adaptation that allows this possibility. So, all their internal organs are attached to their rib cage which means that their organs do not weigh their lungs down and affect their breathing.
The two-toed sloths are usually larger than the three-toed, so the largest sloth is the Hoffman's sloth and the smallest and slowest sloth is the pygmy three-toed sloth.

They may be one of the slowest animals on the planet but they are great swimmers; they actually need to swim as they live in rainforests that seasonally flood, so swimming is essential to their survival.

The pygmy three-toed sloth has a most unusual relationship with an alga and this species of algae only grows on sloths. This alga provides the sloth with camouflage, being green, so the sloth is harder to spot amongst its green vegetation.
These sloths also have additional neck vertebrae which allows them to rotate their heads up to 270 degrees which also allows them to spot their predators better, like jaguars, harpy eagles and snakes.

Adults weigh no more than 3.5 kilos and have grey fur that is darker and longer on the shoulders, and grey-brown hair on their throat.
Their forelimbs bear three digits with large claws that are longer than the hind legs, which also have three digits. The tail is very short and stump like.
Little is known about their reproduction, lifespan, home range or diet, however it is believed they primarily however not exclusively, feed on mangrove leaves.

Due to their mysterious ways and living in the upper most branches of trees, these animals are also very hard to observe and survey their numbers, so population numbers are also mostly unknown.

The pygmy three-toed sloth is found only on a small island off Panama called Isla Escudo de Veraguas. The island has an area of approximately 4.3 km² and is about 17.6 km from the mainland of Panama.
Although previously thought to only live in the red mangroves, recent studies have found them in the central dense tropical forests of the interior of the island.

Despite living in a protected landscape through a governmental resolution in 2009, a number of domestic and international efforts have been mounted to develop tourism infrastructure on the island.

This includes plans for an eco-lodge, a casino, a marina and a banking centre. The current status of the island's custody is vague; a governmental resolution, and thus the protected status of the island, cannot be revoked but no government employee has been appointed specifically to enforce the protection of the island.

Additionally, as pygmy sloths have become more widely recognized internationally, there is growing interest in collecting them for captivity.

The pygmy sloth is listed as critically endangered as this species has a very restricted range, and there is likely to be a continuing decline in the quality of habitat and area used due to habitat degradation.

The pygmy three-toed sloth is endemic, native, to a single island of Panama, which is protected as a wildlife refuge. There is a need to improve the enforcement of this protected area.

A comprehensive conservation plan is underway, bringing together the local community, wildlife authorities in Panama, indigenous authorities and the national and international scientific community to protect the island, using the pygmy sloth as a flagship species.

The hope

The pygmy three-toed sloth was only described scientifically in 2001. A team of conservationists from the Zoological Society of London (ZSL) are surveying them to build the first picture of how these little-known animals are faring.

This project aims to improve the understanding of the pygmy sloth population and the threats to the species, and also to ensure their conservation.

-They will undertake educational programs and workshops to increase local awareness, enhance support for conservation, establish sustainable resource management, and support local authorities in enforcing legal regulations.

Their long-term aim is to develop and implement a management plan that engages everyone involved in the conservation of Escudo and the pygmy sloth.

The island is uninhabited; however, the numbers of seasonal residents is growing, increasing the pressure from small scale logging, fishing and littering. There is also a looming threat of large-scale tourism as the number of visiting holiday-seekers is rapidly increasing.

The field team visits twice a year to monitor the pygmy sloth population and record the number of sloths and other important data on their activity and habitat use. This has occurred since 2014.

The majority of the field team are from the local communities and collaborate with other NGO's and community organisations. Radio collars have been successfully deployed on 10 individuals, and GPS loggers have been tested successfully helping to find out how large an area each sloth needs and which parts of the island they use in different seasons.

In 2016, field team leader, Diorene Smith Cabellos, was awarded the Disney Conservation Hero Award for her impressive dedication and hard work towards the conservation of this species.

The longevity of the project has enabled the team to develop and maintain essential positive relationships with the local communities and authorities.

Rangers from the environment ministry now also attend all field trips, improving the ability to enforce regulation of tourism and pollution.

Some organisations helping this species
IUCN Sloth Specialist Group | Zoological Society of London (ZSL) | Edge of Existence | WWF | Minnesota Zoo.

What you can do to help
Learn more about these animals by contacting the NGO's that are saving them and share with your friends. Make sure that when travelling you don't not take a selfie of yourself and any animal especially a sloth, as usually all these animals have been taken from the wild.
Form a Roots & Shoots group in your school to raise awareness about their plight.
Sponsor a sloth.

Easy Going

BY
Charlotte Kaae

Yarn Isager | Madelinetosh | ITO

Pattern P. 278

Three Tiny Toes

BY
Charlotte Kaae

Yarn Madelinetosh, Vintage

Pattern P. 276

Variable Harlequin frog

We chose this beautiful frog for its most amazing colours which it uses as a warning to all other animals as it is poisonous .

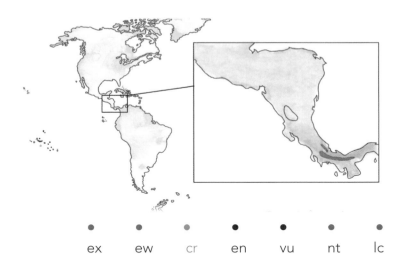

● ● ● ● ● ● ●
ex   ew   cr   en   vu   nt   lc

latin name: Atelopus varius
status: Critically endangered
threats: frog fungus, habitat destruction

Variable Harlequin Frog

The variable harlequin frog (Atelopus varius) is actually a true toad. True toads have a few unique characteristics that make them true toads, one of them being they have no teeth on the upper jaw, whilst most frogs do.
Toads in general have warty skin and relatively short legs for hopping, frogs have smooth skin and long legs for swimming or leaping. There are about 618 species of true toads.

From our frog experts we now understand, that in today's language toads are actually a kind of frog, and they are all now called frogs.
Variable harlequin frogs may also be called harlequin frogs or clown frogs and are found only in Central America, specifically Costa Rica and Panama.

These frogs are a terrestrial species, living only on the ground and in humid lowland and montane forests. They prefer rocky streams in hilly terrain and are usually found along the banks and sitting out on the rocks of small fast-flowing streams.
The variable harlequin frog is diurnal, being active during the day. They are poor swimmers that rarely enter streams other than to lay and fertilise their eggs. They appear to depend on wet surfaces for moisture. They sleep at night on rocks or vegetation.

They feed on small insects, spiders or crustaceans.

What sets these frogs apart is that they are brightly coloured with their dorsal colouration being mottled light and dark. Its colours range from lime-green to yellow-orange to sometimes pink on a black background.
All frogs have various chemicals on their skin that protect them from predators and / or bacterial or fungal infections. Variable harlequin frogs are pretty toxic to avoid predation and their bright colours serve as a warning to predators. Their skin is full of tetrodotoxin which is the same as the toxin found in the puffer fish.

Generally, when going about their daily lives, variable harlequin frogs walk around fairly slowly and deliberately while most frogs will hop from one cover object to another.
Like all amphibians, their eggs do not have the protective shell of birds and reptiles. Frogs and toads lay eggs in jelly-like masses, and unless they are covered in water, they will dry up and die. Variable harlequin frogs lay their white eggs in two sets of strings in the water, attached to rocks.

Variable harlequin frogs were originally found in Costa Rica and Panama. Over 100 populations of this species were known from Costa Rica where it was often quite common. Drastic declines began in Monteverde, Costa Rica in 1988 and the species was thought to have completely disappeared in Costa Rica by 1996.

However, after nearly eight years during which the species was thought to be extinct, a remnant population was discovered near Quepos, on the Pacific coastal range of Costa Rica in 2003 and was surveyed again in 2005 when more individuals were found.
In Panama, some populations have seriously declined.

The major threat to the variable harlequin frog is likely to be the emerging infectious disease chytridiomycosis, caused by a fungus, discovered in 1999, which infects the skins of amphibians and often kills them.

Zoospores of this fungus are motile and can be passed on through frog-to-frog contact as well as through their watery environment.
Infection occurs inside the cells of the outer skin layers which contain keratin. Keratin is the material that makes the outside of the skin tough and resistant to injury and is also what hair and nails in humans are made of.

Their skin becomes thick, and as amphibians "drink" water and absorb important salts through their skin and not their mouths, the disease interrupts normal electrolyte balance and the amphibian dies of cardiac arrest.
This fungus has led to catastrophic amphibian population declines around the world.

Other threats to the species include habitat loss due to the destruction of natural forests, and predation by introduced trout.
The only known site in Costa Rica that contains variable harlequin frogs is under serious threat of a landslide that could potentially destroy the entire stream section where they are presently found.

This frog was collected by the thousands in the 1970s and shipped to Germany as part of the international pet trade.
Listed as critically endangered because of their drastic population decline, estimated to be more than 80% over the last 20 years, this has been inferred from the apparent disappearance of most of the population, most likely due to chytridiomycosis.

Conditions over the past three decades have put frogs at the forefront of another impending mass extinction, with approximately 60% of more than 8,000 described species currently threatened.

Once common along highland streams from western Costa Rica to western Panama, the variable harlequin frog is critically endangered throughout its range, decimated by the amphibian chytrid fungus.

The hope

On January 17, 2018, Smithsonian researchers released approximately 500 frogs at Cobre Panama concession site in Panama's Colon province as a first step toward a potential full-scale reintroduction of this species. This reintroduction is included in Cobre Panama's biodiversity conservation plan as an important part of their environmental commitment.

In order to monitor the released frogs over time, 30 frogs wore miniature radio transmitters. The scientific team also gave each frog an elastomer toe marking that glows under UV light to identify each individual as part of a population monitoring study.
"Before we reintroduce frogs into remote areas, we need to learn how they fare in the wild and what we need to do to increase their chances of survival in places where we can monitor them closely" said Brian Gratwicke, International coordinator of the Panama Amphibian Rescue and Conservation Project (PARC) at the Smithsonian Biology Institute.

Reintroductions may or may not succeed but the lessons learnt will help to understand the challenges faced by a frog as it transitions from captivity into the wild.
PARC brought a number of individuals into the breeding centre between 2013 and 2016 as the fungus continued to impact wild populations.
PARC hopes to secure the future of this frog by reintroducing animals bred in captivity according to an action plan developed with Panama's Ministry of the Environment and the IUCN and other stakeholders.

Some organisations helping this species
IUCN Specialist Frog group | Cheyenne Zoo | Houston Zoo | ZOO New England
The Smithsonian Tropical Research Institution | The Tiger Wood Fund
The Smithsonian Conservation Biology Institute | National Geographic Society
The Tiger Wood Fund | Mohammed bin Zayed Species Conservation fund.

What you can do to help
If this story really interested you, find out more from any of the organisations that are helping this frog and get involved.
Make contact with the Amphibian Survival Alliance www.amphibians.org and Amphibian Ark www.amphibianark.org

Neon Harlequin

BY
Laura Locher

Yarn Kettle Yarn, Islington

Pattern P. 233

Not a Jumper

BY
Laura Locher

Yarn Kettle Yarn, Önling no 1

Pattern P. 231

Antarctica

Blue Whale

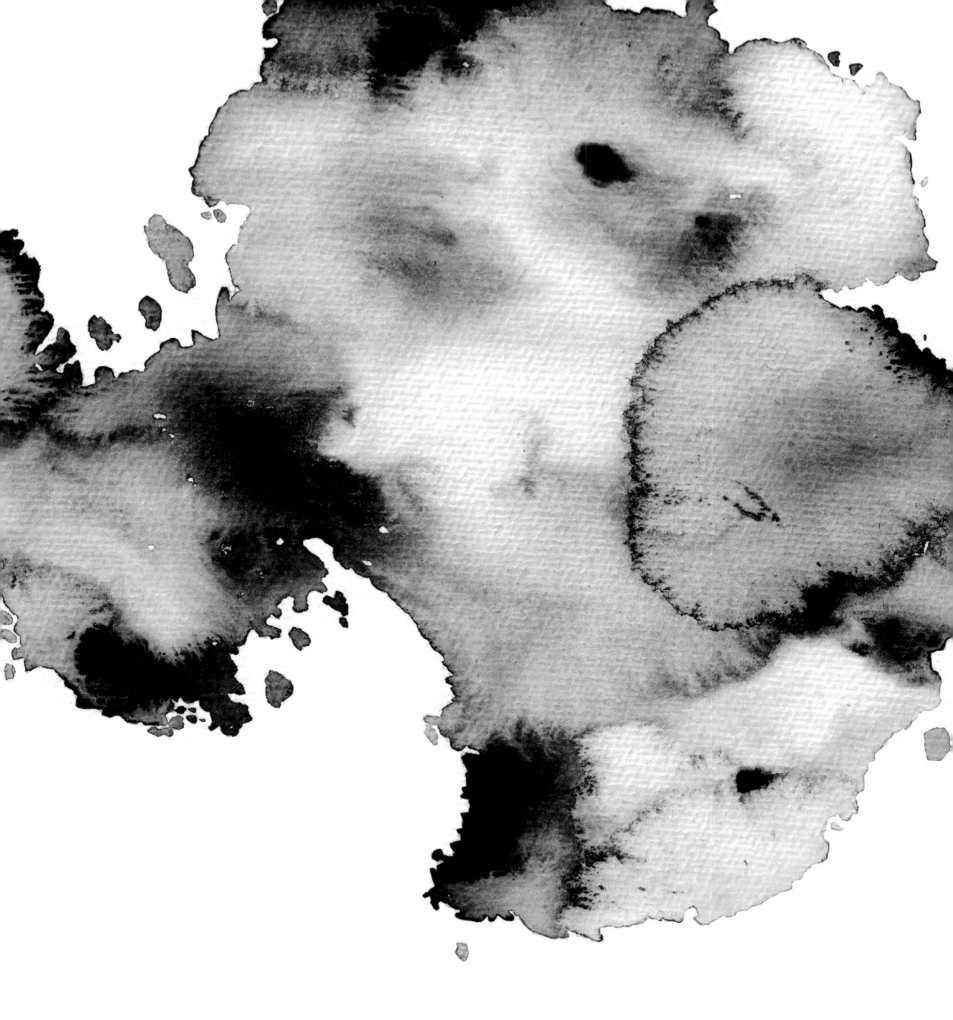

Blue Whale

This majestic creature is the largest animal living on this Earth today.

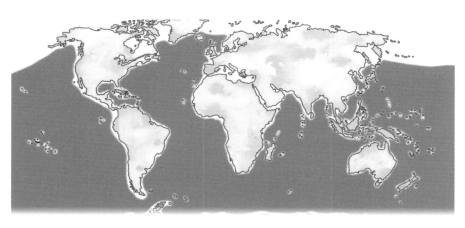

ex   ew   cr   en   vu   nt   lc

latin name: Balaenoptera musculus
status: Endangered
threats: pollution, overfishing for krill, ship strikes

photo Richard Carey

R:E:D: 97

Blue Whale

There are over 90 species of whales, separated into two large groups, the baleen and the toothed whales. Did you know that dolphins and porpoises are toothed whales?

Baleen whales have two blowholes to inhale air and express the air from their lungs, and the toothed whales only have one. It seems that by having two blowholes it allows the 14 baleen whales to be much larger, with the largest being the blue whale. The largest of the 76 species of toothed whales is the sperm whale.
The other interesting difference between these two groups is that the toothed whales seem to be more social, whist the baleen whales don't normally group together in big pods.

Baleen whales are also known as the great whales, and isn't it funny that the largest animals on this planet likes to eat one of the smallest animals, eating up to 40 million tiny krill a day.

Baleen is the bristle-like filter which is also made of the similar substance as our fingernails and animal horns. This filter sifts their food and allows the whale to only swallow its food with the water just passing through.

The blue whale is the largest animal presently on this planet, weighs more than 130,000 kilos and is up to 30 metres long. That is longer than three buses and heavier than three lorries or semi-trailer trucks.

The blue whale's tongue weighs as much as an elephant, its heart is the size of a car and its blood vessels so large you could swim in their veins and arteries.

These blue-grey giants have a very streamlined body, long and slender with a wide head and big powerful flippers, a powerful tail and small dorsal fin.

Blue whales communicate by making a series of super-loud vocalizations. Their calls are the loudest of any creature on the planet and can be heard underwater for hundreds of kilometres.

They migrate seasonally, feeding on krill in the colder polar waters and mate, breed and give birth in the warmer waters.

They live up to 80 to 90 years, and females are generally a metre longer than males. Females give birth, after 10 to 12 months, to a calf that measures around 8 metres long and weigh 2,700 kilos, which is as big as a fully-grown hippopotamus. The blue whale calf will suckle rich fatty milk from their mothers and will gain around 90 kilos a day.

Blue whales can be found in all of the Planet's oceans, and they swim alone or in groups of two to four. However, when there is plenty of food, you will see as many as fifty congregate together.

The migration pattern of blue whales is not well understood; however, it appears to be very diverse.

Blue whales were heavily hunted in the 19th and 20th centuries and despite the ban in 1966, their population has declined by 70 to 90% in the last 150 years. This decline is specific for the Antarctic blue whale, as the North Atlantic, eastern North Pacific and Indian Ocean blue whale populations have fared slightly better.

The whales' only natural predator is the orca.

The main threat to blue whales in the past was direct exploitation, which only became regularly possible in the modern era by using deck-mounted harpoon cannons. Modern blue whale hunting started in the North Atlantic in 1868 and spread to other regions after the North Eastern Atlantic population had been severely reduced. Whaling was temporarily banned in Norway from 1905 and in Iceland from 1915.

The Antarctic and North Atlantic populations were each probably depleted to the low hundreds by the time whaling ceased in the 1960-1970s, but have increased since.

Blue whales have been legally protected worldwide since 1966, although they continued to be caught illegally by former USSR fleets until 1972. The last recorded deliberate catches were off Spain in 1978.

Blue whales off southern Sri Lanka and along the California coast appear to be especially prone to being struck by ships. The southern coast of Sri Lanka is one of the busiest ocean-going shipping lanes in the world; however, the expected frequency of ship strikes on blue whales would be greatly reduced by just moving the shipping lanes slightly further off shore.

The main food of Antarctic blue whales, krill, is predicted to decline during the 21st century due to both the reduced ocean productivity associated with warming and to increasing ocean acidity that limits the krill's shell-building capacity.
Their preferred food source, krill, is also now fished commercially for human consumption, particularly vitamins like the omega oils.

Their recovery from commercial whaling is in direct competition with commercial fishers in the Southern Ocean. As commercial fishery takes more and more krill, the slow increase in numbers of blue whales may stop or even be reversed.

The hope

Oceana is the largest international advocacy organization dedicated solely to ocean conservation. Oceana is rebuilding abundant and biodiverse oceans by winning science-based policies in countries that control one third of the world's wild fish catch. With more than 200 victories that stop overfishing, habitat destruction, pollution and killing of threatened species like turtles and sharks, Oceana's campaigns are delivering results. A restored ocean means that one billion people can enjoy a healthy seafood meal, every day, forever. Visit www.oceana.org to learn more.

Although many organisations are working to save whales, more needs to be done. Conservation efforts need to start locally in order to save endangered whales from extinction, and then followed by a coordinated global approach which includes governments, regional and local communities to ensure the continued survival of the blue whales.

Some organisations helping this species:
IUCN Specialist Whale Group | Sea Shepherd | Greenpeace | WWF | Oceana | Save the Whales

What can you do to help
Disposing of pollutants and hazardous wastes properly. Storm water runoff is one of the leading causes of water pollution. Leaks from vehicles contribute to the problem as oil and antifreeze and other harmful elements wash into small streams and then rivers that eventually end up in the oceans.
Oppose all commercial whaling operations.
Learn more and join organisations dedicated to protecting whales.
Take a whale watching tour from a reputable operation. Tourism dollars spent on whale watching increase the incentive to protect these sea mammals. Research any tour you are thinking of taking to make sure the company follows whale protection guidelines and donates to their conservation.
Support the creation of whale sanctuaries which protect whales from commercial whaling and other fishing threats. In the sanctuaries, whales are safe to breed, birth their calves and feed. Some countries create these areas in places where whales migrate to each year and use eco-tourism dollars to support their maintenance.
Strive for an eco-friendlier lifestyle. Whales are threatened by pollution and ozone depletion. By living a greener lifestyle, you help cut down on these pollution problems and create a healthier planet.

Making Waves

BY
Emalie Dam

Yarn Isager, Highland wool + Alpaca 1

Pattern P. 215

Baleen Beauty

BY
Emalie Dam

Yarn Madelinetosh, Vintage

Pattern P. 212

South America

Green Turtle

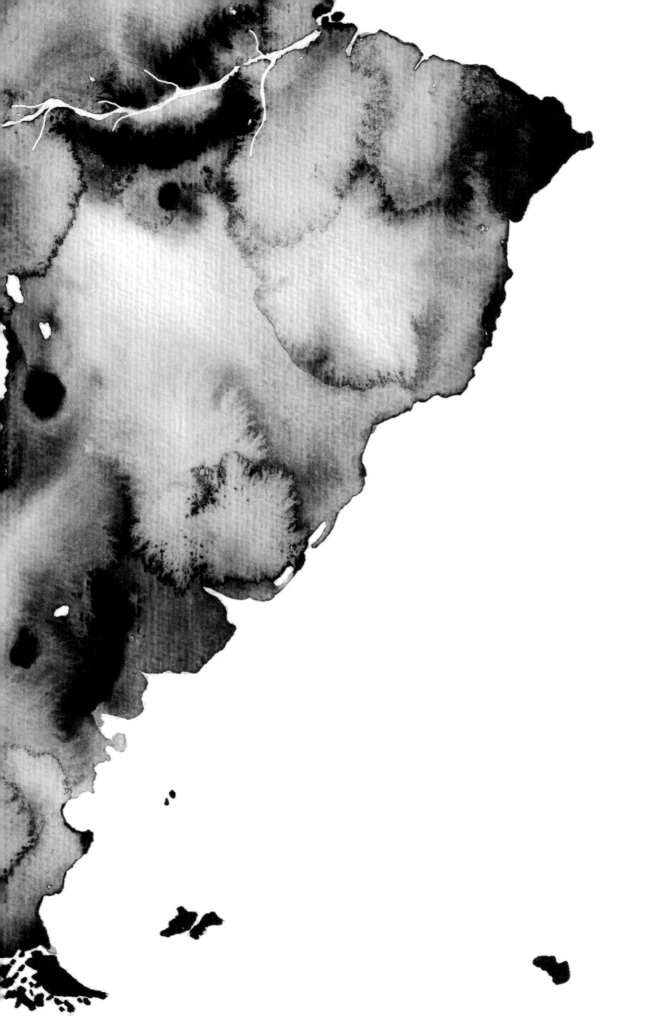

R:E:D: 107

Green Turtle

There are two types of Green sea turtles - the Atlantic and the Eastern Pacific, and it is still unknown if they are separate species.

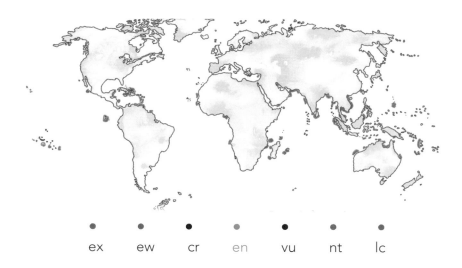

ex   ew   cr   en   vu   nt   lc

latin name: Chelonia mydas
status: Endangered
threats: hunting and collection of eggs, destruction of nesting sites, marine pollution, indiscriminate fishing.

photo Erin Donalson

Green Turtle

Did you know that there are over 356 species of turtles and only seven species are sea turtles? Sea turtles can hold their breath for several hours depending on how active they are. A sleeping or resting sea turtle can stay underwater anything from four to seven hours.

I have always wondered what the difference is between a turtle and a tortoise, and I have found the main difference is that tortoises live exclusively on land whilst turtles live in the water some or most of the time.
The biggest sea turtle is the leatherback turtle, known to weigh up to 900 kilos and measure up to 3 metres. The smallest sea turtle is Kemp's ridley measuring up to 65 cm in length and can weigh up to 45 kilos.

It has been speculated that only 1 out of 1,000 eggs laid by sea turtles survive to adulthood.

Green turtles rely on Earth's magnetic field and ocean currents to find the beaches where they were born to give birth to their own offspring. This is an amazing feat of navigation as they travel the oceans of the world and come right back to where they started their life
Green turtles are one of seven species of sea turtle in the world, all of which are in the class Reptilia and in the family with the hawkesbill and loggerhead turtles. Their shells are streamlined and they have paddle-like flippers, which allow them to swim gracefully and quickly, in fact up to 35 km per hour.
This turtle is not named for its green colour but for the greenish colour of its body fat. It has many names in different parts of the world, such as the black sea turtle or the pacific green turtle.

Green turtles range throughout tropical and subtropical oceans worldwide, and scientists have recently discovered there are over a dozen sub-populations, that nest across all the continents, in over 80 countries having turtles arrive on their beaches, except Antarctica.

To reach their nesting grounds, green turtles may travel long distances. After mating in shallow waters near the shore, females climb onto the beach and lay their eggs in a pit, which they dig with their flippers. They lay 100 to 200 eggs at a time and leave them for two months before they hatch.

Green turtles are well adapted to the sea and they generally only come on land to lay their eggs. Females lay their eggs every two to four years once they are sexually mature.
They are born only 5 cm long and they grow up to 1.2 metres and weigh up to 300 kilos, making them the largest of the hard-shell sea turtles in the world. Hatchlings must crawl to the sea and avoid a multitude of predators that will attack them on their journey from their sandy nests to the ocean.

As juveniles they eat small crabs and other zooplankton, and as adults become herbivores, primarily eating sea grasses and algae.

Like most sea turtles, green turtles are highly migratory.
Upon leaving the nesting beach, it has been hypothesized that hatchlings begin an oceanic phase, perhaps floating passively in major current systems that serve as open-ocean developmental grounds.
After a number of years in the ocean, the turtles migrate to shallower parts of the sea near a coast with rich seagrass and/or marine algae where they can forage and grow until maturity.
Upon attaining sexual maturity, green turtles commence breeding migrations between foraging grounds and nesting areas. Migrations are carried out by both males and females and may traverse oceanic zones, often spanning thousands of kilometres. During non-breeding periods adults reside at coastal feeding areas that sometimes coincide with juvenile developmental habitats.

One of the most detrimental direct human threats to green turtles is the intentional harvest of eggs and adults from nesting beaches and juveniles and adults from foraging grounds. Unfortunately, harvest remains legal in several countries despite substantial declines.

Plastic bags are petroleum-based and do not biodegrade. Green turtles and other marine creatures mistake plastics and other garbage as food (such as jellyfish) and eat it. This mistake causes blockages within their digestive systems and eventually death.
Every time you use a plastic disposable straw, it eventually gets thrown away. Many of these straws, along with other plastic trash, end up in the ocean where they can harm or kill green turtles and many other marine wildlife.
Mortality associated with entanglement in nets is the primary incidental threat; the irresponsible fishing techniques include drift netting, shrimp trawling, dynamite fishing and long-line fishing.

Degradation of both nesting beach habitats and marine habitats through buildings and sand extraction also play a role in the decline of many green turtle numbers.
The presence of lights on or adjacent to nesting beaches alters the behaviour of nesting adults and is often fatal to emerging hatchlings as they are attracted to light sources and are therefore drawn away from the water.

Habitat degradation in the marine environment results from increased effluent and contamination from coastal development, construction of marinas, increased boat traffic and harvest of near shore marine algae resources. Combined, these impacts diminish the health of coastal marine ecosystems and may, in turn, adversely affect green turtles.
The degradation of marine habitats has been implicated in the increasing prevalence of the tumour-causing fibropapilloma disease.
Specific to sea turtles, this disease causes tumours that are usually benign, however it is ultimately debilitating for the turtles, as these tumours can be as large as a grapefruit.

The hope

Green turtles have been afforded legislative protection under a number of international trea-
ties and laws, and as a result of many global designations and agreements, many of the intentional impacts directed at sea turtles have been lessened: harvest of eggs and adults has been
slowed at several nesting areas through nesting beach conservation efforts and an increasing
number of community-based initiatives are in place to slow the taking of turtles in foraging
areas.

However, despite these advances, human impacts continue throughout the world. The lack of
effective monitoring in open seas, and near-shore fisheries operations still allows turtle mortality, and the uncontrolled development of coastal and marine habitats threatens to destroy
the supporting ecosystems of long-lived green turtles.

Some organizations helping this species
IUCN Specialist Sea Turtle group | State of the World's Sea Turtles (SWOT) Program | NOAA
Nat Geo | Green Turtle | Foundation | Sea Turtle | Charity UK | Medasset.

What you can do to help
Visit the bluehabits.org web site for more information
Join the growing community of people who are choosing to reduce or eliminate single-use
plastics from their lives, and reducing their carbon footprint.
Do not purchase any sea turtle products, such as combs and jewellery made from hawksbill
shell which are common in tourist markets in some tropical countries
Protect and clean up your local beach or waterways.
Avoid eating food caught with unsustainable fishing practices.

photo Kleber Cordeiros

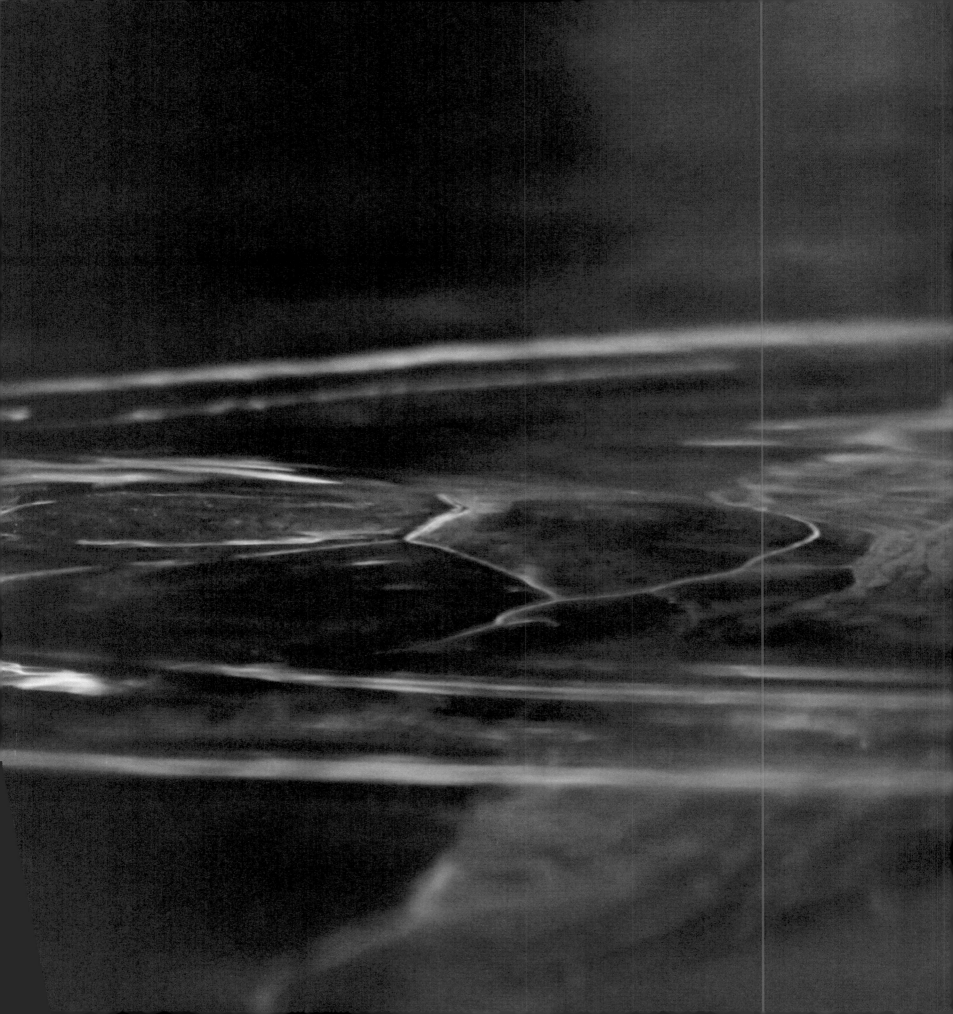

On the Edge

BY
Lisa Renner

Yarn Isager, Alpaca 1

Pattern P. 284

Europe

Goldsteifiger Beetle

Greek Meadow Viper

Atlantic Bluefin Tuna

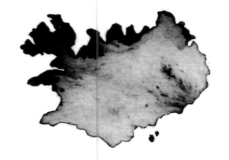

Goldsteifiger Beetle

We chose this most beautiful beetle for its amazing metallic colouring that you may never have seen before.

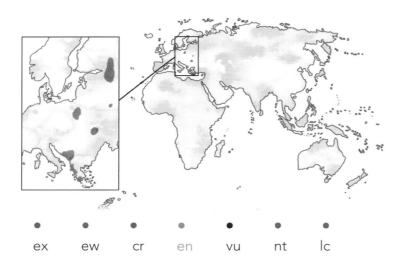

ex   ew   cr   en   vu   nt   lc

latin name: Buprestis splendens
status: Endangered
threats: habitat loss and fragmentation

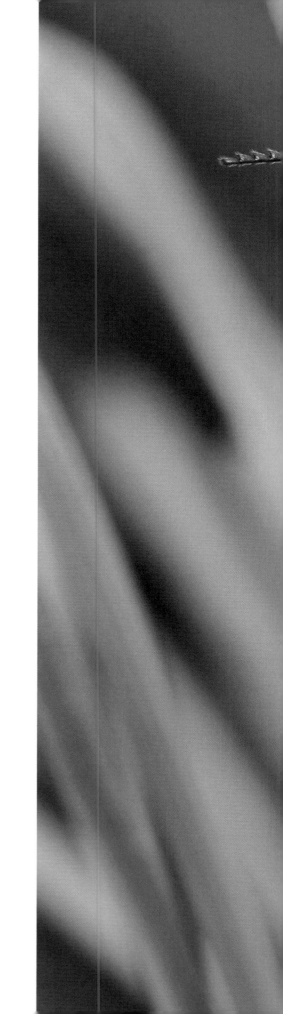

photo Nikola Rahame

Goldsteifiger Beetle

Insects are an incredibly diverse and a very successful group of organisms with 5.5 million species comprising over 75% of the world's animal species. Beetles are the largest group of insects with 1.5 million species. This represents 40% of all insect species, 25% of all animals and one fifth of all known living organisms on Earth.

This strikingly beautiful beetle is part of a large family with over 15,000 species commonly known as jeweled beetles or metallic wood-boring beetles due to their glossy bright colour.

These beetles, along with all insects, spiders, mites and their aquatic cousins the crustaceans are the Arthropods, which is the group of animals that are invertebrates, therefore having no vertebral column. So, they all have a tough semi-transparent shell for support. Members of this group also have jointed appendages and a segmented body. This grouping accounts for over 95% of all animal species.

Within this large group of Arthropods is the insect group which includes the flies, crickets, mosquitoes, butterflies and bees. Like all insects, beetle bodies are divided into three separate sections, the head in front, thorax in the middle, ending with the abdomen.

The head section of beetles has a single pair of antennae, three pairs of mouthparts and a pair of eyes. The thorax contains three parts or segments. Each segment has a pair of legs and the second and third segments have a pair of wings. Some insects like fleas are wingless and flies have one set modified into tiny gyroscopes called "halteres" that allow them to make aerial maneuvers no airplane can ever match. Who ever thought a fly was such an aerial acrobat?

The last part, the abdomen, usually has 7 to 10 visible segments, with its last segment modified with a special extension which could be breeding claspers, stingers or an egg laying tubular organ called an ovipositor.

Beetles have hardened front wings called "elytra" which serve to protect them and a thinner translucent set of back wings they use to fly. Beetles, like butterflies and bees, undergo a complete body change called metamorphosis between hatching from an egg and becoming an adult. Immature beetles are called grubs and they usually look nothing like the adults they will become.

The goldsteifiger beetle is very rare across its European range, and its populations are severely fragmented and still declining.

It might be extinct in the Ukraine, as only one specimen has been seen near Kiev in 60 years. Whilst in Spain, three specimens have been collected in the last 50 years. This beetle is thought to be extinct in Germany, Austria and Sweden.

These beetles are saproxylic invertebrates, which are animals that are dependent on dead or decaying wood. Or they are dependent on the organisms that are themselves dependent on dead wood.
They depend on decaying wood or wood–inhabiting fungi for their development and therefore only live in the relic old growth pine forests of the northern hemisphere.

A new stand of this old forest has been found in Romania, where these beetles may be found.

The main threat to this beetle is the commercial and illegal logging of their forests.
In forests that are protected, these beetles suffer from the slow regrowth in pine forests and are therefore very vulnerable to fires, as well as the removal of dead and dying trees upon which they depend.

This species is also popular with beetle collectors and this is posing an increased threat to their survival.

The major impact on human life from beetles is in agriculture, forestry and horticultural fields as some have become pests, however most beetles do not cause any economic damage. In fact, many beetles are beneficial and help control pests like the ladybug and dung beetles.

There are no groups or organisations known to be working on this beetle's survival; however, we thank the IUCN Invertebrate group for all their work on all invertebrates.

This species is possibly extinct in many countries and it is likely to struggle unless conditions change.

In Romania, the only known population is well preserved in one protected area, as well as this area being very difficult to access.
And there are some small remaining areas In Italy, with one of the localities being a national park.

The IUCN recommends that there be increased monitoring of the last remaining sites and that the development of action plans for this endangered species be developed and implemented.

The hope

Forest Stewardship Council (FSC)
Starting in 1994, FSC is a global not-for-profit organisation that sets the standards for what a responsibly managed forest is, both environmentally and socially. They work to promote environmentally appropriate, socially beneficial and economically viable management of the world's forests.
FSC certified forests have to meet their rigorous standards, which include that the forests are healthy and benefit local communities as well as providing jobs for workers.
FSC tracks the wood from the forest to the shelf, so you can be sure that the furniture or the paper you have just bought came from responsible sources.
FSC helps take care of forests, the people and wildlife who all call the forest their home. So you can keep your life full of forest products while keeping our forests full of life. Forests are good for us. They provide a great environment for activities like hiking, walking and other outdoor pursuits and are even proven to have therapeutic properties.
On a wood or wood-based product, it is your assurance that it is made with, or contains, wood that comes from FSC certified forests or from post-consumer waste.
Products with the FSC label are identified as products with their roots from well-managed forests.
FSC helps forests remain thriving environments for generations to come, by helping you make ethical and responsible choices at your supermarket, bookstore, furniture retailer and beyond.
All this information was provided by FSC website.

Some of the organisations that work to save our forests include:
FSC | Rainforest Alliance | WWF | Greenpeace | Rainforest Rescue.
You can also get involved with your local community council or regional community and help protect your local forest.

What you can do to help
Learn more about forests and help protect them by joining, donating or volunteering with NGO's that are helping conserve our forests.
Join organisations that plant trees in your area.

photo Nikola Rahame

Pixelated View

BY
Bruno Kleist

Yarn Manos Del Uruguay

Pattern P. 252

Shimmering

BY
Bruno Kleist

Yarn Ito, Rokku Tennen + Shio

Pattern P. 249

Greek Meadow Viper

A venemous European snake, that has a moderate venom, yet still decides how much venom it injects, if any into its prey.

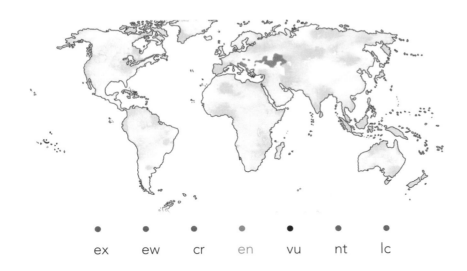

ex   ew   cr   en   vu   nt   lc

latin name: Vipera graeca
status: Endangered
threats: habitat fragmentation, tourism, mining and transportation

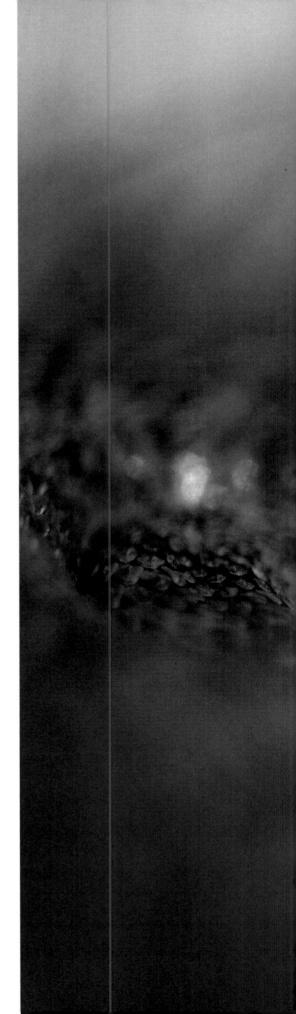

photo Edvárd Mizsei

Greek Meadow Viper

The Greek meadow viper, also called Orsini's viper, is Europe's smallest viper. It is a venomous snake with a beautiful diamond stripe of pinks and browns alerting all its neighbours that it is poisonous. Meadow viper is not a single species but a complex of several species, subspecies from the lowland steppe grasslands and alpine meadows of Eurasia.

The Greek meadow viper is part of the Old World venomous viper group of snakes, which has a very wide range. This group is found from North Africa to just within the Arctic circle and from Great Britain to Pacific Asia, however, this particular species is considered to be very rare. The Greek meadow viper is in the class called Reptilia, better known as reptiles. All reptiles are called cold-blooded, which means they absorb heat from their environment and do not produce their own heat. This is called thermoregulation, when the animal can control body temperature through activity, for example basking when cold, or hiding in shade when it is too hot.

This viper is ovoviviparous, which means the eggs are fertilized and incubate inside the mother and she gives birth to live young, which is most unusual as most reptiles lay eggs. Ovoviviparity is a key evolutionary innovation among vipers, as it allows them to breed in colder environments and not worry about the outside temperature.

Reptiles regularly throw their skin. All reptile scales are made of keratin, the same material that makes human hair and nails, the horns of all rhinoceros species and pangolin scales, just to name a few.

This snake is in the viper family, which includes more than 350 species. This family has two major groups, the old World "true" vipers and the pit vipers, which are found in Asia and the Americas.

Vipers are characterised by large erectile venom-conducting fangs. This efficient venom delivery system allows vipers to eat large (and sometimes dangerous) animals without a struggle that might expose them to harm.
Vipers make a swift strike in which the long hollow, hypodermic needle-like fangs inject venom deep into the prey's body. The viper then waits until the animal dies, tracking it down if necessary, and then calmly swallows it. The venom also has the effect of initiating digestion even
before the prey is ingested. Many vipers do not find it necessary to eat more than once a month.
The venom of these snakes is diverse, being adapted to quickly kill the preferred prey animal of each viper species. The meadow vipers mostly prey on grasshoppers and other insects and rarely hunt small mammals or lizards and consequently their venom is not dangerous to humans, however it hurts like a bee sting.

The four viper sub families are:
Fea's vipers are the most ancient of vipers.

The night adders, only found in sub-Saharan Africa.
The pit vipers, deriving their name from the heat-sensitive pit organ on both sides of the head between nostril and eye, allows them to track prey through infrared radiation images.
And lastly, the true larger pit-less vipers, reaching a maximum length of more than 2 metres, are found throughout Europe, Asia, Africa and the Arctic Circle.

They all strike open mouthed in self–defence and are able to decide how much venom they inject based on the size and species of prey.
Their scales are ridged not smooth, the body is thick build and they have a short tail.

This viper is part of the Eurasian vipers, which are all terrestrial, with the different sexes differing in colour and size in many species. Each type of viper has different head shape, strength, active times and size. Males average about 35 cm long, while females are larger, up to 45 cm in length.
These small vipers are preyed by many other animals, like the red fox, badger, common kestrel and short-toed eagle.

The Greek meadow viper was described as a separate species in 2017 and was undertaken by our very own viper expert Edvard Mizsei.
The Greek meadow viper occurs at high elevations in subalpine meadows, above the tree line of the Hellenides mountain system of southern Albania and central Greece.
The entire distribution is extremely fragmented and each mountain population is completely isolated.

This viper is threatened because populations are completely isolated from each other and occur in highly fragmented small patches of habitat.
There is a continuous decline in habitat quality due to sheep and goat with variable levels of overgrazing. Grazing has an incredible effect on the habitat by destroying its biodiversity, its differences. And this reduces the abundance of the main food source for this viper.

In two areas of suitable habitat in Greece, there is also skiing activity where the habitat has been altered locally by construction of ski resorts and roads to access these resorts. Also, active mining operations affect other areas. This human activity continuously affects the habitat by destroying it either by construction and/or continuous road development for mine access.
Due to global warming, alpine climate zones are shifting upwards on mountain slopes as the tree line rises in elevation, reducing the areas of alpine and subalpine habitats.
The vipers are involved in human-wildlife conflict with local communities, as on average 1-4% of sheep suffer lethal bites every year, while on the other hand shepherds intentionally also kill the snakes.

The hope

There are two in situ conservation projects conducted by the Greek meadow Viper Working Group. The group has established good working relationships with the shepherds in Albania and has studied traditional grazing to find a way to reduce overgrazing.

The crew is researching the dynamic relationship between people, animals and their habitat from locals, and spreading basic knowledge on sustainable land use methods. Furthermore, a large part of the project is for the distribution of educational posters "Snakes of Albania" in schools to raise biodiversity awareness, create a more snake-friendly environment among locals, and build a reputation of conservation actions.
See http://www.speciesconservation.org/case-studies-projects/Greek-meadow-viper/10498.

Another issue is a human-wildlife conflict between shepherds' livestock and Greek meadow viper populations. The project, supported by The Rufford Foundation, helps shepherds and locals to prevent snakebites by informing them about areas where and when vipers are expected to be active, based on habitat preference and yearly/daily activity, to help them avoid encounters.
See http://www.rufford.org/projects/edv%C3%A1rd_mizsei.

Some organisations helping this species
IUCN Viper specialist group | Center for snake conservation | Save the Snakes | The Amphibian and Reptile Conservation | The Orianne Society.

What you can do to help
Do not buy any species that is endangered or even common if it is wild caught.
Report to the authorities any 'seller' you might see either at home or travelling that is selling endangered species.
Get involved with a Viper group that helps conserve these animals
https://www.facebook.com/vipera.graeca.conservation/
Get a group of your friends together, register your group as a Roots & Shoots group on www.roots&shoots.org and you will get help on how to run your group.

photo Edvárd Mizsei

Ranger Danger

BY
Laura Locher

Yarn B C Garn Jaipur silk fino

Pattern P. 239

Warm Embrace

BY
Laura Locher

Yarn Önling, No. 1

Pattern P. 238

Atlantic Bluefin Tuna

This beautiful fish is a slow growing and long lived tuna, that has been heavily exploited across its range.

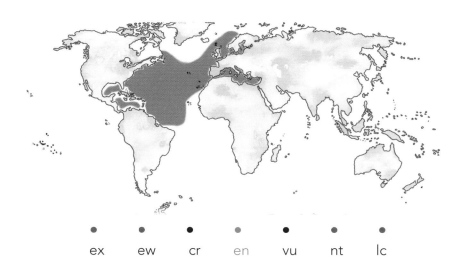

ex   ew   cr   en   vu   nt   lc

latin name: Thunnus thynnus
status: Endangered
threats: overfishing and overexploitation especially for sashimi market

Atlantic Bluefin Tuna

There are eight different species of tunas, and these fish are found in the oceans of the world. The smallest is the blackfin tuna, which only grows to a metre and weighs 21 kilos. The largest is the Atlantic bluefin.

All tunas swim on the surface and are able to dive to depths of over 800 metres looking for food. They sometimes swim along with pods of dolphins, to protect themselves from sharks, as sharks love to eat tuna.
From the 30 million eggs that a female tuna can release in its lifetime, it is proposed that only 2 tunas will survive to adulthood. Think of all the predators that this fish has along the way so it is really amazing that any survive!
Out of the eight species of tuna, three are in danger of extinction all due to overexploitation and overfishing.

The Atlantic bluefin tuna is really built for speed with its streamlined body, it can swim 80+ kilometres an hour. It has a large mouth with well-developed teeth and tiny scales all over its metallic body colouring, a true live torpedo.
The most striking feature of this fish family is that they produce and conserve their own heat, not like most other cold-blooded animals.
Tunas are also negatively buoyant, which means they will sink if they do not swim continuously. The bluefin tuna is in a class of the very diverse ray-finned fishes and all bony fish, the world's largest and most successful group of fish. These fish have their fins strengthened by rays which assist them with their direction and speed – much like a sail on a sailboat. This class of fish comprises 96% of all fish species and more than half of all living vertebrate species.
They are integral to the oceans' food chain and are consumed by other fish, birds, mammals, reptiles, amphibians and invertebrates.

Tunas are found in the open seas and often have wide migratory patterns. Atlantic bluefin tolerates the widest range of water temperatures of any of the tunas ranging from 1 degree to 29 degrees and also show a marked preference and tolerance for high salinity waters. This incredible tolerance to temperature allows the Atlantic bluefin tuna to feed in the northern latitudes up to the Norwegian Sea and the Gulf of Saint Lawrence.

Bluefin tunas spawn only in tropical waters and spend the rest of the year feeding in temperate regions.

Bluefin tunas are active, top ocean predators and sometimes hunt cooperatively, much like wolves. They are opportunistic, non-specialised predators that prey on small schooling fishes like anchovy, squids and red crabs. With streamlined bodies and retractable fins, they can bolt through the water and are capable of crossing oceans in the course of only a few weeks.

Another unique characteristic is that they school by size, so they are aware of how 'old' or big they are and swim together in groups of the same size. Predators of the tuna, beside man, are other larger fish like marlin, sharks and orcas.

The Atlantic bluefin tuna is thought to comprise distinct western and larger eastern Atlantic populations, which primarily spawn in the Gulf of Mexico and Mediterranean, respectively. They are genetically distinct; however, they do mix throughout the north Atlantic sea, especially when feeding.

Historically, it was found in the western Atlantic from Canada to the north to Brazil however populations in Brazil have disappeared and not been observed in 36 years.
The Western Atlantic population is found in the Gulf of Mexico and Caribbean. The Eastern population is found from Norway in the north to as far south as West Africa and in the Mediterranean.
It has been found the eastern and western subspecies usually return to their respective spawning grounds, with females weighing between 270 and 300 kilos and producing as many as 10 million eggs per spawning season.

This tuna is a highly valuable species in the Japanese sashimi market, which has been overfished and overexploited across its range. According to IUCN in 2010, there has been a 51% decline in numbers over the past 40 years.

Human influence has rendered at least five tuna species endangered or vulnerable to extinction, and we need to ensure local, regional and international catch numbers are monitored and policed to enable the tuna to survive.
Since 1970, western Atlantic bluefin tuna has declined by about 70% due to overfishing. In the eastern Atlantic, the majority of the decline has occurred in the past 10 years as they've been caught, without regulatory oversight, for fish farming as there is commercial ranching in the Mediterranean Sea.
Sadly, bluefin tuna remains a prized menu item, with the sushi market keeping prices for tuna high — a single tuna, weighing 278 kilos sold for an astonishing $3.1 million in early 2019.
This also encourages illegal fishing.
Japanese are the biggest consumers of the bluefin tuna and surging worldwide consumption has led to their decline. Despite an outcry from concerned people many sushi restaurants across the globe continue to serve bluefin.
It is estimated that approximately 80% of the Japanese market is supplied by the countries around the Mediterranean.

The hope

The International Commission for the Conservation of Atlantic Tunas (ICCAT) was set up by the 51 fishing nations in 1966 to manage fishing of tuna in the entire Atlantic Ocean and also to address the by-catch from tuna fishing like that of sharks, especially through the use of drift nets.
Drift nets are lengthy, free floating 8-15 metres deep nets each as long as 90 kilometres and ensnare fish by their gills in open waters. These nets are non-selective so their kill (by-catch) includes many other animals like turtles, sharks, seabirds and other marine mammals. These nets are extremely destructive and are used by the world's fisheries.
For the European Union member states, driftnet fishing for tuna has been banned since 1 January 2002; while the ban entered into force in 2004 is still officially permitted in Morocco.

Clearly, an overall reduction in fishing efforts is needed to reverse current trends. We need to protect, monitor and legislate the elimination of illegal fishing and countries need to achieve consensus on bluefin tuna management measures.

Often fishing quotas that are too high, sometimes against scientist recommendations in response to economic and political pressures. Having two distinct populations also makes it hard to manage. The differences in population size and that these two populations mix in their feeding grounds, and their high value, makes for complex challenges.

Organisations helping this species:
Oceana | ICCAT | Sailors for the Sea | WWF | Marine Conservation | Pew Charitable Trust

What you can do to help
Do not buy or consume Atlantic bluefin tuna.

photo Rafael Ben- Ari

Tuna on Parade

BY
Emalie Dam

Yarn Madelinetosh Tosh Merino Light

Pattern P. 222

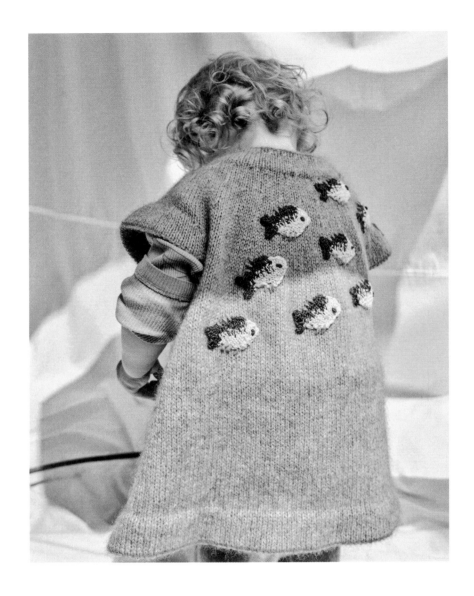

School of Tuna

BY
Emalie Dam

Yarn Zealana, Rimu + Kauri. ITO, Serinshin

Pattern P. 219

Oceania

Fijian Crested Iguana

Orange Bellied Parrot

Numbat

Erect Crested Peguin

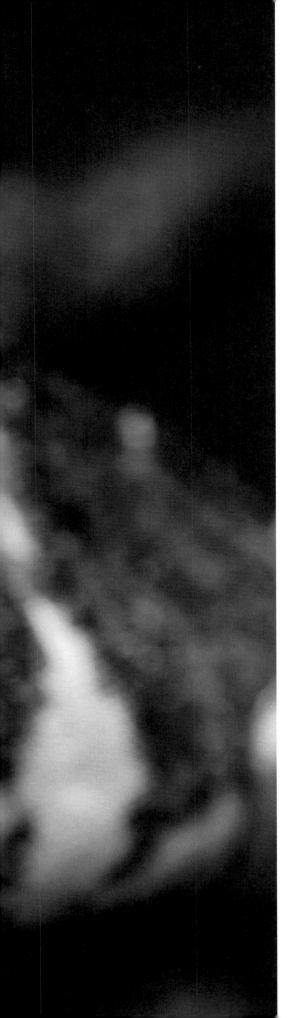

Fijian Crested Iguana

Iguanas are amongst the most popular reptile to have as a pet and are among the world's most endangered animals.

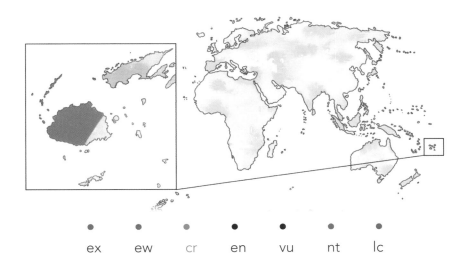

ex   ew   cr   en   vu   nt   lc

latin name: Brachylophus vitiensis
status: Critically endangered
threats: habitat loss, invasive species, habitat degradation

Fijian Crested Iguana

Iguanas are a type of large lizard with a long body of over 1.8 metres, and half of that being its tail; all have strong jaws and razor-sharp teeth. They are found only in Mexico, central and south America, Madagascar, Caribbean, Galapagos and Fijian Islands, and range in habitats from tropical forests to water and desert landscapes.
Iguanas' long, strong, sharp tails are used as whips, in defense against predators, and like most lizards they can also 'lose' their tales in a fight; the tail then gradually regrows.

The variety of habitats where iguanas are found have made each species quite unique, as they have all adapted to their own environment. Those iguanas that have chosen to live up in trees are found at least 13 metres high in the canopy and can actually fall to the ground from that height and not hurt themselves.
Iguanas that have adapted to a marine environment, like the Galapagos iguanas, feed on underwater algae, growing on rocks where they can at times stay underwater for up to 45 minutes! They are also black in color to quickly absorb the sunrays after being in the cold water. Whilst others that live in watery environments actually inflate themselves during a flood and can float away.

Most iguanas are solitary and very independent, whilst males can become extremely territorial. The only exception to this is the social Galapagos iguana that sleeps and sunbathes in large groups without any conflict.
The longest iguana is the green iguana being up to 2 metres long (nose to tail), and the smallest is the spiny tailed iguana from Mexico and Central America measures only 12.5 cm. Iguanas are seed dispersers for many native plants so their protection is vital to the ecosystem's health.

Fijian crested iguanas are very unique as they are known to have one of the longest incubation times of any lizard, taking approximately 9 months for the eggs to hatch. They are also the largest of the living South Pacific iguanas.
They are part of the largest order of reptiles which contains over 10,000 species. Their family includes the Galápagos marine and land spiny-tailed thorntail, rock, desert, green and Chuckwalla iguanas.

All iguanas are relatively large and predominately herbivorous lizards with a spiny crest along the neck and back, with colours that range from grey, green and brown with areas of black, blue, orange and red.

Fiji is home to four species of iguanas which are found nowhere else in the world. They look like neon-coloured dragons with their bright green bodies and small crest spines down their backs. They are perfectly camouflaged to hide in the Fijian forests.

The Fijian iguanas are the only iguanas in the eastern hemisphere, found specifically on the small islands of the Fijian archipelago in the South Pacific. Their closest relatives are from south-western North America and it is believed they dispersed in storm currents across the Pacific Ocean several thousand years ago.

Fijian crested iguanas are an arboreal lizard, living mainly in large bushes and trees, and restricted to coastal dry forests.
Both males and females have a unique pattern of white banding on their backs; their whole body turns darker if they are stressed or agitated by a predator or competitor.

Females lay a single clutch of 2-4 eggs every other year in a carefully excavated burrow on the forest floor.
Fijian crested iguanas are currently known from eight western dry forest islands in Fiji. With the exception of Yadua Taba and possibly the Macuata Islands, their populations have decreased severely, are barely detectable and are expected to become extinct in the next few years. It is estimated the total number of Fijian crested iguanas has declined by at least 80% over the last 40 years.
The iguana's habitat is continuing to be degraded due to goat grazing, presence of feral cats, intentional forest clearing and fires, as well as the spread of invasive alien plant species, village expansion and tourism development.

Because these iguanas are small in size, they are particularly vulnerable to predation by feral cats and perhaps invasive alien black rats. For example, Deviulau Island (23 hectares) has a high proportion of iguana food tree species (69%), yet the presence of cats is likely responsible for the low number of iguanas remaining.

The impact of the recent introduction and spread of the invasive alien common green iguana into Fiji is not yet known for this species, however it has been shown to have significant detrimental effects everywhere they have been introduced.

The hope

The entire island of Yadua Taba is a protected national park and recent natural plant regeneration after goat removal in 2004 has greatly increased the number of iguanas on this island. Recovery efforts like this demonstrate the real potential for recovering iguana populations on other islands.
For example, Monuriki Island has undergone a complete regeneration thanks to the work of many local and international organisations who began removing free-ranging goats and non-native Pacific rats on this island in 2010. These "alien invaders" were eating the iguana eggs and hatchlings and were destroying the iguana's natural food source.

In conjunction, 10 pairs of adult Fijian crested iguanas were transferred to Kula Eco Park on Viti Levu for captive breeding, with assistance and permission from Monuriki Island's local landowners and custodians.

In May 2015, 32 offspring, bred at Kula Eco Park, ranging in age from one to three years old, were released on Monuriki island. This is the first time that Fijian iguanas, bred in captivity, have been released back to the wild as part of conservation efforts.

To protect and restore even one tiny island like Monuriki is a credit to the foresight of the traditional landowners – the Mataqali Vunaivi clan of Yanuya Village.
Recovery of the unique dry forest is seen in the emergence of many young native trees and shrubs which provide essential food and shelter for the iguana and other wildlife.

The Fijian crested iguana is protected from international trade; however, illegal smuggling remains a known threat.

Organisations involved in this recovery program are:
IUCN SSC Iguana Specialist Group | Taronga Conservation Society | Australia Zoo
International Iguana Foundation | San Diego Zoo.

What you can do to help
If you love reptiles and loved this story, learn more about these iguanas through the SSC Iguana specialist group and tell your friends.
If you needed to have a reptile as a pet, make sure that it's a reputable pet shop or aquarium, that you get the proper paper and local authorisation so that you know that any reptile is not illegally traded.

photo Donya Nedomam

My Iguana Friend

BY
Lisa Renner

Yarn Purl Soho, Understory + leftovers

Pattern P. 300

Shy Exhibitionist

BY
Lisa Renner

Yarn Isager, Silk Mohair

Pattern P. 297

Orange Bellied Parrot

This small brightly coloured parrot is one of a few parrots in the world, that migrates to warmer winter grounds far away from its breeding habitat.

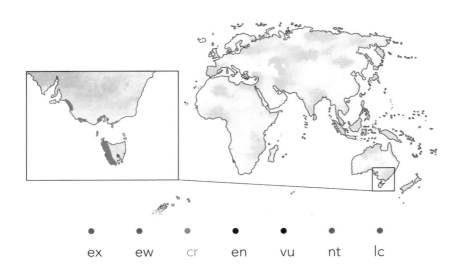

ex · ew · cr · en · vu · nt · lc

latin name: Neophema chrysogaster
status: Critically endangered
threats: habitat fragmentation, diseases

photo Chris Morecroft

Orange Bellied Parrot

Parrots are found all over the world, but not in our polar regions. They are amongst the most intelligent birds and only eat food that they handle with their feet; in fact, they usually prefer to eat with one foot or the other just like we prefer to use our right or left hands. They have very strong beaks, and some parrots can live over 80 years.

The world's largest flying parrot is the South American hyacinth parrot, which has a beak strong enough to crack macadamia nuts considered one of the hardest nuts to crack. The world's largest parrot however, cannot fly and is called the kakapo; it can weigh over 4 kilos and grow over half a metre long – it is the only flightless parrot in the world. It is also the only parrot that is active at night and critically endangered due to introduced species like cats, rats and ferrets into their New Zealand home.

There are more than 360 species of parrots, mostly brightly coloured noisy birds. They include birds like amazons, cockatoos, lorikeets, lories, macaws and parakeets. Many have been domesticated and become household companions and heavily trafficked for pet trade.

The orange bellied parrot is found only in Australia, one of half a dozen species commonly known as grass parrots, which are small, basically green parrots with blue wings in which the male is often enlivened by patches of red or orange.
The orange bellied parrot is distinguished by the intensity of its green plumage and a small patch of bright orange on the belly that is slightly larger on the male, which also has a blue band on his forehead.
They are slightly larger than a small parakeet, being about 20 cm long and weighing up to 50 grams. They have a life expectancy of about four years. When alarmed, they have a distinctive metallic buzzing call. Monogamous, with only one mating partner, they begin breeding in their first year, laying a clutch of three to six eggs.

The orange bellied parrot breeds in south-west Tasmania in patches of eucalypt forest embedded within extensive moorland plains. Nesting occurs in tree hollows and, when breeding, the species feeds on the seeds of a range of grasses and sedges in moorlands. The female cleans out the nest hollow, then lays the eggs about two days apart. She incubates the eggs and broods the nestlings while being fed by the male every two to three hours. The male may feed up to five kilometres away from the nest site. When the young are about 10 days old, the female leaves them during the day and helps the male with feeding. The chicks leave the nest four to five weeks after hatching and are usually fed by their parents before becoming independent.

After breeding, orange bellied parrots migrate north across Bass Strait to saltmarshes, dunes, beaches, pastures and shrub lands close to the coast in central Victoria and South Australia. There, they feed on the ground or in low vegetation, almost exclusively on seeds, mainly of salt-tolerant coastal and saltmarsh plants. Juveniles form small flocks and depart for the mainland about a month later than the adults.

The orange bellied parrot already was extremely rare by 1900, fewer than 200. By the end of the 2015/16 breeding season, there were only 35 and fewer than 20 in 2017 and 2018. Furthermore, the sex ratio was highly skewed, with all but three of the wild birds being females.

Many factors have contributed to the species' rarity. On its breeding grounds there is a strong suspicion the species favoured fire as it prefers to forage in recently burnt areas. Fire was a major feature of Aboriginal land management for millennia, with small burns helping them find food and providing firebreaks so wildfire was contained.

More recently tin miners maintained the tradition in the few areas where the parrots persisted. However, when tin mining ceased, there were several decades when few fires were lit. The managers of the newly created reserve were cautious about lighting fires that would spread over large areas, so preferred to light no fires at all. A consequence appears to have been less feeding habitat for the parrot.

Tree hollows for nesting are also a scarce resource and, in some places, the parrots may have been driven out through competition with introduced European starlings or predation by sugar gliders – a small possum introduced to Tasmania from mainland Australia. Even in their last stronghold they face competition from the native tree martins which also use tree hollows for nesting.

And then on mainland Australia, the fragmentation and degradation of their winter saltmarsh habitat by grazing, as well as agriculture, and urban and industrial development, affect the species even further.

Such effects are made worse by occasional droughts with a ten-year spell of below average rainfall having a severe effect on the health of saltmarsh plants at the turn of the century.

Eventually, with such a tiny population, every source of death becomes a threat. Feral cats, introduced foxes, windfarms, poor weather at the time the parrots cross Bass Strait, all reduce the chances of the species surviving.

The tiny size of modern flocks is also a threat in itself. Birds form flocks so they can share the task of looking for predators. Birds in smaller flocks are therefore more vulnerable to predation. And they even appear to have trouble finding each other to form flocks in the non-breeding season

The hope

Realising the species' rarity, a captive breeding programme was commenced in 1984, by the Recovery Plan group, and more than 300 individuals are now held in seven different breeding centres in Australia and Tasmania.

Captive birds are instrumental in the conservation effort. For example, as the population is severely male biased (six males per one female), females are released in spring at the breeding site to correct the sex ratio imbalance.

Captive-bred birds that have been released have also migrated successfully between their breeding and wintering grounds and back again. Birds released on the wintering grounds have also migrated south to breed. However, survival is poor and many released birds are caught again before migration. Some are also released at wintering sites where they have been joined by birds that have flown there.

The extraordinary effort being made to conserve the orange bellied parrots has undoubtedly prevented its extinction, despite enormous challenges presented by the remoteness of its breeding site and the perils inherent in its migratory behaviour.

Some organisations helping this species
The Australian, Tasmanian, Victorian and South Australian governments and their relevant National Parks | BirdLife Australia | Australian National University | Charles Sturt University | Zoo's and Aquarium Association.

What you can do to help
Contact BirdLife Australia and International, to learn more about the world's birds. Contact the Tasmanian, Victorian and South Australian governments, national parks and regional and local councils, who are also involved.

photo Paul Rushworth

Hopeful Flight

BY
Charlotte Kaae

Yarn Handspun Hope

Pattern P. 282

Parrot Pocket

BY
Charlotte Kaae

Yarn Handspun Hope

Pattern P. 280

Numbat

Even though Numbats are marsupials, best known for having a pouch to rear their young, this species has no pouch.

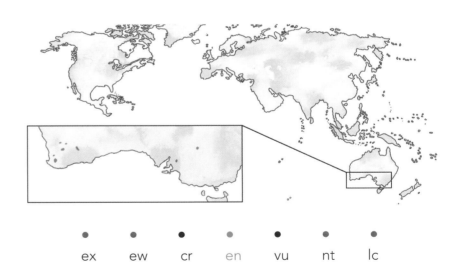

● ● ● ● ● ● ●
ex ew cr en vu nt lc

latin name: Myrmecobius fasciatus
status: Endangered
threats: habitat fragmentation, fox and feral cats, changed fire regimes

photo Isabel Poulin

Numbat

Numbats are a most unusual Australian marsupial; they do not eat plants, like most of the marsupials, and they do not have a pouch to raise their young, most unusual.

The smallest marsupial is a planigale, a tiny mouse-sized animal that despite its small size is a fearless hunter, preying on other animals at least its own size.

The largest living marsupial is the red kangaroo, they can jump over 7 and a half metres in one hop and move for short periods of time at over 56 kilometers an hour. A fully-grown red kangaroo can stand over 180 cm and weigh over 90 kilos.

A marsupial is a group of mammals primarily found in Australia and New Guinea, but there are also some in the Americas. They are identified as a specific group that bear their young at a very early stage of development and the offspring are typically carried, suckle and grow up in a pouch on the mother's belly. However, in numbats the females have no pouch.

The numbat is the only species in the family Myrmecobiidae, meaning ant-eating in Latin, and they can also be called a banded anteater. They are part of the larger group that contains Australia's carnivorous marsupials, like quolls, dunnarts, and the Tasmanian devil; however it has been found that it is more closely related to the extinct Thylacine – the Tasmanian tiger.

The numbat must be one of the most beautiful marsupials found in Australia. With their distinctive reddish-brown coat, four to 11 white stripes across its back, a small narrow delicate head and a pointy snout. They have a long sticky tongue and a very prominent black stripe running from the top of its nose across its eyes, to the base of its ears.

A unique feature of this animal is that it's diurnal – active during the day. Most animals in Australia have adapted to the heat by being active at night. However, their daytime activity is synchronised with their favourite food source, which is active during the day.

The numbats have an unusual diet, with termites forming almost all their food. Numbats do not have very strong claws to destroy termite nests; however, with their strong sense of smell, they find termites by following their scent and the corridors the termites form.

Numbats live in the eucalyptus forests and woodlands in a few small areas of south-western Australia. They are solitary and territorial with large home ranges and spend their daylight hours hunting their prey and sleeping in hollow logs or burrows at night.

They are omnivorous but primarily eat termites, occasionally ants and other small insects, with an adult numbat eating up to 20,000 termites a day, which is 20% of their body weight. Numbats or walpurti as the indigenous peoples call them, usually give birth to four small 2 cm offspring after a gestation period of only a couple of weeks. Once born, they will crawl up to one of the four teats and attach themselves, where they remain for about five months. After they have almost tripled in size they will then be moved to a nest until spring and by the end of spring they will move out to find their own territory.
In captivity numbats live 4-8 years.

Found now only in south-western Australia, the numbat's past distribution was across most of southern Australia. The estimated total population is now only about 1,500 individuals in the wild.

Being active during the day, numbats are exposed to predation by raptors such as wedge-tailed eagles, brown falcons, little eagles and brown goshawks, as well as reptiles such as monitors (goannas) and the carpet python, as well as the introduced fox and feral cats. The introduction of the predatory fox and feral cats has had a profound impact and continues to be a major threat for the numbat.

Changed fire regimes, especially in arid grasslands, and habitat destruction in some areas also contributed to the numbat's decline.

Areas where the species occurs naturally, as well as the reintroduction sites, are all conservation reserves and a recovery plan is being implemented.
A community action group, called Project numbat, has been established in Perth and works with the recovery team to increase awareness of the numbat and its plight, as well as raising significant funding to support numbat conservation.

The hope

"A group of numbat lovers has come to the rare marsupial's rescue in a pocket of south-western, Western Australia.

Robert McLean seems an unlikely conservationist. A meat-truck driver by day, he's a man who loves steak and beer. But most weekends you won't catch him putting his feet up watching the football. Instead you'll find him deep in the Dryandra Woodland on the frontline of a battle to save Western Australia's state animal emblem from extinction.

Robert's passions are photography and numbats, and he has successfully combined the two into a constructive obsession. On weekends he heads inland, driving for several hours from his coastal home to the Dryandra conservation area 170 km south-east of Perth, to find and photograph numbats. His unusual hobby has led him to form a strong bond with three other unlikely conservationists: airline worker Sean Van Alphen; power-company employee Matthew Willett; and John Lawson, caretaker of the Lions Dryandra Woodland Village and former stonemason. The group met on individual searches for the elusive creature after bumping into one another while following the network of old logging tracks that criss-cross Dryandra.

The numbat Taskforce was initially formed to lobby the State government for protection for the numbat from feral cat predation. The four friends set up a Facebook page and now post every numbat image they capture on their cameras. Their efforts have managed to overturn a decision by the State's Environmental Protection Authority not to assess the tip proposal. It was a significant victory for the team."

Information from the Press release is quoted above.

Australian Conservation Heroes

https://www.australiangeographic.com.au/society/awards/2018/10/numbat-task-force-conservationist-of-the-year.

Some organisations involved in this program are:
Project numbat | Nature Conservancy | Australian Wildlife Conservancy | WWF | FAME | The numbat breeding program at Perth Zoo.

What you can do to help
Contact Project numbat or other organisations to see if you can learn more about the numbat and share with friends.
You could adopt a numbat and support in their conservation.
If you live in Australia where cats have no natural predators, do not let your cat out at night or release them as they will prey on native animals.

Hang On

BY
Bruno Kleist

Yarn Purl Soho, Shepherdess Alpaca

Pattern P. 246

Odd Stripes

BY
Bruno Kleist

Yarn Isager, Alpaca 2

Pattern P. 242

Erect Crested Penguin

Climate change will likely affect different penguin species differently, however in the Antarctic, the loss of krill is the penguins major threat.

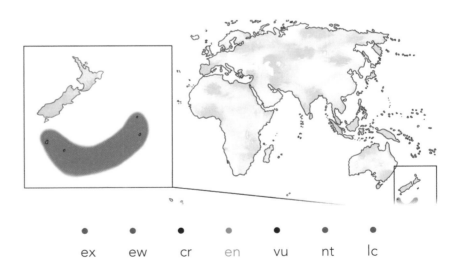

ex   ew   cr   en   vu   nt   lc

latin name: Eudyptes sclateri
status: Endangered
threats: fishing for krill, climate change

photo Duncan Noakes

Erect Crested Penguin

Did you know that penguins are birds that cannot fly?
Their wings have transformed into flippers, which enables them to swim, and they are mostly found in the southern hemisphere of our planet.

All birds have feathers; however, penguins' feathers are much shorter and stiffer, making them more streamlined in water. Their feathers are also able to trap more air, which provide much better insulation. Penguins' bones are not hollow like those of most other birds, penguin bones are denser, to make their diving easier, and they can dive to depths of over 250 metres.

Most penguins eat a variety of seafood like fish, squid and crustaceans, whilst the smaller penguins usually eat krill. As they all eat so much from the sea, they need to cope with high levels of salt. For this they have developed a special gland, located above their eyes, that filters the salt from their bloodstream and is excreted through either sneezing or through their bills.

Emperor penguins are the tallest of all the species of penguin, reaching heights of 1.2 metres. Little penguins, also known as fairy or blue penguins, are the smallest penguins reaching only 33 cm in height.

Penguins are in the Aves class, which are vertebrates and includes all birds. They are in the penguin family, which lives mostly in the southern hemisphere, with only the Galapagos penguin venturing north of the equator. There are 17 to 19 species of penguins in the world, with no penguins in the North Pole.

Crested penguins are in the most diverse group of penguins.
With their yellow feather plumes, red bills and eyes, crested penguins are the most elaborately adorned of all the penguins. They have a wide, bright yellow stripe originating over the eye, which forms a short erect crest.
They share this group with other penguins called fiordland, macaroni, rock hopper, royal and snares penguins.

The erect-crested penguin's feather pattern of black and white, like most penguins, makes them look as if they are wearing a very smart dinner suit. It is a common misconception that this black and white colouring serves as camouflage; however, this is not the case. Other explanations about why the penguins have this black and white look could be for their thermoregulation, keeping warm, protection from abrasion or social signaling.
The erect-crested penguin is a migratory species, travelling many kilometres to other areas at different seasons either to feed or breed. They remain at sea, in the sub-Antarctic over the winter months, which is almost 80% of their lives at sea and the remaining 20% on land, and little is known about their biology and breeding.

Their main predators include leopard seals, sea lions and sharks.

The erect-crested penguin is a bit taller than half a metre and it is a carnivore, eating krill, squid and small fish. They have spikes on their tongues and the roof of their mouth which helps to hold and swallow prey in one piece.

They live in large colonies and communicate via sounds; posturing and displays are the main forms of communication in penguins.
It is not really known if they hunt in groups or on their own; however, they travel hundreds of kilometres to find food. They are offshore foragers, looking for food far away from their breeding grounds, leaving their colonies deserted during non-breeding season.
They nest in large, dense, conspicuous colonies, numbering thousands of pairs, on rocky terrain, often without substantial soil or vegetation, made with stones, grass or mud.
Erect-crested penguins lay two eggs yet incubate and rear only one chick. The second egg is the larger and usually the surviving chick.
Incubation is about a month.

The penguin chick is equipped with several tools to break open the strong eggshell when the time comes to hatch. They have an egg tooth, which is a sharp bump on the top of the bill, used to crack the egg.
They also have a strong neck muscle that provides the force to break the shell. Both the egg tooth and the hatching muscle disappear shortly after hatching.

When chicks are older in the "post guarding phase" and both parents are at sea foraging for food, chicks will huddle in groups called crèches to keep warm and avoid predators. Chicks and parents find each other amid the chaos of crèches through individualized calls that act like an auditory signature.

The average lifespan of erect-crested penguins is unknown; however, it is assumed they may reach 25-30 years.
The erect-crested penguin is only found in New Zealand where it breeds on the Bounty and Antipodes islands. These are nature reserves and part of a World Heritage site designated in 1998.
Population trends indicate a severe decline between the mid-1970s and mid-1990s.
This species' significant decline is attributed to major global-warming-induced changes in the marine environment that have reduced overall ocean productivity and penguin prey. This penguin is also threatened by disease and oil spills. It is unknown at this stage, if microplastics are a problem or could become a problem for these penguins.

The hope

All 17-19 species of penguins are legally protected from hunting and egg collecting.

With a severe lack of data on the species, it is difficult to assess what causes population declines in the species. The absence of introduced terrestrial predators disrupting penguin populations on the mainland points towards sea-based issues, which most likely consist of changes in marine productivity due to ocean warming and, potentially, fisheries interactions.

Apart from infrequent, opportunistic monitoring of population size there are currently no conservation actions underway.

The International penguin Conservation Working Group (IPCWG) was formed in September 2000, to address mounting threats to penguin populations worldwide. It is made up of biologists, research institutes, zoos and aquaria, and other international organisations working in the field of penguin conservation, research and education, sharing ideas and provide international support for local conservation.

The aim of the IPCWG is to promote penguin conservation worldwide, by drawing international attention to the threats facing penguin populations.

They hope to discover more about this species and therefore develop a conservation and management plan for the erect-crested penguin.

Increased and constant surveying of the islands is required, and conducting detailed studies to determine the penguins' foraging ranges, commercial fisheries interactions, and oceanographic or climatic changes also need to be investigated.

Some organisations helping this species
IUCN Specialist penguin group | The Global penguin Society |
International penguin Conservation Working Group | WWF | Penguin Foundation | IFAW.

What you can do to help
Lower your carbon footprint and use of single use plastics.
Learn more about penguins and participate in World penguin Day on April 25.
Volunteer to help penguins – oneworld365.org

Eyes on You

BY
Laura Locher

Yarn Purl Soho, Season Alpaca + Understory

Pattern P. 227

Flying Feathers

BY
Laura Locher

Yarn Madelinetosh, Vintage + Prairie. Ito, Sensai

Pattern P. 224

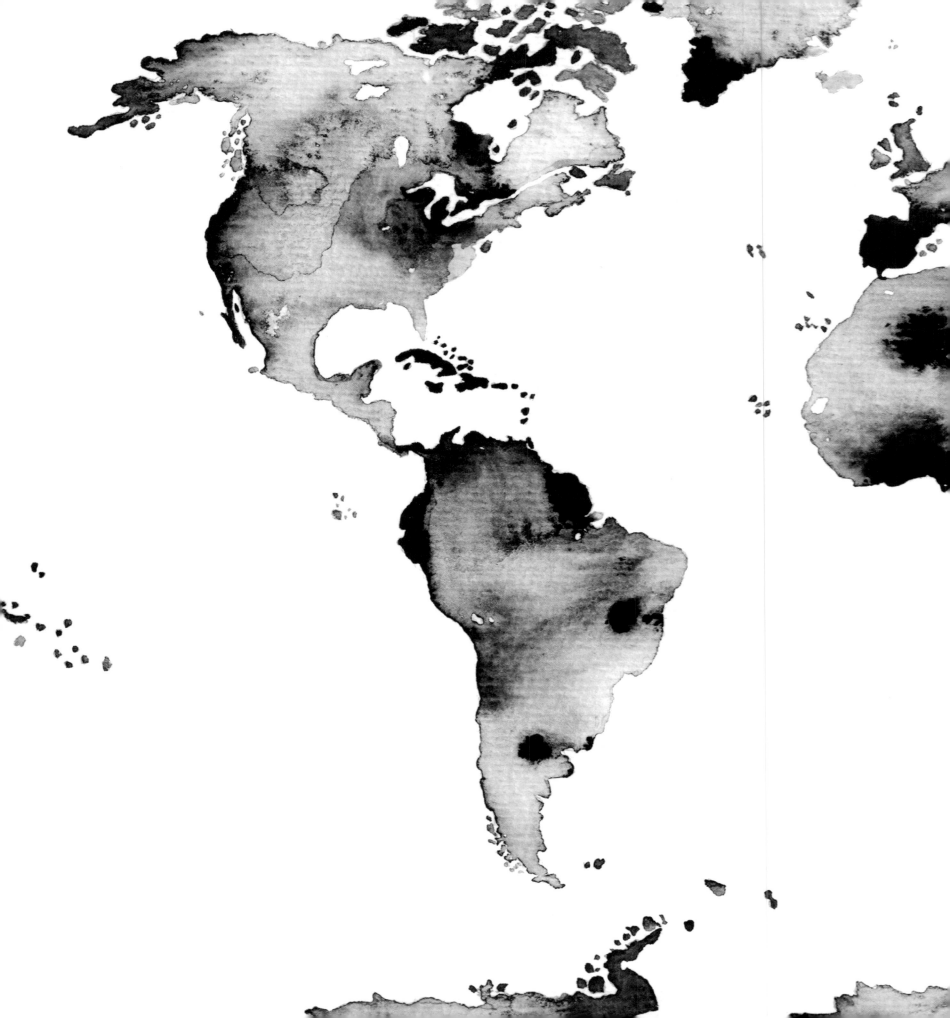

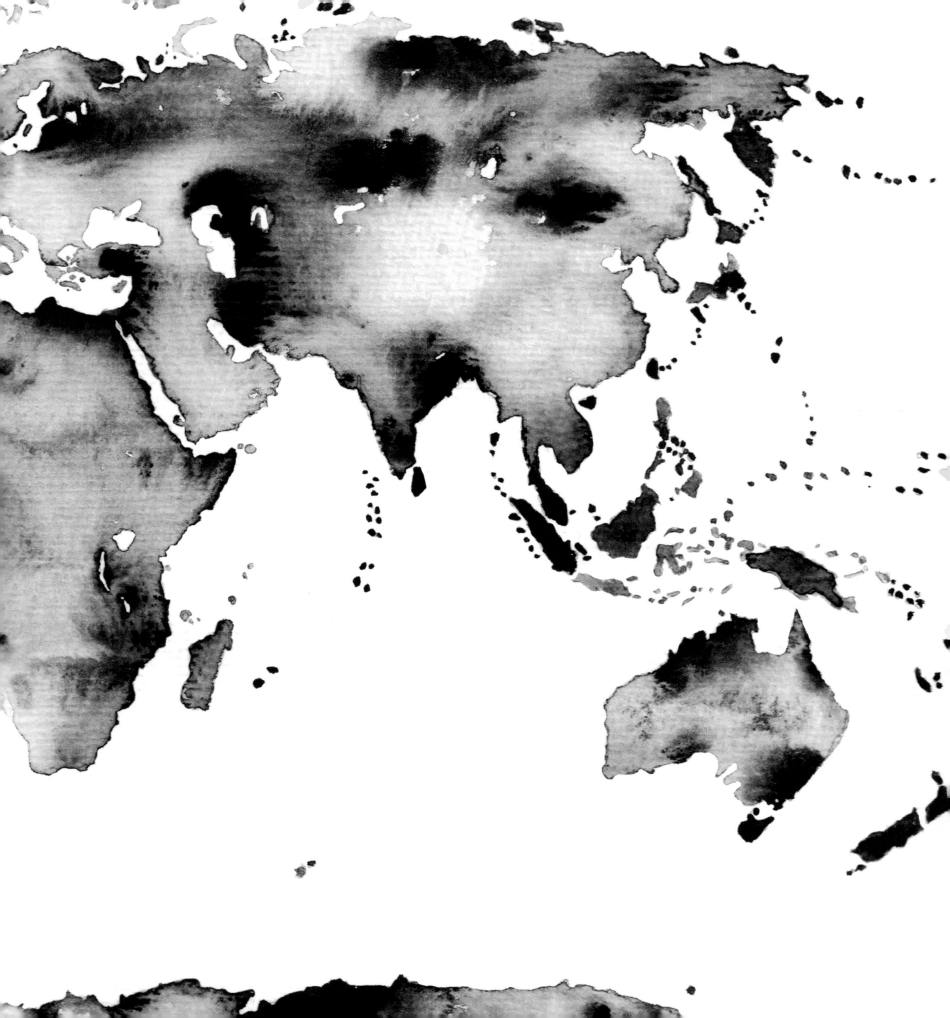

Staghorn Coral

Known as the rainforests of the sea, they occupy less than 1% of the ocean yet they are home to almost 25% of all described marine species.

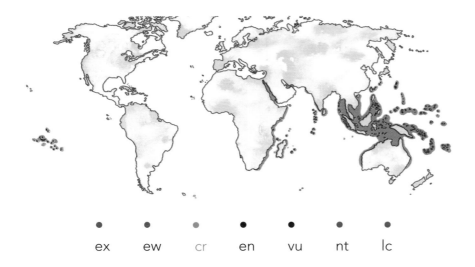

ex   ew   cr   en   vu   nt   lc

latin name: Acropora cervicornis
status: Critically endangered
threats: human development and climate change, shipping and disease

photo John Anderson

Staghorn Coral

There are basically two different types of coral, soft and hard.
Hard corals are reef-building corals, they act as fish nurseries and come in so many different shapes and sizes, resembling deer antlers, trees, giant fans, brains and honeycomb.
Whilst soft corals look more like plants or trees that are colourful and graceful, produce some calcium carbonate that allows them to keep their shape. Most corals grow very slowly.

There are three different types of coral reef formations; fringing, barrier and coral atolls.
Fringing reefs, the most common, are found right along the coastline. Reef building corals are found in shallow, tropical waters running parallel to the coastline, protecting the shallower waters from the open sea. Natural disasters like tsunamis, cyclones and landslides are protected by these barrier reefs.
And coral atolls are rings of coral reef on top of old sunken volcanoes, often mistaken for islands.
There are 25 families of corals, and approximately 1,500 species of coral which are found in over 100 countries around the world.
The Great Barrier Reef is the world's largest coral reef spanning 2,300 kms and can be seen from space. It contains 400 different types of corals and 1,500 different fish species.
Coral reefs stabilize the seabed helping seagrass, seaweed and other marine plants to survive, and they also help to improve water quality.

Corals have been named the medicine cabinets of the 21st century, by the US Department the National Oceanic and Atmospheric Administration (NOAA) – because corals cannot move, they have evolved chemical defense mechanisms to keep their predators at bay. Scientists are still discovering new medical treatments derived from corals to treat cancer, arthritis, Alzheimer's, heart and other diseases.

Unfortunately, 25% of coral reefs are damaged beyond repair.
Corals are made up of small animals with no vertebrae called polyps. They are connected together to form large colonies and actually secrete a calcium carbonate skeleton, which is the rock that you see.
Coral reefs are the most diverse of all marine ecosystems. They are full of life, with perhaps ¼ of all ocean species depending on reefs for food and shelter. Coral reefs cover less than 1% of the earth's surface and due to their diversity are often called the rainforests of the sea.

Staghorn corals are part of a group, or genus, called Acropora, with over 140 other species. They are found in shallow tropical reef ecosystems, liking areas with moderate to low wave exposure, and provide an important complex habitat for other reef animals, especially fish.
These cylindrical, branching, stony coral are attached to the sea–bed. Their larvae disperse as plankton, and the adult coral can live for decades.
The animal part, the polyp, has a symbiotic (mutually beneficial) relationship with a single cell alga, which is a plant called zooxanthellae, which lives in the tissue of the polyps.

This alga produces nutrients which are the corals primary food source.
However, corals can also 'catch' other food, however as coral cannot move, they wait for their food source to come to them and use their stinging cells on their tentacles to sting them.
There are four important stages of development in staghorn corals' reproduction, egg development, settlement and growth.

During the first step mature adults release millions of sperm and egg cells in a unique and synchronized phenomenon known as coral spawning. Floating to the surface the eggs fertilize and can stay on the surface and drift for weeks. At this stage an egg absorbs its alga, which helps it grow into a larva.
The mature larva then sinks to the ocean floor and attaches to a rock surface, where it will transform into a polyp. The polyp will then bud to produce many polyps and secrete the skeleton, and grow to form the adult colony. Like most living organisms, corals take a while before they can reproduce; staghorn coral takes just a few years to fully mature.

The most famous of the staghorn corals, Acropora cervicornis, was found throughout the Caribbean, including the Florida Keys, the Bahamas, and the islands and mainland coasts. But there has been an 80-98% loss of this species in the Caribbean region since the 1980's.

Other species of staghorn corals are found throughout the Pacific and Indian Oceans and are also threatened and declining. For example, since 2016 half of the corals on the Great Barrier Reef have died (source: The Atlantic.com)
Staghorn coral is particularly susceptible to disease and bleaching.
Coral bleaching is the loss of the important algae that live in the coral tissue. The loss of the algae causes the coral to die of starvation, and can increase its vulnerability to disease.

Other major threats include storms and damage by the three-spot damselfish.
All corals are vulnerable to the growing impacts of human activities.
The frequency and duration of coral bleaching and ocean acidification place coral reefs at high risk of collapse. Coral disease, like white-band, has emerged as a serious threat to coral reefs worldwide, often after bleaching events.

Localized threats include dynamite and chemical fishing, human developments like cities, tourism and transportation, pollution from agriculture, industry and domestic pollution, like plastics, increased sedimentation, and human recreation and tourism activities.

Staghorn coral highlights the impact of all these global changes, as one of the most threatened of all coral species worldwide.

The hope

In US waters, it is illegal to harvest corals for commercial purposes. Localized efforts to propagate and reintroduce the species have occurred in Florida, Puerto Rico, Dominican Republic, Jamaica and Honduras. In response to ship grounding and hurricanes, there have been efforts in some areas to salvage damaged corals and reattach them in their habitats.

As an early warning system, coral reefs have been sounding the alarm for years. Bleached white by marine heatwaves, and massive die-offs by the effects of climate change, so a few projects are being trialed to restore the staghorn coral populations.

In the Florida Keys, underwater nurseries offer hope for endangered ecosystems, encouraging growth of coral fragments on fibreglass structures anchored to the sea-bed.

In Australia, Taronga Conservation Society is the lead organisation in applying cryopreservation technologies to reef management, restoration and research for the Great Barrier Reef. Working with the Smithsonian Institute, the Australian Institute of Marine Science (AIMS) and the Great Barrier Reef Foundation, they have been cryobanking keystone coral reef species at annual spawning seasons since 2011.

Some organisations helping the species:
IUCN Coral Specialist group | NOAA | Oceana | Queensland University
Taronga Conservation Society | Smithsonian Institute | AIMS | Great Barrier Reef Foundation
4Ocean | Coral Reef Alliance International Coral Reef Initiative | WWF
Wildlife Conservation Society.

What you can do to help
Don't buy any coral especially when travelling, as it increases the demand for the illegal capture and selling of corals.
Be aware when snorkelling, diving or boating and reduce your carbon footprint.
Support eco-tourism organisations that support coral reef conservation.

Ocean Footprints

BY
Lisa Renner

Yarn Kettle Yarn, Islington

Pattern P. 311

United Nations´ 17 Goals

Sustainable goals for the future

The loss of biodiversity affects us all. It affects the environment, jobs, and livelihoods for people all over the world. We all depend on animals and their habitats, as much as they depend on us to take action in their preservation. And, we have proven that we possess the capabilities to overcome enormous global challenges. Since 1990, world poverty has fallen by almost 75%, nine out of ten children in developing countries are enrolled in school today, twice as many children survive their five-year birthday, and two billion people have access to improved drinking water.

And now, built on these efforts, we have the Sustainable Development Goals. The SDGs were set into effect on the first day of 2016 and committed to by all the UN member states to an unprecedented ambitious and transformative course for sustainable development. The 17 goals are the result of three years of diplomatic efforts and the most comprehensive and transparent consultation process in UN history. Nearly one hundred national and eleven global consultations were held, with contributions from high-level panels, civil society, the private sector, as well as an online survey where 10 million people had their voices heard. Ownership, legitimacy, and representation is the very core of the Sustainable Development Goals, and they apply to every country and work in global, national, and local settings.

The goals are: No Poverty; Zero Hunger; Good Health and Well-being; Quality Education; Gender Equality; Clean Water and Sanitation; Affordable and Clean Energy; Decent Work and Economic Growth; Industry, Innovation and Infrastructure; Reducing Inequality; Sustainable Cities and Communities; Responsible Consumption and Production; Climate Action; Life Below Water; Life on Land; Peace, Justice and Strong Institutions and Partnerships for these Goals.

And this is why a shared responsibility for all to take action in implementing the global goals for sustainable development into all the decisions we make – from our daily routines to global policy make these goals so important.

So, when it comes to the effort we make to preserve biodiversity, what the 17 goals of the SDGs offer, is a common ground in uniting our efforts for a better and sustainable world – and clearly demonstrates how every action we take towards sustainability is supporting the preservation of our incredible animals and nature.
The time to act is now.

Jens Christian Olsen
Student at University of Cph. and intern at UNDP Nordic Office.

R:E:D: 17 Animals

Health Benefits of knitting

It is no wonder that the culture of knitting worldwide is strong. In the past, knitting was a matter of surviving against the weather, and many places around the world it is still a serious factor of daily living.
Besides this, knitting is also about giving and it is known to have a strong and positive impact on your health.

With this book we wish to promote knitting for three main purposes;
Knitting gives a boost of wellbeing and heals your brain and body
Knitting is about giving your loved ones and friends the garments and pieces, you have knitted
And most importantly;
Giving back to nature, while choosing to support endangered animals – by telling people about the threats and how to help; by using yarn from certified dealers; by telling the important stories to our kids; and most of all by taking the steps from hope to action

In the New York Times 2016 a report noted that "there is a surprisingly large body of research showing the health benefits of knitting and what is more surprising is how little known this research is".

The list is long; knitting is known to reduce your blood pressure and to prevent or reduce depression, stress, anxiety, dementia and chronic pain. It gives you a feeling of relaxation, meditation and wellbeing; further to this, it stimulates the whole brain and your cognitive skills. And we haven't even mentioned yet the possibilities of entering into strong social relationships when doing handcrafts in all its different expressions.

The results from a literature review correlating neurological evidence and activities showed that purposeful and meaningful activities could lessen the effects of stress related diseases and reduce the risk of dementia. Specifically, it was found that music, drawing, meditation, reading, arts and crafts (knitting would be an example), and home repairs, for example, can stimulate the neurological system and enhance your health and wellbeing.
(2007 John Wiley & Sons, Ltd.)

Another international survey looked at the benefits of knitting for personal and social well-being in adulthood. The results show a significant relationship between knitting frequency and feeling calm and happy. More frequent knitters also reported higher cognitive functioning. Knitting in a group impacted significantly on perceived happiness, improved social contact and communication with others. (Jill Riley at. all, 2013)

To this we know that hormones of happiness are at a higher level (measured in the blood) when we are giving than when we are receiving.

A study using data from Gallup Poll from a global survey of 234,917 responders found people all over the world experiencing more happiness when spending on others than when spending on themselves.

Researchers from Simon Fraser University in Vancouver tested the idea with an experiment in which they gave 200 students from Canada and South Africa a small amount of money and told them to either buy treats for themselves or for a child in hospital.

The students reported higher levels of well-being after purchasing a goodie bag for a sick child compared to when buying one for themselves.

Lead author Dr Lara Aknin said: "The findings provide the first evidence that the warm glow of spending on someone else rather than on oneself may be a widespread component of human psychology. From an evolutionary perspective, the emotional benefits that people experience when they help others act to encourage generous behavior beneficial to long-term human survival."

A great opportunity is to knit for others and for nature, as well.

In the next section of the book, you will find all the patterns for the jumpers. Enjoy the passion and the health benefits of knitting, enjoy giving the jumper to a teenager or a child and not least, tell the story where you go and where you knit and enjoy the social relationships of knitters and animal lovers.

The knitting patterns

Baleen Beauty

Blue Whale Teen~Adult
Design Emalie Dam
Skill level 4
Photo pg 104 -105

Designer Emalie Dam
- a jacket with an asymmetric opening
#REDbaleenbeauty

Skill level 4
Sizes
EU + UK XS (S) M (L)
To fit bust
82 (88) 94 (100) cm
32¼ (34½) 37 (39½) inches
Actual bust measurement (jumper)
90 (94) 100 (106) cm
35½ (37) 39½ (41¾) inches
Length
68 (71) 74 (77) cm
26¾ (28) 29¼ (30¼) inches
Yarn
Madelinetosh Vintage
100% merino wool, 180 m / 200 yards per skein
3 (3) 3 (4) skeins col A, Then Luna Lovegood
Fed the Thestrals
and
6 (6) 7 (7) skeins col B, Dubrovnik.
Needles
5.5 mm (US 9) circular needle, 80 cm (32 inches)
and 60 cm (24 inches)
5 mm (US 8) dpn for icord edge
13 stitch markers
Long zipper **PLEASE NOTE:** Do not buy one
until the jumper is completely done! It is
important that the zipper has the exact length
as the mid front panel. If you have difficulty
finding the right length, consider shortening
one. You can easily find instructions for this on
You Tube and can try out different lengths first.
Gauge
In stocking stitch on 5.5 mm (US 9) needles: 19
sts x 25 rows = 10 x 10 cm / 4 x 4 inches
In two-coloured 1 x 3 rib on 5.5 mm (US 9)
needles and yarn col A: 32 sts x 25 rows = 10 x
10 cm/4 x 4 inches
Remember to check your gauge for both
patterns and adjust needle size accordingly.
Stitch patterns
Two-coloured 1 x 3 rib as described here and
in the pattern. Where you normally would try
to make sure the yarn on the back should not
be tight, you will here make an effort to hold
the stranded yarn tightly on the back to make
a tighter gauge and the purl sts 'pop up' for a
3D effect.
CO 33sts.

Row 1 (RS) Col B, K1, twist ends of col A and
B. Col A, p3. *col B K1, col A p3*. Repeat *to*.
Twist ends of colour A and B. Last st, col B K1.
Row 2 (WS) Col B p1, twist ends of col A and
B. Col A k3, wyBif (with yarn B in front), *col B
p1 wyAif (with yarn A in front), col A k3 wyBif*.
Repeat *to*. Twist ends of col A and B. Col B
p1.
Repeat row 1-2.

Shown in EU-UK size S with colour A: Then
Luna Lovegood Fed the Thestrals and colour B:
Dubrovnik

Special abbreviations
wyAif = with yarn col A held in front
wyBif = with yarn col B held in front
twist ends = twist ends of colour A and B to
create intarsia

Tip
You need a zipper for the cardigan. The best
is to finish the cardigan first and then select a
zipper that is the exact length of the mid front
colour panel. I suggest basting stitch the zipper
in place using a high-contrast thread before
stitching it finely on the machine or by hand.
To shape the blue whale we are working in
increase/decrease pattern.
As a reference to the baleens of the blue whale
we will be working the fair isle rib pattern in
front, sides and back.

Body
Preparation Wind 2 skeins into 2 mini-skeins
each (4 mini-skeins in total) col A for the fair isle
ribbed panels.

Bottom hem
CO 170 (174) 182 (190) sts loosely using 5.5 mm
(US 9) 80 cm (32 inches) circular needle and
col A to create the folded edge at the bottom
hem.
Row 1 (WS) K2, pm (m9). P 19 (19) 23 (23) sts,
pm (m8). P 29 (30) 30 (32) sts, pm (m7). P 9 sts,
all sizes, pm (m6). P 29 (30) 30 (32) sts, pm (m5).
P 19 (19) 23 (23) sts, pm (m4). P 29 (30) 30 (32)
sts, pm (m3). P 9 sts, pm (m2), p 23 (24) 24 (25)
sts, pm (m1), k2.
Increase/decrease
Row 2 (RS) P2, sm (m1), M1, k to 2 sts before
m2, k2tog, sm. K to m3, sm. K2tog tbl, k to m4,
M1, sm. K to m5, sm. M1, k to 2 sts before m6,

k2tog, sm. K to m7, sm, k2tog tbl, k to m8, M1, sm. K to m9, sm, p2.
Row 3 (WS) Work as set without shaping.
Row 4 (RS) Repeat row 2.
Row 5 (WS) Repeat row 3.

Increase for baleens
Row 6 (RS) P2, sm, M1, k to 2 sts before m2, k2tog, sm. *K1, M1*. Repeat *to* to 1 sts before m3, k1, sm. K2tog tbl, k to m4, M1, sm. *K1, M1*. Repeat *to* to 1 sts before m5, k1, sm. M1, k to 2 sts before m6, k2tog, sm. *K1, M1*. Repeat *to* to 1 sts before m7, k1, sm, k2tog tbl, k to m8, M1, sm. *K1, M1*. Repeat *to* to 1 sts before m9, k1, sm, p2. (52 (52) 60 (60) sts increased)
There are now 222 (226) 242 (250) sts in total.

Folded edge
Row 7 (WS) K all sts to create folded edge.
CO 4 more sts to create the zipper fold. (4 sts increased)
There are now 226 (230) 246 (254) sts in total.
Establish the fair isle rib for baleens
We will now begin the special tight fair isle rib for the baleens of the blue whale.
Row 8 (RS) The baleen panels between markers 2-3 (right side), 4-5 (back), 6-7 (left side) and 8-9 (front) are worked in fair isle knitted ribbing.
NOTE: The gauge of the fair isle ribbing is intentionally tighter than in stocking sts. Make sure you have made a gauge swatch to ensure correct fit.
Change to col B and establish fair isle rib.
P3, k1, p2, sm (m1), k2 tog tbl, k to m2, M1, sm (m2).
K1 col B, twist ends of col A and B (from here described as twist ends), p3 col A. *K1 col B, p3 col A*. Repeat *to* 2 more times. Twist ends.
Col B K1, sm (m3), M1, k to 2 sts before m4, k2tog, sm (m4).
K1 col B, twist ends, p3 col A (a new mini-skein). *K1 col B, p3 col A*. Repeat *to* 7 (7) 9 (9) more times. Twist ends.
Col B K1, sm (m5), k2tog tbl, k to m6, M1, sm (m6).
K1 col B, twist ends, p3 col A (a new mini-skein). *K1 col B, p3 col A*. Repeat *to* 2 more times. Twist ends.
Col B K1, sm (m7), M1, k to 2 sts before m8, k2tog, sm (m8).

K1 col B, twist ends, p3 col A (a new mini-skein). *K1 col B, p3 col A*. Repeat *to* 7 (7) 9 (9) more times. Twist ends.
Col B K1, sm (m9), p2. CO 4 more sts to create the zipper fold. (4 sts increased)
There are now 230 (234) 250 (258) sts in total.
Row 9 (WS) K3, p1, k2, sm. P1 col B, twist ends. K3 col A wyBif. *P1 col B wyAif, k3 col A wyBif*. Repeat *to* 7 (7) 9 (9) more times. Twist ends. Change to col B.
P1, sm, p to m7, sm.
P1 col B, twist ends. K3 col A wyBif, *P1 col B wyAif, k3 col A wyBif*. Repeat *to* 2 more times. Twist ends. Change to col B.
P1, sm, p to m5, sm.
P1 col B, twist ends. K 3 col A wyBif, *P1 col B wyAif, k3 col A wyBif*. Repeat *to* 7 (7) 9 (9) more times. Twist ends. Change to col B.
P1, sm, p to m3, sm.
P1 col B, twist ends. K3 col A wyBif, *P1 col B wyAif, k3 col A wyBif*. Repeat *to* 2 more times. Twist ends. Change to col B.
P1, sm. P to m1, sm, work remaining sts as set.
Repeat row 8 - 9 until work measures 36 (38) 40 (42) cm / 14¼ (15) 15¾ (16½) inches measured from the colour changing/folded edge row. You can shorten or lengthen the body here, please note the yardage needed will change. Finish with a WS row.

Finishing colour work
Row 1 (RS) Make colourwork in sides decrease to shape a triangle as follows:
Work patt as set with the usual incr/dec to m2. K2 col B, twist ends and work as set until 2 sts before m3. Twist ends, k2 col B, sm (3). Work patt as set to m 6. Sm. K2 col B, twist ends and work as set until 2 sts before m7. Twist ends, k2 col B, sm. Work as set to the end.
Row 2 (WS)
Work as set to m7.
P3 col B, twist ends and work as set until 3 sts before m6. Twist ends. P3 col B. Work as set to m3. Sm. P3 col B, twist ends and work as set until 3 sts before m2. Twist ends. Work as set to the end.
Keep incorporating 1 more colour work st in sides until all sts between m2-3 and m6-7 are col B. Finish with a WS row.
Place body on hold while knitting the sleeves. Leave the markers in place.

Right Sleeve
CO 41 (43) 45 (47) sts loosely using 5.5 mm (US 9) 60 cm / 24 inches circular needle and col A. The sleeves are knitted back and forth in stocking stitch and will be stitched together later.
Row 1 (WS) P 15 (16) 17 (18), pm (m2) , p11, pm (m1), p to end.
Row 2 (RS) K1, k2tog tbl, k to m1, M1, sm. K to m2, sm. M1, k to 3 sts before the end, k2tog, k1.
There are now still 41 (43) 45 (47) sts.
Row 3 (WS) Work as set without shaping.
Row 4-5 Repeat rows 1-2.

Increase for baleens
Row 6 (RS) K1, k2tog tbl, k to m1, M1, sm. *K1, M1*. Repeat *-* to 1 sts before m2, k1, sm. M1, k to 3 sts before the end, k2tog, k1. (10 sts increased)
There are now 51 (53) 55 (57) sts in total.
Row 7 (WS) K all to form folded edge.

Establish ribs for baleens
Row 8 (RS) Change to colour B, k1, M1, k to 2 sts before m1, k2tog, sm.
K1 col B, twist ends. P3 col A. *k1 col B, p3 col A*. Repeat *to* 3 more times. Twist ends. Change to col B.
K1, sm, k2tog tbl, k to last sts, M1, k1.
Row 9 (WS) p to m2, sm.
P1 col B, twist ends. K3 col A wyBif. *p1 col B wyAif, k3 col A wyBif*. Repeat *to* 3 more times. Twist ends. Change to col B.
P1 col B, sm, p to end.
Repeat rows 8-9 until work measures 4 (4) 3 (3) cm / 1½ (1½) 1¼ (1¼) inches measured from the colour changing/folded edge row. End with a WS row.

Increases
Row 1 (RS) K1, M1, k to m1, sm. Work in fair isle rib as described above to m2, sm. K to last sts, M1, k1. (2 sts increased)
There are now 53 (55) 57 (59) sts in total.
Row 2 (WS) P to m2, sm. Work in pattern until m1, sm. P to end.
Row 3 (RS) K1, M1, k to 2 sts before m1, k2tog, sm, work in pattern until m2, sm, k2tog tbl, k to last sts, M1, k1.
Row 4 (WS) As row 2.
Row 5 - 8 Repeat row 3 - 4 twice.

Repeat rows 1-8, hereby increasing on every 8th row. Repeat increases 12 (12) 13 (14) more times for a total of 13 (13) 14 (15) increases. There are now 77 (79) 83 (87) sts in total. Afterwards, repeat rows 2-3 until sleeve measures 49 (50) 51 (52) cm / 19¼ (19¾) 20 (20½) inches measured from the colour changing row.

Please note: The sleeves shown are longer on purpose to create the illusion of fins. Alternately, make the sleeves 8 cm shorter (for all sizes) and just ensure all the increases are made before moving on to next section. Leave the markers in their places. Put on hold and knit the left sleeve.

Left Sleeve
Work as right sleeve.

Joining body and sleeves
Start at the beginning of the body RS. Please note that the markers change number and/ or position. Please read carefully and ensure correct numbers.

Row 1 (RS) P3, k1, p2, sm (m1), k2togtbl. K to m2, remove m2, k8.
Now work sts from right sleeve as follows: k2tog, k to two sts before sleeve m1, k2tog, sm (now named m2), work as set to old sleeve m2, sm (now named m3), k2tog tbl, k to 2 sts of sleeve remain, k2togtbl.
Now work sts over the back as follows: K7, k2tog, remove old body m3, k to 2 sts before old body m4 (now again named m4) , k2tog, sm. Work as set to old body m5 (still named m5), sm. K2tog tbl, k to m6, remove m6, k8.
Now work sts from left sleeves as follows: k2tog, k to two sts before old sleeve m1 (now named m6), k2tog, sm (m6), work as set to old sleeve m2, sm (now named m7), k2tog tbl, k to 2 sts of sleeve remain, k2tog tbl.
Now work remaining sts in the front as follows: K7, k2tog, remove m7, k to 2 sts before m8 (still named m8), k2tog, sm, work as set until m9 (still named m9), sm, p2, k1, p3. (14 sts decrease)
There are now 370 (378) 402 (418) sts in total.
Row 2 (WS) Work all sts as set without shaping.

Raglan decrease 1
The raglan is decreased on both sleeves and body on every second row.
Row 1 (RS) P3, k1, p2, sm, k2tog tbl, k to 2 sts before m2, k2tog, sm. Work as set to m3, sm, k2tog tbl, k to 2 sts before m4, k2tog, sm. Work as set to m5, sm, k2tog tbl, k to 2 sts before m6, k2tog, sm. Work as set to m7, sm, k2tog tbl, k to 2 sts before m8, k2tog, sm. Work as set until m9, sm, p2, k1, p3. (8 sts decrease)
There are now 362 (370) 394 (410) sts remaining.
Row 2 (WS) Work all sts as set.
Repeat rows 1-2 25 (26) 27 (29) more times, until there are 162 (162) 178 (178) sts left on needle. Finish with a WS row.

Shortrows
For this section you can use your preferred method of turning. We recommend German short rows or the w&t method described below.
Row 1 (RS) P3, k1, p2, sm, k to m2, (no k2tog on this spot in this row) sm, work as set to m3, sm, k2togtbl, k to 2 sts before m4, k2tog, sm. Work as set to m5, sm, k2tog tbl, k to 2 sts before m6, k2tog, sm. Work as set to 5 sts before m7, w&t wyif.
Row 2 (WS) Work as set without decreases to m3. Work as set to 5 sts before m2, w&t wyif.
Row 3 (RS) Work as set to m3, sm, k2togtbl, k to 2 sts before m4, k2tog, sm. Work as set to m5, sm, k2tog tbl, k to 2 sts before m6, k2tog, sm. Work as set to 4 sts before last turn, w&t wyif.
Row 4 (WS) Work as set to 4 sts before last turn, w&t wyif.
Row 5 - 6 Repeat row 3 and 4
Row 7 (RS) Work as set to m3, sm, k2togtbl, k to 2 sts before m4, k2tog, sm. Work as set to m5, sm, k2tog tbl, k to 2 sts before m6, k2tog, sm. Work as set to m7. Observation: when knitting over the short row 'steps', pick up the wrapped yarn around the st and knit this and the st together. Sm, k2tog tbl, k to 2 sts before m8, k2tog, sm. Work remaining sts as set.
Row 8 (WS) Work all sts as set without decreases. (18 sts decreased during shortrows)
There are now 144 (144) 160 (160) sts in total.
Now move on to icord neckband.

Icord neckband
Preparation row right front (RS) BO the 4 of the edge sts using colour B. Start icord edge row 1 here.
CO 3 sts using one 5 mm (US 8) dpn using colour B. If the edge becomes too tight or loose, adjust needle size accordingly.
Slip all sts one by one from the right hand dpn onto the left hand needle containing the sts from the body. Do not turn the work.
Row A (RS) K2, k2tog tbl. Slip sts from right hand needle to left hand needle without turning. Make sure to pull the yarn tight in the end of each row.
Repeat Row A until you reach m2.
Row B (RS) K2, k3tog tbl. Slip sts from right hand needle to left hand needle without turning. Make sure to pull the yarn tight in the end of each row.
Repeat row B to 1 sts before m3.
Repeat row A to m4.
Repeat row B to 1 sts before m5.
Repeat row A to m6.
Repeat rob B to 1 sts before m7.
Repeat row A to m8.
Repeat row B to 1 sts before m9.
Repeat row A until there are 8 sts remaining in total.
Final row (RS) K2, k2tog tbl, k1, p3.
BO row (WS) BO remaining sts.

Finishing
Sew together the sleeves with mattress stitches in stocking sts, leaving 8 cm open measured from bottom edge to create the 'fin'. Fold bottom and sleeve edges and sew on loosely. Sew in zipper either by hand or on a sewing machine, making sure not to stretch while sewing.
Weave in all ends. Steam your new jacket.

Now you are ready for a walk along the coast....

This amazing animal is disturbed by human activity in the seas. Noises from ships keep the blue whale from hearing the sounds of other whales, which prevents them from mating and makes them very stressed. I wanted to create this style as a tribute to the deep blue ocean, where the blue whale seeks for a quiet moment and when looking up from below, all you see are the beautiful baleens. Sometimes, all you need is some peace and quiet with something beautiful to look at.
Emalie Dam
#REDbaleenbeauty

Making Waves

Blue Whale Child
Design Emalie Dam
Skill level 3
Photo pg 102 - 103

Design Emalie Dam
- a jumper with happy whales...
#REDmakingwaves

Skill level 3 - 4
Sizes
EU 86 (98) 110 (122)
UK 12 - 18 month (2) 4-5 (6-7) years
To fit bust
53 (54.5) 58 (63) cm
20¾ (21 ½) 22¾ (24¾) inches
Actual bust measurement (jumper)
62 (65) 69 (72) cm
24½ (25½) 27¼ (28¼) inches
Length
38 (40) 44 (48) cm
15 (15¾) 17¼ (19) inches
Yarn 1
Isager Highland Wool (mentioned as HL)
100% Wool, 275 m / 300 yards per 50 g
1 (1) 2 (2) x 50 g Ice Blue
1 (1) 1 (2) x 50 g Curry
1 skein all size Charcoal
10 (10) 10 (15) gram actually used
Yarn 2
Isager Alpaca 1
100 % Alpaca, 400m / 432 yds per 50 g
As this is a great jumper for using leftover yarns
we have listed up the grams actually used.
1 skein of following 4 cols all sizes
Col 11: 10 (15) 15 (20) grams actually used
Col 16: 10 (10) 15 (20) grams actually used
Col 54: 10 (10) 15 (20) grams actually used
Col Midnight: 5 (5) 10 (10) grams actually used
Always held together with yarn 1, so you always
knit with two strands of yarn to create a marled/
mottled effect.
Needles
3.5 mm (US 4) and 3mm (US 2.5) circular
needle, 60 cm / 24 inches.
For size 12 - 18 month 40 cm / 16 inches.
3.5 mm (US 4) and 3mm (US 2.5) dpn.
8 stitch markers.
Removable stitch marker (optional)
6 small buttons.
Gauge
In stocking stitch on 3.5 mm (US 4) needles and
1 strand of each yarn 1 and yarn 2: 22 sts x 31
rows = 10 x 10 cm/4 x 4 inches
Remember to check your gauge and adjust
needle size accordingly.
Stitch patterns
The jumper is knitted in garter sts and stocking

sts.
Where the blue whale are swimming, there is a
band of fair isle knitting.

Shown in size 98 / 2-3 years. Colours
mentioned above.

Colour combinations used
Col A: HL Ice Blue + alpaca 1 col 11
Col B: HL Ice Blue + alpaca 1 col 16
Col C: HL Ice Blue + alpaca 1 col 54
Col D: HL Charcoal + alpaca 1 col Midnight
Col E: HL Curry + alpaca 1 col 3

Body
CO 140 (146) 154 (162) sts using 3.5 mm (US 4)
60 cm / 24 inches circular needle and yarn col
A.
Join for working in the round.
Round 1 Pm, k all.
Round 2 Sm, p all.
Round 3 - 11 repeat rows 1 and 2.
Round 12 - 20 (22) 25 (29) Sm, p all.

Col change 1
Round 1 Col B, sm, p all.
Round 2 - 3 Col A, sm, p all.
Round 4 - 5 Col B, sm, p all.
Round 6 Col A, sm, p all. Break alpaca yarn.
Col change 2
Round 1 Change to col B, sm, p all.
Round 2 - 12 (14) 17 (21) sm, p all.
Round 1 Col C. Sm, p all.
Round 2 - 3 Col B, sm, p all.
Round 4 - 5 Col C, sm, p all.
Round 6 Col B, sm, p all. Break alpaca yarn.

Col change 3 and Whale diagram
Change to col C and start Whale diagram
where indicated. For the whales use col D.
Round 1 Sm, work 5 (5) 5 (6) repeats of pattern,
p 0 (1) 4 (0). Whenever you need to twist the
yarns, work a knit st instead of purl. In this way
you will ensure invisibility of contrasting col. It
will also make the uneven texture of waves.
Continue on body according to diagram.
When diagram is finished, work measures
approximately 25 (27) 31 (35) cm and you
continue working sleeve hole.
Sleeve hole
Round 1 Sm, K 68 (71) 75 (79) sts, BO 4 sts
loosely. K to 2 sts before m, BO 4 sts loosely.
The work has now been divided into front and

back with 66 (69) 73 (77) sts on each side. Leave sts on the needle and set the body aside while working the sleeves.

Sleeves
CO 30 (34) 38 (42) sts using 3.5 mm (US 4) dpn and yarn col A. Join for working in the round.
Round 1 pm, k all.
Round 2 sm, p all.
Round 3 - 11 repeat rows 1 and 2.

PLEASE NOTE
From now on, you will work increases and col changes along one another, so be aware and remember to do both at the right time. We recommend using removable stitch markers or similar to keep track of the increases.

Increases
Round 12 Sm, p1, M1p, p to last sts, M1p, p1. There are now 32 (36) 40 (44) sts.
Purl 8 (11) 13 (11) more rounds without any increases and repeat round 12 on every 9th (12th) 14th (12th) round, 7 (6) 6 (6) more times. There are now 46 (48) 52 (56) sts.

AT THE SAME TIME, Col changes
Round 13 - 20 (25) 28 (32) sm, p all.
Col change 1
Round 1 Col B. Sm, p all.
Round 2 - 3 Col A, sm, p all.
Round 4 - 5 Col B, sm, p all.
Round 6 Col A, sm, p all. Break alpaca yarn.

Col change 2
Round 1 Col B, sm, p all.
Round 2 - 15 (20) 23 (27) sm, p all.
Round 1 Col C. Sm, p all.
Round 2 - 3 Col B, sm, p all.
Round 4 - 5 Col C, sm, p all.
Round 6 Col B, sm, p all. Break alpaca yarn.
Round 7 - 10 (15) 18 (22) Col C, sm, p all.
Round 11 (16) 19 (23) Col C, sm, k all.
Round 12 (17) 20 (24) Sm, p all.
Round 13 (18) 21 (25) - 17 (22) 25 (29) Repeat two previous rounds.

Col Change 3
Round 1 Col E. Sm, k all.
Repeat round 1 until sleeve measures 24 (28) 32 (36) cm / 9 ½ (11) 12 ½ (14) inches
Last round Sm, k to 2 sts before m. BO 4 sts loosely.
There are now 42 (44) 48 (52) sts.

Knit the other sleeve in the same way.

Joining body and sleeves
Using the circular needle from the body. Begin where the yarn was left off before knitting the sleeves. Working Col E.
Round 1 Pm (m1). K all 66 (69) 73 (77) sts (back). Pm (m2). K all 42 (44) 48 (52) sts from the first sleeve onto the same circular needle (left sleeve).
Pm(m3). K all 66 (69) 73 (77) front sts.
Pm (m4). K all 42 (44) 48 (52) from the second sleeve onto the same circular needle (right sleeve).
All 216 (226) 242 (258) sts are now joined on one needle.
Round 2 - 3 K all.

Decrease 1
Round 1 Work decreases on both sleeves and body like this. Sm1, k2, k2tog, k to 4 sts before m2. K2tog tbl, k2, sm2, k2, k2tog. K to 4 sts before m3. K2tog tbl, k2, sm3, k2, k2tog. K to 4 sts before m4. K2tog tbl, k2, sm4, k2, k2tog. K to 4 sts before m1. K2tog tbl, k2. 8 sts dec. There are now 208 (218) 234 (250) sts.
Round 2 K all sts without any shaping.
Repeat rounds 1 - 2 another 7 (7) 8 (8) times. There are now 50 (53) 55 (59) sts front and back. 26 (28) 30 (34) sts each sleeve. 152 (162) 170 (186) sts in total.

Decrease 2
Round 1 Work decreases on sleeves only. Sm1, k to m2. Sm2, k2, k2tog. K to 4 sts before m3. K2tog tbl, k2, sm3. K to m4, sm4, k2, k2tog. K to 4 sts before m1. K2tog tbl, k2. 4 sts dec. There are now 148 (158) 166 (182) sts.
Round 2 K without any shaping.
Repeat rounds 1 - 2 another 6 (5) 5 (6) times. Ending with a round 1.There are now 12 (16) 18 (20) sts in each sleeve and 124 (138) 146 (158) sts remaining in total.

Neck
Row 1 (RS) Sm1, k to m2, sm2, k to m3, sm3. K 15 (17) 17 (18). W&t wyif.
Row 2 (WS) P to m3, sm3, p2, p2tog tbl. P to 4 sts before m2, p2tog, p2, sm2. P to m1, sm1, p2, p2tog tbl. P to 4 sts before m4, p2tog, p2, sm4. P 15 (17) 17 (18). W&t wyib. 4 sts dec. There are now 120 (134) 142 (154) sts.
Row 3 (RS) K to m4, sm4, k2, k2tog. K to 4 sts before m1, k2tog tbl, k2, sm1. K to m2, sm2, k2,

k2tog. K to 4 sts before m3, k2tog tbl, k2, sm3. K 12 (14) 14 (15). W&t wyif. 4 sts dec. There are now 116 (130) 138 (150) sts.
Row 4 (WS) P to m3, sm3, p2, p2tog tbl. P to 4 sts before m2, p2tog, p2, sm2. P to m1, sm1, p2, p2tog tbl. P to 4 sts before m4, p2tog, p2, sm4. P 12 (14) 14 (15). W&t wyib. 4 sts dec. There are now 112 (126) 134 (146) sts.
Only size (98) 110 (122):
Row 5 (RS) K to m4, sm4, k2, k2tog. K to 4 sts before m1, k2tog tbl, k2, sm1. K to m2, sm2, k2, k2tog. K to 4 sts before m3, k2tog tbl, k2, sm3. K -- (13) 13 (14). W&t wyif. 4 sts dec. There are now -- (122) 130 (142) sts.
Only size (98) 110 (122):
Row 6 (WS) P to m3, sm3, p2, p2tog. P to 4 sts before m2, p2tog, p2, sm2. P to m1, sm1, p2, p2tog. P to 4 sts before m4, p2tog, p2, sm4. P -- (13) 13 (14). W&t wyib. 4 sts dec. There are now -- (118) 126 (138) sts.
Only size 110 (122):
Row 7 (RS) K to m4, sm4, k2, k2tog. K to 4 sts before m1, k2tog tbl, k2, sm1. K to m2, sm2, k2, k2tog. K to 4 sts before m3, k2tog tbl, k2, sm3. K -- (--) 12 (13). W&t wyif. 4sts dec. There are -- (--) 122 (134) sts.
Only size 110:
Row 8 (WS) Work as set without further shaping to m4, sm4. P -- (--) 12 (--). W&t wyib.
Only size (122):
Row 8 (WS) P to m3, sm3, p2, p2tog. P to 4 sts before m2, p2tog, p2, sm2. P to m1, sm1, p2, p2tog. P to 4 sts before m4, p2tog, p2, sm4. P -- (--) -- (13). W&t wyib. 4 sts dec. There are -- (--) -- (130) sts.
In all sizes, there are 6 sts remaining in the sleeve, which will be used for button bands.

Shortrows Right Front Shoulder
Row 1 (RS) K to 3 sts before m4, w&t wyif.
Only size 86 (98):
Row 2 (WS) P 8 (9) -- (--), pm (m5), w&t wyib.
Only size 110 (122):
Row 2 (WS) P -- (--) 9 (10). pm (m5). Turn.
All sizes
Row 3 (RS) K to 3 sts before last turn, w&t wyif.
Row 4 (WS) P to m5, turn.
Row 5 (RS) K to 3 sts before last turn, w&t wyif.
Row 6 (WS) P to m5, turn.
Row 7 (RS) K all sts to m4. Break yarn. Slip sts from left needle to right needle until m1.

Shortrows Right Back Shoulder
The sts on the neckside are placed on hold as

you w&t to create the neckline shaping.
Row 1 (RS) Start at m1. K 13 (14) 14 (15). W&t wyif.
Row 2 (WS) P to 3 sts before m1, w&t wyib.
Row 3 (RS) K 8 (9) 9 (10). pm (m6), w&t wyif.
Row 4 (WS) P to 3 sts before last turn, w&t wyib.
Row 5 (RS) K to m6, turn.
Row 6 (WS) P to 3 sts before last turn, w&t wyib.
Row 7 (RS) K to m6, turn.
Row 8 (WS) P all sts to m1. Break yarn. Now, slip sts from right needle until 13 (14) 14 (15) sts after m2. Turn. Start short rows left back shoulder here.

Shortrows Left Back Shoulder
The sts on the neckside are placed on hold as you w&t to create the neckline shaping.
Row 1 (RS) K to 3 sts before m2, w&t wyif.
Row 2 (WS) p 8 (9) 9 (10), pm (m7), w&t wyib.
Row 3 (RS) K to 3 sts before last turn, w&t wyif.
Row 4 (WS) P to m7, turn.
Row 5 (RS) K to 3 sts before last turn, w&t wyif.
Row 6 (WS) P to m7, turn.
Row 7 (RS) K all sts to m2. Break yarn. Slip sts from left needle to right needle until m3.

Shortrows Left Front Shoulder
Only size 86 (98):
Row 1 (RS) Start at m3. K 11 (12) -- (--), pm (m8), w&t wyif.
Only size 110 (122):
Row 1 (RS) Start at m3. K -- (--) 12 (13), pm (m8). Turn.
Row 2 (WS) P to 3 sts before m3, w&t wyib.
Row 3 (RS) K to m8, turn.
Row 4 (WS) P to 3 sts before last turn, w&t wyib.
Row 5 (RS) K to m8, turn.
Row 6 (WS) P to 3 sts before last turn, w&t wyib.
Row 7 (RS) K to m8, turn.
Row 8 (WS) P all sts to m3. Start knitting the button band here.

Left Button band
The button band is worked over the 6 sleeve sts between m3 and m2. They are worked in garter sts.
Row 1 (WS) Using 3mm (US 2.5) dpn, start at

m3. Remove m3. K 1 (0) 0 (1), pm (m3), k 4 (5) 5 (4), Dbe1. Turn.
Row 2 (RS) Dbe1, K to m3, sm, K2tog tbl, w&t wyif.
Row 3 (WS) K1, sm, k to last st, Dbe1. Turn.
Repeat rows 2 - 3 until you reach m8. Finish with a WS row and place sts on hold. You will later start the front neckband here. Knit remaining button under-/overlays first.

Left Button band with button holes
Row 1 (RS) Using 3mm (US 2.5) double pointed needles, start at m2. Pick up and knit 6 sts over the left button band in between m2 and where m3 used to be.
Row 2 (WS) K 5 (6) 6 (5), move m2 to here. K2tog tbl, w&t wyib.
Row 3 (RS) K 1, sm, k to last st, Dbe1.
Row 4 (WS) Dbe1, K to m2, sm, k2tog tbl, w&t wyib.
Repeat rows 3 - 4 until you reach m7.
AT THE SAME TIME on row 7, start buttonholes as follows:
Row 7 (RS) K1, sm, k1, k2tog, yo, k1 (2) 2 (1), Dbe1.
Repeat buttonhole on row 17 (17) 17 (19).

Finish button band on a WS row and place sts on hold.

Right Button band
The button band is worked over the 6 sts between m4 and m1 in garter sts.
Row 1 (RS) Using 3mm (US 2.5) double pointed needles, start at m4. K5, Dbe1.
Row 2 (WS) Dbe1, k 4 (5) (5) 4, move m4 to here. k2tog, w&t wyib.
Row 3 (RS) K 1, sm, k to last st, dbe1.
Row 4 (WS) 1dbe, k to m4, sm, k2tog, w&t wyib.
Repeat rows 3 - 4 until you reach m5. Finish with a WS row and place sts on hold.

Right Button band with button holes
Row 1 (RS) Using 3mm (US 2.5) dpn, start at where m4 used to be. Pick up and knit 6 sts over the right button band in between m1 and m4.
Row 2 (WS) K5, dbe1.
Row 3 (RS) 1dbe, K 4 (5) 5 (4), move m1 to here. K2tog tbl, w&t wyif.
Row 4 (WS) K 1, sm, k to last st, Dbe1.
Row 5 (RS) Dbe1, K to m1, sm, k2tog tbl, w&t wyif.

Repeat rows 4 - 5 until you reach m6.
AT THE SAME TIME, on row 7, start buttonholes as follows:
Row 7 (RS) Dbe1, k 1 (2) 2 (1), yo, k2tog, k to m1, sm, k2tog tbl, w&t wyif.
Repeat buttonhole on row 17 (17) 17 (19).
Finish button band on a RS row. Begin neck band here.

Back Neckband
The neckband is worked in garter sts in two parts, one front and one back.
Row 1 (RS) Using 3mm (US 2.5) 60 cm / 24 inches circular needle. Dbe1, k to m, remove marker. Pick up and knit 3 (3) 4 (4) sts. K over the 28 (29) 31 (33) sts on hold on the back. Pick up and knit 3 (3) 4 (4) sts before m2. Knit over the remaining sts from the left button band to last st. dbe1. There are now 46 (49) 51 (51) sts.
Row 2 (WS) Dbe1, k over all sts and remove all markers to last st. Dbe1.
Row 3 (RS) Button hole Dbe1, k 1 (2) 2 (1), yo, k2tog. K to 4 (5) 5 (4) sts before end of row. K2 tog, yo, k 1 (2) 2 (1). Dbe1.
Row 4 (WS) Dbe1, k to last st, Dbe1.
Rows 5 - 8 Repeat row 4 on both RS and WS. BO all back neckband sts.

Front Neckband
Begin at the edge of left button band.
Row 1 (RS) Using 3mm (US 2.5) 60 cm / 24 inches circular needle, 1dbe, k to m3, remove marker. Pick up and knit 5 (5) 6 (6) sts. K over the 28 (29) 31 (33) sts on hold on the front. Pick up and knit 5 (5) 6 (6) sts before m4. Knit to last st. dbe1. There are now 50 (53) 55 (55) sts.
Row 2 (WS) Dbe1, k over all sts and remove all markers to last st. Dbe1.
Row 3 (RS) Dbe1, k to 1 sts before end, Dbe1.
Rows 4 - 8 Repeat row 3 on both RS and WS. BO all back neckband sts.

Finishing
Graft together sts under sleeve. Weave in ends and sew on buttons under the buttonholes on the underlay. Steam new whale sweater and let it get out in the open and swim.

Whale diagram

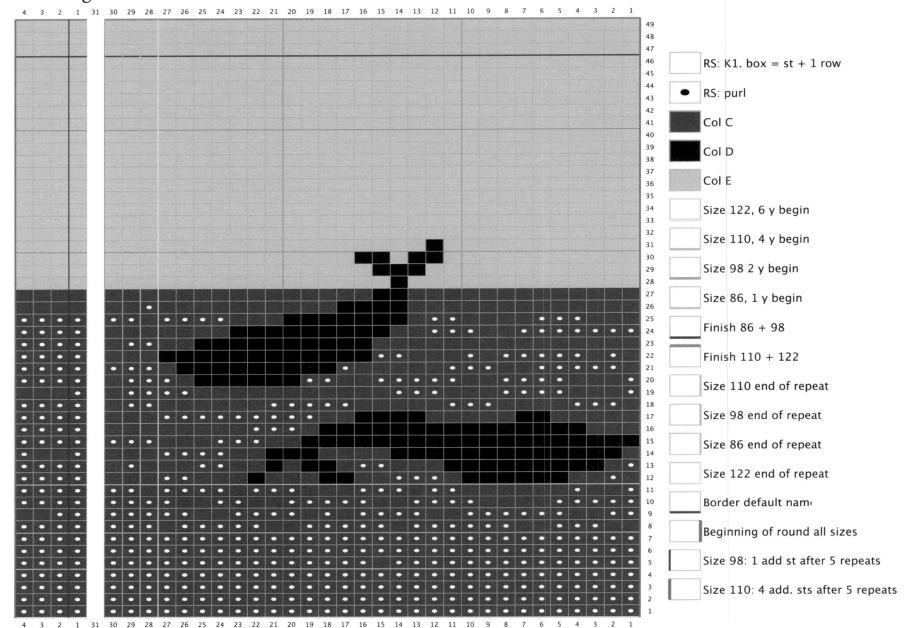

RS: K1. box = st + 1 row

● RS: purl

Col C

Col D

Col E

Size 122, 6 y begin

Size 110, 4 y begin

Size 98 2 y begin

Size 86, 1 y begin

Finish 86 + 98

Finish 110 + 122

Size 110 end of repeat

Size 98 end of repeat

Size 86 end of repeat

Size 122 end of repeat

Border default name

Beginning of round all sizes

Size 98: 1 add st after 5 repeats

Size 110: 4 add. sts after 5 repeats

I was inspired by the lives of the blue whales from my traveling at sea and observing marine life from a distance. I admire these wonderful huge animals, who have such a grace and incredible strength and an easily recognisable shape. This jumper is created to give the little children a flock of blue whales of their own without having to seek the horizon. Instead, they can get close to them and become friends with them.
Emalie Dam
#REDmakingwaves

R:E:D: 218

School of Tuna

Atlantic Bluefin Tuna Child
Design Emalie Dam
Skill level 3
Photo pg 148 - 149

Design Emalie Dam
-a tunic to keep the body warm...
#REDschooloftuna

Skill level 3
Sizes
EU 86 (98) 110 (122)
UK 18 month (2) 4-5 (6-7) years
To fit bust
53 (54.5) 58 (63) cm
21 (21½) 23 (25) inches
Actual bust measurement (vest)
62 (64) 68 (72) cm
24½ (25¼) 27 (28¼) inches
Length
34 (37) 43 (48) cm
13½ (14½) 17 (19) inches
Yarn A (Col A)
Zealana Rimu
60% fine NZ merino, 40% brushtail possum, 153 m / 167 yards per 40g
1 (1) 2 (2) skeins
Yarn B (Col B)
Zealana Kauri
60% fine NZ merino, 30% brushtail possum, 10% mulberry silk, 153 m / 167 yards per 40g
2 (3) 3 (3) skeins
Yarn C, for tiny tuna
ITO Serishin
100% silk, 290 m / 317 yards per 50g
(Col C)
1 (1) 1 (1) skein (used 20 g) 105 Orient Blue
(Col D) 35 gram total
1 (1) 1 (1) skein (used 20 g) 108 Snow Grey
Needles
4.5 mm (US 7) circular needles 80 cm / 36 inches
2 of 4.5 mm (US 7) circular holding needles optional whether 40 cm / 16 inches or 60 cm /24 inches.
4.5 mm (US 7) dpn
2.5 mm (US 2) dpn
2 stitch Wmarkers.
1 removeable stitch marker.
4 (4) 5 (5) sew-on snap fasteners, 15 mm
Gauge
In stocking stitch on 4.5 mm (US 7) needles in yarn B: 22 sts x 31 rows = 10 x 10 cm/4 x 4 inches.
Remember to check your gauge and adjust needle size accordingly.
Stitch patterns
Stocking sts with applied small tunas.

Shown in size 110 / 4-5 years. Yarn A, colour Kiwicrush. Yarn B, colour Natural. Tunas colour 105 Orient Blue. 108 Snow Grey.

This vest is worked bottom up, worked in one piece back and forth. It is made with folded bottom edge in contrast colour and folded edges in the front opening, along the neckline and in the sleeve hole. The tiny tunas are worked separately and will be sewed on by hand in the end.

Body, folded edge
Preparations: Roll two mini skeins approx equal size for the folded edge col A.
CO 136 (141) 150 (158) sts loosely using 4.5 mm (US 7) 80 cm / 36 inches circular needle and Col A to create the folded edge.
Row 1 (WS) P all sts.
Increases
We will now make the increases to ensure the edge is possible to fold beautifully.
Row 2 (RS) K2, M1, k to 2 sts remaining. M1, k2.
There are now 138 (143) 152 (160) sts.
Row 3 - 10 Repeat rows 1 - 2. Increased by a total of 10 sts.
There are now 146 (151) 160 (168) sts.
Row 11 (WS) K all sts to create a hem to fold the edge around.

Body front side
We will now add the second colour.
Row 12 (RS) K2, M1, pm (m1). P1, k1, p1. Change to Col B and twist the two yarns around one another. K to 5 sts remaining. Change to Col A (the second mini skein) and twist the yarns as before. P1, k1, p1, pm (m2), M1, K2.
There are now 148 (153) 162 (170) sts.
Row 13 (WS) P to m2, sm. K1, p1, k1. Change to Col B and twist yarn. P to 3 sts before m1. Change to Col A and twist yarn. K1, p1, k1, sm. P to end.
Row 14 (RS) K2, M1, k to m1, sm. P1, k1, p1. Change to Col B and twist yarn. K to 3 sts before m2. Change to Col A and twist yarn. P1, k1, p1, sm. K to 2 sts before end. M1, K2.
There are now 150 (155) 164 (172) sts.
Row 15 - 21 Repeat row 13 and 14.
On the last sts on row 21 work dbe1. Increased by another 6 sts.
There are now 156 (161) 170 (178) sts.

Row 22 (RS) Dbe1, k to m1. Remove marker. P1, k1, p1, pm (m1). Change to Col B and twist yarn. K to 3 sts before m2. Change to Col A and twist yarn. Move m2 to here. P1, k1, p1, k to last sts, dbe1.
PLEASE NOTE: we have now moved the stitch markers 3 sts towards the centre of the vest.
Row 23 (WS) Dbe1, work as set to m2, sm. Change to Col B and twist yarn. P to m1, sm. Change to Col A and twist yarn. Work as set to last sts, dbe1.
Row 24 (RS) Dbe1, work as set to m1, sm. Change to Col B and twist yarn. K to m2, sm. Change to Col A and twist yarn. Work as set to last sts, dbe1.
Continue repeating rows 23 - 24 until work measures 24 (26) 30 (34) cm / 9½ (10¼) 12 (13½) inches measured from CO edge. Ending with a WS row.

Preparation for Yoke
Row 1 (RS) Dbe1. Work as set to m1, sm. Change to Col B and twist yarn. K 56 (59) 61 (65) sts (front). Knit next 8 (8) 10 (10) sts onto the 4.5 mm (US 7) dpn holding needle. K 56 (58) 61 (65) sts (back). Knit next 8 (8) 10 (10) sts onto another 4.5 mm (US 7) dpn holding needle. K8 st to m2, sm. Change to Col A and twist yarn. Work as set to last sts, dbe1.
There are now 140 (145) 150 (158) sts on the circular needle.
Leave body for now until 'Joining for yoke'.

Finishing sts on holding needles
Begin at the 8 (8) 10 (10) sts on one holding needle left side and work these sts only.
Row 1 (RS) Using Col A: BO all 8 sts.
Repeat for the other 8 (8) 10 (10) sts set aside on the other holding needle.

Sleeve underlay
CO 38 (39) 40 (43) sts loosely using 4.5 mm (US 7) dpn and Col A to create the folded edge for the sleeve.
Row 1 (WS) P to last sts, dbe1.
Row 2 (RS) Dbe1. K1, M1, K to last 2 sts, M1, k1, dbe1.
There are now 40 (41) 42 (45) sts.
Row 3 - 10 Repeat rows 1 - 2. Work first and last st as dbe1. Increased by a total of 10 sts. There are now 48 (49) 50 (53) sts.
Row 11 (WS) P all sts.
Row 12 (RS) Purl all sts on this RS. Leave sts on needle for the joining.

Repeat steps to make a second underlay.

Joining for yoke
Row 1 (WS) Starting where we left off with the body.
Dbe1. Work as set to m2, sm. Change to Col B and twist yarn. P8 to the cast off sts. Now p over the 48 (49) 50 (53) sts from the first sleeve underlay; make sure to begin at the WS of the underlay. P 56 (58) 61 (65) sts over the back to the cast off sts. Now p over the 48 (49) 50 (53) sts from second sleeve underlay WS. P to m1, sm. Change to Col A and twist yarn. Work as set to last sts, dbe1.
There are now 236 (243) 250 (264) sts gathered on the same needle.
PLEASE NOTE: Length of yoke will be measured from this round. We recommend placing a removable stitch marker to measure from.
Row 2 (RS) Dbe1. Work as set to m1, sm. Change to Col B and twist yarn. K to m2, sm. Change to Col A and twist yarn. Work as set to last sts, dbe1.
Row 3 (WS) Dbe1. Work as set to m2, sm. Change to Col B and twist yarn. P to m1, sm. Change to Col A and twist yarn. Work as set to last sts, dbe1.
Work in patt and Col as set for another 6 (6) 6 (6) rows.

Decrease 1
Row 1 (RS) Dbe1. Work as set to m1, sm. Change to Col B and twist yarn. K3, *k5, k2tog*. Repeat *to* 30 (31) 32 (34) times in total. K3, sm. Change to Col A and twist yarn. Work as set to last sts, dbe1. We have decreased 30 (31) 32 (34) sts.
There are now 206 (212) 218 (230) sts.
Work in patt and Col as set for another 7 (7) 9 (9) rows.

Decrease 2
Row 1 (RS) Dbe1. Work as set to m1, sm. Change to Col B and twist yarn. K3, *k 4, k2tog*. Repeat *to* 30 (31) 32 (34) times in total. K3, sm. Change to Col A and twist yarn. Work as set to last sts, dbe1. We have decreased 30 (31) 32 (34). There are now 176 (181) 186 (196) sts.
Work in patt and Col as set for another 5 (7) 7 (9) rows.

Decrease 3
Note that during these following 10 rows, you will have to start with edge decreases as described.

Row 1 (RS) Dbe1. Work as set to m1, sm. Change to Col B and twist yarn. K3, *k 3, k2tog*. Repeat *to* 30 (31) 32 (34) times in total. K3, sm. Change to Col A and twist yarn. Work as set to last sts, dbe1. We have decreased 30 (31) 32 (34) sts.
There are now 146 (150) 154 (162) sts.
Work in patt and Col as set for another 5 (7) 7 (9) rows.
AT THE SAME TIME: When yoke measures 8.5 (9.5) 11 (12.5) cm / 3¼ (3 ¾) 4¼ (5) inches, begin working edge decreases as described below, still keeping count on rows worked since decrease 3.
Yoke now measures 9.6 (10.4) 11.6 (12.8) cm / 3 ¾ (4) 4½ (5) inches. Move on to decrease 4 and 5 while continuing edge decreases.

MEANWHILE, Edge decreases
When yoke (sleeve) measures 8.5 (9.5) 11 (12.5) cm / 3¼ (3 ¾) 4¼ (5) inches, begin working edge decreases on every RS row as follows:
Row 1 (RS) k1, k2tog tbl, work as set to m1, sm. Change yarn to Col B and twist ends. K to m2, sm. Change yarn to Col A and twist ends. Work as set to last 3 sts, k2tog, k1.
Repeat edge decrease on every RS rows 4 more times while continuing with decrease 4 and 5.
NOTE: the edge decrease is not described in decrease 4 and 5, so remember to work both decreases. And where dbe1 was knitted before, this will be a regular k edge to make seaming easier.

Decrease 4
Note that during this bit, you will continue with edge decreases as described above, even though they are not described. Also note that the number of sts mentioned in each decrease is without the decreased sts and therefore only a rough guideline.
Row 1 (RS) Dbe1. Work as set to m1, sm. Change to Col B and twist yarn. K3, *k 2, k2tog*. Repeat *to* 30 (31) 32 (34) times in total. K3, sm. Change to Col A and twist yarn. Work as set to last sts, dbe1. We have decreased 30 (31) 32 (34) sts.
There are now 116 (119) 122 (128) sts.
Work in patt and Col as set for another 5 (7) 7 (9) rows. Yoke now measures approx 12 (13) 14.5 (16) cm / 4¾ (5) 5¾ (6¼) inches from first row.

Decrease 5
Row 1 (RS) Dbe1. Work as set to m1, sm.

Change to Col B and twist yarn. K3, *k 1, k2tog*. Repeat *to* 30 (31) 32 (34) times in total. K3, sm. Change to Col A and twist yarn. Work as set to last sts, dbe1. We have decreased 30 (31) 32 (34) sts.

There are now 86 (88) 90 (94) sts.

Row 2 (WS) In this row work Col A only, as the neckband is knitted in yarn A only. Dbe1. Work as set to m2, sm, p to m1, sm, work as set to last sts, dbe1. Remove all markers as you go.

Neckband

Row 1 (RS) K1, **purl** (to make a folding edge)to last sts, k1.

Row 2 (WS) P all sts.

Row 3 (RS) K1, k2tog, k to 3 sts remaining, k2tog tbl, k1.

Row 4 (WS) P all sts.

Row 5-12 Repeat rows 3 - 4. We have then decreased a total of 10 sts. There are now 66 (68) 70 (74) sts.

Row 13 (RS) BO all sts very very loosely.

Decoration Tunas

For the decoration tunas, there is a diagram included. We recommend you knit the first few using both the description and the diagram until you are familiar with knitting from the diagram only. Before beginning, wind some silk into a skein, as you will need two strands of each colour. The tunas are knitted in stocking stitch with the WS shown, sewn on as shown in diagram 2.

Tiny Tuna

CO 2 sts loosely using 2.5 mm (US 2) dpn and two strands of Col D in 108 Snow Grey (white in diagram).

Row 1 (WS) P1, yo, p1.

Row 2 (RS) K1, k1 but leave the sts on left needle, k1 tbl, leave sts on left needle, k1 and slip sts, k1. (2 sts increased to 5 sts in total)

Row 3 - 5 Work sts in stocking sts (k on RS and p on WS).

Row 6 (RS) K1, M1, k3. Leave one strand in colour grey and start with a strand in colour blue, so you now have one strand of each colour (light blue in diagram). M1. Leave the grey strand and start with the second strand blue, so you are now knitting with two in blue (dark blue in diagram). K1. 2 sts increased to 7 sts in total.

Row 7 (WS) P all in colour work as shown on diagram, using the colour change method described above.

Note: This method of exchanging strands of colour will be used throughout and hereafter only described as colourwork - always following pattern on the diagram.

Row 8 (RS) K1, M1, k to last sts in colourwork, M1, k1. 2 sts increased to 9 sts in total.

Row 9 -11 work stocking sts in colourwork as per diagram.

Row 12 (RS) K2tog tbl, k to last 2 sts in colourwork, k2tog. 2 sts decreased to 7 sts in total.

Row 13 (WS) P all in colourwork.

Row 14 (RS) K2tog tbl, k to last 2 sts in colourwork, k2tog. 2 sts decreased to 5 sts in total.

Row 15 (WS) P all in colourowork.

Row 16 (RS) K2tog tbl, k to last 2 sts in colourwork, k2tog. 2 sts decreased to 3 sts in total.

Row 17 (WS) P all i colourwork, now work only with two strands of blue.

Row 18 (RS) K1, M1, k1, M1, k1. 2 sts increased to 5 sts in total.

Row 19 (WS) P1, M1p, p to last sts, M1p, p1. 2 sts increased to 7 sts in total.

Row 20 (RS) K1, k2tog, slip sts, k2tog tbl, pull the slipped sts over, k1. 3 sts decreased to 4 sts in total.

Row 21 (WS) P2tog, turn without working the last two sts. 1 sts decreased to 3 sts in total.

Row 22 (RS) K1 st, break the yarn and pull thread through st. Return to remaining two sts on opposite finn.

Row 23 (RS) K2tog, turn work.

Row 24 (WS) P st, break the yarn and pull thread through st.

Make an eye on the tuna using two strands of dark blue by doing a French knot.

Darn in all ends on the RS of the fish, as the WS will be the one featured.

Repeat 21 more times for a total of 22 fish. Amount of fish can be adjusted according to taste. We also recommend the fish as patches for holes in jeans, jumpers etc or simply for decoration - an excellent way of using any leftover yarn.

Finish

Sew in- and decrease edges together using mattress stitches to form neat corners on your vest. Sew all edges loosely to the back of work, folding at bottom, top and side edges. Sew

edges of the underlays loosely to the back of work.

Weave in all ends and sew on snap fasteners evenly along the edges.

Steam the little tunic.

And let us see if can dance...

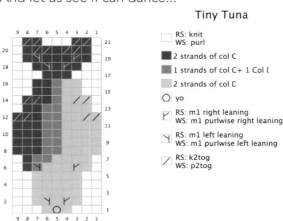

Tiny Tuna

☐	RS: knit / WS: purl
■	2 strands of col C
▦	1 strands of col C+ 1 Col D
▨	2 strands of col D
O	yo
⅄	RS: m1 right leaning / WS: m1 purlwise right leaning
⅄	RS: m1 left leaning / WS: m1 purlwise left leaning
⧄	RS: k2tog / WS: p2tog

With this design, I was inspired by how modern overfishing targets entire schools of tuna with none left in the ocean. I wanted to recreate the schools of tunas on a children's tunic to play with the idea of family and the easily recognisable shape of fish. Even though the school is enclosed by a yellow line of knitting representing danger, it is still free – which is how it should be.

Emalie Dam
#REDschooloftuna

Tuna on Parade

Atlantic Bluefin Tuna Teen~Adult
Design Emalie Dam
Skill level 3
Photo pg 146 - 147

Design Emalie Dam
- tuna jumper in stripes
#REDtunaonparade

Skill level 3
Sizes
EU 34 (36) 38 (40) UK 8 (10) 12 (14)
To fit bust
80 (84) 88 (92) cm
31½ (33) 34½ (36 ¼) inches
Actual bust measurement (jumper)
116 (120) 124 (128) cm
45¾ (47½) 48¾ (50½) inches
Waist measurements (jumper)
38 (42) 46 (50) cm
15 (16½) 18¼ (19¾) inches
Length
46 (48) 50 (52) cm
18 (19) 19¾ (20½) inches
Yarn
Madelinetosh Merino Light
100% merino wool, 384 m / 420 yds per skein,
app. 112 g.
1 (2) 2 (2) skeins in col A Oeste
1 (1) 1 (2) skeins in col B Sulfur
1 (1) 1 (1) skein in col C Danger
1 (1) 1 (1) skein in col D Antler
1 (1) 1 (1) skein in col E Carbon Dating
Needles
4 mm (UK 8) (US 6) circular needle, 100 cm/32
inches and 60 cm/24 inches.
4 mm (UK 8) (US 6) double pointed needles.
4 stitch markers.
Gauge
In stocking stitch on 4 mm (UK 8) (US 6) needles
and Col A: 24 sts x 35 rows = 10 x 10 cm/4 x 4
inches.
Remember to check your gauge and adjust
needle size accordingly. Note: The gauge
row-wise is particularly important as the
increases along the edges of panel 1 and
sleeves are spread out evenly based upon this.

Stitch patterns
The stitch patterns for this pattern are stocking
stitch, garter stitch and ribbing. The technique
of Icord is used and explained. Further
instructions for the technique can easily be
found on You Tube.

Shown in EU size 36 / UK size 10.

Tip In this pattern we use the technique for
seaming called "Grafting" or "Sew together
stitchwise". This is good fun because the
seam becomes entirely invisible. However it
is optional. You can have a nice Tuna Parade
jumper if you choose to sew the jumper
together in your preferred way.

Front Panel 1
CO 34 (36) 38 (40) sts using 4 mm (UK 8) (US
6) circular needle Col A. This panel is worked
in stocking stitch with increases as described
below:
Row 1 (WS) P all.
Row 2 (RS) K all.
Row 3 (WS) P all.
Row 4 (RS) K1, M1. K to last st, M1, K1 (2sts
increased).
Repeat rows 1 - 4 another 33 (35) 37 (39).
There are now 102 (108) 114 (120) sts.
Now work measures approx. 42 (44) 46 (48) cm /
16½ (17¼) 18 (19) inches.
We will now work each shoulder separately.

Right shoulder
Row 1 (WS) P 43 (45) 47 (49), w&t wyif.
Row 2 (RS) K to the end.
Row 3 (WS) P 38 (40) 42 (44), w&t wyif.
Row 4 (RS) K to last st, M1, K1. (1sts increased).
Row 5 (WS) P 36 (38) 40 (42), w&t wyif.
Row 6 (RS) K to the end.
Row 7 (WS) P 35 (37) 39 (41), w&t wyif.
Row 8 (RS) K to last st, M1, K1 (1sts increased).
Row 9 (WS) P 35 (37) 39 (41), pm (m1) w&t wyif.
Now 35 (37) 39 (41) sts remain. Work short rows
as described below to shape the shoulder.

Short rows
The short rows are worked over the remaining
35 (37) 39 (41) sts.
Row 10 (RS) K 28 (30) 32 (34), w&t wyif.
Row 11 (WS) P to m1.
Row 12 (RS) K to 4 sts before last turn, w&t
wyif.
Rows 13 - 22 Repeat rows 11 and 12 another 5
(5) 5 (5) times.
Row 23 (WS) P to m1.
Row 24 (RS) K all 35 (37) 39 (41) sts.
Leave sts on hold while working left shoulder.

Left shoulder
Row 1 (RS) K 43 (45) 47 (49), w&t wyif.
Row 2 (WS) P to the end.
Row 3 (RS) K 38 (40) 42 (44), w&t wyif.
Row 4 (WS) P to last st, M1p, P1 (1sts
increased).
Row 5 (RS) K 36 (38) 40 (42), w&t wyif.
Row 6 (WS) P to the end.
Row 7 (RS) P 35 (37) 39 (41), w&t wyif.

Row 8 (WS) P to last st, M1p, P1 (1sts increased).
Row 9 (RS) K 35 (37) 39 (41), pm (m2) w&t wyif. Now 35 (37) 39 (41) sts remain. Work short rows as described below to shape the shoulder.

Shortrows
The short rows are worked over the remaining 35 (37) 39 (41) sts.
Row 10 (WS) P 28 (30) 32 (34), w&t wyif.
Row 11 (RS) K to m2.
Row 12 (WS) P to 4 sts before last turn, w&t wyif.
Rows 13 - 22 Repeat rows 11 and 12 another 5 (5) 5 (5) times.
Row 23 (RS) K to m2.
Row 24 (WS) P all 35 (37) 39 (41) sts.
The front panel 1 is now finished. The sts between m1 and m2 will become the neck opening. Move all front sts to spare needle, while working the back. Remove all markers.

Back Panel 1
Repeat panel 1 as for the front in Col A.
Graft together shoulder sts from front and back panel on both shoulders to form one knitted piece. Grafting is marked with dashed lines in diagram A. From now on, panel one front and back are described as just panel 1.

***Right side Panel 2
Row 1 (RS) Using Col B and 4 mm (UK 8) (US 6) circular needle, 100 cm/39 inches, pick up and knit 220 (230) 240 (250) sts evenly along the long, right side of panel 1. Panel 2 is worked in garter stitch and the pick up line is marked in blue on diagram A.
PLEASE NOTE To make a nice and even "pick up and knit edge" work this in the second st and not in the first edge st.
Row 2 (WS) K all.
Row 3 (RS) K all.
Repeat rows 2 and 3 until the panel measures 8 (9) 9 (10) cm / 3¼ (3½) 3½ (4) inches from pick up edge.
Meanwhile on the last row (RS)
K 84 (86) 88 (90) sts. Pm (m3). K another 52 (58) 64 (70) sts, they will become sleeves. Now use 4 mm (UK 8) (US 6) circular needle, 60 cm/24 inches for knitting the remaining 84 (86) 88 (90) sts.
These last 84 (86) 88 (90) sts will be used for panel 3 right side.

Right side Panel 3
Row 1 (WS) Change to Col C and establish rib

on the 84 (86) 88 (90) sts as follows: P3 (4) 5 (6), *K1, P6*. Repeat from *to* until there are 4 (5) 6 (0) sts remaining, K1, P3 (4) 5 (0).
Row 2 (RS) K all.
Repeat rows 1 and 2 working rib as set until panel 3 measures 12 (12) 14 (14) cm / 4¾ (4 ¾) 5½ (5½) inches.
Graft together the 84 (86) 88 (90) sts from the newly knitted panel with the 84 (86) 88 (90) sts on the back of panel 2.

Right sleeve
The sleeves are knitted over the 52 (58) 64 (70) sts remaining from panel 2 and some new sts we are now going to pick up:
Using Col D and the same 4 mm (UK 8) (US 6) needle the 52 (58) 64 (70) sts are left on. Pm (m2). Pick up and knit 26 (26) 30 (30) sts along the top edge of panel 3 to shape the armhole. There are 78 (84) 94 (100) sts in total. The sleeves are worked in stocking stitch and will eventually be joined in the round.
Row 1 (RS) Start at m3. Remove m3. Continue Col D. K2, pm1, K to 2 sts before m2. Move m2 to this point. K2tog tbl twice, (2 sts decreased) w&t wyib.
Row 2 (WS) P2, sm. P to m1, sm, P2tog twice (2 sts decreased) w&t wyib.
Row 3 (RS) K2, sm. K to m2, sm. K2tog tbl twice, (2 sts decreased) w&t wyib.
Repeat rows 2 and 3 until all stitches from panel 3 have been integrated to the sleeve and there are 52 (58) 64 (70) sts remaining. Join for working in the round, remove stitch markers.
Round 1 pm (m1). K all.
Repeat round 1, until sleeve measures 14 (14) 15 (15) cm / 5½ (5½) 6 (6) inches measured from the Col Change from Col B to Col D.

Decreases
Round 1 - 9 Sm. K all.
Round 10 (decrease round) Sm. K1, k2tog tbl. K to 3 sts before m1. K2tog, k1. (2 sts decreased, 50 (56) 62 (68) sts remaining).
Repeat round 1 - 10 4 (5) 5 (6) more times until there are 42 (46) 52 (56) sts remaining.
Continue in stocking stitch without decreases until sleeves measure 37 (38) 39 (40) cm / 14½ (15) 15½ (16) inches measured from the Col Change from B to D, or your prefered length.
Last round Change to Col E. Sm. K all.

Icord edge right sleeve
CO 6sts on dpn 4 mm (UK 8) (US 6). If the edge becomes too tight or loose, adjust needle size accordingly.
Remove m1.
Slip all CO sts one by one from the right hand dpn onto the left hand needle containing the sleeve sts. Do not turn the work.
Row 1 (RS) K5, k2tog tbl (that is: k tog last sts of icord together with first st of the sleeve). Slip sts from right hand needle back to left hand needle without turning.
Repeat Row 1 ignoring that the wool is in the "wrong" place, when beginning the row, continue repeating row 1 until all sleeve sts have been worked.
Make sure to pull the yarn tight in the end of each row. Graft together the remaining 6 icord sts and the CO edge.***

Left side Panel 2
To work left side of the jumper repeat pattern from ***to***.

Finishing bottom hem
Icord edge
Using Col E and 4 mm (UK 8) (US 6) circular needle, 100 cm / 39 inches, pick up and knit 228 (246) 264 (282) sts along bottom edge. Start at an edge of panel 1 on the back.
CO 6 sts on dpn 4 mm (UK 8) (US 6) with Col E and work icord edge as for the sleeves.
Graft together the remaining 6 icord sts and the CO edge.

Finishing neckband, icord
Start at backside neck opening at sts on hold. Using col E and 4 mm (UK 8) (US 6) circular needle 60 cm/ 24 inches. Pm (m1). Work held 36 (38) 40 (42) sts in knit. Pick up and knit 36 sts (all sizes) before reaching front sts on hold. Knit front sts. Pick up and knit 36 sts (all sizes) before m1.
There are now 138 (142) 146 (150) sts around the neck in Col E.
CO 6sts on dpn 4 mm (UK 8) (US 6) using Col E and work icord as for sleeves and bottom hem. Graft together the remaining 6 icord sts and the CO edge.

Finishing
Weave in all ends. Steam your new Jumper. And take the jumper on parade...

Flying Feathers

Penguin Child
Design Laura Locher
Skill level 3
Photo page 187 - 192 - 193

Desing Laura Locher
- a jumper with crests, moving when jumping...
#REDflyingfeathers

Sizes
EU 86 (98) 110 (122)
UK UK 12-18 month (2-3) 4-5 (6-7) years
To fit bust, body
53 (55) 59 (63) cm
21 (21.5) 23 (25) inches
1 (2) 4 (6) years
Actual bust measurement, jumper
64 (66) 70 (74) cm
25 (26) 27½ (29) inches
Length
38 (40) 44 (48) cm
13 ½ (15 ¾) 18 (20 ½) inches
Yarn A
Madelinetosh Vintage
100 % Merino wool, 182 m / 200 yds per 100
gram 4 (4) 5 (6) x 100 gram Col: T`Challa
Yarn B
Tosh merino Light Madelinetosh 384 m / Yards
112 gram. Col Antler.
1 unicorn tale all sizes. 42 meter / 46 yards.

Yarn penguin feathers
Yarn A: Madelinetosh Prairie 100 % merino
wool 768 m / 112 gram
40 (40) 40 (40) gram
Yarn B: ITO Sensai
1 skein all sizes
Needles
4.5 (US 7) and z4.5 (US 7) and 5 mm (US 8) dpn.
4 stitch markers.
Gauge
In stocking stitch on 5 mm (US 8) needles and
yarn A: 17 sts x 25 rows = 10 x 10 cm / 4 x 4
inches.
Remember to check your gauge and adjust needle size accordingly.
Stitch patterns
Brioche rib pattern
Worked in the round:
Round 1 Col A K1, sl1yo.
Round 2 Col A K1, s1yo2.
Round 3 Col B K1, brk1^2.

Stocking stitches
Worked forth and back:
RS Knit all stitches
WS Purl all stitches
Worked in the round: Knit all stitches

Shown in size 110 / 4-5 years

Tip
This jumper is worked bottom up. The body is
worked in the round on circular needles. The
sleeves are the worked on dpn.
From the sleevehole and upwards all pieces are
gathered on the same needle and worked in

the round. So there will be a minimun of finish
afterwards.

Body, rib pattern
CO 88 (94) 100 (110) sts using 4.5 mm (US 7)
circular needle and yarn A.

Set up round
Join for working in the round and k all sts.

Brioche rib pattern
Round 1 Col A *K1, sl1yo*. Repeat *to* to the
end.
Round 2 Col A *K1, s1yo2*. Repeat *to* to the
end.
Round 3 Col B *K1, brk1^2*. Repeat *to* to
the end.
Repeat round 1 - 3 another 5 times.

Body, stocking stitch and Increase
Round 1 Change to 5 mm (US 8) circular
needle. K 4 (2) 0 (1). *K4 (5) 5 (6), M1*. Repeat
to to 4 (2) 0 (1) sts before end. K to end.
There are now 108 (112) 120 (128) sts. Continue
in stocking stitch. Work straight until work
measures 25 (26) 29 (32) cm / 10 (10¼) 11½ (12
½) inches.

Armhole
Row 1 Pm (m1) K 53 (55) 59 (63) sts. BO 2 sts
loosely. K to 1 st before m1. BO 2 sts loosely.
The work has now been divided into front
and back with 52 (54) 58 (62) sts on each side.
Remove m1.
Leave sts on hold while working the sleeves.

Sleeve
CO 20 (22) 24 (26) sts using 4.5 mm (US 7) dpn
and yarn A. Join for working in the round.

Set up round K all sts.

Brioche Rib pattern
Round 1 Col A *K1, s1 yo*. Repeat *to* to the
end.

Round 2 Col A *K1, s1 yo2*. Repeat *to* to the
end.
Round 3 Col B *K1, brk*. Repeat *to* to the
end.

Repeat round 1 - 3 another 3 times.

Stoking stitch and increases
Round 1 Change to needle 5 mm (US 8). Pm
(m1). K 1 (2) 3 (4) *K3, M1*. Repeat *to* to 1 (2)
3 (4) sts before end. K to end. There are now 26
(28) 30 (32) sts.
Round 2 - 5 Knit all sts.

Increase

Round 1 K1, M1. K to last st. M1, K1.
There are now 28 (30) 32 (34) sts.
Round 2 - 5 Knit all sts.
Repeat round 1-5 another 7 (8) 9 (10) times.
There are now 42 (46) 50 (54) sts. Continue straight without further increases to a total measurement of 21 (23) 27 (31) cm / 8 (9) 10½ (12) inches.

Armhole
Work to 1 st before m1. BO 2 sts loosely. There are now 40 (44) 48 (52) sts. Leave sts on hold while working the other sleeve the same way.

Joining all pieces
Joining round (RS) Using the needle from the body was resting on. Beginnig where the needles and yarn is. This will now be the back. Work back sts like this:
Pm (m1). K1, p1. Patt to last 2 back sts. P1, k1.
Pm (m2). Knit the sts of one sleeve onto the same needle.
Pm (m3). Work front sts onto same needle: K1, p1, k to last 2 sts. P1, k1.
Pm (m4). Knit the sts of the other sleeve onto the needle to end.
All sts are now joined on the same needle and joined for working in the round. There are now sts 184 (196) 212 (228) sts.
Round 1 (RS) Sm. Sl1. K to 1 st before m2. Sl1, sm. K to m 3. Sm. Sl1. K to last st before m4. Sl1, sm. K sts to m1.
Round 2 (RS) Sm. K1, p1. K to 2 sts before m2. P1 k1, sm. P1. K to 1 st before m 3. P1, sm. K1, p1. K to 2 sts before m4. P1, k1, sm. P1. K to 1 st before m1. P1. You now have established a pattern for the raglan line.

Raglan decreases
Round 3 (RS) Sm. Sl1, k1. K2tog. Patt to 4 sts before m2. K2tog tbl. K1, sl1, sm, k1, k2tog. K to 3 sts before m3. K2tog tbl, k1, sm, sl1, k1, k2tog. K to 4 sts before m4. K2tog tbl, k1, sl1, sm, k1, k2tog. K to 3 sts before m1. K2tog tbl, k1. (red. 8 sts)
Round 4 (RS) Sm. K1, p1. K to 2 sts before m2. P1, k1, sm. P1. K to 1 st before m3. P1, sm. K1, p1. K to 2 sts before m4. P1, k1, sm. P1. K sts to 1 st before m1. P1.

Repeat row 3 - 4 until there are 14 (16)16 (18) sts remaining in the sleeve part (between m2 and m3 and between m4 and m1).

Short rows
In order to make the jumper comfortable to wear, we will work short rows to have a neckopening that is lower in front, than in the back.
Row 1 (RS) Sm. Sl1, k1. K2tog. K to 4 sts before m2. K2tog tbl. K1, sl1, sm, k1, k2tog. K 7 (8) 8 (9)

st, w&t. (red. 3 sts).
Row 2 (WS) P to 1 st before m2. K1, sm, p1, k1. P to 2 sts before m1. K1, p1, sm, k1. P2tog. P 7 (8) 8 (9) st, w&t.(red. 1 sts)
Row 3 (RS) K to m1. Sm. Sl1, k1. K2tog. K to 4 sts before m2. K2tog tbl. K1, sl1, sm, k1, k2tog. K 4 (5) 5 (6) st, w&t. (red. 3 sts).
Row 4 (WS) P to 1 st before m2. K1, sm, p1, k1. P to 2 sts before m1. k1, p1, sm, k1. P2tog. P 4 (5) 5 (6) st, w&t. (red. 1 sts).

Hoodie
Row 1 (RS) Remowe m1. K 11 (11) 11(12) sts. Pm (m1)midt back. K all sts till 8 (7) 7 (7) sts before m4, remove m2 and m3 as you meet them. Now work dbe1. Pm (m2). Turn work.This is now the left opening of the hoodie.
Row 2 (WS) Dbe1. P all sts to m2. (Remove m4 as you meet it).
Sm (m2) Using dpn 4.5 (US 7), below the following 8 (10) 10 (12) sts pick up 8 (10) 10 (12) sts on the WS of work.
Then again using the circular needle, purl 7 (9) 9 (11) sts, dbe1. Turn work. These 80 (86) 86 (96) sts will become the hoodie.
The marker m2 indicates the opening of the hoodie, you can remove this marker, when you do not need to indicate the opening anymore. The marker m1 indicates midt back of hoodie and that one stays in place.
Row 3 (RS) Dbe1. K all sts till 1 st before you meet m2 again. Dbe1. Turn work.
Row 4 (WS) Dbe1. P to 1 st before end. Dbe1.
Shaping the hoodie
Row 1 (RS) Dbe1. K to 1 sts before m1. M1, k1, sm, k1, M1. K to last st, dbe1. There are 82 (88) 88 (98) sts.
Row 2 (WS) Dbe1. P to last st. Dbe1.
Row 3 (RS) Dbe1. K to last st. Dbe1.
Row 4 (WS) Dbe1. P to last st. Dbe1.
Repeat row 1 - 4 another 5 times.
There are now 92 (98) 98 (108) sts.
Continue straight till the hood measures 15 (16) 17 (19) cm/ inches.
Decrease, shaping hoodie
Row 1 (RS) Dbe1. K to 3 sts before m1. K2tog tbl, k1, sm, k1, k2tog. K to last st. Dbe1.
Row 2 - 4 Work as set without shaping.
Repeat row 1 - 4 twice more.
There are now 86 (92) 92 (102) sts.

Bind of
BO all sts in knit togehter-bind-off methode as descibed below. First: Move all sts after m1 to a spare needle.
Now fold the hoodie WS to WS.
K2tog using 1 st from main needle and 1 st from spare needle.*k2tog using 1 st from main needle and 1 st from spare needle, slip first the st on right hand needle over the second st* Rep *to* to the end. Break yarn and drag the

yarn end through the last st.

Needles
5 mm (US 8) circular needle, 60 cm (24 inches).
Note: we are not working in the round, just using circular needles as they are more comfortable for our shoulders.

Gauge
In garter st on needle 5 mm (US 8) in Yarn A + Yarn B,
18 st = 10 cm / 4 inches.

Tip
For the feathers we are using the knitted cast on method, where nothing else is mentioned. There are lots of good videos on the web but you can also watch ours:
LINK TO BE PUT IN

Feathers
CO 60 (70) 80 (90) sts (in your usual way) using needle 5mm and Yarn A only.

Feather 1
Row 1 (RS) Yarn A+B K 14 (16) 18 (20) st, leave Yarn B. K to the end.
*****Row 2 (WS)** K until you get to Yarn B. Add Yarn B, K to last st. Dbe 1.
Row 3 (RS) K 22 (24) 26 (28), leave Yarn B, K to last st. Dbe 1.
Row 4 (WS) As row 2.
Row 5 (RS) Button hole. K 3, yo k2tog. K 13 (15) 17 (19), leave Yarn B. K to 15 sts before end, w&t.
Row 6 (WS) As row 2.
Row 7 (RS) K 10 (12) 14 (18), leave Yarn B. K to 15 sts before last wrapped st, w&t.
Row 8 (WS) As row 2.
Row 9 (RS) K 16 (18) 20 (22), leave Yarn B. K4, w&t.
Row 10 (WS) As row 2.
Row 11 (RS) K 18 (20) 22 (24) st leave Yarn B. K all sts to the end.
Row 12 (WS) BO 42 (50) 58 (66) sts using only yarn A. Yarn A + B, K to last st. Dbe 1. There are now 18 (20) 22 (24) sts.

Feather 2
Row 1 (RS) K 14 (16) 18 (20) sts, leave Yarn B. K 4. CO 26 (34) 42 (50) sts. There are now 44 (54) 64 (74) sts.
Row 2 (WS) K till you meet Yarn B. Ad Yarn B, k to last st. Dbe 1.
Row 3 (RS) K 10 (12) 14 16 sts, leave Yarn B, k to last st. Dbe 1.
Row 4 (WS) As row 2.
Row 5 (RS) Button hole
K 3, yo k2tog. K 9 (11) 13 (15) sts, leave Yarn B. K to 15 sts before end, W&t.
Row 6 (WS) As row 2.

Row 7 (RS) K 10 (12) 14 (16) sts, leave Yarn B. K to 8 sts before last wrapped st, W&t.
Row 8 (WS) As row 2.
Row 9 (RS) K 14 (16) 18 (20), W&t.
Row 10 (WS) As row 2.
Row 11 (RS) K 12 (13) 14 (15) st leave Yarn B. K all sts to the end.
Row 12 (WS) BO 32 (41) 50 (59) sts. K to last st. Dbe 1. There are now 12 (13) 14 (15) sts.

Feather 3
Row 1 (RS) K 10 (11) 12 (13) st, leave Yarn B. K 2. CO 48 (57) 66 (75) sts. There are now 60 (70) 80 (90) sts.
Row 2 (WS) K till you meet Yarn B. Ad Yarn B, k to last st. Dbe 1.
Row 3 (RS) K 12 (14) 16 (18) sts, leave Yarn B, k to last st. Dbe 1.
Row 4 (WS) As row 2.
Row 5 (RS) Button hole
K 3, yo k2tog. K 13 (15) 17 (19) sts, leave Yarn B. K to 15 sts before end, W&t.
Row 6 (WS) K till you meet Yarn B. Ad Yarn B, k to 10 sts before end, w&t (now on the WS).
Row 7 (RS) Leave Yarn B. K to 15 sts before last wrapped st, W&t.
Row 8 (WS) As row 2.
Row 9 (RS) K 4 its before last wrapped st, W&t.

Row 10 (WS) K to 8 sts before end, w&t (now on the WS).
Row 11 (RS) K 14 (16) 18 (20) st leave Yarn B. K all sts to the end.
Row 12 (WS) BO 46 (54) 62 (70) sts using only yarn A. Yarn A + B, K to last st. Dbe 1. There are now 14 (16) 18 (20) sts.

Feather 4
Row 1 (RS) K 8 (9) 10 (11) st, leave Yarn B. K to end. CO 38 (46) 54 (62) sts. There are now 52 (62) 72 (82) sts.
Row 2 (WS) K till you meet Yarn B. Ad Yarn B, k to last st. Dbe 1.
Row 3 (RS) K 12 (14) 16 (18) sts, leave Yarn B, k to last st. Dbe 1.
Row 4 (WS) As row 2.
Row 5 (RS) Button hole K 3, yo k2tog. K 9 (11) 13 (15), leave Yarn B. K to 15 sts before end, W&t.
Row 6 (WS) K till you meet Yarn B. Ad Yarn B, k to 10 sts before end, w&t (now on the WS).
Row 7 (RS) Leave Yarn B. K to 15 sts before last wrapped st, W&t.
Row 8 (WS) As row 2.
Row 9 (RS) K 14 (16) 18 (20). Leave Yarn B. K all sts to the end.
Row 10 (WS) BO 38 (46) 54 (62) sts using only yarn A. Yarn A + B, K to last st. Dbe 1. There are now 14 (16) 18 (20) sts.
Feather 1
You are now ready to repeat from feather 1 again. Just the first row is work like this:

Row 1 (RS) Yarn A+B K 10 (12) 14 (16) st leave Yarn B. K to the end. CO 38 (40) 42 (44) sts. There are now 60 (70) 80 (90) sts.***
Rep from * to ***** to work maesures 42 (46) 50 (56) cm. BO all its from a (WS).

Finish
Weave in all ends. Close the little gab under the sleeve hole. Drag a linen band through the holes i the top line of the feather cape.
Sew in a button midt back and on each top of front raglan line. Button the cape on to the jumper…

And here you are … ready to fly.

When you jump my feathers will fly around you like a crest!
Laura Locher
#REDflyingfeathers

Eyes on You

Erect Crested Penguin Teen~Adult
Design Laura Locher
Skill level 4
Photo page 188 - 189 - 190
front cover

Design Laura Locher
- a unisex Jumper
#REDeyesonyou

Skill level 4
Sizes
S M L XL
To fit bust
84 94 106 120 cm
33 (37) 42 (47) inches
Actual bust measurement (jumper)
90 (100) 112 (126) cm
35½ (39½) 44 (49½) inches
Please note this pattern makes a very stretchy jumper.
Length
54 (58) 67 (74) cm
21¼ (22¾) 26¼ (29) inches
Yarn A
Season Alpaca, Purl Soho
100 % Baby Alpaca, 200 m / 218 yards per 100 g
3 (4) 4 (5) x 100 g
Yarn B
Understory, Purl Soho
50 % Baby Alpaca, 25 Baby Yak, 25 % Silk, 228 m / 250 yards per 100 g
3 (4) 4 (5) x 100 g

Yarn for eyes
We have used 4 Contrast colours (CC): Keetle Yarn Beyul, Orchid and Rhubarb and Tosh merino Light Col Penumbra and Hi-Lo.
Needles size S and L
4.5 mm (US 7) and 4 mm (US 6) circular needle, 80 cm (32 inches).
4.5 mm (US 7) dpns.
4 stitch markers.
Gauge size S and L
In two colour brioche patt on 4.5 mm (US 7) needles: 18 sts x 38 rows = 10 x 10 cm/4 x 4 inches.
Needles size M and XL
5 mm (US 8) and 4.5 mm (US 7) circular needle, 80 cm (32 inches).
5 mm (US 8) dpns.

4 stitch markers.
Gauge size M and XL
In two colour brioche patt on 5 mm (US 8) needles: 16 sts x 36 rows = 10 x 10 cm/4 x 4 inches.

Remember to check your gauge and adjust needle size accordingly.

Shown in S
Dark Colour, Stillwater blue.
Light Colour, Heirloom white

Patterns used
Two colour rib patt: knit in dark, purl in light colour.
Brioche patt: Brk1, dark. Brp1 light colour.

Knitting swatch
CO 21 sts using col A and 4.5 (5) 4.5 (5) mm (US 7 (8) 7 (8)) dpn.
Setting up row (WS) K1, p to last st. K1.
Row 1 using col A (RS) K1. Sl1yo *K1, sl1yo*. Repeat *-* to last st. K1. Slide.
Row 2 using col B (RS) K1. Brp1 *Sl1yo, brp 1*. Repeat *-* to last st. K1. Turn work.
Row 3 using col A (WS) K1. sl1yo. *Brp1, sl1yo*. Repeat *-* to last st. K1. Slide.
Row 4 using col B (WS) K1. Brk1 *sl1yo*. Repeat *-* to last st. K1. Turn work.
Repeat Rows 1 - 4 until work measures 11 cm / 4¼ inches, however in row 1 it is from now on *brk1, sl1yo*.

Tip
Whenever there has been worked a **brkyobrk** on the previous row, these 3 sts will have to be worked: **Sl1yo, p1, sl1yo** on the following row.

Tips
Prepare yarn for eyes. Measure a piece of CC yarn of 150cm / 60 inches. Make sure to distribute colours of eyes in a random way.

Special abbreviations
brkRsl dec = brioche 2 st decrease which leans to the right, worked over three sts. Slip the first st knit wise, knit into the next st, pass the sl st over, pass the st back to left needle and sl next st over, pass st back to right needle.

brkyobrk = brioche 2 st increase - brk1, leave the st on left needle, bring yarn forward to create a yarn over a brk1 into the same st. Three sts are created from one st, work these as separate sts on following row.

brkyobrkRsl dec = brioche 2 st increase and 2 st decrease at the same time. Slip the first st knit wise, brkyobrk into next st, pass the sl st over these three sts, pass the sts back to left needle and sl next st over, pass st back to right needle.

Body rib
Body, two colour rib pattern
CO 160 (160) **200 (200)** sts for size S and L using 4.5 mm (US 7).
For size M and XL using 5 mm (US 8) circular needle, 80 cm (32 inches) and yarn A Join for working in the round.
Round 1 (RS) Set up round
* using col. A k1, change to col B, **k1**.
Repeat *-* to end of round.
Round 2 (RS)
Work two colour rib patt: * using col. A k1, change to col B, p1*. Repeat *-* to end of round. Continue in two colour rib patt until work measures 2.5 cm / 1 inch.

Body, brioche pattern
Setting up rounds
Round 1 using col A Pm (m1) *K1, sl1yo*. Repeat *-* for a total of 80 (80) **100 (100)** sts. Pm (m2). Repeat *-* to the end of the round.
Round 2 using col B *Sl1yo, brp1*.
Repeat *-* to the end of the round.
Round 3 using col A *Brk1, sl1yo*.
Repeat *-* to the end of the round.
Round 4 using col B *Sl1yo, brp1*.
Repeat *-* to the end of the round.

Feather and eye pattern, body
Round 1 using col A *brkyobrk, (sl1yo, brk1)x7, sl1yo, brRsl dec, sl1yo*. Repeat *-* to the end.
Round 2 using col B *Sl1yo, brp1*.
Repeat *-* to the end.
Round 3 using col A *Brk1, sl1yo*.
Repeat *-* to the end.

Round 4 using col B *Sl1yo, brp1*.
Repeat *-* to the end.

Round 5 using col A *brk1, sl1yo, brkyobrk, (sl1yo, brk1)x6, sl1yo, brRsl dec, sl1yo*. Repeat *-* to the end.
Round 6 using col B As round 2.
Round 7 using col A As round 3.
Round 8 using col B As round 4.

Round 9 using col A *(Brk1, sl1yo)x2, brkyobrk, (sl1yo, brk1)x5, sl1yo, brRsl dec, sl1yo*. Repeat *-* to the end.
Round 10 using col B As round 2.
Round 11 using col A As round 3.
Round 12 using col B As round 4.

Round 13 using col A *(Brk1, sl1yo)x3, brkyobrk, (sl1yo, brk1)x4, sl1yo, brRsl dec, sl1yo*. Repeat *-* to the end of the round.
Round 14 using col B As round 2.
Round 15 using col A As round 3.
Round 16 using col B As round 4.

Round 17 using col A *(Brk1, sl1yo)x4, brkyobrk, (sl1yo, brk1)x3, sl1yo, brRsl dec, sl1yo*. Repeat *-* to the end.
Round 18 using col B As round 2.
Round 19 using col A As round 3.
Round 20 using col B As round 4.

Round 21 using col A *(Brk1, sl1yo)x5, brkyobrk, (sl1yo, brk1)x2, sl1yo, brRsl dec, sl1yo *. Repeat *-* to the end of the round.
Round 22 using col B As round 2.
Round 23 using col A Eyes
Prepare yarn for 8 (8) 10 (10) eyes (see TIPS)
*(Brk1, sl1yo)x7. Change to CC held double.
K3, w&t.
(WS) P3, w&t.
(RS) K4. Turn (without wrap).
(WS) P4. Turn (without wrap).
(RS) Pick up col A, twist CC and Col A still using CC: k2, twist col A around CC, still using CC: k2, twist col A and CC. Change to col A, brk, sl1yo*. Repeat *-* to the end of the round.
Round 24 using col B Work as round 4 until

you reach the CC sts: Still using col B: K4.
Continue in brioche sts patt as round 4, till you meet the next sts in CC. K4. Keep working in brioche patt and whenever meeting CC sts, work K4. Work like this to the end of the round.

Round 25 using col A Eyes ending
*(Brk1, sl1yo)x6, brkyobrk, sl1yo, k1, sl1yo, brRsl dec, sl1yo *. Repeat *-* to the end of the round.
Round 26 using col B As round 2.
Round 27 using col A As round 3.
Round 28 using col B As round 4.

Repeat feather and eye pattern, body from round 1-28 another 4 (4)5 (6) times.
There will now be a total of 5 (5) 6 (7) set of eye patterns.
Approx length of the body at 39 (43) 46 (51)cm /15.5 (17) **18¼ (20)** inches.

Divide work in front and back
From now on we will be working back and forth.
Whenever a col A row is worked, you will slide the knitting back and work your col B row. Then the work is ready to be turned.
Continue working the 'eye and feather' pattern as described below.

Front
Preparation to work front
Sm. ***M1(pick up the loop before next st LC using LH needle going from the back, using col B p1 on this loop). Move the new st from RH needle back to LH needle.
This st now belongs to the front.
Row 1 (RS) using col A Decrease / Increase
Sl1yo, brk1, (sl1yo, brk1)x7, sl1yo, brRsl dec, sl1yo. *brkyobrk, (sl1yo, brk1)x7, sl1yo, brRsl dec, sl1yo*. Repeat *-* another 2 (2) 3 (3) times.
M1 (pick up loop before next st col A, k this loop tbl).
Remove m2.
Now slip all back sts onto spare needle until you meet m1. Remove m1.
The work is now divided into back and front.
Leave the back sts on hold on the spare needle, while working the front.
There are now
82 (82) 102 (102) sts front.
80 (80) 100 (100) sts back.
Row 2 (RS) using col B Brp. *sl1yo, brp*.
Repeat *-* to last st. Sl1yo, M1 (pick up loop

before next st col B, k this loop tbl). Turn work. There are now 83 (83) 103 (103) sts.
Row 3 (WS) using col A *Sl1yo, brp*. Repeat *-* to last st. Sl1yo. Do not turn. Slide.
Row 4 (WS) using col B *Brk, Sl1yo*. Repeat *-* to last st. Brk. Turn.

Round 5 (RS) using col A
Sl1yo, brkyobrk, (sl1yo, brk1)x6, sl1yo, brRsl dec, sl1yo, brk. Repeat *-* last st. Sl1yo. Slide.
Row 6 (RS) using col B Brp *sl1yo, brp*. Repeat *-* to the end. Turn work.
Row 7 (WS) using col A *Sl1yo, brp*. Repeat *-* to last st. Sl1yo. Do not turn. Slide.
Row 8 (WS) using col B *Brk, Sl1yo*. Repeat *-* to last st. Brk. Turn.

Row 9 (RS) using col A
Sl1yo, brk1, sl1yo, brkyobrk, (sl1yo, brk1) x5, sl1yo, brRsl dec, sl1yo, brk. Repeat *-*last st. Sl1yo. Slide.
Row 10 (RS) using col B As row 6.
Row 11 (WS) using col A As row 7.
Row 12 (WS) using col B As row 8.

Row 13 (RS) using col A *Sl1yo, (brk1, sl1yo)x2, brkyobrk, (sl1yo, brk1)x4, sl1yo, brRsl dec, sl1yo, brk*. Repeat *-* last st. Sl1yo. Slide.
Row 14 (RS) using col B As row 6.
Row 15 (WS) using col A As row 7.
Row 16 (WS) using col B As row 8.

Row 17 (RS) using col A *Sl1yo, (brk1, sl1yo)x3, brkyobrk, (sl1yo, brk1)x3, sl1yo, brRsl dec, sl1yo, brk*. Repeat *-*last st. Sl1yo. Slide.
Row 18 (RS) using col B As row 6.
Row 19 (WS) using col A As row 7.
Row 20 (WS) using col B As row 8.

Row 21 using col A (RS) *Sl1yo, (brk1, sl1yo)x4, brkyobrk, (sl1yo, brk1)x2, sl1yo, brRsl dec, sl1yo, brk*. Repeat *-*last st.

Sl1yo. Slide.
Row 22 using col B (RS) As row 6.
The eyes will now be worked beginning from the WS like this:
Row 23 (WS) using col A Sl1yo,* (brp1, sl1yo) x2. Move Col A yarn to WS.
Change to CC held double.
P3, w&t.
(RS) k4. Turn (without wrap).
(WS) P4. W&t.
(RS) K4.
(WS) Pick up col A, twist CC and Col A still using CC: p2, twist col A around CC, still using CC: p2, twist col A and CC. Change to col A Sl1yo. (brp1, sl1yo)x6*.
Repeat *-* another 3 (3) 4 (4) times. Slide.
Row 24 (WS) using col B Work as row 8 until you reach the CC sts: Still using col B: P4. Keep working in brioche patt and whenever meeting CC sts, work P4. Continue to end.

Row 25 (RS) using col A
sl1yo, (brk1, sl1yo)x5, brkyobrk, sl1yo, brk1, sl1yo, brRsl dec, sl1yo, brk1. Repeat *-*last st. Sl1yo. Slide.
Row 26 (RS) using col B brp1, *sl1yo, brp1* Repeat to the end. Turn.
Row 27 (WS) using col A Sl1yo, *brp1, sl1yo*. Repeat to the end. Slide.
Row 28 (WS) using col B Brp1, *sl1yo, brk1*. Repeat *-* to the end. Turn.
There are now
81 **(81) 101** (101) sts front.***

Continue in two colour brioche patt without making eyes to a measurement of 14 (15) 16 (17.5) cm / 5½ (6) 6¼ (7) inches from sleeve hole, ending with as (WS) col B.

Neck opening front
Left front
Row 1 (RS) using col A Patt 28 (27) 29 (29) sts. Slip 25 (27) 29 (29) sts onto spare needle. Slide left front sts.
Row 2 (RS) using col B Patt 28 (27) 29 (29) sts. Turn.
Row 3 (WS) using col A Sl 2 st onto spare needle. Work as set to end. Slide.
Row 4 (WS) using col B Work as set to end. Turn.
Repeat the 4 brioche rows twice more; every time Sl 2 sts onto spare needle in the beg of

row 3.
Continue without further shaping until work measures 20 (21) 22.5 (24) cm / 8 (8 ¼) 8¾ (9½) inches from sleeve hole; ending with a (WS) col B. BO all sts using col A.

Right front
Row 1 (RS) using col A Patt 28 (27) 29 (29) sts to end. Slide.
Row 2 (RS) using col B Patt 28 (27) 29 (29) sts. Turn.
Row 3 (WS) using col A Work as set to end. Slide.
Row 4 (WS) using col B Work as set to 2 sts before end. Sl 2 sts onto spare needle. Turn. Repeat the 4 brioche rows twice more; every time Sl 2 sts onto spare needle in the end of row 4.
Continue without further shaping until work measures 20 (21) 22.5 (24) cm / 8 (8 ¼) 8¾ (9½) inches from sleeve hole, ending with a (WS) col B. BO all sts using col A.

Back
Repeat from as for front from ***to*
Thereafter** repeat the eyes and feather patt from row 1 - 28 (without the extra increases in beg and end of row 1 - 3) to a measurement of 19 (20) 21 (22.5) cm / 7½ (8) 8¼ (9) inches from sleeve hole, ending with as (WS) col B.

Neck opening front
Right Back
Row 1 (RS) using col A Patt 22 (21) 23 (23) sts. Slip 37 (39) 41 (41) sts onto spare needle. Slide left front sts.
Row 2 (RS) using col B Patt 22 (21) 23 (23) sts. Turn.

Continue two col brioche patt without further shaping until work measures 21 (22) 23.5 (25) cm / 8¼ (8½) 9¼ (9¾) inches from sleeve hole; ending with a (WS) col B.
BO all sts using col A.

Left back
Row 1 (RS) using col A Patt 22 (21) 23 (23) sts to end. Slide.
Row 2 (RS) using col B Patt 22 (21) 23 (23) sts. Turn.
Continue without further shaping until work measures 21 (22) 23.5 (25) cm / 8¼ (8½) 9¼ (9¾)

inches from sleeve hole; ending with a (WS) col B.
BO all sts using col A.

Sleeve, two colour rib pattern
CO 42 42 (44) 46 sts using 4.5 mm (US 7) dpn and yarn A. Join for working in the round.
Round 1 Set up round using col. A K1, Change to col B, **k1***. Repeat *-* to end.
Round 2
Work two colour rib patt: *Using col. A K1, Change to col B, p1*. Repeat *-* to end. Continue in two colour rib patt until work measures 2.5 cm / 1 inches.

Sleeve, brioche pattern
Setting up rounds
Round 1 using col A Pm (m1) *K1, sl1yo*. Repeat *-* for a total of 40 sts. Pm (m2) Repeat *-* to the end.
Round 2 using col B *Sl1yo, brp 1*. Repeat *-* to the end.
Round 3 using col A *Brk1, sl1yo*. Repeat *-* to the end.
Round 4 using col B *Sl1yo, brp 1*. Repeat *-* to the end.

Feather and eye pattern, sleeves
Round 1 using col A *Brkyobrk, (sl1yo, brk1) x7, sl1yo, brRsl dec, sl1yo*. Repeat *-* m2. Sm. Work brk1, sl1yo, to m1. Sm.
Round 2 using col B *Sl1yo, brp1*. Repeat *-* to the end.
Round 3 using col A *Brk1, sl1yo*. Repeat *-* to the end.
Round 4 using col B *Sl1yo, brp1*. Repeat *-* to the end.

Round 5 using col A *Brk1, sl1yo, brkyobrk, (sl1yo, brk1)x6, sl1yo, brRsl dec, sl1yo*. Repeat *-* m2. Sm. Work brk1, sl1yo, to m1. Sm.
Round 6 using col B As round 2.
Round 7 using col A As round 3.
Round 8 using col B As round 4.

Round 9 using col A *(Brk1, sl1yo)x2, brkyobrk, (sl1yo, brk1)x5, sl1yo, brRsl dec, sl1yo*. Repeat *-* m2. Sm. Work brk1, sl1yo, to m 1. Sm.
Round 10 using col B As round 2.
Round 11 using col A As round 3.
Round 12 using col B As round 4.

Round 13 using col A *(Brk1, sl1yo)x3, brkyobrk, (sl1yo, brk1)x4, sl1yo, brRsl dec,

sl1yo*. Repeat *-* m2. Sm Work brk1, sl1yo, to m 1. Sm.
Round 14 using col B As round 2.
Round 15 using col A As round 3.
Round 16 using col B As round 4.

Round 17 using col A *(Brk1, sl1yo)x4, brkyobrk, (sl1yo, brk1)x3, sl1yo, brRsl dec, sl1yo*. Repeat *-* m2. Sm. Work brk1, sl1yo, to m 1.
Round 18 using col B As round 2.
Round 19 using col A As round 3.
Round 20 using col B As round 4.

Round 21 using col A *(Brk1, sl1yo)x5, brkyobrk, (sl1yo, brk1)x2, sl1yo, brRsl dec, sl1yo *. Repeat *-* m2. Work brk1, sl1yo, to m 1.
Round 22 using col B As round 2.
Round 23 using col A Eyes
Prepare yarn for 8 eyes (see TIPS)
*(Brk1, sl1yo)x7. Change to CC held double. K3, w&t.
(WS) P3, w&t.
(RS) K4. Turn (without wrap).
(WS) P4. Turn (without wrap).
(RS) Pick up col A Twist CC and Col A Still using CC: k2, twist col A around CC, still using CC: k2, twist col A and CC. Change to col A, brk, sl1yo*. Repeat *-* to m2. Work brk1, sl1yo, to m1.
Round 24 using col B Work as round 4 till you reach the CC sts: Still using col B: K4. Keep working in brioche patt and whenever meeting CC sts, work K4. Work to end.

Round 25 using col A Eyes ending
*(Brk1, sl1yo)x6, brkyobrk, sl1yo, k1, sl1yo, brRsl dec, sl1yo *. Repeat *-* m2. Work brk1, sl1yo, to m 1.
Round 26 using col B As round 2.
Round 27 using col A As round 3.
Round 28 using col B As round 4.

Repeat 'eye and feather' pattern, sleeve from round 1-28.
AT THE SAME TIME
When the sleeve reaches at measurement of 20 (15) 10 (10) cm /8 (6) 4 (4) inches: work sleeve increases on a col A round, where the patt does not change (on a round 3 or as a round 3).
Sleeve increases
Work pattern as set to m2. Sm. brkyobrk, sl1yo. Work *brk1, sl1yo* to m1.
(2 sts increased)

There are now 44 (44) 46 (48) sts.
Work 11 rounds without increases, then on the 12th round repeat increases 3 (4) 6 (7) times more.
There are now 50 52 (58) 62 sts.
Continue without further increases to a total measurement at 44 (46) 50 (52) cm /17.5 (18) 19.5 (20.5) inches.
BO all sts loosely using col A.

Finish Seam together shoulder seams and set in sleeves. Be careful not to set in too tight. We prefer to do this from the RS. If you take your time to finish well you will be able to wear this jumper inside-out.

Neckband
Using 4.5 mm (US 7) circular needle 40 cm / 16 inches . Begin at left shoulder.
Row 1 (RS) using col A Pick up and k 12 (14) 14 (16) st before the front side holding needle. Work the st from hold *sl1yo, k1* Repeat to last st. Sl1yo. Pick up and k 12 (14) 14 (16) st before the right shoulder.
Pick up and k 4 (6) 6 (7) st before the sts on holding needle. Work the st from hold *sl1yo, k1*. Repeat to last st. Sl1yo.
Pick up and k 4 (6) 6 (7) st before the left shoulder. Adjust number of sts if uneven.
Work two colour rib patt for 6 (6) 7 (8) rounds.
BO all sts tight.
Weave in remaining ends.

Now the many eyes are ready to go look at the world…

Our eyes are on you, watching what you are doing to our world.
Laura Locher
#REDeyesonyou

Not a Jumper

Frog Child
Design Laura Locher
Skill level 4
Photo page 89 - 92 - 93

Designer Laura Locher
- a jumper with eyes...
#REDnotajumper

Skill level 2
Sizes
EU 86 (98) 110 (122)
UK 12-18 month (2-3) 4-5 (6-7) years
To fit bust
53 (55) 59 (63) cm
21 (21½) 23 (25) inches
Actual bust measurement (jumper)
64 (66) 70 (76) cm
25 (26) 27½ (30) inches
Length
38 (40) 44 (48) cm
13½ (15¾) 18 (20½) inches
Yarn Önling 1
75% Merino Superfine 25% Angora. 180m / 197
yds per 50 gram
Col A Pink 3 (3) 4 (5) x 50 gram skeins
Col B Grå 1 (1) 2 (2) x 50 gram skeins
Needles
4 mm (US 6) and 4.5 mm (US 7) circular needle,
60 cm / (24 inches).
4 mm (US 6) and 4.5 mm (US 7) circular needle,
60 cm / (24 inches) and dpn.
Gauge
In garter stitch on 4.5 mm (US 7) needles.
19 sts x 36 rows = 10 x 10 cm / 4 x 4 inches.
Remember to check your gauge and adjust
needle size accordingly.

Shown in size 110 / 4 years
Col base Pink.

Body, rib pattern Front
Using 4 mm (US 6) needles and Col A, CO 46
(50) 58 (66) sts.
***Rib pattern, front
Row 1 (WS) K1. *k4, p4*. Repeat *-* to last st.
K1.
Row 2 (RS) Sl1p wyif, *k4, p4*. Repeat *-* to
last st, k1.
Repeat row 2 on as well WS as RS until the rib
measures 7 cm / 2¾ inches.
Last row must be a WS row.

Body
Row 1 (RS) Change to needle 4.5 mm (US 7)
Sl1p wyif, k to the end of row.
Repeat row 1 on RS was well as WS till work
measures 11 cm / 4¼ inches all sizes. Last row

must be a WS row.
Increase 1
Row 1 (RS) Sl1p wyif. K1, M1. K to 2 sts before
end. M1, k2.
There are now 48 (52) 60 (68) sts.
Row 2 - 6 (6) 8 (8) Sl1p wyif, k to the end of
row.

Repeat row 1 - 6 (6) 8 (8) another 4 times.
There are now 56 (60) 68 (76) sts.

Increase 2
Row 1 (RS) Sl1p wyif. K1, M1. K to 2 sts before
end. M1, k2.
There are now 58 (62) 70 (78) sts.
Rows 2 - 12 (12) 16 (16) Sl1p wyif, k to the end
of row.
Repeat rows 1 - 12 (12) 16 (16) twice more.
There are now 62 (66) 74 (82) sts ***

Continue without increases to a total
measurement of 31 (33) 35 (37) cm / 12.25 (13)
14 (14½) inches.
Change to col B.
Work another 3 cm/ 1¼ inches to a total
measurement of 34 (36) 38 (40) cm / 13½ (14¼)
15 (15¾) inches.

****Shaping for eyes, short rows, front
Left eye
Row 1 (RS) Sl1p wyif. K 16 (17) 19 (21) sts. W&t.
Row 2 (WS) K to the end of row.
Row 3 (RS) Sl1p wyif. K to 2 sts before last
wrapped st. W&t.
Row 4 (WS) K to the end of row.
Row 5 - 10 Repeat row 3 and 4 another three
times.
Row 11 (RS) Sl1p wyif. K to the **first** wrapped
st you meet. K the wrapped st. W&t.
Row 12 + 14 + 16 + 28 (WS) K to the end of
row.
Row 13 (RS) Sl1p wyif. K to **second** wrapped
st. K the wrapped st. W&t.
Row 15 (RS) Sl1p wyif. K to **third** wrapped st. K
the wrapped st. W&t.
Row 17 (RS) Sl1p wyif. K to **fourth** wrapped st.
K the wrapped st. W&t.
Row 19 (RS) Sl1p wyif. K all the way to the end
of row.

Right eye
Row 1 (WS) Sl1p wyif. K 16 (17) 19 (21) sts. W&t.
Row 2 (RS) K to the end of row.

Row 3 (WS) Sl1p wyif. K to 2 sts before last wrapped st. W&t.
Row 4 (RS) K to the end of row.
Row 5 - 10 Repeat row 3 and 4 another 3 times.
Row 11 (WS) Sl1p wyif. K to the **first** wrapped st, you meet. K the wrapped st. W&t.
Row 12 + 14 + 16 + 18 (RS) K to the end of row.
Row 13 (WS) Sl1p wyif. K to **second** wrapped st. K the wrapped st. W&t.
Row 15 (WS) Sl1p wyif. K to **third** wrapped st. K the wrapped st. W&t.
Row 17 (WS) Sl1p wyif. K to **fourth** wrapped st. K the wrapped st. W&t.
Row 19 (RS) Sl1p wyif. K to the end of row. BO all sts.
Leave a 1 m tail for finishing.****

Back
Work the back as the front from *** to ***.
Continue without increases to a total measurement of
33 (35) 37 (39) cm / 13 (14) 14½ (15¼) inches. Change to col B.
Work another 3 cm / 1¼ inches to a total measurement of 34 (36) 38 (40) cm / 14¼ (15¼) 16¼ (17) inches.

Shaping for eyes, short rows, back
Work as for front from ****-****.

Sleeve
While working the sleeves we will work the first and the last st as a k1.
Using 4.5 mm (US 7) needle dpn or 60 cm / 24 inches and col B (grey) CO 28 (28) 32 (32) sts.
Set up row (WS) K 1, p to last st, k1.
Row 1 (RS) K to the end of row.
Row 2 - 8 Repeat row 1.
Row 9 - 12 Change to Col A and repeat row 2.

Increase
Row 1 (RS) K2, M1. K to 2 sts before end. M1, k2. There are now 30 (30) 34 (34) sts.
Row 2 - 6 K to the end of row.
Repeat row 1 - 6 another 4 (6) 7(9) times.
There are now 38 (42) 48 (52) sts.
Continue straight without further increases to a total measurement of 21 (24) 27(30) cm / 8¼ (9 ½) 10 ½ (12) inches.

Frog mouth
Using circular needle 4.5 mm (US7) and col B (grey) CO 64 (72) 84 (92) sts.

Row 1 (WS) *K2tog tbl*. Repeat *-* on all sts to end of row.
There are now 32 (36) 42 (46) sts.
Row 2 (RS) Sl1p wyif. K to the end of row.
Row 3 (WS) Sl1p wyif. K to last st. M1. K1.
There are now 33 (37) 43 (47) sts.
Row 4 (RS) Sl1p wyif. K to last st. M1. K1.
There are now 34 (38) 44 (48) sts.
Row 5 (WS) Sl1p wyif. K to the end of row. Change to col A (pink).
Row 6 (RS) Sl1p wyif. K to the end of row.
Row 7 (WS) Sl1p wyif. K to the end of row. Change to col B (grey).
Row 8 (RS) Sl1p wyif. K to the end of row.
Row 9 (WS) Sl1p wyif. K2tog. K to last three sts. K2tog. K1.
Row 10 - 11 Sl1p wyif. K to the end of row.
Row 12 (RS) *K2tog tbl*. Repeat *-* on all sts to end of row.
Row 13 (WS) BO all sts in purl. Leave a yarn end of approx. 50 cm for finishing.

Eyes
Using col B (grey) and 4.5 (US 7) dpn. CO 20 st.
Row 1 (RS) K to the end of row.
Row 2 - 4 Sl1p wyif. K to the end of row.
Row 5 (RS) Sl 7 sts onto RH needle. Change to Col C (off white). K6. W&t.
Row 6 (WS) K6 sts. W&t.
Row 7 (RS) K to last wrapped st. K1. W&t.
Row 8 - 14 Repeat row 7 (there are now 14 sts worked in col C).
Row 15 (RS) Sl 4 sts onto RH needle. Change to Col B (grey). K6. W&t.
Row 16 (WS) K7 sts. W&t.
Row 17 (RS) K to last wrapped st. K1. W&t.
Row 18 -19 Repeat row 17.
Row 20 (WS) K to last wrapped st. K1. Slip remaining sts to RH needle without knitting them. Do not break yarn.
Row 21 (RS) K all sts to the end of row.
Row 22 (WS) as row 21.
Row 23 (RS) Wyib: Slip 5 sts to RH Needle. Make sure the yarn is not to tight when you begin knitting. K 10 sts. W&t.
Row 24 (WS) K9. W&t.
Row 25 (RS) K8. W&t.
Row 26 (WS) K7. W&t.
Row 27 (WS) K6. W&t.
Row 28 (WS) K6. Sl 4 sts. Turn.
Row 29 (RS) Change to col C. K 14 sts. W&t.
Row 30 (WS) K12. W&t.
Row 31 (RS) K10. W&t.

Row 32 (WS) K8. W&t.
Row 33 (RS) K6. W&t.
Row 34 (WS) K4. Break Yarn. Slip all st to RH needle. Turn work.

Row 35 (RS) Col B. Making sure col B yarn is not too tight, pick up and knit 3 sts in the right side edge of the work. Now k all sts to the end, and pick up and knit 3 sts in the left side edge. There are now 24 sts.
Row 36 - 38 Sl1p wyif. K to the end of row.
Row 39 BO all its.
Make the other eye in the same way.

Finish
Weave in ends. Seam together the sleeves, seam front to back in the side. Leave the opening for the sleeves to be places with the top of sleeve 2.5 cm / 1 inc into the dark part. Sew together the shoulder seam (that is the top of the eyes). Set in sleeves. Before weaving in these ends make sure the child's head will fit in the opening.

Have you ever seen a pink frog?? For this jumper you can choose your favorite colour!
It's a frog that doesn't jump, let's hope it will keep sitting there for a long time.
Laura Locher
#REDnotajumper

Neon Harlequin

Variable Harlequin Frog Teen~Adult
Design Laura Locher
Skill level 3
Photo page 90 - 91

Designer Laura Locher
#REDneonharlequin
- ajumper to nurse your skin

Skill level 3
Sizes EU (UK) Sizes S (M) L (XL)
To fit bust 82 (88) 94 (100) cm
32.2 (34½) 37 (39½) inches
Actual bust measurement (jumper)
92 98 102 110 cm
36¼ (38½) 40 (43¼) inches
Length
63 (65) 67 (69) cm
25 (25½) 26½ (27¼) inches
Yarn Kettle Yarn Co, Islington. Merino wool /
Silk 400 m / 437 yards per 100 g
Col A, Light Colour (Col A), Padparadscha,
Pink.
2 (3) 3 (3) skeins
Col B, Dark Colour (Col B), Old Smoke
2 (3) 3 (3) skeins
Needles 3 mm (US 2.5) circular needle 80 cm /
32 inches + dpn.
4 mm (US 6) circular needle 80 cm / 32 inches +
dpn + 40 cm/ 16 inches + 60 cm / 24 inches. 4
stitch markers
Gauge Weaving pattern 3/1 on needle 4 mm /
(US 6): 23st x 32 rows = 10 x 10 cm / 4 x 4 inches
Shown in Small

TIP: We are using circular needles for working
in the round as well as for working back and
forth. This is to protect your shoulders from the
tense muscles that may appear from knitting
with the old-fashioned straight needles. We will
be working intarsia knitting. This means that we
are using two colors. For each spot of a colour
we will have a separate bundle of wool. With
every color change the two strands of wool will
be twisted, to prevent holes from appearing in
the knitting.
Patterns used Two patterns are used. Stocking
stitch patt: Knit on RS, purl on WS, and a
weaving knit patt. We name it: Weaving patt
(for short W-patt).
Row 1 (RS) *K2, sl1 wyif, k1*. Repeat *-*. **Row 2
(WS)** P all.
Row 3 (RS) *Sl1 wyif, k3*. Repeat *-*. **Row 4
(WS)** P all.
Weaving pattern worked back and forth
For the knitting swatch CO 30 sts Col B. **Set up
row** P all sts.
Row 1 (RS) K1 *K2, sl1 wyif, k1*. Repeat *-* to

last st. K1
Row 2 (WS) K1. P to last st. K1.
Row 3 (RS) K1. *Sl1 wyif, k3*. Repeat *-* to last
st. K1.
Row 4 (WS) K1. P to last st. K1.
Repeat row 1 - 4 until work measures 15 cm
/ 6 inches. Check whether the center 23 sts
measure 10 cm / 4 inches. (Do not measure
over edge sts.) Check whether the center 32
rows measure 10 cm / 4 inches.

Body, front
Edge Using Col A and 3 mm (US 2.5) circular
needles CO 106 (114) 122 (126) sts loosely.
(Loosely because you will have to pick up sts
along the CO edge later on.)
Row 1 (WS) P to last st. Dbe1.
Row 2 (RS) Dbe1, k to last st. Dbe1.
Row 3 (WS) Dbe1. P to last st. Dbe1.
Row 4 - 9 Repeat row 2 - 3.
Row 10 (RS) Dbe1, k to last st. Dbe1.**Row 11
(WS)** Dbe1, **k** to last st. Dbe1. This is to create
a line of purl sts upon the RS to fold the edge
around.
Row 12 - 21 Repeat row 2 - 3 (10 rows).

Folded edge
Row 22 (RS) Using a 2.5 - or 3 mm (US 1 - 2)
circular needle, pick up 106 (114) 122 (126) sts
along the CO edge (do not pick up and knit –
just pick up sts directly from the edge onto the
needle). This is a little tricky but will contribute
to a really neat edge. Fold the edge WS to WS
to make the two needles lie parallel on top of
each other. Work 1 st from larger needle tog
with 1 st from smaller needle. Repeat all the
way across the sts to join the folded edge.
Make sure that the first st on the smaller needle
corresponds with – or is the same st as – the
first st of the round to prevent the edge from
twisting.
Row 23 (WS) Change to 4 mm (US 6) circular
needle 60 cm / 24 inches. Dbe1. P to last st.
Dbe1.

Establish Weaving pattern**
Row 1 (RS) Dbe1. *K2, sl1 wyif, k1*. Repeat *-*
to last st. Dbe1.
Row 2 (WS) Dbe1. P to last st. Dbe1.
Row 3 (RS) Dbe1. *Sl1 wyif, k3*. Repeat *-* to
last st. Dbe1.
Row 4 (WS) Dbe1. P to last st. Dbe1.These four
rows make up the patt.

Repeat row 1 - 4 another 2 (3) 4 (5) times.**Continue from "Front Diagram" from line 1 to line 36 (38) 40 (42).

Please note about the working in two colour knitting:
1. Prepare little yarn bundles for each spot of colour.
2. Twist yarn around one another in all colour changes.
3. All colour changes happen on the RS. On the WS you simply purl as the colours appear.
4. On the WS you have to be aware of where to use the particular colour in the next row and bring the yarn to that place as mentioned below:.
This will appear for the first time in diagram line 3
WS: Col B, grey.
Work like this: Dbe1, W-patt 5 (9) 13 (15). Twist yarn. Change to col A pink. Work W-patt 4 sts, twist yarn, still using Col A. Continue as patt shows to the end. Now col B is ready to be used in line 4. Continue in this way until you have worked line 37 (39) 41 (43) back and forth. Leave sts on a hold and work back piece.

Back
Work folded edge as for the front from **row 1 - row 22.** Establish W-patt as for the front from **to**. Now work "Back Diagram" from line 1 until you have worked line 37 **(39) 41**(43) back and forth. Leave sts on hold and work sleeves.

Sleeve
Edge
Using Col A and needle 3 mm (US 2) circular needles CO
50 (50) 54 (54) sts loosely. (Loosely because you will have to pick up sts along the CO edge later on.)
Row 1 (WS) P to last st. Dbe1.
Row 2 (RS) Dbe1, k to last st. Dbe1.
Row 3 (WS) Dbe1. P to last st. Dbe1.
Row 4 - 9 Repeat row 2 - 3.
Row 10 (RS) Dbe1, k to last st. Dbe1.
Row 11 (WS) Dbe1, **k** to last st. Dbe1.
Row 12 - 21 Repeat row 2 - 3 (10 rows).

Folded edge
Row 22 (RS) Using a 2.5 or 3 mm (US 1- 2) circular needle, pick up 50 **(50) 54** (54) sts along the CO edge and work folded edge as for front and back.
Row 23 (WS) Change to 4 mm (US 6) circular needle 60 cm / 24 inches. Dbe1. P4 (4) 6 (6) *P4,

M1p*. Repeat *to* another 9 times. P4 (4) 6 (6). Dbe1.
There are now
60 (60) 64 (64) sts in the sleeve.

Frog Diagram sleeves
In the sleeves we begin the diagram right after the folded edge.
Follow Sleeve Diagram from line 1 and establish the W-patt at the same time like this.

Establish Weaving pattern in 4 rows as for the front row 1 - row 4.
Row 5 Dbe1, k1, M1. Work W-patt to last 2 sts. M1, k1. Dbe1.
There are now 62 (62) 66 (66) sts
Continue sleeve until line 47 (51) 55 (59) is worked back and forth.
Work increases as row 5, when shown in diagram until
there are 92 (94) 100 (104) sts.
Leave sleeve sts on hold.
Work another sleeve in the same way.

Joining all pieces for working in the round
Please note: After joining, the upper part of the jumper is worked back and forth in order to be able to work the frog diagram. The simultaneous joining in the round is achieved by working a particular "turning maneuver". Do not forget to twist the yarns around each other at each colour change. We strongly recommend you keep your yarn bundles tied like in the picture, to prevent the yarn from tangling too much.

Row 1 (RS) Beg at left sleeve.
Pm (m1). Using 4 mm (US 6) circular needle, k3. Work left sleeve sts according to sleeve diagram and existing weaving patt to last 3 sleeve sts, k3.
Pm (m2). Work front sts onto the same needle as follows: K2. Patt across front sts according to front diagram and existing weaving patt to last 2 front sts, k2.
Pm (m3). Work right sleeve sts onto the same needle as follows: K3. Work right sleeve sts according to sleeve diagram and existing weaving patt to last 3 sleeve sts, k3.
Pm (m4). Work back sts as follows: K2. Patt across back according to back diagram and existing weaving patt to last 2 sts before m1, k2. Sm (m1). Pick up the loop of yarn before next st with the left needle and k the loop tbl –

this will be the turning st. Turn to work the next row from the WS on the "inside" of the round.
Row 2 (WS) Sm. P all sts to 1 st before m1. W&t wyif (on the turning st).
Row 3 (RS) Sl1 wyif. K2. Patt to 3 st before m2. K2, sl1 wyif. Sm. K2. Patt to 2 sts before m3. K2. Sm, Sl1 wyif. K2. Patt to 3 st before m4. K2, sl1 wyif. Sm. K2. Patt to 2 sts before m1. K2. Sm. W&t wyif (on the turning st).
Row 4 (WS) Sm. P all sts to 1 st before m1. W&t on the turning st.

Decrease type 1
Row 1 (RS) Sl1 wyif, k1, k2tog, patt to 4 sts before m2.
K2tog tbl, k1, sl1 wyif. Sm. K1. K2tog.
Patt to 3 sts before m3.
K2tog tbl, k1. Sm. Sl1 wyif, k1, k2tog. Patt to 4 sts before m4.
K2tog tbl, k1, sl1 wyif. Sm. K1. K2tog. Work to 3 sts before m1.
K2tog tbl, k1. Sm. K1 (= turning st). Turn. (8 sts decreased.)
There are now
104 (112) 120 (124) sts each on front and back and
90 (92) 98 (102) sts on each sleeve.
Row 2 (WS) Sl 1 purl wise wyif (= turning st). Sm. P to last sts before m1. W&t wyif (on the turning st).
Rows 3 (RS) Sl1 wyif. K2. Patt to 3 st before m2. K2, sl1 wyif. Sm. K2. Patt to 2 sts before m3. K2. Sm, Sl1 wyif. K2. Patt to 3 st before m4. K2, sl1 wyif. Sm. K2. Patt to 2 sts before m1. K2. Sm. W&t wyif (on the turning st).
Rows 4 (WS) Sm. Work as row 2.
Row 5 - 48 Repeat rows 1- 4 another 11 times, so that the decrease row has been worked a total of 12 times.
Regarding the turning stitch: The turning stitch is only actually worked (in knit) at the end of every other RS row, that is on every 4th row. On all other rows the turning stitch is wrapped and turned. This makes the stitch relax into the pattern and appear like a seam.

Decreases type 2
Continue now decreases on every RS row 12 times in total.
Continue decrease until you have finished line 80 (89) 90 (91).

Neck opening
Row 1 (RS) Work patt as set with the usual

decreases to 14 sts after m2. Slip 20 sts onto spare needle. Work in patt as set with the usual decreases to m1. Break yarn.
Now continue from left shoulder WS.
Row 2 (WS) Sl 1 st onto the spare needle. P to 2 st before m1. P2tog to close the turning st. P all the way to last st before spare needle at front. Slip 1 st onto spare needle.
Row 3 (RS) Sl 1 st onto the spare needle. Work in patt as set with decreases all the way to last st before spare needle at front. Slip 1 st onto spare needle.
Row 4 -12 Continue repeating row 2 and 3. Break yarn.

Neckband
Round 1 (RS) Using Col A (pink) and 4 (US 6) 40 cm / 16 inches circular needle.
Beg at m1. K all sts until you meet the spare needle. Pick up and k 3 sts in the part before the spare needle. K the st from spare needle: *K1, pick up and k1 st*. Repeat *-* another 5 times.
K20 sts. Repeat *-* 6 times.
Pick up and k3 sts before the sts at ready for right front shoulder. K to m1.
Round 2 (RS) *K3, sl1 purl wise wyif*. Repeat *to* to the end.
Round 3 (RS) *P1, sl1 purl wise wyib, p2*. Repeat *to* to the end.
Round 4 - 10 Repeat row 2 and 3 . BO all sts.

Frog Sleeve Diagram

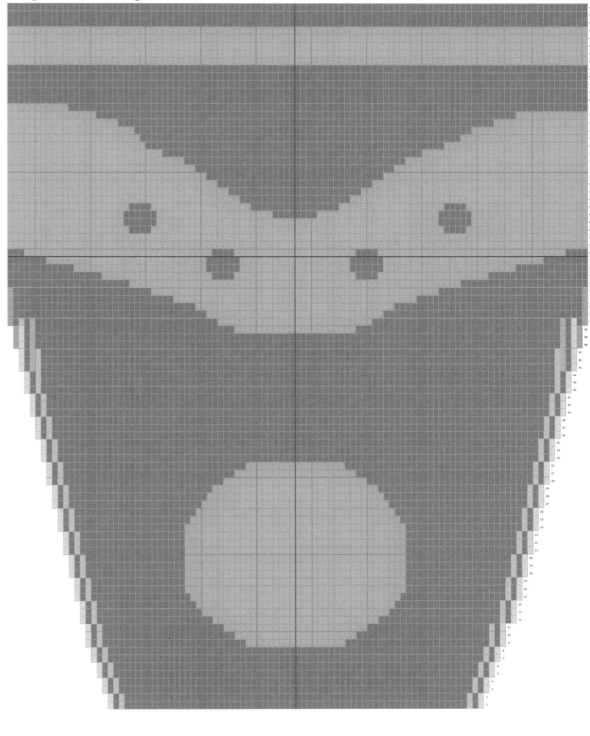

☐	= 1 st+ 2 row
☐	RS: knit / WS: purl
▨	Col A, pink
▦	Col B, grey
▨	Small
▨	Medium
▨	Large
▨	X Large
℧	m1
/	k2tog
▯	Midt
▯	Small
▯	Medium
▯	Large
▯	X Large

The pattern on each of these frogs is unique and so stunning! It inspired to the flashy look of this jumper; to give more attention to this little endangered neon beauty.
Laura Locher
#REDneonharlequin

Frog Back Diagram

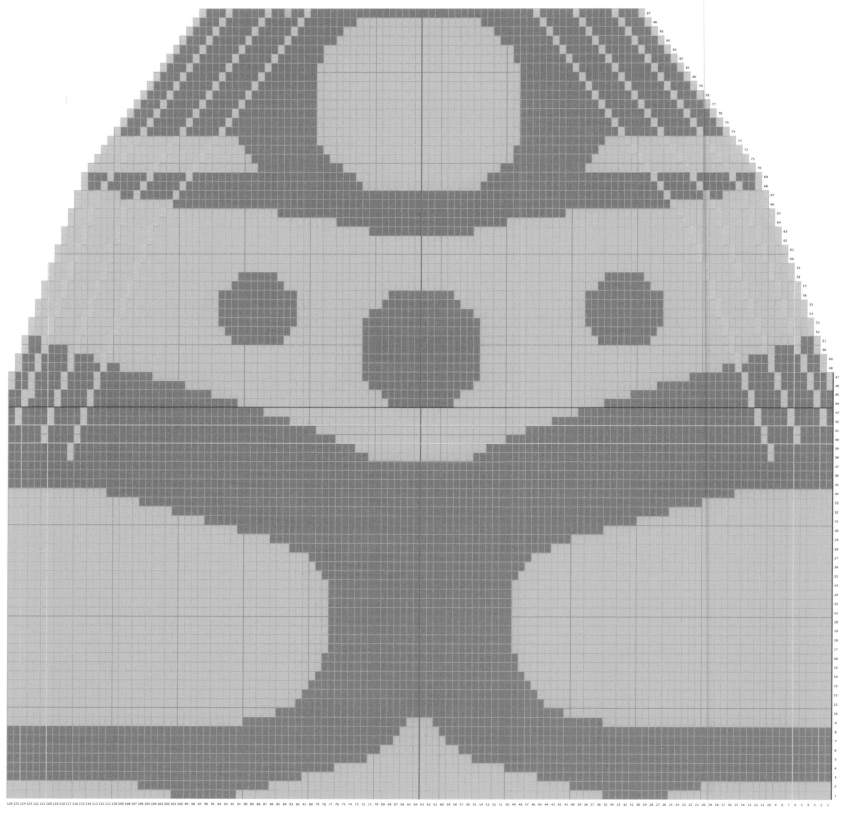

R:E:D: 236

Frog Front Diagram

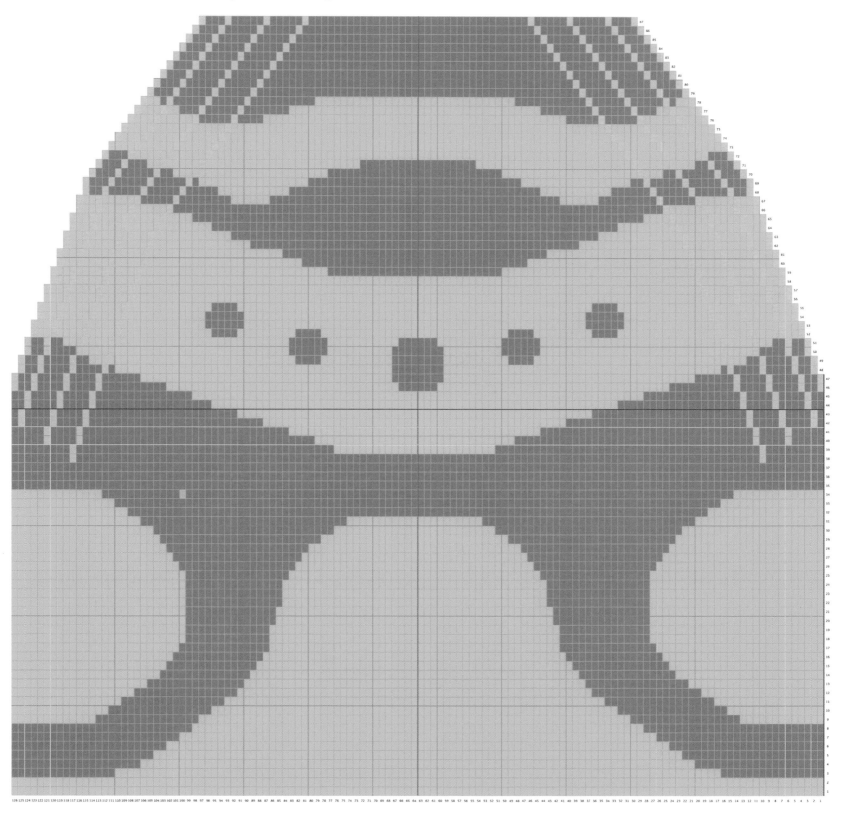

R:E:D: 237

Warm Embrace

Greek Viper Child
Design Laura Locher
Skill level 2
Photo page 138 - 139

Design Laura Locher
-a vest worked in one piece...
#REDwarmembrase

Skill level 2
Sizes
EU 86 (98) 110 (122)
UK 12-18 month (2-3) 4-5 (6-7) years
To fit bust
53 (55) 59 (63) cm
21 (21½) 23 (25) inches
To fit waist
54 (56) 60 (64) cm / 21¼ (22) 23½ (25¼) inches
Actual bust measurement (vest)
56 (58) 62 (66) cm / 22 (22¾) 24½ (26) inches
Length
36 (38) 42 (45) cm / 14¾ (15) 16½ (18) inches.
Longer at the back, a bit shorter at the front.
Yarn Önling 1
75% Merino Superfine 25% Angora.
180m / 197 yards per 50 g
Col A Grey all sizes 1 x 50 g skein
Col B Peach 1 (1) 2 (2) x 50 g skeins
Col C Warm grey 1 (1) 1 (2) x 50 g skeins
Needles
4.5 mm (US 7) dpn.
Gauge In garter stitch on 4.5 mm (US 7)
needles. 19 sts x 36 rows = 10 x 10 cm / 4 x 4
inches.
Remember to check your gauge and adjust
needle size accordingly.

Tip
We will be working in stripe pattern. Do not
break the yarn in colour changes, but leave it
hanging on the WS of work to be used next
time when this colour appears.
Shown in size 122 / 6 years
Col A Col B Col C.

Snake Tail
Using 4.5 mm (US 7) dpn and Col A, CO 15 (19)
15 (19) sts.
Row 1 (WS) Change to Col B. P to last st.
Dbe1.
Row 2 (RS) Dbe1, sks. K 4 (6) 4 (6). M1L. K1,
M1R. K 4 (6) 4 (6), k2tog tbl, dbe1.
Row 3 (WS) Dbe1. P to last st. Dbe1.
Row 4 - 7 Repeat row 2 and 3.
Row 8 (RS) Repeat row 2.
Row 9 (WS) Move col B yarn to the back.
Change to Col A Dbe1. P to last st. Dbe1.

Row 10 - 15 Leave Col A at WS. Change to
Col C and repeat row 2 and row 3.
Row 16 (RS) Leave col C yarn at the WS.
Change to Col A and work as row 2.
Repeat patt from row 1 - 16, though now first st
on row 1 is worked as dbe1.

Increase the tail
Row 1(WS) Change to Col B. P to last st. Dbe1.
Row 2 (RS) Dbe1, k 6 (8) 6 (8). M1L. Pm (m1).
K1, M1R. K to last st. Dbe1.
There are now 17 (21) 17 (21) sts.
Row 3 (WS) Dbe1. P to last st. Dbe1.
Row 4 (RS) Dbe1, k to m1. M1L. Sm. K1, M1R.
K to last st. Dbe1.
There are now 19 (23) 19 (23) sts.
Row 5 - 8 Repeat row 3 and 4.
There are now 23 (27) 23 (27) sts.
Row 9 (WS) Move Col B yarn to the back.
Change to Col A Dbe1. P to last st. Dbe1.
Row 10 (RS) Leave Col A at WS. Change to
Col C. K to m1. M1L. Sm. K1, M1R. K to last st.
Dbe1.
There are now 25 (29) 25 (29) sts.
Row 11 (WS) Dbe1. P to last st. Dbe1.
Row 12 - 15 Repeat row 10 - 11 twice.
There are now 29 (33) 29 (33) sts.

Body
From now on the body has got the desired
dimensions.
Continue now repeating rows 1 and 2 as they
are mentioned below.
AT THE SAME TIME repeating the striped
pattern already established:
1 row col A
8 rows col B
1 row Col A
6 rows col C.
Place a strand of yarn in contrast colour in the
first st of the following row. In this way you will
be able to identify and measure from this first
row of the body later on.

Row 1 (RS) Dbe1. K1. *M1R, k 4 (5) 4 (5), k2tog
tbl, pull yarn tight (in order to bring the 2 knit
together sts to lay "shoulder by shoulder"),
k2tog, k 4 (5) 4 (5), M1L*. K1 (centerstitch).
Repeat *to* to last 2 sts. K1. Dbe1.
Row 2 (WS) Dbe1. P to last st. Dbe1.
Repeat row 1 - 2 until work measures approx.
56 (58) 62 (66) cm / 22 (22¾) 24½ (26) inches.

-pattern continues pg 240

Ranger Danger

Greek Meadow Viper Teen~Adult
Design Laura Locher
Skill level 2
Photo pg 135 - 136 - 241w

Designer Laura Locher
- a silky top to wind around your body
#REDrangerdanger

Skill level 2
Sizes EU ~ UK S (M) L (XL)
Sizes
XS (S) M (L)
To fit bust
80 (86) 92 (98) cm / 32 (34) 36 (38½) inches
Actual bust measurement top
72 (78) 84 (90) cm / 28¼ (30¾) 33 (35½) inches
Length top
50 (52) 54 (56) cm /19½ (20½) 21¼ (22) inches
Yarn
Jaipur Silk Fino, B C Garn 100 % Mulberry Silk,
300 m / 328 yds per 50 g
3 (4) 4 (5) x 50 g C
Needles
3 mm (US 2) dpn
Gauge
In stocking stitches on 3 mm (US 2) needles: 31
sts x 36 rows = 10 x 10 cm/ 4 x 4 inches.
To be able to measure accurately, make a
swatch with at least 37 sts and 40 rows and
measure over the center 31 sts x 36 rows.

Always check your gauge and adjust needle
size accordingly.

Shown in EU size S / UK size 10.

TIPS
For this top, take your time to get familiar with
the Double edge stitch, mentioned: Dbe1.
We hope you will love this stitch as we do.
Learn it from the Abbreviations or watch the
videos we made specially for the R:E:D: book
on You Tube.
We will be working cable knitting. If you have
not done this before, do not worry. It is easy
and is fun.
This top is worked as one long piece "a snake
winding around the body".
When we have done the first round, the work
will gradually be gathered for a top. This will be
described as you go.
It will be like knitting a scarf, that will then
eventually wind around the body...in silk! -have
fun.

Body Rib pattern

Using 3 mm (US 2) dpn CO 52 (54) 56 (58) sts.
Set-up row (WS) K 4 (5) 6 (7). *P4, k4*. Repeat
to 8 (1) 10 (11) sts before end.
P 4 (0) 4 (4), k 3 (0) 5 (6). Dbe1.
Row 1 (RS) Dbe1, p 3 (4) 5 (6). *K4, p4*. Repeat
to 8 (1) 10 (11) sts before end.
K 4 (0) 4 (4), p 3 (0) 5 (6). Dbe1.
Row 2 (WS) Dbe1, k 3 (4) 5 (6). *P4, k4*. Repeat
to 8 (1) 10 (11) sts before end.
P 4 (0) 4 (4), k 3 (0) 5 (6). Dbe1.
Row 3 - 4 Repeat rows 1 - 2.
Row 5 The cable knit begins.
Dbe1, P 3 (4) 5 (6). K4, p4, k4.
Cable: Work as shown on diagram 1. Beg at
row 5: P2, sl 8 sts onto cable needle, hold at
back. Work the following 8 sts as they appear:
p2, k4, p2. Now work the sts from the cable
needle as they appear: p2, k4, p2. P2. Continue
the remaining sts on needle: k4, p4, k4, p 3 (4) 5
(6). Dbe 1.
Row 6 (WS) Dbe1, k 3 (4) 5 (6). *p4, k4*. Repeat
to 8 (1) 10 (11) sts before end.
P 4 (0) 4 (4), k 3 (0) 5 (6). Dbe1.
Row 7 - 14 Repeat row 1 - 2.
Repeat rows 1 - 14 until work measures
65 (72) 78 (85) cm / 25½ (28¼) 30¾ (33½) inches.
Make sure to end working a WS row..

Gather the top whilst working
Row 1 (RS) Work in patt as set until last st.
Work dbe1. Do not turn work.
Using the left end of your RH dpn, pick up the
two loops of the dbe st from the first row of
your work (RS, right edge of work) slip all four
loops at the end of the row back to LH needle
and k4tog tbl. Turn work.
Row 2 (WS) Slip first st purlwise wyif. Work in
patt as set to last st. Dbe1.
Repeat rows 1 and 2 until you have worked
the knit together for two total rounds and
another 10 (11) 13 (15) cm / 4 (4¼) 5 (6) inches.

Opening for neckband
Now we will continue working the viper back
and forth without the knit together in the
end of the RS. This will become the right side
shoulder strap.

Row 1 (RS) Dbe1, work in patt as set to last st.
Dbe1.
Row 2 (WS) Dbe1, work in patt as set to last st.
Dbe1.

Repeat rows 1 - 2 until the strap has a total measurement of 41 (44) 46 (48) cm / 16¼ (17¼) 18 (19) inches. Mark this spot with a thread or a removable marker.

Decreases
We will now be working decreases every 10 rows. This will become the left shoulder strap.
Row 1 (RS) Dbe1, p 3 (4) 5 (6), k2tog, k2, p4, k2tog. Work patt as set to14 (15) 16 (17) sts before end. K2tog tbl, p4, k2, k2tog tbl. Patt to last st. Dbe1. (red 4sts)
Row 2 (WS) Dbe1. Work in patt as set to last st. Dbe1.
Row 3 - 10 Repeat row 2.
Row 11 (RS) Dbe1, p 3 (4) 5 (6), k2tog, k1, p4, k2tog. Work patt as set to13 (14) 15 (16) sts before end. K2tog tbl, p4, k1, k2tog tbl. Patt to last st. Dbe1. (red 4sts)
Row 12 - 20 Repeat row 2.
Row 21 (RS) Dbe1, p 3 (4) 5 (6), k2, p2, p2tog, Work patt as set to 10 (11) 12 (13) sts before end. P2tog. Patt to last st. Dbe1. (red 2sts)
Row 22 - 30 Repeat row 2.
Row 31 (RS) Dbe1, p 3 (4) 5 (6). k2tog, p3, k2tog. Work patt as set to 11 (12) 13 (14) sts before end. K2tog tbl, p3, k2tog tbl. Patt to last st. Dbe1. (red 4sts)
Row 32 - 40 Repeat row 2.
Row 41 (RS) Dbe1, p 3 (4) 5 (6), k1, p1, p2tog, Work patt as set to 7 (8) 9 (10) sts before end. P2tog. Patt to last st. Dbe1. (red 2sts)
Row 42 - 50 Repeat row 2.
There are now 36 (38) 40 (42) sts.
Continue in patt without decrease until the left shoulder strap measures 30 (32) 34 (36) cm /

11¾ (12½) 13¼ (14) inches from the beginning of the decreases. BO all sts in patt

Finish
Try the top on. Get a friend to help you needling down the back middle 12½ cm / 5 inches. Make sure to begin 12½ cm / 5 inches prior to the decrease start and end where the decreases begins.
Also fasten the shoulder strap left shoulder with needles where it fits you best. Now sew these two seams.

Your personal Ranger Danger is ready to take you out there into the jungle

Warm Embrace,

Continued from pg 238
from first row of the body, make sure to end where you have just finished 8 rows in col B.

Gather the top while working
We will now turn this long tail into the beginning of our vest.
The working row will now be knit together with the base of the body step by step.

Row 1 (RS) Work patt as set until last st. Dbe1. Do not turn. Using RH dpn, pick up one loop of the dbe st from the first row of the base of the body (RS, right edge of work). Turn work.
Row 2 (WS) Sl1 purl wise. K2tog, pass slipped st over.

Work in patt as set to last st. Dbe1.
Repeat Row 1 and 2 until you have gathered the vest for 1 round and continue another 10 (11) 12 (13) cm / 4 (4¼) 4¾ (5) inches.

Shoulder strap
Now we will again be working the snake (viper) without the knit together in the end of each RS row in order to create a shoulder strap for left shoulder.
Continue repeating rows 1 and 2 until the strap measures approx. 24 (26) 28 (30) cm / 9½ (10¼) 11 (11¾) inches from the beginning of the strap, though make sure to end working a Col B stripe to the end.

The head
Change to Col A. Work 1 row in Col A RS/WS depending where you exactly are in the patt.
Next row: Change to Col B and work patt as set for another 14 rows.
Change to Col A and BO all sts. Make sure to BO in k if you are working a RS row rows or if you are working a WS row, then BO in p.

Finish
Fold the corners of the head to WS to shape the snake with a triangular head. Sew corner to the WS.
Embroider the eyes and sew in a button.
Now take your snake out sneaking about in the wild.

Diagram 1
16 mixed cable = Slip 8 sts onto cable needle, hold at back. P2, k4, p2.
Work sts from cable needle: p2, k4, p2.

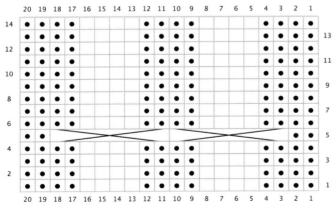

Key

☐	RS: knit / WS: purl
✕	16 stitch mixed cabl
☐•	RS: purl / WS: knit
☐	Repeat from row

Viper Child
Imagine having your own personal snake. One you can wear and that will keep you warm.
Laura Locher

#REDwarmembrace

Viper Teen
Who is more dangerous? The ranger or the viper? This garment winds around your body to bring you closer to this fascinating animal even though it can seem scary.
Laura Locher

#REDrangerdanger

Odd Stripes

Numbat Teen~Adult
Design Bruno Kleist
Skill level 3 - 4
Photo pg 177 - 180 - 181

Designer Bruno Kleist
- a jumper in two-coloured brioche...
#REDoddstripes

Sizes
EU - UK: S (M) L (XL)
To fit bust
82 (88) 94 (100) cm
32½ (34½) 37 (40) inches
Actual bust measurement (jumper)
98 (104) 110 (116) cm
38½ (41) 43½ (45½) inches
Length
67 (69) 71 (73) cm
26 (27) 28 (29) inches
Yarn
Isager, Alpaca 2
50% Wool, 50% Alpaca, 273 yards / 250 meters
per 50 g.
Col A,Gold
3 (4) 4 (4) x 50 g, Shade 3
Col B, Dark Grey
4 (5) 5 (6) x 50 g, Eco 4S
Col C, White
1 (1) 1 (1) x 50 g, Eco 0
Needles
4 mm (US 6) circular needle, 80 cm (32 inches)
and 60 cm (24 inches).
4 mm (US 6) dpn.
4 stitch markers.
Gauge
In Brioche stitch on 4 mm (US 6) needles: 22 sts
x 28 rows* = 10 x 10 cm/4 x 4 inches. *1 row = 1
row in LC and 1 row in DC.
Remember to check your gauge and adjust
needle size accordingly.

Shown in size L

Tip
This jumper will be worked with Brioche
stitches.
Two colour Brioche pattern
Brioche knit, Light col (LC) colour A, Gold.
Brioche purl, Dark col (DC) colour B, Dark Grey.
Knitting swatch
CO 31 sts using Col A and 4 mm (US 6) mm
dpn.
Setting up row (WS) K1, p to last st. K1.
Row 1 Using col A (RS) K1. Sl1yo *K1, sl1yo*.
Repeat *-* to last st. K1. Slide.
Row 2 Using col B (RS) K1. Brp1 *Sl1yo, brp1*.
Repeat *-* to last st. K1. Turn work.
Row 3 Using col A (WS) K1. Sl1yo. *Brp1,
sl1yo*. Repeat *-* to last st. K1. Slide.
Row 4 Using col B (WS) K1. Brk1 *sl1yo, brk1*.

Repeat *-* to last st. K1. Turn work.
Repeat Row 1 - 4 until work measures 11 cm
/ 4½ inches, however in row 1 it is from now on
***brk1**, sl1yo* .

Twy: Twisting yarn
When twisting the yarn; always twist old over
new. This means the yarn you were knitting with
should be twisted over the new yarn you will
start working with.

Body front
CO 140 (150) 160 (170) sts using 4 mm (US 6) 80
cm (32 inches) circular needle using one strand
of each yarn A and B.
Join for working in 1by1 rib in round.
Round 1 (RS) *K1, p1*. repeat *to* to end.
Repeat round 1 to rib measures 4.5 (4.5) 4.5
(4.5) cm / 1¾ (1¾) 1¾ (1¾) inches in total.

**Establish the two colour Brioche pattern as
described below.**
Establishing round using col A (RS) *K2, M1*.
Repeat *-* to end. In size M and XL, do not
make the last M1. You now have 210 (224) 240
(254) sts.
Round 1 Using col A (RS) Pm (m1). *K1, sl1yo*.
Repeat *-* to end. Twy. At the same time: Pm
(m2) after 105 (112) 120 (127) sts.
Round 2 Using col B (RS) *Sl1yo, brp 1*.
Repeat *-* to end. Twy.
Round 3 Using col A (RS) *Brk1, sl1yo*.
Repeat *-* to end. Twy.
Round 4 Using col B (RS) *Sl1yo, brp 1*.
Repeat *-* to end. Twy.
Continue knitting Brioche patt repeating round
3 - 4 for another 3 (4) 5 (6) times ending with a
round 2 using col B.
Start making the patterns in yarn C following
the diagram as described below:
Please note: When working the diagram the
jumper will be worked in short rows. Twisting
the yarn will ensure that there will be no hole to
the side seams.
Row 1 Using col A (RS) Work in col A *Brk1,
sl1yo*. Repeat *-* until diagram shows col
C begins. Change to col C and work until
diagram shows shows col C ends. Change to
col A. (make sure to twist col C with col A for
as many sts as you will need, so you have col C
ready when you return to this point on the WS)
Work to m1 following the diagram. Twy with col
B.
Row 2 Using col B (RS) *Sl1yo, brp 1*. Repeat
- to end. Twy. TURN.
Now you will work from the WS.
Row 3 Using col A (WS) *Sl1yo, brp1*. Repeat
- until diagram shows col A ends. **Change to**

col C (make sure to twist col C with col A for as many sts as you will need, so you have yarn C ready when you return to this point on the WS) Work to m1 following the diagram. Twy.

Row 4 Using col B. (WS) *Brk 1, sl1yo*. Repeat *-* to end. Twy. TURN.

These 4 rows will form the routine of the Brioche patt.

Please note: You will only be changing the shape on every 4th row that is row 1.

Continue knitting Brioche patt following diagram until the line marking your size and work measures approx. 43 (45) 47 (49) x 17 (17½) 18½ (19½) inches. Make sure to end working a col A round.

Armhole

Round 1 (RS) Using col B Work to 1 st before m2. BO 3 sts loosely. Work to 1 st before m1, BO 3 sts loosely. Place last st on left needle. The work has now been divided into front and back with 102 (109) 117 (124) sts on each side. Leave sts on hold while working the sleeves.

Sleeves

CO 30 (32) 34 (36) sts using 4 mm (US 6) dpn using one strand of each yarn A and B.

Join for working in 1by1 rib in round.

Round 1 (RS) *K1, p1*. Repeat *-* to end. Repeat round 1 to rib measures 4,5 cm / 1¾ inches in total.

Establish the two colour Brioche pattern as on body. Work entire sleeve in col A and B.

Establishing round using col A (RS) *K2, M1*. Repeat *-* to end. You now have 45 (47) **51** (55) sts. Size M and size XL repeat to 2 sts before end. K2.

Round 1 Using col A (RS) Pm (m1). *K1, sl1yo*. Repeat *-* to last st. K1. Twy.

Round 2 Using col B (RS) *Sl1yo, brp1*. Repeat *-* to last st. S1yo. Twy.

Round 3 Using col A (RS) *Brk1, sl1yo*. Repeat *-* to last st. Brk1. Twy.

Round 4 Increase round using col A Brk1, sl1yo, M2. *Brk1, sl1yo*. Repeat *-* to 3 sts before last st, M2, brk1, sl1yo. Brk1 (4 sts increased)

Round 5 Using col B (RS) Work in Brioche patt.

Sl1yo, brp1, sl1yo, p1. *Sl1yo, brp1*. Repeat *-* to 5 sts before end. Sl1yo, p1, sl1yo, brp1, sl1yo. Twy.

Working the increase round on every 14th (14th) 14th (14th) round to a total of 81 (85) 89 (93) sts.

Continue knitting Brioche patt until work measures 50 (51) 52 (53) cm / 19½ (20) 20½ (21) inches.

Make sure to end working a col A round.

Sleevehole

Using col B Work as set to 3 sts before end, BO 4 sts loosely.

There are now 77 (81) 85 (89) sts.

Set the sleeve aside while working the other sleeve the same way.

Joining all pieces for working in the round.

Round 1 using col A and the needle where the back and front sts are resting on.

Beg at left sleeve. Pm (m1). Work brioche patt 77 (81) 85 (89) sts of one sleeve onto the needle. Pm (m2).

Work front sts onto same needle like this: Work 102 (109) 117 (124) front sts in brioche patt as set following diagram. Pm (m3). Using the same needle, work all 77 (81) 85 (89) right sleeve sts in brioche patt as set. Pm (m4). Using still the same needle, work brioche patt across back 102 (109) 117 (124) sts. All 358 (380) 404 (426) sts are now joined on one needle.

Round 2 Using col B

Work all sts in brioche patt as set.

Decreases

Round 3 Using col A

Sm. Sl1yo, sks. Work to 3 sts before m2. K2tog, Sl1yo. Sm, brk1, sl1yo. Sks.

Work as set to 4 sts before m3. K2tog, Sl1yo, brk1. Sm, Sl1yo, sks.

Work to 3 sts before m4. K2tog, Sl1yo. Sm, brk1, Sl1yo, sks.

Work to 4 sts before m1. K2tog, Sl1yo, brk1. Twy. (8 sts decreased)

PLEASE NOTE WHILE WORKING DECREASES: You will sometimes need to work two sl1yo in a row; when that happens, you only yo the first of them. Then the second st: sl1 (no yo). Then when meeting them again for working brk or brp: brk1/brp1, lift up the yarn over loop and place it on the needle and work the second brk1/brp1 as well.

Round 4 Using col B Work all sts in Brioche patt as set.

Row 5 (RS) Using col A Follow chart. We will now again work back and forth.

Work brioche patt as set to diagram shows col

A ends. **Change to col C,** make sure to twist col C with col A for as many sts as you will need, so you have col C ready when you return to this point on the WS. Work to m1 following the diagram. Twy.

Row 6 Using col B (RS) Work all sts in Brioche patt as set. Twy. Turn.

Row 7 Using col A (WS) Work brioche patt as the diagram shows. **Change to col C** (make sure to twist col C with col A for as many sts as you will need, so you have yarn C ready when you return to this point on the WS) Work to m1 following the diagram. Twy. Turn.

Row 8 Using col B (RS) Work all sts in Brioche patt as set. Twy. Turn.

Row 9 (RS) Using col A (RS) Repeat the decrease as described in Round 3, at the same time work to m1 following the diagram. Twy.

Row 10 Using col B (RS)

Work all sts in Brioche patt as set. Twy. Turn.

Row 11 Using col A (WS) Work brioche patt as the diagram shows.

Continue following the diagram and at the same time work decreases on every second col A row.

Col B rows are worked in patt as set without decreases, always col B and alway from the RS.

Continue until 35 sts remain in sleeves in all sizes.

There are now 60 (63) 67 (70) sts in front and back.

There are 190 (196) 204 (210) sts in total.

Decrease type 2

Now continue following the diagram and at the same time work decreases on **every** col A row in a total of 7 times.

There now 21 sts in the sleeves all sizes and 47 (49) 53 (56) sts in front and back all sizes.

Shaping the neck

Row 1 Using col A (RS) Work as set with the usual decreases to 9 sts after m2. Slip 33 (33) 33 (35) sts onto spare needle (from front).

Using the main needle, move sts from right needle to left needle until you are back at m1 where you have your col B.

Row 2 Using col B (RS)

Work brioche without decreases to 9 sts after m2. Turn.

Now continue from left shoulder WS.

Numbat chart adult

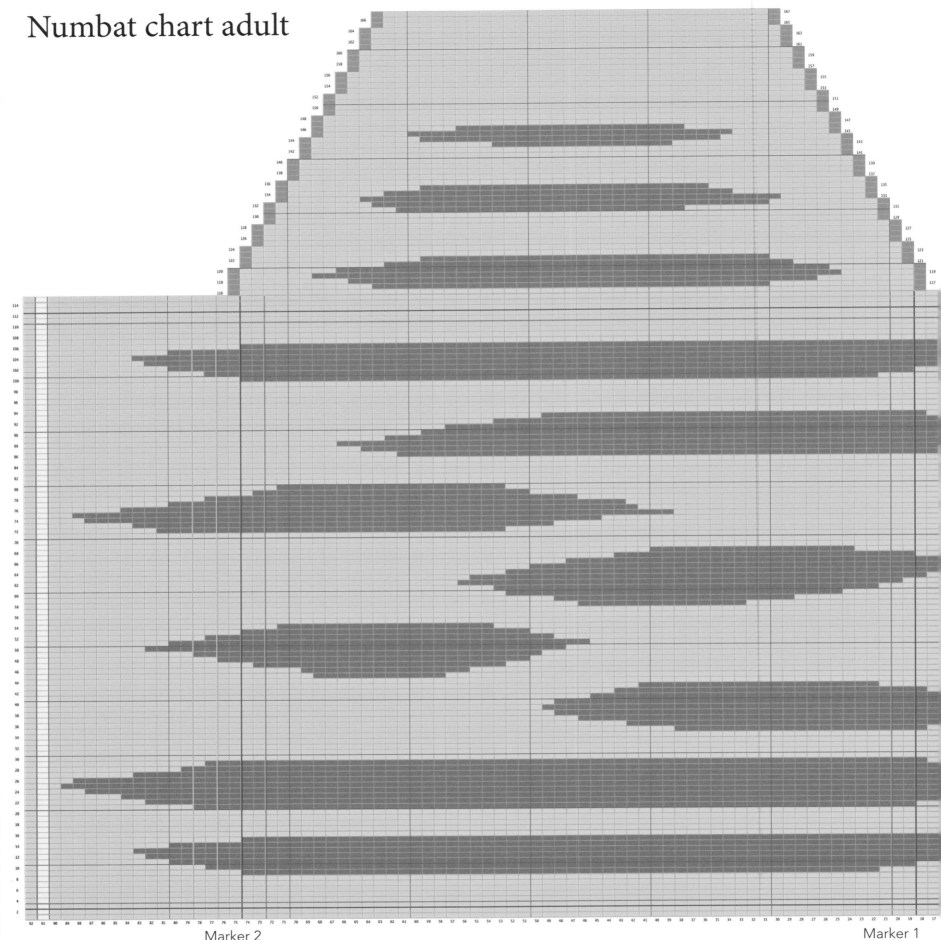

Marker 2

Marker 1

R:E:D: 244

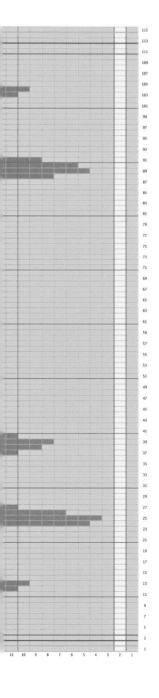

= 2 sts and 2 rows

Size S

Size M

Size L

Size XL

Col A

Col C

Border approx.

Work in col as as mentioned

Sts not counted

grey no stitch

Beg + end Size S

Beg + end Size M

Beg + end Size L

Beg + end Size XL

Row 3 Using col A (WS) Sl 1 st onto the spare needle. Work as set across left shoulder, back and right shoulder to spare needle at front. Slide.

Row 4 Using col B (WS) Sl 1 st onto the spare needle. Work as set across left shoulder, back and right shoulder to spare needle at front. Turn

Row 5 Using col A (RS) Sl 1 st onto the spare needle. Work as set across right shoulder, back and left shoulder to spare needle at front. ON THIS ROW MAKE THE USUAL DECREASES. Slide.

Row 6 Using col B (RS) Sl 1 st onto the spare needle. Work as set across right shoulder, back and left shoulder to spare needle at front. Turn. **Repeat Row 3-6** two more times.

Neckline
Round 1 (RS) Using col A *K3, k2tog*. Repeat *-* across all sts including the ones on the spare needle to end. Make sure the sts around the front-sleeve area are very tight to ensure there are no holes here.
Round 2 (RS) Using one strand of each col A and col B *K1, p1*. repeat *-* to end.
Repeat round 2 to rib measures 3 (3) 3 (3) cm / 1 (1) 1 (1) inches in total.
BO all sts.

Finishing
Close the hole under the arms.
Weave in all ends.
Steam your new sweater.

The stripes on its back are defining the numbat and each one has a unique set, which can be compared to our fingerprints.
Bruno Kleist

#REDoddstripes

Hang on

Numbat Child
Design Bruno Kleist
Skill level 2 - 3
Photo pg 178 -179

Design Bruno Kleist
-a jumper with a comfortable opening
#REDhangon

Skill level 2
Sizes
EU 86 (98) 110 (122)
UK 18 month (2-3) 4-5 (6-7) years
To fit bust
53 (54.5) 58 (63) cm
12 – 18 month, (2-3) 4-5 (6-7) years
21 (21½) 23 (25) inches
Actual bust measurement (jumper)
64 (67) 70 (76) cm
25 (26½) 28 (30) inches
Length
34 (36) 40 (44) cm
14 (15) 16 (17) inches
Yarn A
Purl Soho, Shepherdess Alpaca
100% Alpaca, Undyed + Handspun, 55 meters
/60 yards per 100 g.
4 (5) 5 (6) x 100 g col 0030SA, Bantam Hen.
Yarn B
Isager, Silk Mohair
75% Kid Mohair, 25% Silk, 212 m per 25 g.
2 threads
1 (1) 1 (1) x 100 g col 35, Grey
Yarn C
Manos del Uruguay, Silk Blend
30% Silk, 70% Merino Extrafine Wool, 150 yards
| 135 meters per 50 g.
1 (1) 1 (1) x 50 g col White. Used 20 gram.
Or similar yarn suitable for needle 3, use any
small leftover yarn you have.
Yarn D
Mohair: 3 different col, use left over if you have.
One strand of each:
1 (1) 1 (1) x 20 g col Red
1 (1) 1 (1) x 20 g col Rose
2 strands of:
1 (1) 1 (1) x 20 g col Peach
Black thread for eyes and details.
Needles
6mm (US 10) circular needle 60 cm (24 inches)
6mm (US 10) double pointed needles
4mm (US 6) dpn. 5 stitch markers.

Gauge
In stocking stitch on 6mm (US 10) needles and
yarn A: 13 sts x 18 rows = 10 x 10 cm / 4 x 4
inches.
Remember to check your gauge and adjust
needle size accordingly.

Shown in size 86 / 12 – 18 month.
Body
CO 84 (88) 92 (100) sts using 6mm (US 10)
circular needle 60 cm (24 inches) and yarn A.
Join for working in the round.
Round 1 (RS) Pm (m1). *K2, p2*, repeat to end.
At the same time, Pm (m2) after 42 (44) 46 (50)
sts.
Round (RS) 2 - 4 (4) 6 (6) Work rib patt as set.

Turning maneuver
Please note: The jumper is worked back and
forth in order to be able to work the patt with
mohair on the numbat. This is achieved by
working a particular "turning maneuver".
Preparations rounds
Work in purl without diagram for 0 (2) 4 (6)
rounds.

The Numbat comes in
We will now begin working th diagram from
line 1 in Numbat diagram child. Remember to
add yarn B (two strands), when indicated on
diagram.
Row 1 (RS) Patt across front to m2, sm, purl to
m1. Sm. Pick up the strand of yarn between sts
with the left needle and k the strand tbl – **this
will be the turning st.** Turn to work the next
row from the WS on the "inside" of the round.
Row 2 (WS) Sl 1 pwise wyif (= turning st) Knit
to m2. Patt across front to 2 sts before m1. K1.
W&t wyif (on the turning st).
Row 3 (RS) Patt across front to m2, sm, purl to
m1. Sm. P1 (on the turning st). Turn.
Row 4 (WS) Sl 1 pwise wyif (= turning st). Sm.
Knit to m2. Patt across front to 2 sts before m1.
K1. W&t wyif (on the turning st).
Repeat row 3 - 4 but note regarding the
turning stitch: The turning stitch is only actually
worked (purled) at the end of every other RS
row, that is on every 4th row. On all other rows
the turning stitch is w&t. This makes the stitch
relax into the pattern and appear like a seam.
Work as diagram on front. On back work
stocking stitch purl side out (wrong side out).
Continue without any increases to armhole
indication on diagram.
Armhole
Work to 1 st before m2 following diagram. BO
2 sts loosely. Purl to 1 st before m1, BO 3 sts
loosely. (3 sts in order to close the turning st)
The work has now been divided into front and
back with 40 (42) 44 (48) sts on each side.
Leave sts on hold while working the sleeves.

Sleeves

CO 20 (20) 24 (24) sts using 6mm (US 10) dpn's and yarn A. Join for working in the round.
Round 1 (RS) *K2, p2*, repeat *to* to end.
Round 2 - 4 Work rib as set.
Round 5 Pm m1. Purl to end. Work stocking stitch, purl side, out from here onwards.

Increase
Round 6
P1, M1p. P to last st, M1p, p1. 2 sts increased. There are now 22 (22) 26 (26) sts.
Working the increase round on every 8th (8th) 9th (9th) round to a total of 30 (32) 34 (38) sts. Continue straight until work measures 24 (28) 32 (36) cm / 9½ (11) 12½ (14¼) inches.
K to last st. BO 2 sts loosely.
There are now 28 (30) 32 (36) sts.
Break the yarn with 1 m left to use for closing the armhole in the end.
Set the sleeve aside while working the other sleeve the same way.

Joining all pieces for working back and forth in the round
Please note: After joining, the upper part of the jumper with the sleeves you will work in rounds. Mohair yarn for the numbat will be in loops on the backside of the work.
Round 1 (RS)
Beg at working front sts as follows: Pm (m1) K1, patt across front 38 (40) 42 (46) sts. K1.
Work right sleeve sts onto the same needle as follows: Pm (m2). K1, purl 26 (28) 30 (34) sts. K1.
Work back sts as follows: Pm (m3). K1, purl across back 38 (40) 42 (46) sts. K1.
Work left sleeve sts onto the same needle as follows: Pm (m4). K1, purl 26 (28) 30 (34) sts. K1.
All 136 (144) 152 (168) sts are now joined on one needle.
Round 2 (RS) Work as set.
Round 3 (RS) Decrease round
K1, p2tog. Patt across front to 3 sts before m2. P2tog tbl, k1, sm, k1, p2tog. Purl to 3 sts before m3. P2tog tbl, k1, sm, k1, p2tog. P to 3 sts before m4. P2tog tbl, k1, sm, k1, p2tog. P to 3 sts before m1. P2tog tbl, k1. (8 sts decreased)
Round 4 Work as set
Round 5-6 Repeat rows 3-4.

Splitting the work
From here on the jumper is worked back and forth.
Row 7 (RS) K1. Purl to front opening indication on diagram. Break the yarn. Pm m(5) on right

hand needle.
Continue on RS CO 14 (14) 16 (16) sts using knitted cast on, working the new sts on the left hand needle. Work the sts of the diagram to m(2). Work as set all the way to m(1). Sm. Work to m(5). Turn. M5 indicates the opening on the front. Remove marker, when you do not need it anymore.
Row 8 (WS) BO2. Work as set to end at m5. Turn.

Decreases 2
Row 9 (RS) BO 2. P to 3 sts before m2. P2tog tbl, k1, sm, k1, p2tog. Purl to 3 sts before m3. P2tog tbl, k1, sm, k1, p2tog. P to 3 sts before m4. P2tog tbl, k1, sm, k1, p2tog. P to 3 sts before m1. P2tog tbl, k1, sm, k1, p2tog. Work to end. (8 sts decreased)
Row 10 (WS) BO 2. K to 1 sts before m1. P1, sm, p1, k2tog. Knit to 3 sts before m4. K2tog tbl, p1, sm, p1. Knit to 1 sts before m3. P1, sm, p1, k2tog. Knit to 3 sts before m2. K2tog tbl, p1, sm, k to end. Turn. (4 sts decreased on sleeves only).
Repeat row 9-10 for 2 more times.
Row 15 (RS) BO 2. Work as set without decreases.
Row 16 (WS) BO 2. Work as set with decreases only on sleeves.
Repeat row 15 - 16 for another 2 (3) 4 (5) times. In size (98) 110 (122) the (2) 4 (6) last rows are without BO 2 at the beginning of each row.

Separating the work
Row 1 (RS) Work to m2. BO 6 (6) 8 (8) loosely, closing right sleeve.
Work to m4. BO 6 (6) 8 (8) loosely, closing left sleeve. Work to end.
Work is now separated in back and 2 front panels. (Front panels 9 (10) 12 (13) sts. Back 30 (32) 34 (36) sts.)

Left front
Row 1 (WS) BO 2. Knit to end.
Row 2 (RS) BO all sts loosely.

Right front
Row 1 (RS) BO 2. Purl to end.
Row 2 (WS) BO all sts loosely.
Back
Row 1 (RS) K1, purl 8 (9) 10 (11). BO 12 (12) 12 (12). Purl 8 (9) 10 (11). K1.

Left Back

Row 1 (WS) Knit to end.
Row 2 (RS) BO all sts loosely.

Right Back
Row 1 (RS) Purl to end.
Row 2 (WS) BO all sts loosely.

Finish
Sew shoulder seams together.
Attach the 6 (6) 8 (8) sts of the sleeve to the shoulder.
I-cord neckband
Using a 4 mm (US 6) dpn, CO 4 sts in yarn C + yarn D. Without turning, slide the sts back to the beg of the needle.
Row 1 (RS) Using another dpn, k3, M1 through the neck opening edge. Begin at inside flap RS (underlay). Then slip 1 st from right dpn onto the left dpn. K2tog. (you now have 4 sts)
Slide (Without turning, push the sts back to the beg of the needle)
Row 2 (RS) K1 tbl, k2, M1 through the neck opening edge. Slip 1 st from right dpn onto the left dpn. K2tog. Slide.
Repeat row 2 until all neckline is made. Take your time to ensure the I-cord is tight enough and not too tight. This will make the best result. BO all 4 sts. Sew the end of the tongue (red I-cord) to the tip of the numbats nose.

Finishing
Close the armhole. Weave in all ends. Steam your new sweater. And find a tree to climb.

The tiny numbat is holding on to us with its long tongue, hoping we will give it a chance to survive.
Bruno Kleist

#REDhangon

Numbat chart child

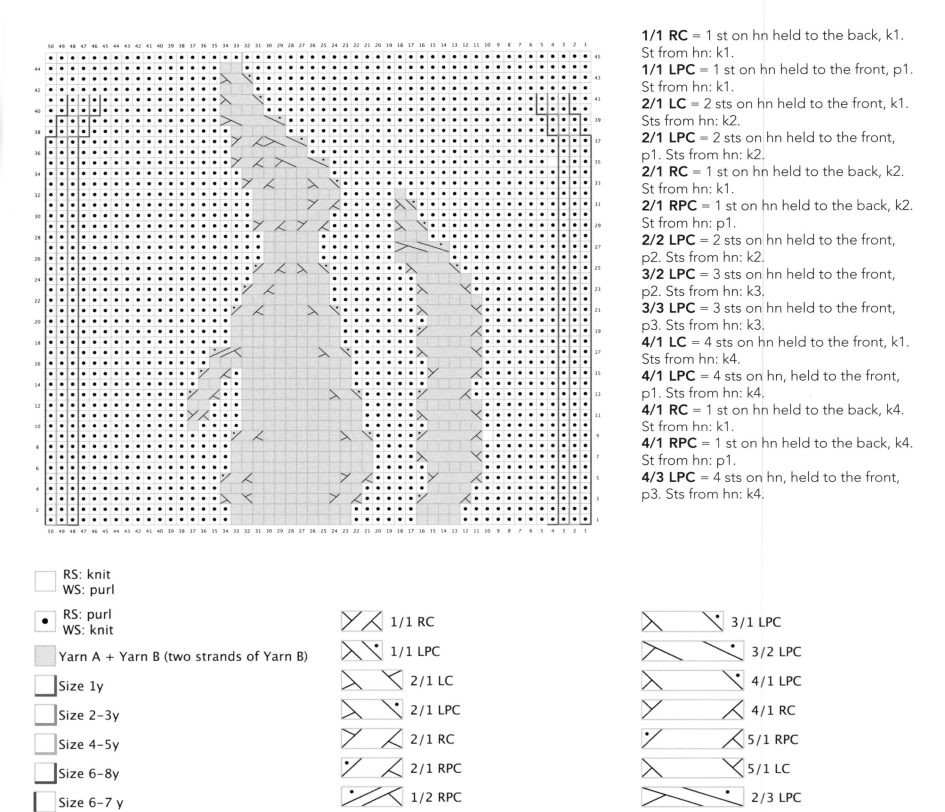

1/1 RC = 1 st on hn held to the back, k1. St from hn: k1.

1/1 LPC = 1 st on hn held to the front, p1. St from hn: k1.

2/1 LC = 2 sts on hn held to the front, k1. Sts from hn: k2.

2/1 LPC = 2 sts on hn held to the front, p1. Sts from hn: k2.

2/1 RC = 1 st on hn held to the back, k2. St from hn: k1.

2/1 RPC = 1 st on hn held to the back, k2. St from hn: p1.

2/2 LPC = 2 sts on hn held to the front, p2. Sts from hn: k2.

3/2 LPC = 3 sts on hn held to the front, p2. Sts from hn: k3.

3/3 LPC = 3 sts on hn held to the front, p3. Sts from hn: k3.

4/1 LC = 4 sts on hn held to the front, k1. Sts from hn: k4.

4/1 LPC = 4 sts on hn, held to the front, p1. Sts from hn: k4.

4/1 RC = 1 st on hn held to the back, k4. St from hn: k1.

4/1 RPC = 1 st on hn held to the back, k4. St from hn: p1.

4/3 LPC = 4 sts on hn, held to the front, p3. Sts from hn: k4.

Legend

- ☐ RS: knit / WS: purl
- • RS: purl / WS: knit
- ▨ Yarn A + Yarn B (two strands of Yarn B)
- ☐ Size 1y
- ☐ Size 2–3y
- ☐ Size 4–5y
- ☐ Size 6–8y
- ☐ Size 6–7 y
- ☐ Marking front opening

- 1/1 RC
- 1/1 LPC
- 2/1 LC
- 2/1 LPC
- 2/1 RC
- 2/1 RPC
- 1/2 RPC
- 2/2 LPC

- 3/1 LPC
- 3/2 LPC
- 4/1 LPC
- 4/1 RC
- 5/1 RPC
- 5/1 LC
- 2/3 LPC
- 4/2 LPC

R:E:D: 248

Shimmering

Beetle Child
Design Bruno Kleist
Skill level 2 - 3
Photo pg 128 - 129 - 210

Designer Bruno Kleist
-a jumper to celebrate the colours...
#REDshimmering

Skill level 2
Sizes
EU 86 (98) 110 (122)
UK 18 month (2) 4-5 (6-7) years
To fit bust
53 (54.5) 58 (63) cm
21 (21½) 23 (25) inches
Actual bust measurement (jumper)
64 (66) 70 (74) cm
25¼ (26) 27½ (29¼) inches
Length
38 (40) 44 (48) cm
15 (15¾) 17¼ (18¾) inches
Main Yarn (from now on called MY)
ITO, Rokku Tennen
100% Wool, 328 yards / 300 meters per 100 g.
3 (3) 4 (4) 100 g in 299, Natural Brown.
Contrast Yarn (from now on called CY)
ITO, Shio
100% Wool, 525 yards / 480 meters per 40 g.
Colour 1: 2 (2) 2 (2) x 40 g in 570, Balsam (petroleum)
Colour 2: 1 (1) 1 (1) x 40 g in 582, Lemon
Colour 3: 1 (1) 1 (1) x 40 g in 450, Denim
Colour 4: 1 (1) 1 (1) x 40 g in 588, Persimmon (orange)
Colour 5: 1 (1) 1 (1) x 40 g in 459, Navy
Colour 6: 1 (1) 1 (2) x 40 g in 587, Mustard
Colour 7: 1 (1) 1 (1) x 40 g in 572, Mint
Colour 8: 1 (1) 2 (2) x 40 g in 447, Gold oak (bronze)

Needles
4 mm (US 6) circular needle, 80 cm (32 inches)
3.5 mm (US 4) circular needle, 80 cm (32 inches)
3.5 mm (US 4) double pointed needles
4 stitch markers.

Gauge
In rib pattern on 4 mm (US 6) needles and yarn
MY + CY1 + CY2 + CY3 (total of 4 threads): 26
sts x 32 rows = 10 x 10 cm/4 x 4 inches
In moss stitch on 4 mm (US 6) needles and yarn
MY + CY1 + CY2 + CY3 (total of 4 threads): 21
sts x 36 rows = 10 x 10 cm/4 x 4 inches
Remember to check your gauge and adjust
needle size accordingly.

Shown in size 122, 6-7 years.

PLEASE NOTE: Moss Stitch is the UK
terminology and is the same as Seed Stitch, the
US terminology.

Body
CO 168 (174) 180 (192) sts using 3.5 mm (US 4)
circular needle, and MY + CY1. Now working
with a total of 2 threads. Join for working in the
round.
Round 1 Pm (m1). *K1, p1*. Repeat to end.
Round 2 - 5 As round 1.
Round 6 - 10 Add yarn CY colour 5 . Now
working with a total of 3 threads.
Round 11 Add additional yarn CY colour 8.
Now working with a total of 4 threads. Continue
as set until work measures 3 (3) 4 (4.5) cm / 1¼
(1¼) 1½ (1½) inches.

Broken Rib pattern:
Change to 4 mm (US 6) circular needle, 80 cm
(32 inches).
Round 1 *P3, k1, p1, k1*. Repeat *-* to end.
Round 2 *P1, k1, p1, k3*. Repeat *-* to end.
Repeat round 1 - 2 until work measures 25
(26.5) 29.5 (32) cm / 9¾ (10½) 11½ (12½) inches
in total.
AT THE SAME TIME:
Follow diagram for CY selection while working
the Broken Rib pattern.

Armhole
Work 82 (85) 88 (94) sts as set. BO 4 sts loosely.
Knit to 2 st before m1, BO 4 sts.
The work has now been divided into front and
back with 80 (83) 86 (92) sts on each side.
Leave sts on hold while working the sleeves.

Sleeves
CO 32 (34) 38 (42) sts using 3.5 mm (US 4)
double pointed needles and MY + CY1 (total of
2 threads). Join for working in the round.
Round 1 Pm (m1). *K1, p1*. Repeat to end.
Round 2 - 5 As round 1
Round 6 - 10 Add yarn CY5 . Now working with
a total of 3 threads.
Round 11 Add additional yarn CY8. Now
working with a total of 4 threads. Continue as
set until work measures 3 (3) 4 (4) cm. 1¼ (1¼)
1½ (1½) inches.
Change to 4 mm (US 6) circular needle, 80 cm
(32 inches).
Round 1 - 6 Work moss stitches.
AT THE SAME TIME:

Follow diagram for CY selection while working the moss stitch pattern.

Increase

Round 7 (RS) Patt 1, M1. Work moss stitches to 1 st before m1, M1, patt 1. There are now 32 (34) 38 (42) sts.

Continue in moss stitch patt, working the increase round on every 5th (6th) 6th (6th) round to a total of 48 (50) 56 (64) sts. Continue straight until work measures 20 (24) 28 (32) cm / 7¾ (9½) 11 (12½) inches.

K to last sts, BO 2 sts loosely.

There are now 46 (48) 54 (62) sts.

Set the sleeve aside while working the other sleeve the same way.

Joining all pieces for working in the round

We will now work moss stitch patt on sleeves as well as body.

Round 1 (RS)

Using the 4 mm (US 6) circular needle, where the body sts are resting. Beg at left sleeve. Pm (m1). Work moss stitch 46 (48) 54 (62) sts of one sleeve onto the needle. Pm (m2).

Work moss stitch across front 80 (83) 86 (92) sts onto the same needle as set. Pm (m3).

Work moss stitch 46 (48) 54 (62) sts of right sleeve sts onto the same needle. Pm (m4).

Work moss stitch across back 80 (83) 86 (92) sts.

All 252 (262) 280 (308) sts are now joined on one needle.

Round 2 (RS) K1, patt to 1 st before m2. K2. Patt to 1 st before m3. K2. Patt to 1 st before m4. K2. Patt to 1 st before m1. K1.

Continuing in moss stitch patt on front, back and sleeves. Thought the sts on both sides of the all four markers will be worked in knit from now on.

Raglan decreases

Round 3 K1, k2tog. Work to 3 sts before m2. K2tog tbl, k2, k2tog. Work to 3 sts before m3. K2tog tbl, k2, k2tog. Work to 3 sts before m4. K2tog tbl, k2, k2tog. Work to 3 sts before m1. K2tog tbl, k1. (8 sts decreased)

Round 4 Work as set without any decreases.

Round 5 - 16 Repeat round 3 - 4 (for another 6 (6) 6 (6) times).

Raglan decreases, sleeves only

We will now be working the decreases in only the sleeve not in the body part.

Round 17 K1, k2tog. Work to 3 sts before m2. K2tog tbl. Work to 1 sts after m3. k2tog. Work to 3 sts before m4. K2tog tbl. Work to m1. K2tog tbl, k1. (4 sts decreased)

Round 18 Work as set without decreases.

Repeat row 17 - 18 until there are 14 sts remaining in sleeves in all sizes.

There are now 66 (69) 72 (78) sts on front and back.

Splitting the work

Round 1 Place sts from left sleeve on hold. You will finish the sleeve later. Keep front sts on needle. Place sts from right sleeve on hold. You will finish the sleeve later. Place sts from back on hold. You will finish the back later.

Left Front shaping

Work front i short rows creating the neck shape and shoulder overlapping.

Row 1 (RS) K1. Work moss stitch 29 (30) 32 (34) sts. Turn.

Row 2 (WS) Work moss stitch to 1 st before end. P1.

Row 3 (RS) K1. Work moss stitch to 3 st before last turn. Turn work.

Repeat row 2 - 3 for 2 (2) 2 (2) more times.

Row 8 (WS) Work moss stitch to 1 st before end. P1.

Row 9 (RS) K1. Work moss stitch to 2 st before last turn. Turn work.

Repeat row 8 - 9 for 3 (3) 3 (4) more times.

Continue shaping left front

Row 1 (WS) Work moss stitch to 1 st before end. P1.

Row 2 (RS) K1. Work moss stitch to 1 st before last turn. Turn work.

Repeat row 1 - 2 for 2 (2) 4 (4) more times.

End of shaping left front

Row 1 (WS) Work moss stitch to 1 st before end. P1.

Row 2 (RS) K1. Work moss stitch across the entire front to 1 st before end. K1.

Right Front shaping

Row 1 (WS) P1. Work moss stitch 29 (30) 32 (34) sts. Turn

Row 2 (RS) Work moss stitch to 1 st before end. K1.

Row 3 (WS) P1. Work moss stitch to 3 st before last turn. Turn work.

Repeat row 2 - 3 for 2 (2) 2 (2) more times.

Row 8 (RS) Work moss stitch to 1 st before end. K1.

Row 9 (WS) P1. Work moss stitch to 2 st before last turn. Turn work.

Repeat row 8 - 9 for 3 (3) 3 (4) more times.

Continue shaping right front

Row 1 (RS) Work moss stitch to 1 st before end. K1.

Row 2 (WS) P1. Work moss stitch to 1 st before last turn. Turn work.

Repeat row 1 - 2 for 2 (2) 4 (4) more times.

End shaping right front

Row 1 (RS) Work moss stitch to 1 st before end. K1.

Row 2 (WS) P1. Work moss stitch across the entire front to 1 st before end. P1.

Neck Rib front

Change to needle 3.5 mm (US 4) circular needle, 80 cm (32 inches) and MY + CY 5 (Navy).

Row 1 (RS) *K1, p1*. Repeat *to* to end.

Row 2 - 8 Work 1by1 rib as set.

BO all sts loosely.

Back

Using the 4 mm (US 6) circular needle pick up the 66 (69) 72 (78) back sts and work the back in short rows shaping the neckline as follows. Use same yarn as were you left. Begin with a RS row.

Row 1 (RS) K1, work moss stitch to 1 st before end. K1.

Row 2 (WS) P1, work moss stitch to 1 st before end. P1.

Repeat row 1 - 2 4 (4) 4 (6) more times.

Right Back shaping

Row 1 (RS) K1. Work moss stitch 18 (19) 24 (24) sts. Turn.

Row 2 (WS) Work moss stitch to 1 st before end. P1.

Row 3 (RS) K1. Work moss stitch to 2 st before last turning. Turn work.

Repeat row 2 - 3 for 2 (2) 2 (2) more times.

Row 8 (WS) Work moss stitch to 1 st before end. P1.

Row 9 (RS) K1. Work moss stitch to 1 st before last turning. Turn work.

Repeat row 8 - 9 for 3 (4) 7 (7) more times.

End shaping right back

Row 1 (WS) Work moss stitch to 1 st before end. P1.

Row 2 (RS) K1. Work moss stitch across the entire back to 1 st before end. K1.

Left Back

Row 1 (WS) P1. Work moss stitch 18 (19) 24 (24) sts. Turn.

Row 2 (RS) Work moss stitch to 1 st before end. K1.

Row 3 (WS) P1. Work moss stitch to 2 st before last turning. Turn work.

Repeat row 2 - 3 for 2 (2) 2 (2) more times.

Row 8 (RS) Work moss stitch to 1 st before end. K1.

Row 9 (WS) P1. Work moss stitch to 1 st before last. Turn.
Repeat row 8-9 for 3 (4) 7 (7) more times.

End shaping left back
Row 1 (RS) Work moss stitch to 1 st before end. K1.
Row 2 (WS) P1. Work moss stitch across the entire back to 1 st before end. P1.

Neck Rib back
Change to needle 3.5 mm (US 4) circular needle, 80 cm (32 inches) and MY + CY 5 (Navy).
Row 1 (RS) *K1, p1*, repeat to end.
Row 2 - 3 work 1by1 rib as set.

Buttonholes
Row 4 (WS)
Work 6 (6) 8 (8) sts. 2yo (not too tightly), p2tog, p2tog. Work to 10 (10) 12 (12) sts before end. 2yo (not too tightly), p2tog, p2tog. Work to end.
Row 5 Work rib as set. When meeting the two yo: k1 on the first loop, then k1 tbl on the second loop .
Row 6 - 8 Work rib as set. Work the reestablished sts into patt.
BO all sts loosely.

Left sleeve cap
Pick up the 14 (14) 14 (14) sts from left sleeve.
Row 1 (RS) K1, k2tog, k to 3 sts before end. k2tog tbl, K1.
Row 2 (WS) Work as set to end.
Repeat row 1-2 for 2 more times.
BO all the remaining 8 sts loosely.

Right sleeve cap
Work sleeve cap as for left sleeve.

Finishing
Join the front and back and sleeve cap. The back should overlap the front just enough to meet the point where the work was split.
Sew on the 2 buttons on the front.
Join armhole openings.
Weave in all ends.
Steam your new sweater.

Take the beautiful colours for a walk in the sun...

Beetle Contrast yarn selection

Rib (Body)				
row 1-5	C1	-	-	1by1 rib
row 6-10	C1	C5	-	1by1 rib
row 11-15	C1	C5	C8	1by1 rib
row 16-22	C1	C5	C8	Broken rib
row 23	C1	C3	C7	Broken rib
row 24	C1	C5	C8	Broken rib
row 25-30	C1	C3	C7	Broken rib
row 31	C1	C2	C5	Broken rib
row 32	C1	C3	C7	Broken rib
row 33-38	C1	C2	C5	Broken rib
row 39	C1	C6	C3	Broken rib
row 40	C1	C2	C5	Broken rib
row 41-46	C1	C6	C3	Broken rib
row 47	C1	C5	C7	Broken rib
row 48	C1	C6	C3	Broken rib
row 49-54	C1	C5	C7	Broken rib
row 55	C1	C2	C3	Broken rib
row 56	C1	C5	C7	Broken rib
row 57-62	C1	C2	C3	Broken rib
row 63	C1	C7	C4	Broken rib
row 64	C1	C2	C3	Broken rib
row 65-70	C1	C7	C4	Broken rib
row 71	C1	C6	C5	Broken rib
row 72	C1	C7	C4	Broken rib
row 73-78	C1	C6	C5	Broken rib
row 79	C1	C8	C3	Broken rib
row 80	C1	C6	C5	Broken rib
row 81-86	C1	C8	C3	Broken rib
row 87	C1	C2	C6	Broken rib
row 88	C1	C8	C3	Broken rib
row 89-94	C1	C2	C6	Broken rib
row 95	C1	C7	C5	Broken rib
row 96	C1	C2	C6	Broken rib
row 97-102	C1	C7	C5	Broken rib
moss stitch yoke				
row 1-7	C6	C8	C8	Moss stitch
row 8-14	C6	C8	C4	Moss stitch
row 15	C6	C4	C2	Moss stitch
row 16	C6	C8	C4	Moss stitch
row 17-26	C6	C4	C2	Moss stitch

The metallic shimmer from the beetle creates many different shades. Depending on the angle and light you will get a unique view.

Bruno Kleist

#REDshimmering

Pixelated View

Beetle Teen~Adult
Design Bruno Kleist
Skill level 2 - 3
Photo page126 - 127

Designer Bruno Kleist
- a plain jumper with an extraordinary animal.
#REDpixelatedwiev

Skill level 3
Sizes
EU + UK XS (**S**) M (L)
To fit bust
82 (88) 94 (100) cm
32¼ (34½) 37 (39½) inches
Actual bust measurement (jumper)
98 (104) 110 (116) cm
38½ (41) 43¼ (45½) inches
Length
63 (**65**) 67 (69) cm
24¾ (25½) 26½ (27) inches
Yarn A
Mano del Uruguay, Silk Blend
30% Silk, 70% Merino Extrafine Wool, 150
yards / 135 meters per 50 g.
9 (9) 10 (10) x 50 g in Natural SB3014.
Yarn B
Mano del Uruguay, Silk Blend
1 (1) 1 (1) x 50 g in Oxygen, SB3214.
Yarn C
Mano del Uruguay, Silk Blend
1 (1) 1 (1) x 50 g in Pewter, SB3064.
Yarn D
Mano del Uruguay, Silk Blend
1 (1) 1 (1) x 50 g in Topaz, SB300X.
Yarn E
Mano del Uruguay, Silk Blend
1 (1) 1 (1) x 50 g in Juniper, SB3043.
Yarn F
Mano del Uruguay, Silk Blend
1 (1) 1 (1) x 50 g in Tahiti, SB3210.
Yarn G
Mano del Uruguay, Silk Blend
1 (1) 1 (1) x 50 g in Nickel, SB3031.
Yarn H
Mano del Uruguay, Silk Blend
1 (1) 1 (1) x 50 g in Citric, SB3068.
Needles
3.5 mm (US 4) circular needle, 80 cm (32
inches). 3.5 mm (US 4) dpn.
3 mm (US 3) circular needle, 80 cm (32
inches). 3 mm (US 3) dpn. 4 stitch markers.

Gauge
In stocking stitch using 3.5 mm (US 4) needles
and yarn A: 26 sts x 34 rows = 10 x 10 cm / 4 x
4 inches.

Remember to check your gauge and adjust
needle size accordingly.

Shown in size Small.

Tip
This jumper will be worked with small
patches so prepare mini skeins to use
according to diagram.

Front body rib
CO 122 (134) 146 (158) sts using long 3 mm
(US 3) circular needle and yarn A.
Work Rib
Row 1 (WS) Dbe1. *K1, p1, k1, p3*. Repeat
to to last st. Dbe1.
Repeat row 1 on RS and WS to rib measures
6 cm / 2¼ inches in total (all size).

Front Body
Change to 3.5 mm (US 4) 80 cm (32 inches)
circular needle.
Row 1 (RS) Dbe1. K to last st. Dbe1.
Row 2 (WS) Dbe1. P to last st. Dbe1.
Continue knitting stocking stitch for 2.5
(2.5) 4.5 (6.5) cm / 1 (1) 2 (3) inches. First and
last st are worked as dbe1; this will not be
mentioned again.

Work beetle diagram
Please note: The jumper is worked according
to the diagram as described on the following
row. Twist yarn as described. Always twisting
the old yarn (the one you just came from)
over the new yarn (the colour you are about
to knit). This will make a nice transition from
each colour.
Row 1 (RS) Knit to diagram shows colour. K1
in contrast yarn. Twist yarn A over contrast
yarn. K5 in contrast yarn. Twist contrast yarn
over yarn A. Knit to end.
All coloured squares are 6 sts x 8 rows. This
will make approx 2.4 x 2.4 cm / 1 x 1 inch.
Pattern length approx 48 cm / 19 inches.

Continue straight following diagram until
work measures 51 (53) 55 (57) cm / 20 (20¾)
21½ (22½) inches.
Neck opening
Begin shaping the neck.
Row 1 (RS) Knit 57 (62) 67 (72) sts. BO 8 (10)
12 (14) sts. Knit to end. Front is now divided

into right and left front.

Right front
Row 1 (WS) Purl to end.
Row 2 (RS) BO 3 sts. Knit to end.
Row 3 (WS) Purl to end.
Repeat row 2 - 3 for 2 (2) 2 (2) more times.
Row 8 (RS) BO 2 sts. Knit to end.
Row 9 (WS) Purl to end.
Repeat row 8 - 9 for 3 (3) 3 (3) more times.
Row 16 (RS) BO 1 sts. Knit to end.
Make decreases as row 16 on every 5th (5th) 5th (6th) 3 more times.
There are now 36 (41) 46 (51) sts.

Shoulder slanting
Row 1 (RS) Knit to 5 (5) 6 (6) sts before end. W&t.
Row 2 (WS) Purl to end. Turn.
Row 3 (RS) Knit to 10 (10) 12 (12) sts before end. W&t.
Row 4 (WS) Purl to end. Turn.
Row 5 (RS) Knit to 15 (15) 18 (18) sts before end. W&t.
Row 6 (WS) Purl to end. Turn.
Row 7 (RS) Knit to 20 (20) 24 (24) sts before end. W&t.
Row 8 (WS) Purl to end.
Row 9 (RS) Knit all sts to end. The hole that appeared from the w&t will now be closed.
Row 10 (WS) Purl to end.
BO all sts loosely.

Left front
Row 1 (WS) Purl to end.
Row 2 (RS) Knit to end.
Row 3 (WS) BO 3 sts. Purl to end.
Repeat row 2-3 for 2 (2) 2 (2) more times.
Row 8 (RS) Knit to end.
Row 9 (WS) BO 2 sts. Purl to end.
Repeat row 8 - 9 for 3 (3) 3 (3) more times.
Row 16 (RS) Knit to end.
Row 17 (WS) BO 1 sts. Purl to end.
Make decreases as row 17 on every 5th (5th) 5th (6th) 3 more times.
There are now 36 (41) 46 (51) sts.
Shoulder slanting
Row 1 (WS) Purl to 5 (5) 6 (6) sts before end. W&t.
Row 2 (RS) Knit to end. Turn.

Row 3 (WS) Purl to 10 (10) 12 (12) sts before end. W&t.
Row 4 (RS) Knit to end. Turn.
Row 5 (WS) Purl to 15 (15) 18 (18) sts before end. W&t.
Row 6 (RS) Knit to end. Turn.
Row 7 (WS) Purl to 20 (20) 24 (24) sts before end. W&t.
Row 8 (RS) Knit to end. Turn.
Row 9 (WS) Purl all sts to end. The hole that appeared from the w&t will now be closed. BO all sts loosely.

Back body rib
CO 122 (134) 146 (158) sts using 3 mm (US 3) 80 cm (32 inches) circular needle and yarn A.
Work Rib
Row 1 (WS) Dbe1. *P3, k1, p1, k1*. Repeat *to* to last st. Dbe1.
Repeat row 1 on RS and WS to rib measures 6 (6) 6 (6) cm / 2¼ (2¼) 2¼ (2¼) inches in total.
Back body
Change to 3.5 mm (US 4) circular needle.
Row 1 (RS) Dbe1. K to last st. Dbe1.
Row 2 (WS) Dbe1. P to last st. Dbe1.
Continue stocking stitch straight without diagram until work measures 60 (62) 64 (66) cm / 23½ (24¼) 25¼ (26) inches.

Neck opening and shoulder slanting
Row 1 (RS) Knit to 5 (5) 6 (6) sts before end. W&t.
Row 2 (WS) Purl to 5 (5) 6 (6) sts before end. W&t.
Row 3 (RS) Knit to 10 (10) 12 (12) sts before end. W&t.
Row 4 (WS) Purl to 10 (10) 12 (12) sts before end. W&t.
Row 5 (RS) Knit to 15 (15) 18 (18) sts before end. W&t.
Row 6 (WS) Purl to 15 (15) 18 (18) sts before end. W&t.
Row 7 (RS) K 31 (36) 38 (43) sts. BO 30 (32) 34 (36) sts. K to 20 (20) 24 (24) sts before end. Turn.
Row 1 (WS) Purl to end. Work is now divided. 46 (51) 56 (61) sts on both sides.

Left Back
Row 1 (WS) Purl to end.
Row 2 (RS) BO 5 sts. Knit to 25 (25) 32 (32) sts before end. W&t.
Row 3 (WS) Purl to end.
Row 4 (RS) BO 5 sts. K all sts to end. The hole that appeared from the w&t will now be closed.
Row 5 (WS) Purl to end.
You now have 36 (41) 46 (51) sts.
BO all sts loosely.

Right Back
Row 1 (WS) Purl to 20 (20) 24 (24) sts before end. W&t.
Row 2 (RS) Knit to end.
Row 3 (WS) BO 5 sts. Purl to 25 (25) 32 (32) sts before end. W&t.
Row 4 (RS) Knit to end.
Row 5 (WS) BO 5 sts. Purl all sts to end. The hole that appeared from the w&t will now be closed.
Row 6 (RS) Knit to end.
You now have 36 (41) 46 (51) sts. **BO all sts loosely.**

Neckline
Sew shoulder seam together before making the neckline.
Collect 108 (108) 108 (116) sts around the neckline with 3 mm (US 3) circular needle and yarn A.
Round 1 *P3, k1, p1, k1*. repeat *-* to end.
Round 2 *P1, k1, p1, k3*. repeat *-* to end.
Repeat round 1-2 to rib measures 3 (3) 3 (3) cm / 1¼ (1¼) 1¼ (1¼) inches in total.
BO all sts as each st shows. (P st BO purlwise. K st BO knitwise)

Sleeves
CO 42 (42) 48 (48) sts using 3 mm (US 3) dpn and yarn A. Join for working in the round.
Round 1 *P3, k1, p1, k1*. Repeat *to* to end.
Round 2 *P1, k1, p1, k3*. Repeat *to* to end.

Repeat round 1- 2 to rib measures 6 (6) 6 (6) cm / 2¼ (2¼) 2¼ (2¼) inches in total. Change to 3.5 mm (US 4) circular needle. From now on work in stocking stitch whilst making increases.

Increases

Round 6 Pm (m1). K1, M1. Knit to 1 st before m1, M1, k1. (2 sts increased to 44 (44) 50 (50))
Continue in stocking stitch, working the increase round on every 5th (5th) 5th (5th) round to a total of 94 (98) 104 (108) sts. Continue straight until work measures 51 (52) 53 (54) cm / 20 (20½) 20¾ (21¼) inches.

Sleeve Cap

We will now be working back and forth.
Round 1 (RS) Knit to 10 sts before m1. W&t.
Round 2 (WS) Purl to 10 sts before m1. W&t.
Round 3 (RS) Knit to 20 sts before m1. W&t.
Round 4 (WS) Purl to 20 sts before m1. W&t.
Round 5 (RS) Knit to 30 sts before m1. W&t.
Round 6 (WS) Purl to 30 sts before m1. W&t.
Round 7 (RS) Knit to 40 sts before m1. W&t.
Round 8 (WS) Purl to 40 sts before m1. W&t.
Round 9 (RS) Knit to m1.
Round 10 (RS) Remove marker. BO all sts.
Work the other sleeve the same way.

Finishing

Attach sleeves to body.
Weave in all ends. This will take some time :)
Steam your new sweater.

Ready to take this new jumper for a walk in the park.

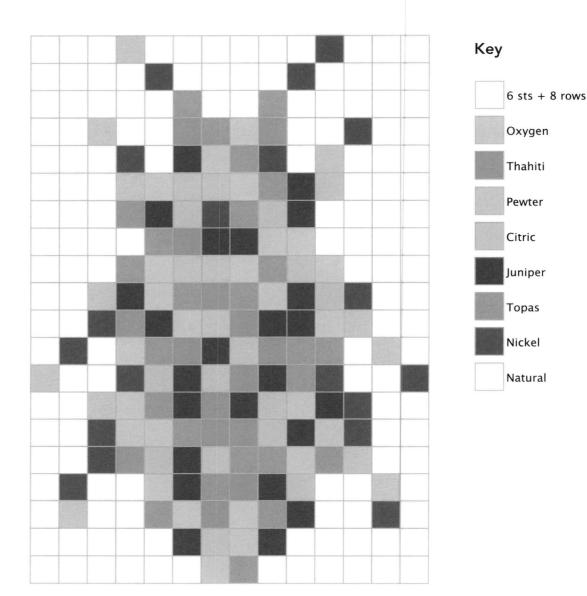

Key

⬜	6 sts + 8 rows
🟦	Oxygen
🟫	Thahiti
🟦	Pewter
⬜	Citric
⬛	Juniper
🟦	Topas
🟫	Nickel
⬜	Natural

The beetle is not easy to find out there but if we try to focus, we will hopefully find more of them in time.

Bruno Kleist

#REDpixelatedwiev

Gold Within

Javan Rhino Child
Design Mea Andresen
Skill level 3
Photo page 54 - 55

Design Mea Andresen
- a jumper with face and ears.
#REDgoldwithin

Skill level 3
Sizes
EU 86 (98) 110 (122)
UK 12 – 18 month (2-3) 4-5 (6-7) years
To fit bust
53 (54.5) 58 (63) cm
12 – 18 month, (2-3) 4-5 (6-7) years
21 (21½) 23 (25) inches
Actual bust measurement (jumper)
66 (68) 72 (77) cm
26 (26¾) 28¼ (30¼) inches
Length
32 (38) 44 (50) cm
12½ (15) 17½ (20) inches
Yarn A
Madeline Tosh A.S.A.P
100% Merino Wool, 90 yards / 82 meters per
130 g.
4 (4) 5 (6) x 120 g in Kitten 316, grey.
Yarn B
Purl Soho Spun Silk
100% Silk, 202 yards / 184 meters
1 (1) 1 (1) x 50 g in Golden Pear 7040, Gold
Black thread for eyes, mouth and details.
Needles
8 mm (US 11) circular needle 60 cm (24 inches)
8 mm (US 11) dpns.
3.5 mm (US 4) circular needle 60 cm (24 inches)
3.5 mm (US 4) dpns.
3.5 mm (US 4) crochet hook
4 stitch markers.
Gauge
In stocking stitch on 8 mm (US 11) needles
and yarn A: 11 sts x 17 rows = 10 x 10 cm/4 x
4 inches. Remember to check your gauge and
adjust needle size accordingly.
In stocking stitch on 3.5 mm (US 4) needle and
yarn B: approx 22 sts = 10 cm. Rows are not
important in this yarn. Since it is only used for
very small areas, there is no need to be exact in
yarn B gauges.

Shown in size 98 / 2-3 years

Tip, Horn
Once the jumper is done we will be knitting the
horn of gold with 2 threads of fine silk. When
winding Yarn B divide into 2 balls to make it
easier to knit with 2 threads at the same time.

For this jumper, make sure to learn the Dbe
(see abbreviations). It is a beautiful edge stitch
that provides this jumper with a unique finish.

Body Front
CO 74 (76) 80 (84) sts using 3.5 mm (US 4) 60 cm
(24 inches) circular needle and yarn B 1 thread
only.
Knit stocking stitches back and forth.
Row 1 (WS) P to last 1 sts. Dbe1.
Row 2 (RS) Dbe1. K to last st. Dbe1.
Row 2 - 6 Repeat rows 1 - 2. First and last stitch
is worked as dbe1.
Row 7 (WS) Dbe1. P to end. (no dbe).

Change to 8 mm (US 11) circular needle and
yarn A.
Row 1 (RS) *K2tog*, repeat *-* to end reducing
to 37 (38) 40 (42) sts.
Row 2 (WS) K to last 1 sts. Dbe1. (making a
row with p on RS to fold around, from here on
called fold-line)
Row 3 (RS) Dbe1. K to last 1 sts. Dbe1.
Continue in stocking stitch, working dbe1 at
end and beg of each row.
Work straight until work measures 20.5 (25) 29.5
(34) cm / 8 (9¾) 11½ (13½) inches, measured
from fold-line.
Row 1 (RS) BO 1 sts loosely. K to 1 st before
end, BO 1 st loosely. 35 (36) 38 (40)
Set front aside and work the back.

Body Back:
Make front and back identical.
Set front and back aside and work the sleeves.

Sleeves
CO 16 **(16)** 18 (18) sts using 8 mm (US 11) dpns
and yarn A. Join for working in the round.
Round 1 P to end.
Round 2 K to end.
Round 3 P to end.
Round 4 K to end.
Size EU 86 (98): Work stocking stitch from here.
Size EU 110 (122): Make these 2 rounds:
Round 5 P to end
Round 6 K to end. Work stocking stitch from
here.
Increases
**On all sizes start increasing on round 6 as
follows:**
Round 6 (increase round) K1, M1. K to last st,
M1, k1. (2 sts increased to 18 (18) 18 (20))

Working the increase round on every 4th (5th) 5th (6th) round to a total of 28 (30) 32 (34) sts. Continue straight until work measures 20 (23) 27 (31) cm / 7¾ (9) 10½ (12¼) inches.

Armhole
K to last sts. BO 2 sts loosely.
There are now 26 (28) 30 (32) sts.
Set the sleeve aside while working the other sleeve the same way.

Joining body and sleeves
We will now join front, back and sleeves on the 8 mm (US 11) circular needle.
Round 1 Pm (m1). K 26 (28) 30 (32) sts of one sleeve onto the needle (left sleeve).
Pm (m2). K 35 (36) 38 (40) front sts.
Pm (m3). K 26 (28) 30 (32) sts of the other sleeve onto the same needle (right sleeve).
Pm (m4). K 35 (36) 38 (40) back sts.
All 122 (128) 136 (144) sts are now joined on one needle.

Round 2 Sm. P1. K 24 (26) 28 (30). P1. Sm. P1. K 33 (34) 36 (38). P1. Sm. P1. K 24 (26) 28 (30). P1. Sm. P1. K 33 (34) 36 (38). P1.

Raglan decrease
Round 3 Sm p1, k2tog. K to 3 sts before m2. K2tog ssk, p2, k2tog. K to 3 sts before m3. K2tog ssk, p2, k2tog. K to 3 sts before m4. K2tog ssk, p2, k2tog. K to 3 sts before m1. K2tog ssk, p1. (8 sts decreased)
Round 4 Work as set without any shaping.
Work decreases on every 2nd round for another 9 (10) 11 (11) times.

HOWEVER, only decrease on body **and** sleeves for another 1 (1) 1 (2) more decrease rounds.
After this there are 31 (32) 34 (36) sts each on front and back. From here on, work increases **only** on the sleeves. That is:
After m1,
Before m2
After m3
Before m4.
AT THE SAME TIME
When work measures 26 (30) 36 (42) cm / 10¼ (11¾) 14¼ (16½) inches from fold-line, divide the work, making back slit.

Work back and forth for back slit
You will now work a few rows back and forth to create back slit and raise neckline in the back.
Continue working the raglan decreases as

before (only on every RS row in sleeves sts).
Row 1 (RS) Work as set with the usual decreases to m4. Sm. P1. K 13 (14) 15 (16), dbe1. Turn. (back slit).
Row 2 (WS) Dbe1. Work as the sts show (p on p and k on k) to m1. Sm. K1. P 14 (14) 15 (16), Dbe1. Turn.
Row 3 - 4 repeat rows 1-2.

Neck opening front
Row 1 (RS) Dbe1. Work as set to 13 (13) 14 (15) sts after m2. K 5 (6) 6 (6) sts onto spare needle. Work to last st. Dbe1.

Right shoulder, front and back
Row 1 (WS) Dbe1. Work as set to 13 (13) 14 (15) sts after m3. Turn.
Row 2 (RS) Place 1 sts on holder. Work to last st. Dbe1.
Row 3 (WS) Dbe1. Work as set to 12 (12) 13 (14) sts after m3. Turn.
Row 4 (RS) Place 1 sts on holder. Work to last st. Dbe1.
Row 5 (WS) Dbe1. Work as set to 11 (11) 12 (13) sts after m3. Turn.
Row 6 (RS) Place 1 sts on holder. Work to last st. Dbe1.
After row 6, there will be 8 (9) 9 (9) sts on holder.
Row 7 - 8 Work as set with no further shaping. Remember dbe1 only on back slit side.
Row 9 (WS) Dbe1. Work to m4. BO sts from sleeve 8 (8) 8 (10). You have now reached m3. Work as set to the end.
Front and back is now divided on right sleeve side.
Row 10 Front (RS) Work the 10 (10) 11 (12) sts as set.
Set aside these sts for later making the ear. Break yarn, leave an end of 13 m / 14 yards for working the ears.
Row 10 Back (RS) P1, k 9 (9) 10 (11).
Row 11 Back (WS) P 9 (9) 10 (11), k1.
Row 12 Back (RS) BO loosely knitwise.

Left shoulder, front and back starting at center back slit.
Row 1 (RS) Work as set to 13 (13) 14 (15) sts after m2. Turn.
Row 2 (WS) Place 1 sts on holder. Work to last st. Dbe1. Turn.
Row 3 (RS) Dbe1. Work as set to 12 (12) 13 (14) sts after m2. Turn.
Row 4 (WS) Place 1 sts on holder. Work to last

st. Dbe1. Turn.
Row 5 (RS) Dbe1. Work as set to 11 (11) 12 (13) sts after m2. Turn.
Row 6 (WS) Place 1 sts on holder. Work to last st. Dbe1. Turn.
After row 6, there will be 11 (12) 12 (12) sts on holder.
Row 7 - 8 Work as set. Remember dbe1 only on back slit side.
Row 9 (RS) Dbe1. Work to m1. BO sts from sleeve 8 (8) 8 (10) purlwise. You have now reached m2. Work as set.
Front and back is now divided on left sleeve side.
Row 10 Front (WS) Work the 10 (10) 11 (12) sts as set, last st dbe1.
Set aside these sts for later making the ear. Break yarn, leave an end of 13 m / 14 yards for working the ears.
Row 10 Back (WS) K1, p 8 (8) 9 (10). Dbe1.
Row 11 Back (RS) Dbe1. K 8 (8) 9 (10), p1.
Row 12 Back (WS) BO loosely knitwise.

Shaping the right ear
Using the sts set aside from front shoulder, RS, working from the neck towards the arm 10 (10) 11 (12) sts.
Row 1 (RS) Dbe1 (that is: Unravel first st so that you have a loop and a st. Work dbe1 on the loop and the st). K to 3 sts before end. M1, p2, dbe1.
Row 2 (WS) Dbe1. P to last st. Dbe1.
Row 3 - 10 (10) 12 (14) Repeat row 1 and 2 (First st in row 1 is worked dbe1).
Ending ear
Row 1 (RS) Dbe1. P to last st. Dbe1.
Row 2 - 5 Repeat row 1.
Row 6 (WS) BO all sts loosely. Break the yarn, leaving an end of 1 meter / 1.2 yards for fastening the ear to the body.
Fold top of ear down to the front and attach to front body as in picture.

Shaping the left ear
Using the sts set aside from front shoulder, left side, working from the neck towards the arm 10 (10) 11 (12) sts.
Row 1 (WS) Dbe1 (that is: Unravel first st so that you have a loop and a st. Work dbe1 on the loop and the st). P to 3 before end. M1p, k2, dbe1.
Row 2 (RS) Dbe1. K to 1 before end, Dbe1.
Repeat rows 1-2 until 10 (10) 12 (14) rows in total.

Row 1 (WS) Dbe1. P to last st. Dbe1.
Rows 2 - 5 Repeat row 1.
Row 6 (RS) BO all sts loosely using p sts. Break the yarn, leaving an end of 1 meter / 1.2 yards for fastening the ear to the body.
Fold top of ear down to the front and attach to front body as in picture.

Shoulder finishing

Attach back shoulder to front shoulder, showing no visible stitches on front.
Attach top sleeve cap 8 (8) 8 (10) to shoulder.

Neckband

The neckband is worked in back and forth.
Row 1 (RS) Beg at center back slit, pick up and k 24 (24) 26 (28) sts using 8 mm (US 11) circular needle and yarn A.
Row 2 (WS) K to last sts.
Row 3 (RS) Change to needle size 3.5 mm (US 4) and yarn B.
K1 tbl, keeping the old sts in yarn A on left needle, k1, repeat *-* to end increase to 48 (48) 52 (56) sts.
Row 4 (WS) P to last st. Dbe1.
Row 5 (RS) Dbe1. *K2, M1*, repeat *-* to last st. Dbe1.
Row 6 (WS) Dbe1. P to last st. Dbe1.
Row 7 (RS) BO all sts loosely.
Fold golden neckband to the WS of work and stitch down in yarn B.

Side seam panel

CO 12 sts using 3.5 mm (US 4) double pointed needles and yarn B.
Row 1 (WS) K1. P2, k2, p2, k2, p2, dbe1.
Row 2 (RS) Dbe1. K2, p2, k2, p2, k2, dbe1.
Continue in rib until work measures 20.5 (25) 29.5 (34) cm / 8 (9¾) 11½ (13½) inches.
Make one more the same way.

Finish side seam

Close armhole and first 2 cm (¾ inch) of side seam from armhole towards bottom hem with Yarn A.
Attach the silk side seam panels at front and back side seam piece from wrong side.
Front and back piece should almost touch each other so silk will only be visible when the child is moving. See picture.

Loop at Center Back

Using crochet hook 3.5 mm (US 4) and 2 threads of yarn B make loop at center back. Pick up 1 sts. Crochet 10 times. BO and sew the other end in to create the loop.
Attach 1 button.

Horn:

After knitting the jumper you knit the horn as follows:
Pick up stitches in yarn B, 2 threads, with crochet hook 3.5 mm (US 4) and place on dpn spare needles along the shape. See picture.
Picking up these stitches shapes the horn outline, so be careful to pick up the stitches in the right place. Transfer the stitches from the bottom horizontal line onto a dpn needle 3.5 mm (US 4). Work in stocking stitch collecting stitches from the crochet needle on beginning and end of each row following diagram.
Add padding if wanted when the horn is ¾ finished.
Embroider with black thread the eyes, mouth and details following picture.
Weave in all ends.
Steam your new sweater, jump into it and get into your wellingtons and see if you can find another Rhino out there and become friends..

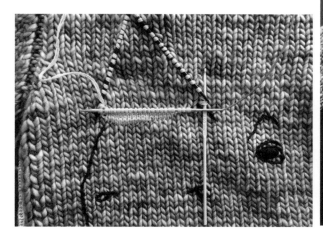

On the black market my horn is worth more than gold. But in reality I'm worth much more alive and free.

Mea Andresen

#REDgoldwithin

Simply Surviving

Javan Rhino Teen~Adult
Design Mea Andresen
Skill level 3
Photo pg 56 -57

Designer Mea Andresen
-a kimono i silk
#REDsimplysurivng

Skill level 3
Sizes
EU 34 (36) 38 (40)
UK 8 (10) 12 (14)
To fit bust
80 (84) 88 (92) cm
31½ (33) 34½ (36) inches
Actual bust measurement (jumper)
112 (116) 120 (124) cm
44 (45½) 47¼ (48¾) inches
Length
56 (58) 60 (62) cm
22 (22¾) 23½ (24¼) inches
Yarn
Purl Soho, Spun Silk
100% Silk, 202 yards / 185 meters per 50 g.
Col A 8 (9) 10 (10) 50 g 7090, Gray.
Col B 2 (2) 2 (2) x 50 g 7000, White.
Needle
3 mm (US 2) circular needle, 80 cm (32 inches)
3 mm (US 2) dpn. 4 stitch markers.
Gauge
In stocking stitch on 3 mm (US 2) needles and
yarn A: 30 sts x 38 rows = 10 x 10 cm/4 x 4
inches
Remember to check your gauge and adjust
needle size accordingly.

Shown in size 34

Tip
This cardigan will be worked front and back
and front in one piece. Shaping around
the shoulders will be worked in short rows.
Attach the collar afterwards.
Chest embroidery will be applied as
embroidery at the end.
Special Abbreviations
Loop-CO = CO as follows: *holding the
needle with the sts on your right hand. Make
a loop with the yarn in your left hand. Place
the loop on the right needle.*

Body
CO 340 (352) 364 (376) sts using 3 mm (US 2)
circular needle and Col B.
Row 1 (WS) P to end.
Row 2 (RS) Dbe1. K to last st. Dbe1.

Row 3 (WS) Dbe1. P to last st. Dbe1.
4 - 5 Repeat rows 2 - 3.
Change to Col A.

Fold line
Row 6 (RS) Dbe1. P to last st. Dbe1.
Row 7 (WS) Loop-CO 21 sts. (holding work
on RS) Turn work. P to end (no Dbe1). Loop-
CO 21 sts.
There are now 382 (394) 406 (418) sts.
Row 8 (RS) Dbe1. P 10 sts. K to 11 before
end. P 10 sts. Dbe1.
Row 9 (WS) Dbe1. K 10 sts. P to 11 before
end. K 10 sts. Dbe1.
Continue as set to work measures 16 cm / 6¼
inches (all sizes) from fold line.

Waistband tunnel
Row 1 (RS) Place 30 sts on spare needle.
Change to Col B. K to 31 sts before end.
Dbe1. Leave 30 sts on spare needle. Turn
(important not to wrap).
Row 2 (WS) Dbe1 *P3, sl1 **wyib***. Repeat
to to 5 sts before sts on spare needle. P4.
Dbe1.
Row 3 (RS) Dbe1. K1 *K3, sl1 **wyif***. Repeat
to to 4 st before turn. K3, Dbe1.
Row 4 - 8 Repeat rows 2 - 3.
Row 9 (RS) Dbe1. K all sts to 1st before
turn. Dbe1. Break the yarn. Place the 30 sts
from left spare needle on the right needle.
Slide all sts to the left on your needle and
slip all sts from spare needle onto working
needle right in front of the sts just worked as
waistband tunnel. Do not turn work.
Row 10 (RS) Change to Col A. Dbe1. P 10
sts. K across all sts to 11 before end. P 10 sts,
Dbe1.
Row 11 (WS) Work sts as set.

Decrease
Row 1 (RS) Dbe1. P 10 sts, k2tog. K to 11
before end. K2tog. P 10 sts, Dbe1.
Continue as set, working the decrease row
on every 10th (10th) 11th (11th) row to a total
of 370 (382) 394 (406) sts. Continue as set to
work measures 33 (34) 35 (36) cm / 13 (13½)
13¾ (14¼) inches from fold line, ending with
a WS row.

Armhole
(RS) Work 96 (99) 102 (105) sts, BO 4 sts

loosely. K 170 (176) 182 (188), BO 4 sts loosely. Work to end.
The work has now been divided into right front, back and left front. We will now work each part at a time, beginning with the left front.

Left Front
Row 1 (WS) Work to end as set.
Row 2 (RS) BO 2 (2) 2 (2) sts loosely. Work to end as set.
Row 3 (WS) Work to end as set.
Repeat rows 2 - 3 for another 9 times.
Work as set without decreases until work measures 51 (53) 55 (58) cm / 20 (21) 21½ (22¾) inches, ending with a WS row.

Shoulder slanting
Row 1 (RS) Work to end as set.
Row 2 (WS) Work as set to 3 (3) 3 (3) sts before end. W&t.
Row 3 (RS) Work to end as set.
Row 4 (WS) Work as set to 3 sts before last wrapped st. W&t.
Repeat row 3 - 4 another 8 times.

Collar, left front
Row 1 (RS) Work as set across all sts to end.
Row 2 (WS) Work as set across all sts to end.
Closing the sts for the shoulder seam
Row 3 (RS) BO 27 (29) 30 (32) sts loosely. Work as set to end.
Row 4 (WS) Work as set to end. Loop-CO 30 (33) 36 (39) sts.
Row 5 (RS) K the new 30 (33) 36 (39) sts. Work as set to end.
Row 6 (WS) Work as set to end. (new sts worked in p)
Work as set to collar measures 10 cm / 4 inches.
Row 1 (RS) Work to end.
Row 2 (WS) BO 11 sts. Change to yarn B. **K** to end.
Row 3 (RS) 1 dbe, k to 1 st before end, 1 dbe.
Continue in stocking stitch for 4 more cm / 1 more inches.
BO all sts loosely.
Right Front
Row 1 (WS) Work to end as set.
Row 2 (RS) Work to end as set.

Row 3 (WS) BO 2 (2) 2 (2) sts loosely. Work to end as set.
Repeat row 2 - 3 for another 9 times.
Work as set without decreases until work measures 51 (53) 55 (58) cm / 20 (21) 21½ (22¾) inches, ending with a WS row.

Shoulder slanting
Row 1 (RS) Work as set to 3 (3) 3 (3) sts before end. W&t.
Row 2 (WS) Work to end as set.
Row 3 (RS) Work as set to 3 sts before last wrapped st. W&t.
Row 4 (WS) Work to end as set.
Repeat row 3 - 4 for another 8 times.

Collar, right front
Row 1 (RS) Work as set across all sts to end, **meanwhile** whenever you meet a wrapped st: lift up the "wrap", place it on the left needle and work a k2tog tbl on the wrap and the st.
Closing the sts for the shoulder seam
Row 2 (WS) BO 27 (29) 30 (32) sts loosely. Work as set to end.
Row 3 (RS) Work as set to end. Loop-CO 30 (33) 36 (39) sts. Turn work.
Row 4 (WS) P the new 30 (33) 36 (39) sts. Work as set to end.
Row 5 (RS) Work as set to end.
Work as set until collar measures 10 cm / 4 inches.
Row 1 (RS) BO 11 sts. Change to yarn B. **P** to end.
Row 2 (WS) 1 dbe, p to 1 st before end, 1 dbe.
Continue in stocking stitch for 4 more cm / 1 more inch.
BO all sts loosely.

Back
Row 1 (RS) BO 2 (2) 2 (2) sts loosely. K to end.
Row 2 (WS) BO 2 (2) 2 (2) sts loosely. P to end.
Repeat row 1 - 2 for 9 more times.
Work as set without decreases until work measures 51 (53) 55 (58) cm / 20 (21) 21½ (22¾) inches.

Shoulder slanting
Row 1 (RS) K to 3 (3) 3 (3) sts before end. W&t.

Row 2 (WS) P to 3 (3) 3 (3) sts before end. W&t.
Row 3 (RS) K to 3 sts before last wrapped st. W&t.
Row 4 (WS) P to 3 sts before last wrapped st. W&t.
Repeat row 3 - 4 for another 8 times.
Row 1 (RS) K all sts to end, **meanwhile** whenever you meet a wrapped st: lift up the "wrap", place it on the left needle and work a k2tog tbl on the wrap and the st.
Row 2 (WS) P all sts.
BO all sts loosely. Please Note: As silk yarn is very smooth, you will have to be aware not to tighten the yarn in the BO.

Sleeves
CO 90 (96) 102 (108) sts using 3 mm (US 2) circular needle and yarn B. Join for working in rounds.
Round 1 K to end.
Round 2 - 15 Work in stocking sts.
Change to yarn A.
Round 16 Fold line. **P** to end.
Continue in stocking sts for another 16 rounds.

Increase
Round 33 K1, M1. K to last st, M1, k1. (2 sts increased).
Continue in stocking sts, working the increase round on every 11th (12th) 12th (13th) round to a total of 9 times. 108 (114) 120 (126) sts. Continue straight until work measures 33 (34) 35 (36) cm / 13 (13½) 14 (14½) inches.

Shaping the sleeve cap
Row 1 (RS) BO 3 (3) 3 (3) sts loosely. Patt to end. Turn.
Row 2 (WS) BO 3 (3) 3 (3) sts loosely. Patt to end. Turn.
Repeat rows 1 - 2 until you have 6 (6) 6 (6) sts left. BO all sts loosely.

Sleeve 2
Work the other sleeve the same way.

I-cord string:
Using a 3 mm (US 2) dpn, CO 6 sts in yarn B. Without turning, push the sts back to the

Horn Embroidery

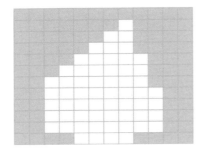

☐ =1 st+ 1 rov

☐ White

■ Light grey

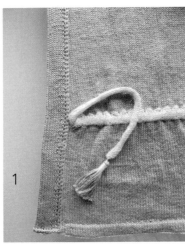

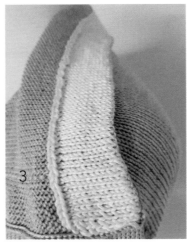

beg of the needle.
Row 1 (RS) Using another dpn, k6. Slide.
Row 2 (RS) K1 tbl (hold the yarn tight), k5, slide.
Repeat Row 2 until string measures 140 (144) 148 (152) cm / 55 (57) 58 (60) inches.
BO all 6 sts.
Make 2 tassels. See picture 1.
Attach each tassels to string ends.

Horn embroidery
Make embroidery of horn on chest as diagram (picture 2) using yarn B and a soft pointed needle.

Finishing
Sew the shoulder seams together. Sew the two collar sides together and attach the collar to the back neck. See picture 3.
Attach sleeves to body.
Steam the front placket and overlap it so it is on the outside. Sew down the front placket. See picture 4.
Sew down the collar, bottom hem and cuffs invisibly so the areas knitted in yarn B are not visible on the outside.
Weave in all ends. Steam your new kimono.
Add the I-cord string to the waistband tunnel.

A simple statement. Crying tears over the way humans are treating animals. Wearing the horn to hope for a better future.

Mea Andresen

REDsimplysurviving

Thumbs Up

Chimpanzee Child
Design Mea Andresen
Skill level 2
Photo pg 30 - 31

Designer Mea Andresen
-a cardigan with gloves and ears...
#REDthumbsup

Skill level 2
Sizes
EU 86 **(98)** 110 (122)
UK 12 – 18 months, (2-3) 4-5 (6-7) years
To fit bust
53 (54.5) 58 (63) cm
21 (21½) 23 (25) inches
Actual bust measurement (jumper)
62 (64) 68 (72) cm
24½ (25¼) 26¾ (28¼) inches
Length
34 (36) 40 (44) cm
13½ (14½) 15¾ (17½) inches
Yarn A
Zealana, Air
40% Brushtail Possum fiber, 40% Cashmere,
20% Mulberry Silk
191 yards / 175 meters per 25 g.
Col A 3 (3) 4 (4) x 25 g in Natural A04, Beige.
Col B 3 (3) 4 (4) x 25 g in Charcoal A01,
Charcoal.
Needles
3 mm (US 2) circular needle, 80 cm (32
inches).
3 mm (US 2) dpn.
7 buttons.
Gauge
In garter stitch on 3 mm (US 2) needles and
yarn A: 28 sts x 55 rows = 10 x 10 cm / 4 x 4
inches.

Shown in size 98 / 2-3 years

Tip
This cardigan is knitted in one piece, starting
at back body.
For the hands there are special gloves, easy
to put on. Cosy to play with for the little
hands.
These gloves will emerge from the sleeves
being longer on the back side than on the
front.

Body Back
CO 89 (91) 97 (103) sts using 3 mm (US 2)
needles, 80 cm (32 inches) circular needle, col

A.
Row 1 (RS) K to end 1 sts. Dbe1.
Row 2 (WS) Dbe1. K to 1 st before end.
Dbe1.
Row 3-5 repeat row 2. Working in garter
stitch.
Row 6 (WS) Dbe1. P1. *K1, P1*. Repeat *-*
to 2 sts before end. P1, Dbe1.
Continue in rib as set until work measures 4
(4.5) 5 (5) cm / 1½ (1¾) 2 (2) inches.
Row 1 (RS) Dbe1. K to end 1 sts. Dbe1.
Continue in garter stitch as row 1 until work
measures 20 (21.5) 25 (28.5) cm / 7¾ (8½) 9 ¾
(11¼) inches.

Armhole and sleeves:
**We will now increase the stitches to be
able to work the right sleeves, back and
left sleeve in one piece.**
**Row 1 (RS) Creating left sleeve. Change to
Col B.**
Dbe1. K to last sts. K1. CO, using the Loop-
CO method as follows: *holding the needle
with the sts in your RH. Make a loop with the
yarn in your LH. Place the loop on the right
needle.* Repeat *-* 77 (89) 101 (113) times.
Increasing with 78 (90) 102 (114) sts. Turn.
Row 2 (WS) Creating right sleeve.
K the new 78 (88) 98 (108) sts. Pm (m2). K to
last sts. K1. Pm (m1). Loop-CO as follows:
Repeat *-* for a total of 78 (90) 102 (114)
times. Turn.
Now we have increased to the total number
of sts for working all in one: right sleeve, back
and left sleeve.
There are now 245 (271) 301 (331) sts.
Row 3 (RS) Shaping the sleeves
K to m2. K 4 (5) 5 (6) sts. w&t.
Row 4 (WS) K to m1. K 4 (5) 6 (6) sts. w&t.
Row 5 (RS) K to 4 (5) 6 (6) sts after last
wrapped st. w&t.
Row 6 (WS) K to 4 (5) 6 (6) sts after last
wrapped st. w&t
Repeat row 5 - 6 another 14 (14) 14 (15)
times.
Row 1 (RS) K to end.
Row 2 (WS) K all sts.
Continue in garter stitch until sleeve
measures 8 (8.5) 9.5 (10.5) cm / 3¼ (3½) 3¾
(4¼) inches at sleeve opening.

Outer shoulder and back neck opening

Row 1 (RS) BO 14 (14) 17 (20) sts loosely. K to end.

Row 2 (WS) BO 14 (14) 17 (20) sts loosely. K 10 sts. BO 5 (5) 6 (6) sts (making a hole for the left thumb). K to 26 (26) 28 (30) sts after m2. K 38 (39) 41 (43) sts onto spare needle. Place those sts on thread and put on hold for later (creating neck-opening). K to 15 (15) 16 (16) sts before end. BO 5 (5) 6 (6) sts (making a hole for the right thumb). K to 1 st before end. Dbe1.

The work is now divided in Right Front and Left Front and in the middle sts are put on hold.

Right Front: Change to Col A

Row 1 (RS) Dbe1. K to thumb hole. Loop-CO 5 (5) 6 (6) sts. K to 1 st before end. Dbe1.

Row 2 (WS) Dbe1. K to 1 st before end. Dbe1.

Row 3-4 Work as row 2.

Front Neckline

Row 5 (RS) Dbe1. K to end. Pm (m3). Loop-CO 25 (25) 27 (29) sts. Turn work.

Row 6 (WS) K1. K to last st. Dbe1.

Row 7 (RS) Dbe1. K to m3. K2. w&t.

Row 8 (WS) K to last st. Dbe1.

Row 9 (RS) Dbe1. K to 2 sts after last wrapped st. w&t.

Repeat row 8 - 9 another 8 (8) 9 (10) times.

Row 1 (WS) Dbe1. K to last st. Dbe1.

Row 2 (RS) Dbe1. K to last st. Dbe1.

Row 3 (WS) Buttonholes
Dbe1. K2, yo (not too tight), k2tog. K to 1 st before end. Dbe1.

Continue in garter stitch until sleeve part in Col A measures 8 (8.5) 9.5 (10.5) cm / 3¼ (3½) 3¾ (4¼) inches at sleeve opening. Ending with a RS row.

AT THE SAME TIME MAKE:
Make buttonholes every 4 (4.5) 5.2 (6.5) cm / 1½ (1¾) 2 (2½) inches. (7 buttonholes in total) Place last buttonhole 1.5 cm / ½ inch before bottom hem.

Shaping the sleeves

Row 1 (WS) Dbe1. K to 4 (5) 5 (6) sts before end. w&t.

Row 2 (RS) K to last st. Dbe1.

Row 3 (WS) Dbe1. K to 4 (5) 5 (6) sts before last wrapped st. w&t.

Repeat row 2 - 3 another 13 (13) 14 (14) times.

Armhole

Row 1 (WS) Dbe1. K all sts to last st. Dbe1.

Row 2 (RS) BO all sts until m1 loosely. K to 1 st before end. Dbe1. You now have 51 (51) 55 (59) sts.

Continue in garter stitch until work measures 15 (16) 19 (22.5) cm / 7¾ (8½) 9 ¾ (11¼) inches from armhole. Ending with a WS row.

Row 1 (RS) Dbe1. P1. *K1, P1*. Repeat *-* to 2 sts before end. P1, Dbe1.

Continue in rib as set until rib measures 4 (4.5) 5 (5) cm / 1½ (1¾) 2 (2) inches. Ending with a WS row.

Row 1 (RS) Dbe1. K to last st. Dbe1.

Row 2 (WS) Dbe1. K to last st. Dbe1.

Row 3-5 Repeat row 2. Working in Garter stitch.
BO all sts loosely.

Left Front: Use Col A

Row 1 (RS) Begin at the sts set as side for left sleeve. K1. K to thumb hole. Loop-CO 5 (5) 6 (6) sts. K to last st. Dbe1.

Row 2 (WS) Dbe1. K to 1 st before end. Dbe1.

Row 3-5 Work as row 2.

Front Neckline

Row 6 (WS) Dbe1. K to last st. K1. Pm m4. Loop-CO 25 (25) 27 (29) sts.

Row 7 (RS) Dbe1. K to last st. Dbe1.

Row 8 (WS) Dbe1. K to m4. K2. w&t.

Row 9 (RS) K to last st. Dbe1.

Row 10 (WS) Dbe1. K to 2 **after** last wrapped st. w&t.

Repeat row 9 - 10 another 8 (8) 9 (10) times.

Row 1 (RS) Dbe1. K to last st. Dbe1.

Row 2 (WS) Dbe1. K to last st. Dbe1.

Continue in garter stitch until sleeve part in Col A measures 8 (8.5) 9.5 (10.5) cm / 3¼ (3½) 3¾ (4¼) inches at sleeve opening. Ending with a WS row.

Shaping the sleeves

Row 1 (RS) Dbe1. K to 4 (5) 5 (6) sts before end. w&t.

Row 2 (WS) K to last st. Dbe1.

Row 3 (RS) Dbe1. K to 4 (5) 5 (6) sts before last wrapped st. w&t.

Repeat row 2 - 3 another 13 (13) 14 (14) times.

Armhole

Row 1 (RS) Dbe1. K all sts to last st. Dbe1.

Row 2 (WS) BO all sts until m2 loosely. K to 1 st before end. Dbe1. You now have 51 (51) 55 (59) sts.

Continue in garter stitch to work measures 15 (16) 19 (22.5) cm / 7¾ (8½) 9 ¾ (11¼) inches from armhole. Ending with a RS row.

Row 1 (WS) Dbe1. P1. *K1, P1*. Repeat *-* to 2 sts before end. P1, Dbe1.

Continue in rib as set until rib measures 4 (4.5) 5 (5) cm / 1½ (1¾) 2 (2) inches. Ending with a WS row.

Row 1 (RS) Dbe1. K to last st. Dbe1.

Row 2 - 5 repeat row 1. Working in Garter stitch.
BO all sts loosely.

Thumb

Pick up 14 (14) 16 (16) sts along thumb edge using 3 mm (US 2) needles, dpn, Col B. Join for working in the round.

Round 1 Pm m1. K7. Pm m2. K7.

Round 2 P all.

Round 3 K all.

Repeat round 2 and 3, (ending with a round 2) until thumb measures 2.5 (3.5) 4.5 (5) cm / 1 (1¼) 1¾ (2) inches.

Decrease

Round 1 K2tog, k to m2, k2tog, k to end.

Round 2 Purl to end.

Repeat round 1-2 until 6 sts remain.
BO all sts and sew the tip of the thumb tog. Work the other thumb the same way.

Hood

Use 3 mm (US 2) needles, 80 cm (32 inches) circular needle, Col B.

Row 1 (RS) Starting from the right front pick up and k33 (33) 35 (37) sts. K the 38 **(39)** 41 (43) sts from back neck spare needle. Pick up and k34 (34) 36 (38) sts (one more than the other side) along the left front. There are now 105 (106) 112 (118) sts.

Row 2 (WS) To work a Dbe1 on this particular place: K2tog tbl. k52 (53) 56 (59) Pm m1. K to last st. Dbe1. There are now 104 (105) 111 (117) sts.

Increase

Row 3 (RS) Dbe1. K to 1 before m1. M1, k2, M1. K to last st. Dbe1.
Repeat row 2 - 3 for 5 more times. (Dbe1 on first and last st.)
Row 14 - 25 work Garter stitch without further increases.
AT THE SAME TIME
Row 15 (RS) Buttonhole Dbe1. K2, yo (not too tight), k2tog. K to last st. Dbe1.
Hood edge
Row 26 (WS) BO 2 sts. K to last st. Dbe1.
Row 27 (RS) BO 2 sts. K to last st. Dbe1.
Repeat row 26-27 for another 6 more times. Continue in Garter stitch without shaping until hood measures 18 (19) 20 (21) cm / 7 (7½) 8 (8¼) inches.
Row 1 (RS) BO 30 (30) 33 (36) sts. K 28 (29) 29 (29). BO 30 (30) 33 (36) sts.
Row 2 (WS) Rejoin yarn. K to last st. Dbe1. Continue without shaping in Garter stitch until hood measures 12 (12) 13 (14) cm, 4¾ (4¾) 5¼ (5½) inches from cast off sts, ending with a WS row.
BO all sts loosely.
Join side edge at top of hood to 28 (29) 29 (29) cast off sts.

CO 13 sts using 3 mm (US 2) dpn and Col A. (Beige)
Row 1 (RS) K to last st. Dbe1.
Row 2 (WS) Dbe1. M1. K to last st. Dbe1.
Row 3 (RS) Dbe1. K to last st. Dbe1.
Repeat row 2-3 another 4 times.
Continue in Garter stitch until work measures 8.5 cm / 3¼ inches.
Row 1 (RS) Dbe1. K to last st. Dbe1.
Row 2 (WS) Dbe1. K2tog. K to last st. Dbe1.
Repeat row 1-2 another 4 times.
Row 11 (RS) Dbe1. K to last st. Dbe1.
BO all sts loosely. Work other ear the same way.

Finishing
Attach ears to hood with a little fold before stitching.
Weave in all ends.
Fold the longer bit of the sleeve (in col B) to the front and attach in the sides as shown in photo.

Steam your new cardigan and get out to play in the jungle.

Ear

A mother chimpanzee will do anything to protect her child from the poacher. Are we really that different?

Mea Andresen

#REDthumbsup

David Greybeard

Chimpanzee Teen~Adult
Design Mea Andresen
Skill level 5
Photo pg 32 - 33 - 34 - 35

Design Mea Andresen
-loose reversible bomber jacket.
#REDdavidgreybeard

Skill level 5
Sizes
S **(M)** L (XL)
To fit bust
80 (84) 88 (92) cm
31½ (33) 34½ (36) inches
Actual bust measurement (jumper)
104 (108) **112** (116) cm
41 (42½) 44 (45½) inches
Length
58 (60) 62 (64) cm
22¾ (23½) 24¼ (25) inches
Yarn
Önling, No. 1
75% Superfine Wool 25% Selected Angora, 197
yards / 180 meters per 50 g.
Col A Navy, no 3339
6 (7) 8 (9) x 50 grams.
Col B Off White, no 3622
6 (7) 8 (9) x 50 grams.

Zip 46 (48) 50 (52) cm / 18 (19) 19 (20) inches
reversible zipper. Make sure the zipper is 1 cm
shorter than zipper-opening. This way you will
avoid that the zipper is bulky after attaching the
zipper to the front. Therefore buying the zipper
after knitting the jumper is advised.
Elastic 70 (76) 82 (88) cm / 27½ (30) 32½ (35)
inches for body and 2x 21 (22) 23 (24) cm / 8¼
(8¾) 9¼ (10) inches for cuffs. 3 cm/ 1¼ inches in
width for both.
Needles
4.5 mm (US 7) circular needle, 80 cm / 32 inches
+ 60 cm/24 inches.
4.5 mm (US 7) dpn
6 stitch markers
Gauge
In double knitting on 4.5 mm (US 7) needles
and col A + col B: 18 dbs x 26 rows = 10 x 10
cm / 4 x 4 inches.
Remember to check your gauge and adjust
needle size accordingly.
A gauge test for this jacket can be made
following diagram A. This way you will have a
nice hand after making the test.

Knitting sample
Using col A hold double and 4.5 mm (US 7) dpn
CO 32 sts in your usual CO method.
From now on col A is used in single thread.
Row 1 (WS)

Turning CO into double knitting:
Pick up both colours with left hand: Col B is
held to the right and over as well index finger
as long finger. Col A is held to the left as usual
(only over the index finger, see photo.)
*Using Col B work a k1 on one loop of the st.
Moving working yarn to the back, using RH
needle: go behind **both** threads and work a
p1 with Col A on the second loop of the st*.
Repeat *-* to a total of 32 times. *-* is now
called dbsB, as col B is in front in this row.
The 32 sts are now turned into 32 dbs.
Recap.
So this does the trick: *K1 yarn A, go behind
both threads, P1 yarn B*. Repeat from *to*
The "go behind both threads" when working
the p1, is the trick that makes this double
knitting.
The threads travel together to make the
stitches whatever knitting style is used, and
only the correct colour is used.

Row 2 (RS)
Using col A K1 wyib. Using col B P1 wyif.
repeat *-* to a total of 31 times. *-* is now
called **dbsA**, as col A is in front in this row. Last
dbs: Dbye1
Row 3 (WS) Slip 1 st purlwise, work dbsB 30.
Dbye1.
Row 4 (RS) Slip 1 st purlwise, work dbsA 30.
Dbye1
Ro w 5 (WS) Slip 1 st purlwise, work dbsB 30.
Dbye1
Row 6 (RS) Slip 1 st purlwise, work dbsA 15.
Work diagram A. Work dbsA to 1 before end.
Dbye1.
Continue in patt to diagram A is finished. Make
5 more rows as row 3 and 4.
BO all sts loosely using the BOdb.

**Special abbreviations for this pattern
(suggest moving this nearer the beginning
of the text)**
dbs = double stitch
dbsA = double stitch with yarn A in front.
dbsB = double stitch with yarn B in front.
FyC = Front side yarn colour.
ByC = Back side yarn colour.
dbye1 = Double yarn edge stitch. Using both
threads working a k1 on the last st through
both loops
dbe-dk1 = 1 double edge stitch in double
knitting
**dbe-dk1 at the end of a row with yarn B in
front:** Using the LH needle, pick up the strand

of yarn in col B just before the last col B st slip wyib, pick up a strand of yarn col A just before the last col A st slip wyif. Turn work.

1 dbe-dk at the beginning of a row with yarn A in front: Using Ktog col A st and loop tbl wyib. Using col B Ktog col B st and loop tbl wyif. Please note: Work the dbe-dk very loosely.

BOdb = BO by knitting both yarns through both loops.

BO dbk = BO col A sts with col A. BO col b sts with col B.

M1dbs = Make 1 double st. Pick up loop before next st from the front in FyC, k the loop tbl. Pick up loop before next st from the back in ByC, p the loop tbl. (1 dbs increased.)

W&t-dbs = wrap and turn with yarn in double knitting: Holding the front yarn to the front, holding the back yarn at the back now slip next st (FyC) to the RH as if to purl. Bring the yarn to the back. Holding back side yarn to the front, now slip next st (ByC) to RH needle. Move back side yarn to the back. Turn work.

Holding both yarns to the front, slip first st to the RH needle. Move same col yarn to the back. Slip next st to RH needle whilst holding same col yarn to the front. Move that yarn to the back.

The yarn will now be wrapped around the slipped stitch. A small hole will develop at the turning point, but this will close again after working over that spot.

This is how to double knit.
What is double knitting
Double knitting is double the fun and double the trouble. It will take double time before finished, you will however be double proud once completed. You do get two bomber jackets in one. It is simply possible to wear a double knitted jumper with either side in or out.
The trick is to work both sides at the same time.

Who can knit this jacket?
Is it possible to knit this bomber jacket if you never before tried to work in double knitting. If you know how to work k1 and p1, you can do it. We will take you through the technique below.

Important
Working in double knitting, we always have to distinguish between stitches as you know them and double stitches. Double stitches are for short named dbs, and by dbs1 we always mean to mention
one pair of sts: 1st from the RS-layer and 1st from the WS-layer.
It is always worked k1 on the RS and p1 on the WS.
You can never stop half way through a pair in double knitting sts, unless you are increasing or decreasing.
Now let us get to it.
In the chapter Knitting sample, you can learn the technique.

Tip
This jumper will be worked back and forth. Colour A will be on the outside, but as it is reversible you can use both sides out as you please.

Shown in size M

Body
Using col A two strands CO 154 (162) 170 (178) sts using 4.5 (US 7) 80 cm / 32 inches circular needle.

Bottom hem
Row 1 (WS)
Establish the double knitting as in the knitting sample.
The 154 (162) 170 (178) **sts** are now turned into 154 (162) 170 (178) **dbs.**
Row 2 (RS) Work dbsB 153 (161) 169 (177). Dbe-dk1.
Row 3 (WS) Dbe-dk1. Work dbeA 152 (160) 168 (176). Dbe-dk1.
Row 4 (RS) Dbe-dk1. Work dbeB 152 (160) 168 (176). Dbe-dk1.
From now on knit the double edge stitches as on row 3 and 4 if nothing else is indicated. This finish will allow you to attach the zipper between the layers and give you a nice finish.
Row 5-8 Work as row 3 - 4.
Body with pattern
Row 9 (WS) Change colours as follows. Dbe-dk1. Work dbsA 2. *DbsB 1. <u>Twist the yarn</u>*. Repeat *-* to 3 sts before end. DbsA 2. Dbe-dk1.
PLEASE NOTE twisting the yarn is part of the repeat and is important, since this will make sure the elastic stays in place.
Increases
Row 10 (RS) Dbe-dk1. DbsB 2. *M1dbs,
dbsA4*. Repeat *-* to 3 st before end. M1dbs. DbsB 2. Dbe-dk1.
Increase with 38 (49) 42 (44) sts to a total of 192 (202) 212 (222) sts.
From here on continue in double knit following the diagram for the hands and use markers as guidelines.
Placing side seam markers
Row 11 (WS) Dbe-dk1. DbsA 2. Work dbsB 45 (48) 50 (53) sts pm (m2). Work dbsB 96 (100) 106 (110) sts pm (m1). Work dbsB to 3 sts before end. DbsA 2. Dbe-dk1.

Start working diagram for hand 1 and 2
Row 1 (RS) Dbe-dk1. DbsB 2. Work DbsA to 8 (10) 12 (14) sts after (m1). Pm (m3). Work diagram A, starting at **row 19.** Work dbsA to 32 sts before end. Pm (m4). Work diagram A, starting now at **row 4**. DbsA to 3 sts before end. DbsB 2, Dbe-dk1.
Continue following diagrams until work measures 10 (11) 12 (13) cm / 4 (4¼) 4¾ (5) inches.

Start working diagram for the 3rd hand
Row 1 (RS) Dbe-dk1. DbsB 2. Work as set dbsA to 25 (27) 29 (31) sts before (m2). Pm (m5). Work diagram B. Work as set to 3 sts before end. DbsB 2, Dbe-dk1.
Continue following diagrams until work measures 23 (25) 27 (29) cm / 9 (9¾) 10½ (11½) inches. Remove marker when a diagram is finished.

Start working diagram for the 4th hand
Row 1 (RS) Dbe-dk1. DbsB 2. Work as set dbsA to 18 (20) 22 (24) sts after (m1). Pm (m3). Work diagram A. Work as set to 3 sts before end. DbsB 2, Dbe-dk1.
Continue following diagrams until work measures 24 (26) 28 (30) cm / 9½ (10¼) 11 (11¾) inches.

Start working diagram for the 5th hand
Row 1 (RS) Dbe-dk1. DbsB 2. Work as set dbsA 11 sts. Pm (m4). Work diagram B. Work as set to 3 sts before end. DbsB 2, Dbe-dk1.
Continue following diagrams until work measures 34 (36) 38 (40) cm.
AT THE SAME TIME
When work measures 33 (35) 37 (39) cm / 13 (13¾) 14½ (15¼) inches, work armholes from
***

Start working diagram for the 6th hand
Row 1 (RS) Dbe-dk1. DbsB 2. Work as set dbsA to 40 sts before end. Pm (m5). Work diagram A. Work as set to 3 sts before end. DbsB 2, Dbe-dk1.
Continue following diagrams until work measures 37 (39) 41 (43) cm / 14½ (15¼) 16¼ (17) inches.

Start working diagram for the 7th hand
Row 1 (RS) Dbe-dk1. DbsB 2. Work as set dbsA to 23 (25) 27 (29) sts before m2. Pm (mG). Work diagram B. When you reach 2 dbs before m2 end diagram. Work as set to 3 sts before end. DbsB 2, Dbe-dk1.

***Armholes
PLEASE NOTE hands diagram should end 2 dbs before armhole markers.
Row 1 (RS) Work as set 47 (49) 51 (54) dbs, BO 4 dbs loosely: *Place 1 st col A on spare needle in front of work and 1 sts col B on spare needle in back of work to a total of 5 sts on each spare needle. BO 4 in col A loosely. Keep the 5th st on right needle. BO 4 in yarn B loosely. Keep the 5th st on right needle.*
Work 92 (96) 102 (106) sts (inc the st on right needle from before), BO 4 sts loosely by repeating *-*. Work to end.
The work has now been divided into left front, right front and back. 46 (49) 51 (54) sts on front and 92 (96) 102 (106) sts on back.
Set body aside and work the sleeves.

Sleeve
Using col A hold double CO 50 (50) 50 (55) sts using 4.5 (US 7) circular needle working back and forth.
Cuff panel
Row 1 (WS) Now add colour B and establish double knit as for body. Work dbsA 50 (50) 50 (55).
Row 2 (RS) Work dbsB 49 (49) 49 (54) sts. Dbe-dk1.
Row 3 (WS) Dbe-dk1. Work dbsA 48 (48) 48 (53) sts. Dbe-dk1.
Row 4 (RS) Dbe-dk1. Work dbsB 48 (48) 48 (53) sts. Dbe-dk1.
Row 5-8 Knit as row 3-4.
Row 9 (WS) Dbe-dk1. *DbsB 1. Twist the yarn* repeat *-* to 1 st before end. Dbe-dk1. It is important to twist the yarn.
Join the work and continue in round.

Sleeve
Round 1 (RS) Change colours as follows
Pm (m1). DbsA 2. *M1dbs, dbsA 5*. Repeat *-* to 3 st before end. M1dbs. DbsA 3.
There are now 60 (60) 60 (67) dbs.
Round 2 (RS) Work dbsA on all sts.
Round 3-9 continue in dbsA.
Increases
Round 10 DbsA 2. M1dbs. Work dbsA to 2 st before end. M1dbs. DbsA 2. There are now 62 (62) 62 (69) dbs.
Continue in dbsA. Work the increase round on every 10th (10th) 10th (10th) round to a total of 70 (74) 78 (82) dbs. Continue straight until work measures 49 (50) 51 (52) cm / 19¼ (19½) 20 (20¼) inches.
Last round Patt to 2 sts before end. BO 4 sts as follows. *BO 1 st in yarn B knitwise. Place this st on spare needle. BO 1 st in yarn A purlwise.* repeat *-* 3 more times. Set work aside and work the other sleeve in the same way.

Joining body and sleeves
Join front, back and sleeves on the circular needle.
We will now place new markers.
Row 1 (RS) Begin at right front.
Patt across front 46 (49) 51 (54) dbs. Pm (m1). Work dbsA right sleeve 66 (70) 74 (78) dbs onto same needle. Pm (m2).
Patt across back 92 (96) 102 (106) dbs. Pm (m3). Work dbsA left sleeve 66 (70) 74 (78) dbs onto same needle. Pm (m4).
Patt across left front. 46 (49) 51 (54) dbs.
All 316 (334) 352 (370) dbs are now joined on one needle.
Row 2 (WS) Patt across all sts as set.
Decreases, raglan
Row 3 (RS) Patt to 3 sts before m1. *K2dbtog, dbsA 1, sm, dbsA 1, K2dbtog*. Repeat *-* at 3 sts before m2, m3 and m4. (8 sts decreased, 304 (322) 340 (358) dbs)
Row 4 (WS) Work as set without decreases.
Repeat row 3 - 4 until 12 (12) 12 (12) dbs remain on each sleeve, 19 (20) 20 (21) dbs on front, 38 (38) 40 (40) dbs on back.

Shaping neck opening
Still continue the raglan decreases.
Row 1 (RS) Patt to 14 dbs before end. W&t-dbs.
Row 2 (WS) Pat to 14 dbs before end. W&t-dbs.
Row 3 (RS) Patt to 6 dbs before last. W&t-dbs.
Row 4 (WS) Patt to 6 dbs before lats. W&t-dbs.

Repeat row 3 - 4 for another 2 (2) 2 (2) times. BOdb all sts tight. Tight to give the jacket a firm collar that will stay in shape.

Collar
Using col A two strands CO 150 (150) 152 (152) sts using 4.5mm (US 7) circular needle working back and forth.
Row 1 (WS) Now add colour B and establish double knit by working dbsA 150 (150) 152 (152) sts.
Row 2 (RS) Work dbsB to 4 dbs before end. Turn
Row 3 (WS) Work dbsA to 4 dbs before end. Turn
Row 4 (RS) Work dbsB to 2 dbs before last. Turn
Row 5 (WS) Work dbsA to 2 dbs before last. Turn
Repeat row 4 - 5 for 1 more time.
Row 8 (RS) Work dbsB across all sts.
Separating the two layers
Row 9 (WS) *Using col A K1 wyib, using spare needle and col B P1* repeat *-* to end.
Work is now separated with sts in yarn A on one needle and sts in yarn B on another.
BO all sts from main needle in yarn A. BO all sts from spare needle in yarn B.

Finishing
Attach collar outside neck opening on both the inside and the outside. This will hide the **BOdb** at the neck. Sew down the collar from both sides.

Attach the zipper by placing the zipper between the two layers. See pictures for guide in zipper placement. Sew down the inner layer to the zipper. Sew the elastic at the bottom hem to the zipper. Sew down the outer layer to the zipper. By this the elastic is hidden in the bottom hem panel.
Place the elastic in the cuff rib panel. Sew the two ends together. Close the panel opening. Repeat this on the other sleeve.

Weave in all ends.
Steam your new jacket.
Your new bomber jacket is ready for work in town. Find your favorite side for the day.

Diagram A

Diagram B

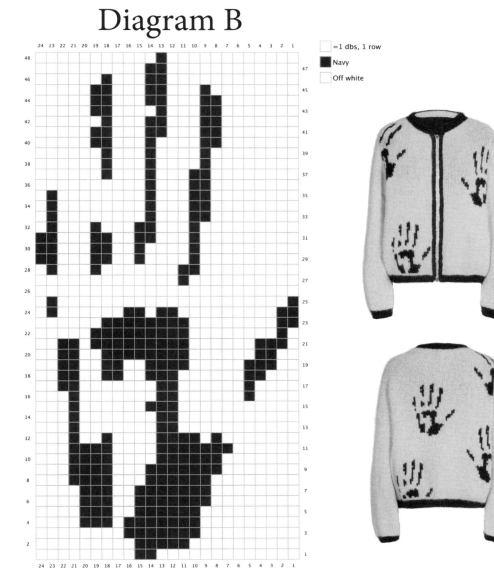

= 1 dbs, 1 row

Navy

Off white

David Greybeard, the first Chimpanzee, that allowed Dr Jane Goodall enter into their world.
Is it the hand of a human or a chimpanzee? You tell me.

Mea Andresen, designer

#REDdavidgreybeard

Peek-a-boo

Wild Dog Child
Design Mea Andresen
Skill level 3
Photo pg 20 - 21

Design Mea Andresen
-a jumper with raglan sleeves and separate ears
you can play Peek-a-boo with.
#REDpeekaboo

Skill level 2
Sizes
EU 86 **(98)** 110 (122)
UK 12 – 18 months (2-3) 4-5 (6-7) years
To fit bust
53 (54.5) 58 (63) cm
20¾ (21½) 22¾ (25¼) inches
Actual bust measurement (jumper)
64 (67) 70 (76) cm
25¼ (26¼) 27½ (30) inches
Length
34 (36) 40 (44) cm
13½ (14¼) 15¾ (17½) inches
Yarn
Isager, Alpaca 1
100% Alpaca, 437 yards / 400 m per 50 g.
Colour A: 1 (1) 1 (1) x 50 g Shade 3, Mustard
Colour B: 1 (2) 2 (2) x 50 g Shade 61, Old Rose
Colour C: 1 (1) 1 (1) x 50 g ECO 0, White
Colour D: 1 (1) 1 (1) x 50 g ECO 8S, Brown
Colour E: 1 (1) 1 (1) x 50 g Shade 30, Black
Needles
3 mm (US 2) circular needle, 40 cm (16 inches)
or 60 cm (24 inches).
3 mm (US 2) dpn
4 st markers.

PLEASE NOTE: Moss Stitch is the UK
terminology and is the same as Seed Stitch, the
US terminology.

Gauge
In moss st on 3 mm (US 2) needles and 2
threads of yarn: 23 sts x 50 rows = 10 x 10 cm/4
x 4 inches.
Remember to check your gauge and adjust
needle size accordingly.
Patterns used
2by2 rib patt.
Row 1 k2, p2.
Row 2 k2, p2.
Moss st patt
Row 1 k1, p1.
Row 2 p1, k1.
To continue in moss st patt:
Always work P st over a knit st and knit st over a
P st.
Shown in size 98 (UK 2-3 years)
Tip: In this jumper we will change Cols
gradually always following this patt:

Round 1 New Yarn Col
Round 2 Old Yarn Col
Round 3 Old Yarn Col
Round 4 New Yarn Col
Round 5 New Yarn Col
Round 6 Old Yarn Col
Round 7 New Yarn Col

Body
CO 148 (152) 162 (170) sts using 3 mm (US 2) 40
(40) 60 (60) cm / 16 (16) 24 (24) inches circular
needle and yarn in Col A+A (2 threads of
Mustard). Join for working in the round.

Rib pattern
Round 1 Pm (m1). *K2, p2*. Repeat to end.
Round 2 - 12 Work rib patt as set.

Moss stitch pattern and increase
From now on we will work the moss st patt.
Round 13 *K1, p1*. Repeat to end. M1.
There are now 149 (153) 163 (171) sts.
The uneven number makes it easier to maintain
the moss st patt.
Round 14 *P1, k1*. Repeat to end.
Please note: The jumper is worked in moss st
from now on.
Follow instructions below regarding yarn colour
changes.
Continue in Col A+A until work measures 5 (6) 7
(8) cm / 2 (2½) 3 (3½) inches.
Change to Cols: A+B. Follow the tip to how you
change the Cols.
Continue in Col A+B until work measures 8 (9)
10.5 (12) cm / 3 (3½) 4 (4½) inches. Change to
Col B+B.
Continue in Col B+B until work measures 16
(18) 20.5 (23) cm / 6 (7) 8 (9) inches. Change to
Col B+C.
Continue in Col B+C until work measures 19
(21) 23.5 (27) cm / 7½ (8½) 9½ (10½) inches.
Change to Col C+C.
Continue in Col C+C until work measures 22
(24) 27 (30.5) cm / 8½ (9½) 10½ (12) inches.
Change to Col C+D.
Continue in Col C+D until work measures 24
(25.5) 29 (31.5) cm / 9½ (10½) 11½ (12½) inches.
Change to Col D+E, BUT here you need to do
it a different way:
Round 1 D+E
Round 2 D+D
Round 3 D+D
Round 4 D+E
Round 5 D+E
Round 6 D+D

Round 7 and on D+E
Continue until work measures 25.5 (27) 30.5 (34) cm / 10 (10½) 12 (13½) inches.

Armhole
Work 74 (76) 81 (85) sts. BO 2 sts loosely. Work to 1 st before m1, BO 3 sts loosely.
The work has now been divided into front and back with 72 (74) 79 (83) sts on each side.
Leave sts on hold while working the sleeves.

Sleeves
CO 34 (36) 40 (46) sts using 3 mm (US 2.5) dpns and yarn in Col A+A (2 threads of Mustard).
Join for working in the round.
Round 1 *K2, p2*. Repeat *-* to end.
Round 2 - 4 Work rib as set.

Moss stitch pattern and increase
From now on we will work the moss st patt.
Round 5 *K1, p1*. Repeat to end. M1.
There are now 35 (37) 41 (47) st.
Round 6 *P1, k1*. Repeat to end.

Increases
Round 1 Work 1 sts as set, M1. Work to last st, M1, work 1st. (2 sts increased)
There are now 37 (39) 43 (49) sts.
Round 2 - 9 (10) 11 (13) Work in patt as set without increases.
Repeat row 1 - 9 (10) 11 (13) thus working the increase round on every 9th (10th) 11th (13th) round to a total of 55 (57) 61 (67) sts.

Follow instructions below regarding yarn Col changes.
Continue in Col A+A until work measures 5 (6) 7 (8) cm / 2 (2½) 3 (3½) inches.
Change to Cols: A+B. Follow the tip to how you change the Cols.
Continue in Col A+B until work measures 8 (9) 10.5 (12) cm / 3 (3½) 4 (4½) inches. Change to Col B+B.
Continue in Col B+B until work measures 16 (18) 20.5 (23) cm / 6 (7) 8 (9) inches. Change to Col B+C.
Continue in Col B+C until work measures 19 (21) 23.5 (27) cm / 7½ (8½) 9½ (10½) inches. Change to Col C+C.
Continue in Col C+C until work measures 22 (24) 27 (30.5) cm / 8½ (9½) 10½ (12) inches. Change to Col C+D.
Continue in Col C+D until work measures 24

(25.5) 29 (31.5) cm / 9½ (10½) 11½ (12½) inches.
Change to Col D+E, BUT here you need to do it a different way:
Round 1 D+E
Round 2 D+D
Round 3 D+D
Round 4 D+E
Round 5 D+E
Round 6 D+D
Round 7 and on D+E
Continue straight until sleeve measures 24 (28) 32 (36) cm / 9½ (11) 12½ (14¼) inches.
Sleevehole:
Work as set to last 1 sts, BO 2 sts loosely.
There are 53 (55) 59 (65) sts.
Set the sleeve aside while working the other sleeve the same way.

Joining all pieces for working in the round use yarn D+E
Round 1 (RS)
Beg at left sleeve using the needle where the body sts are resting: 3 mm (US 2.5) circular needle, 60 cm (24 inches).
Pm (m1). Work moss st patt all 53 (55) 59 (65) sts of one sleeve onto the needle (left sleeve).
Pm (m2) Work moss st patt as set across all front 72 (74) 79 (83) sts onto the same needle.
Pm (m3) Work moss st patt all 53 (55) 59 (65) sts of right sleeve sts onto the same needle.
Pm (m4). Work moss st patt across all back 72 (74) 79 (83) sts.
All 250 (258) 276 (296) sts are now joined on one needle.
Round 2 K2, work to 2 st before m2. K4. Work to 2 st before m3. K4. Work to 2 st before m4. K4. Work to 2 st before m1. K2.
Round 3 decreases K2, k2tog. Work to 4 sts before m2. K2tog tbl, k4, k2tog. Work to 4 sts before m3. K2tog tbl, k4, k2tog. Work to 4 sts before m4. K2tog tbl, k4, k2tog. Work to 4 sts before m1. K2tog tbl, k2. (8 sts decreased)
When making the decreases follow your moss st patt making k2tog or p2tog suiting the following moss st.
Repeat round 2 - 3 until work measures 29 (31) 35 (39) cm / 11½ (12) 13½ (15) inches.
Splitting the work
We will now separate the front from the rest.
Row 1 (RS) Work to m2. Remove marker. Turn.
Still working the 2 sts before and after m4 and m1 RS: k2, WS: p2 from here on.
Row 2 (WS) CO 6 sts using knitted CO. Work

new sts: p6. Work patt as set to m3. Remove marker. Turn.
Row 3 (RS) CO 6 sts using knitted CO. Work new sts: k6. Work patt as set to last st. Dbe1.
Front is now separated from the rest. Place sts from front on spare needle.
Row 4 (WS) Dbe1. p7, work moss st to 8 sts before end. P7, Dbe1.
Row 5 (RS) Dbe1. k7, k2tog. Work to 4 sts before m4. K2tog tbl, k4, k2tog.
Work to 4 sts before m1. K2tog tbl, k4, k2tog.
Work to 10 sts before end. K2tog tbl, k7, Dbe1.
When making the decreases follow your moss st patt making k2tog or p2tog suiting the following moss st.
Row 6 (WS) Dbe1. p7. Work to 8 sts before end. P7, Dbe1.
Repeat row 3 - 4 another 4 times.
Row 1 (RS) as Row 5.
Row 2 (WS) Dbe1. k7. *K3, k2tog*. Repeat from *-* to 8 sts before end while removing m4 and m1. K7. Dbe1.

Neckline, sleeves and back
You can choose to make normal easy 2by2 rib from here or make the special double tuckstich rib. Do what suits your desire and skills.
Double tuck st is described in this text:
Row 1 (RS) Col D+E (black+brown) Dbe1. k7. *k1, sl1yo*. Repeat from *-* to 8 sts before end. K7, Dbe1.
PLEASE NOTE: The yarn over is worked on the same st in row 1 and two. Then in row 3 it is worked as a brioche st (ktog).
On row 4 and 5 the yarn over is worked on the same st again. On row 6 it is worked as a brioche knit/purl (brk/brp).
Row 2 (WS) Col D+E (black+brown) Dbe1. p7, *sl1yo2, p1*. Repeat from *-* to 8 sts before end. P7. Dbe1.
Row 3 (RS) Slip 8 sts from left needle to right needle without knitting them. Change to **Col B+C** (white + rose) *k1, brk1*. Rep from *-* to 8 sts before end. Slip 8 sts from left needle to right needle without knitting them. Do not turn, make next row also from RS.
Row 4 (RS) Col D+E Dbe1. K7, *k1, sl1yo*. Repeat from *-* to 8 sts before end. K7. Dbe1.
Row 5 (WS) Col D+E Dbe1. p7, *sl1yo2, p1*. Repeat from *-* to 8 sts before end. P7. Dbe1.
Do not turn, make next row also from WS.
Row 6 (WS) Slip 8 sts from left needle to right needle without working them. Change to **Col**

B+C,*brp1, p1*. Repeat from *-* to 8 sts before end. Slip 8 sts from left needle to right needle without knitting them.
Row 7-12 repeat row 1 - 6.
Row 13 (RS) Col D+E. BO all sts loosely.

Front

Use the sts you placed on the spare needle when splitting the work.
Row 1 (RS) CO 4 sts using knitted CO. Work new sts: k4.
K2, k2tog. Work moss st patt to 4 sts before end. K2tog tbl, k2.
Row 2 (WS) CO 4 sts using knitted CO. Work new sts: p4.
P2, work moss st patt to 6 sts before end. P5. Dbe1.
Row 3 (RS) Dbe1. k5, k2tog. Work to 8 sts before end. K2tog tbl, k5, Dbe1.
Row 4 (WS) Dbe1. p5. Work to 6 sts before end. P5, Dbe1.
Repeat row 3 - 4 another 4 times.
AT THE SAME TIME
Make Buttonholes on row 7 like this: Dbe1. k1, 2yo. BO 2, k2. Work to 6 before end. K2, 2yo, BO 2, k1. Dbe1. Row 8 Work 2 new sts on the 2 yo at each end.
Row 13 (RS) Work as row 3, but with buttonholes.
Row 14 (WS) Dbe1. k5. *K3, k2tog*. Repeat from *-* to 6 sts before end. K5. Dbe1.

Neckline, front

Work 2by2 rib or double tuck st. We will describe the double tuck st.
Row 1 (RS) Col D+E (black+brown) Dbe1. k5. *k1, sl1yo*. Repeat from *-* to 6 sts before end. K5, Dbe1.
Row 2 (WS) Col D+E (black+brown) Dbe1. p5, *sl1yo2, p1*. Repeat from *-* to 6 sts before end. P5. Dbe1.
Row 3 (RS) Slip 6 sts from left needle to right needle without knitting them. Change to **Col B+C** (white + rose) *k1, brk1*. Rep from *-* to 6 sts before end. Slip 6 sts from left needle to right needle without knitting them. Do not turn, make next row also from RS.
Row 4 (RS) Col D+E Dbe1. K5, *k1, sl1yo*. Repeat from *-* to 6 sts before end. K5, Dbe1.
Row 5 (WS) Col D+E Dbe1. p5, *sl1yo2, p1*. Repeat from *-* to 6 sts before end. P5. Dbe1. Do not turn, make next row also from WS.
Row 6 (WS) Slip 6 sts from left needle to right needle without working them. Change to **Col**

B+C,*brp1, p1*. Repeat from *-* to 6 sts before end. Slip 6 sts from left needle to right needle without knitting them.
Row 7-12 repeat row 1 - 6.
Row 13 (RS) Col D+E. BO all sts loosely.

AT THE SAME TIME
Make Buttonholes in the neckline on row 7. Dbe1. k1, 2yo. BO 2, k2. Work to 6 before end. K2, 2yo, BO 2, k1. Dbe1.

Ears

CO 32 (35) 41 (44) sts using 3 mm (US 2.5) dpns and yarn in Col D+E (Brown and Black)
Row 1 (WS) P to end.
Row 2 (RS) Col D+E Dbe1. k5. *k1, sl1yo*. Repeat from *-* to 6 sts before end. K5. Dbe1. Continue working double tuck st for 11 more rows, same number of sts and colours as for neckline front.
AT THE SAME TIME
Make Buttonholes on row 7. Dbe1. k1, 2yo. BO 2, k2. Work to 6 before end. K2, 2yo, BO 2, k1. Dbe1.
From here on use only Col D+E.
Row 13 (RS) Dbe1. k5. *k3, M1*. Repeat from *-* to 6 sts before end. K5. Dbe1.
Increase with 6 (7) 9 (10) sts.
Row 14 (WS) Dbe1. p5. Work moss st patt to 6 before end. P5. Dbe1.
Work 8 more rows as set.
Row 23 (RS) Dbe1. k5, M1, work moss st patt to 6 sts before end. M1, k5. Dbe1.
Row 24 (WS) Work as set.
Repeat Row 23 - 24 for 2 more times.
Work 2 rows as set without increase.
Repeat row 23 - 24. 46 (50) 58 (62) sts.

Splitting to two ears

Row 1 (RS) Work 21 (23) 27 (29) sts as set. BO 4 sts. Work to end.

Left ear

Row 2 (WS) Work 21 (23) 27 (29) sts. Turn.
Row 3 (RS) CO 6 sts using knitted CO. Work new sts in k. K1, M1, work moss st patt to 6 before end, M1, k5. Dbe1.
Row 4 (WS) Work as set to 6 sts before end. P6.
Row 5 (RS) K 6 sts. K1, M1, work moss st patt to 6 before end, M1, k5. Dbe1.
Row 6 (WS) Work as set to 6 sts before end.
Row 7 - 8 Repeat 5 - 6.
Work 22 rows as set without increases.
*Row 1 (RS)** Dbe1. K5, p2tog. Moss st patt to 8 before end. P2tog, K5. Dbe1.

Row 2 - 4 without decreases.
Row 5 (RS) Dbe1. K5, p2tog, work to end.
Row 6 - 8 Work patt as set without decreases.*
Repeat *-* until you have 23 sts left.
Row 1 (RS) Dbe1. K5, p2tog, Moss st patt to 8 before end. P2tog, k5. Dbe1.
Row 2 (WS) Work as set without decreases.
Repeat row 1-2 until you have 13 sts left.
Stitch the last 13 sts tog with mattress st allowing the edge to roll.

Right ear

Row 1 (RS) Work the 21 (23) 27 (29) sts. Turn.
Row 2 (WS) CO 6 sts using knitted CO. Work new sts in P. P1, work moss st patt to 6 before end, p5. Dbe1.
Row 3 (RS) Dbe1. K5, M1, work moss st patt to 6 before end, M1, k5. Dbe1.
Row 4 (WS) Work as set.
Row 5 - 8 Repeat row 3 and 4.
Work 22 rows as set without increases.
*Row 1 (RS)** Dbe1. K5, p2tog. Moss st patt to 8 before end. P2tog, k5. Dbe1.
Row 2 - 4 without decreases.
Row 5 (RS) Work to 8 before end. P2tog, K5. Dbe1.
Row 6 - 8 Work patt as set without decreases.*
Repeat *-* until you have 23 sts left.
Row 1 (RS) Dbe1. K5, p2tog. Moss st patt to 8 before end. P2tog, K5. Dbe1.
Row 2 (WS) Work as set without decreases.
Repeat row 1 - 2 until 13 sts remain.
Stitch the last 13 sts tog with mattress st allowing the edge to roll.

Finishing

Fold the neckline placket from the sleeve side halfway vertically and sew.
Attach the neckline placket from the front on top of the placket from the sleeve. Sew on the 6 buttons on the neckline placket.
Sew the end of both ears at the center of the ear piece.
Close the holes under the arms.
Weave in all ends.
Steam your new sweater.
Attach the ears and play Peek-a-boo.

Peek-a-boo is my favourite game. Where are you?
Mea Andresen

#REDpeekaboo

Unseen

African Wild Dog Teen~Adult
Design Mea Andresen
Skill level 3
Photo pg 22 - 23

Design Mea Andresen
- a loose jumper with dropped shoulders..
#REDunseen

Skill level 4
Sizes
EU 34 (36) 38 (40)
UK 8 (10) 12 (14)
To fit bust
80 (84) 88 (92) cm
31½ (33) 34½ (36) inches
Actual bust measurement (jumper)
104 (108) 112 (116) cm
41 (42½) 44 (45½) inches
Actual waist measurement (jumper)
88 (92) 96 (100) cm
34½ (36¼) 38 (39½) inches
Length
58 (60) 62 (64) cm
22¾ (23½) 24¼ (25) inches
Yarn A
MadelinetTosh, Tosh Merino Light
100% Merino Wool, 420 yards / 384 meters per
112 g.
2 (2) 2 (2) x 112 g in Modern Fair Isle 306,
Cream.
Yarn B
MadelinetTosh, Tosh Merino Light
100% Merino Wool, 420 yards / 384 meters per
112 g.
1 (1) 1 (1) x 112 g in The Wildlings 440, Purple.
Yarn C
MadelinetTosh, Prairie. You will be using 2
threads of this yarn.
100% Merino Wool, 840 yards / 768 meters per
112 g.
2 (2) 2 (3) x 112 g in Whiskey Barrel 255, Brown.
Needles
4 mm (US 6) circular needle, 80 cm (32 inches)
4 mm (US 6) circular needle, 40 cm (16 inches)
3.5 mm (US 4) circular needle, 40 cm (16 inches)
3.5 mm (US 4) circular needle + dpn
4 stitch markers.
Gauge
In stocking stitch on 4 mm (US 6) needles and
yarn A: 24 sts x 33 rows = 10 x 10 cm / 4 x 4
inches.
In moss stitch pattern* on 4 mm (US 6) needles
and yarn A: 24 sts x 42 rows = 10 x 10 cm / 4 x 4
inches.
In double tuck stitch on 4 mm (US 6) needles
and yarn A: 21 sts = 10 cm/ 4 inches. Height on
rows in double tuck stitch is not important.

*) PLEASE NOTE: Moss Stitch is the UK
terminology and is the same as Seed Stitch, the
US terminology.

Remember to check your gauge and adjust
needle size accordingly.

Shown in size 38.

Tip
This jumper will be back and forth in intarsia.
Intarsia: working with **color** spots created by
separate mini skeins that are **not** "traveling
along on the WS of the knitting" (as it is for
Fair Isle knitting), but one mini skein only to be
used on this particular spot. Prepare mini skeins
to use where the patterns demand it.
This pattern is very complex and even for the
most skilled knitter, there will be small flaws.
Don't go back and remake if you made one
brown stitch where you were supposed to
have a white. This will only make your jumper
unique, and remember no wild dog has the
exact same pattern.

Sleeves
Beginning with the sleeves you will be familiar
with the technique of knitting this complex
pattern before working the full body.
CO 44 (44) 44 (48) sts using 3.5 mm (US 4) dpn
and 2 threads of yarn C.
Round 1 (WS) P to end. Gather for working in
the round on the dpn.
Tuck stitch patterns
Round 1 Yarn A, White. *k1, sl1yo*. Rrepeat
from *-* to end.
Round 2 Yarn A, White. *k1, sl1yo2*. Rrepeat
from *-* to end.
Round 3 Yarn C, Brown, 2 threads. *k1,
brk1^2*. Repeat from *-* to end.
Round 4 Yarn A, White. *k1, sl1yo*. Repeat
from *-* to end.
Round 5 Yarn A, White. *k1, sl1yo2*. Repeat
from *-* to end.
Row 6 Yarn C, Brown, 2 threads. *k1,
brk1^2*. Repeat from *-* to end.
Repeat round 1 - 6 until work measures 5 cm /
2 inches.
Round 1 (RS) Yarn C, Brown, 2 threads. K to
end. Break the yarn.
Change to 4 mm (US 6) circular needle, 40 cm
(16 inches) and yarn A.
We are using circular needles even though we
are back and forth.

This is better for your hands and shoulders.
Row 1 (RS) *K5, M1*. Rrepeat ***-*** to end. (increase with 8 sts) Turn.
Row 2 (WS) P all sts to the end.
Row 3 - 6 Continue in stocking stitch.

Increase
Row 7 (RS) Work 1, M1. Work to last st, M1, work 1. (increase with 2 sts)
Continue in stocking stitch patt, working the increase round on every 8th (8th) 8th (8th) row to a total of 88 (92) 96 (100) sts. Continue straight until work measures 45 (47) 49 (50) cm / 17¾ (18½) 19¼ (19¾) inches.
AT THE SAME TIME
When you reach increase number 5 begin:
Sleeves diagram for Wild dog
From now on work in back and forth following the diagram. Please remember to twist yarn in **colour** changes. When the diagram ends, continue in Yarn C moss st patt as established.

Shaping the sleeve cap
Row 1 (RS) BO 11 (12) 13 (14) sts loosely. Patt to end.
Row 2 (WS) BO 11 (12) 13 (14) sts loosely. Patt to end.
Row 3 (RS) BO 10 (10) 10 (10) sts loosely. Patt to end.
Row 4 (WS) BO 10 (10) 10 (10) sts loosely. Patt to end.
Row 5 (RS) BO 10 (10) 10 (10) sts loosely. Patt to end.
Row 6 (WS) BO 10 (10) 10 (10) sts loosely. Patt to end.
Row 7 (RS) BO 26 (28) 30 (32) sts loosely. BO all remaining sts loosely.

Work the other sleeve in exactly the same way. In this way the sleeves will be identical and not inverted, and that is intentional. Once we sew the sleeves to the body it will have this deliberately non-symmetrical look.

Body
CO 212 (220) 232 (240) sts using 4 mm (US 6) 80 cm (32 inches) circular needle and yarn A. Gather for working in the round.
Work Rib
Round 1 Pm m1, *K2, p2*. Repeat *-* to end.
Round 2 Work rib as set until work measures 4 (4) 4 (4) cm / 1½ (1½) 1½ (1½) inches.

Change to moss rib pattern.

Round 1 *K4, p1, k1, p1, k1, p1, p1* repeat ***-*** to end.
Round 2 *K4, p1, p1, k1, p1, k1, p1* repeat ***-*** to end.
These two rounds will make the moss rib patt.
Repeat round 1 - 2 until work measures 7 (7) 7 (7) cm / 2¾ (2¾) 2¾ (2¾) inches in total.

Body
We will now work the "turning maneuver"
Please note: The jumper is worked back and forth in order to be able to work the patt. This is achieved by working a particular "turning maneuver".
Row 1 (RS) Pm (m1). K106 (110) **116** (120) sts. Pm (m2). K to end. Sm. Pick up the loop before next sts with the left needle and k the loop tbl – this will be the turning st. Turn to work the next row from the WS on the "inside" of the round. This new st is referred to as "the turning st" and will not be counted in the st number.
Row 2 (WS) P to 2 sts before m1. P1. W&t wyif (on the turning st).
Row 3 (RS) K to m1. Sm. P1 (= turning st). Turn.
Row 4 (WS) Sl 1 purlwise wyif (= turning st). Sm. P to 2 sts before m1, k1. W&t wyif.
Recap
Regarding the turning stitch: The turning stitch is only actually worked (purled) at the end of every other RS row (as row 3), that is on every 4th row. On all other rows the turning stitch is wrapped and turned. This makes the stitch relax into the pattern and appear like a seam. Continue working this turning maneuver.

AT THE SAME TIME
When work measures 10 (10) 10 (10) cm / 4 (4) 4 (4) inches from the bottom edge, start making increases.

Increase
Row 1 (RS) Work 1, M1, patt across front to 1 sts before m2. M1, work 1. Sm. Work 1, M1, patt across back to 1 sts before m1. M1, work 1. There are now 216 (224) 236 (244) sts.
Row 2 -12 Work patt without increases.
Continue in patt, working the increase row on every 12th row to a total of 252 (260) 272 (280) sts.
AT THE SAME TIME
Row 7 From now on follow Body diagram from line 1 in diagram. Work the front sts according to diagram and then repeat diagram on the back sts.
Continue straight until work measures 38 (39) 40 (41) cm / 15 (15½) 16 (16½) inches.

Sleeve hole
Work to 2 sts before m2. BO 4 sts loosely. Work to last 2 sts, BO 5 sts loosely (removing the turning stitch). Working all stitches as indicated by diagram.
The work has now been divided into front and back with 122 (126) 132 (136) sts on each side. Continue shaping front and back separate still following the patt. When diagram ends continue in Moss stitch in yarn C.

Body Front
Continue in patt following diagram for another 13 (13) 15 (15) rows without shaping.
PLEASE NOTE: When the diagram ends, continue in Yarn C moss st patt as established.

Increase
Row 1 (RS)
Work 1, M1. Patt across front to 2 sts before end. M1, work 1. (2 st increase)
Working the increase row on every 14th (14th) 16th (16th) row to a total of 132 (136) 142 (146) sts.

Neck opening
When work measures 45.5 (47) 49 (51) cm / 18 (18½) 19¼ (20) inches begin shaping the neck.
Row 1 (RS) Patt 55 (57) 59 (61) sts. BO 16 (16) 18 (18) sts. Patt to end. Front is now divided into right and left front.

Right front
PLEASE NOTE: Remember to make the increases at the armhole.
Row 2 (WS) Patt to end.
Row 3 (RS) BO 2 sts. Patt to end.
Repeat row 2 - 3 another 4 times.
Row 12 (RS) BO 1 sts. Patt to end.
Make decreases as row 12 on every 4th (4th) 6th (6th) row in total of 5 times.
There are now 43 (45) 47 (49) sts.
Continue without decreases until work measures 56 (58) 60 (62) cm /22 (22¾) 23½ (24½) inches.

Shoulder slanting
Row 1 (RS) Patt to 10 sts before end. W&t.
Row 2 (WS) Patt to end.
Row 3 (RS) Patt to 20 sts before end. W&t.
Row 4 (WS) Patt to end.
Row 5 (RS) Patt to 30 sts before end. W&t.
Row 6 (WS) Patt to end.
Row 7 (RS) Patt across all sts to end.

Row 8 (WS) BO all sts loosely.

Left front
PLEASE NOTE: Remember to make the increases at the armhole.
Row 1 (RS) Patt to end.
Row 2 (WS) BO 2 sts. Patt to end.
Repeat row 1-2 another 4 times.
Row 11 (RS) Patt to end.
Row 12 (WS) BO 1 sts. Patt to end.
Make decreases as row 12 on every 4th (4th) 6th (6th) row in total 5 times.
You now have 43 (45) 47 (49) sts.
Continue without decreases until work measures 56 (58) 60 (62) cm /22 (22¾) 23½ (24½) inches.

Shoulder slanting
Row 1 (WS) Patt to 10 sts before end. W&t.
Row 2 (RS) Patt to end.
Row 3 (WS) Patt to 20 sts before end. W&t.
Row 4 (RS) Patt to end.
Row 5 (WS) Patt to 30 sts before end. W&t.
Row 6 (RS) Patt to end.
Row 7 (WS) Patt across all sts to end.
Row 8 (RS) BO all sts loosely.

Body Back
Beginning on WS.
Continue in patt following diagram for 13 (13) 15 (15) rows.
PLEASE NOTE: When the diagram ends, continue in Yarn C moss st patt as established.

Increase
Row 1 (RS) Work 1. M1. Patt across back to 2 sts before end. M1. Work 1. (2 st increase)
Work the increase row on every 14th (14th) 16th (16th) row to a total of 132 (136) 142 (146) sts.

Neck opening back
When work measures 53.5 (55.5) 57.5 (59.5) cm / 21 (21¾) 22½ (23½) inches begin shaping the neck. Make sure to end with a WS row.
Row 1 (RS) Patt 52 (54) 56 (58) sts. BO 28 (28) 30 (30) sts. Patt to end. Back is now divided into right and left back.

Left Back
Row 2 (WS) Patt to end.
Row 3 (RS) BO 2 sts. Patt to end.
Repeat row 2 - 3 another 3 times.

Row 10 (WS) Patt to end.
Row 11 (RS) BO 1 st. Patt to end.
Row 12 (WS) Patt to end.

Shoulder slanting
Row 1 (RS) Patt to 10 sts before end. W&t.
Row 2 (WS) Patt to end.
Row 3 (RS) Patt to 20 sts before end. W&t.
Row 4 (WS) Patt to end.
Row 5 (RS) Patt to 30 sts before end. W&t.
Row 6 (WS) Patt to end.
Row 7 (RS) Patt across all sts to end.
There are now 43 (45) 47 (49) sts.
BO all sts loosely.

Right Back
Row 1 (RS) Patt to end.
Row 2 (WS) BO 2 sts. Patt to end.
Repeat row 1 - 2 another 3 times.
Row 9 (RS) Patt to end.
Row 10 (WS) BO 1 sts. Patt to end.
Row 11 (RS) Patt to end.

Shoulder slanting
Row 1 (WS) Patt to 10 sts before end. W&t.
Row 2 (RS) Patt to end.
Row 3 (WS) Patt to 20 sts before end. W&t.
Row 4 (RS) Patt to end.
Row 5 (WS) Patt to 30 sts before end. W&t.
Row 6 (RS) Patt to end.
Row 7 (WS) Patt across all sts to end.
There are now 43 (45) 47 (49) sts.
BO all sts loosely.

Neckline
Sew shoulder seam together before making the neckline.
Using 3.5 mm (US 4) circular needle and yarn C 2 threads, pick up and K120 (124) 124 (128) sts along the neckline.
Place m1 at left shoulder point.
Round 1 (RS) *K3, k2tog*. Repeat *-* to end.
You now have 98 (100) 100 (102) sts.
Tuck stitch patterns
Round 1 Yarn A, White. *k1, sl1yo*. Repeat from *-* to end.
Round 2 Yarn A, White. *k1, sl1yo*. Repeat from *-* to end.
Round 3 Yarn C, Brown 2 threads. *k1, brk1^2*. Repeat from *-* to end.
Round 4 Yarn A, White. *k1, sl1yo*. Repeat from *-* to end.

Round 5 Yarn A, White. *k1, sl1yo*. Repeat from *-* to end.
Row 6 Yarn C, Brown, 2 threads. *k1, brk1^2*. Repeat from *-* to end.
BO all sts tight in Yarn C.

Finishing
Close sleeve and attach to body.
Weave in all ends.
Steam your new sweater and sneak out in the wild....

Wild warrior. Sensitive, shy survivor. Camouflaged but still outstanding.

Mea Andresen

#REDunseen

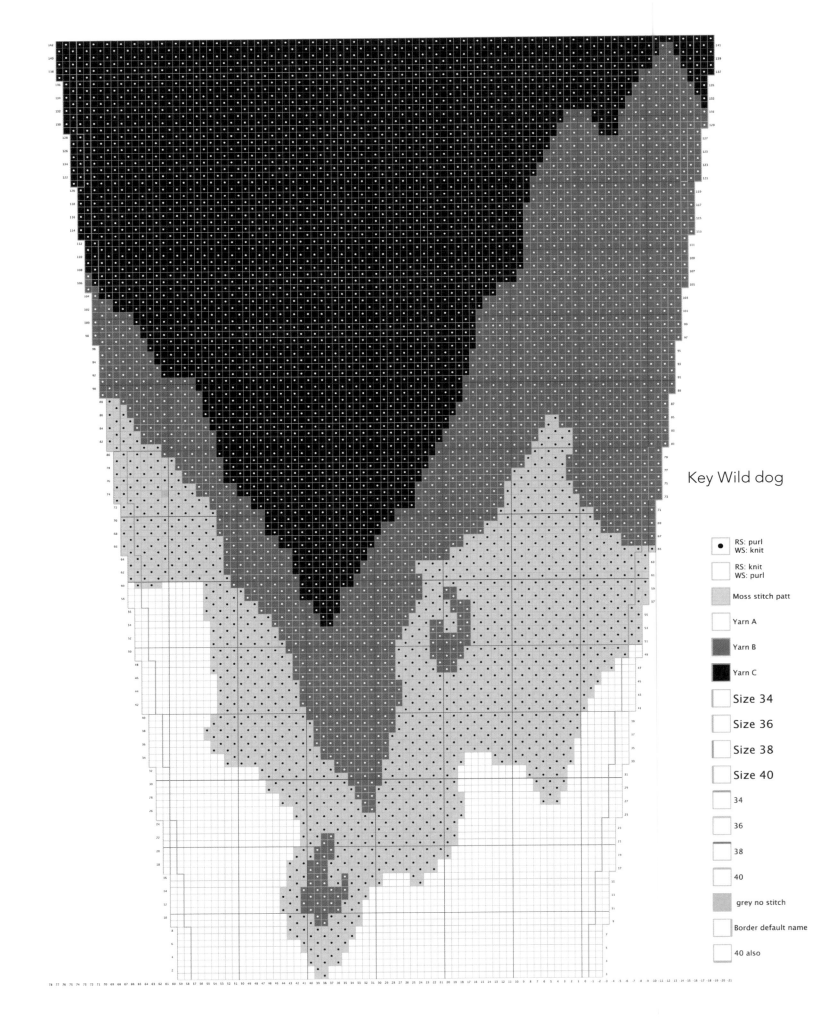

Key Wild dog

- RS: purl
  WS: knit
- RS: knit
  WS: purl
- Moss stitch patt
- Yarn A
- Yarn B
- Yarn C

Size 34
Size 36
Size 38
Size 40

34
36
38
40

grey no stitch
Border default name
40 also

R:E:D: 274

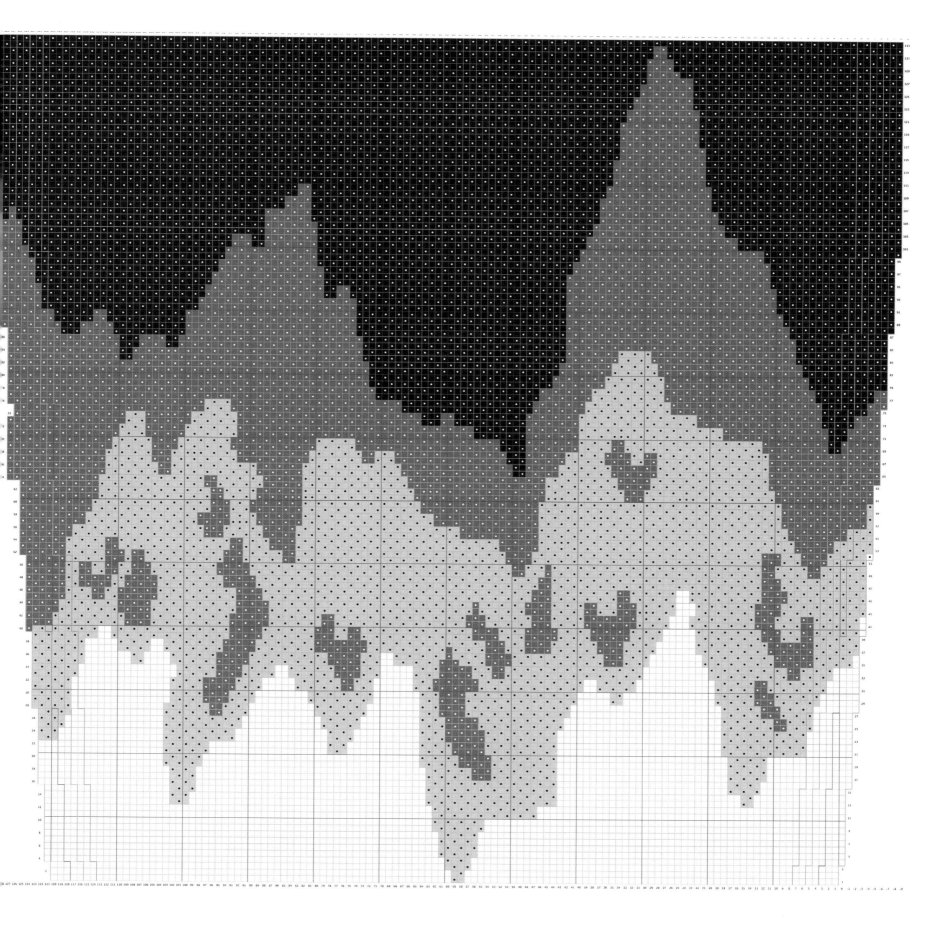

R:E:D: 275

Three Tiny Toes

Pygmy Three-toed Sloth Child
Design Charlotte Kaae
Skill level 3
Photo pg 82 - 83

Designer Charlotte Kaae
- a plain jumper with an extraordinary animal…
#REDthreetinytoes

Skill level 3
Sizes
EU 86 (98) 110 (122)
UK 12–18 month (2-3) 4-5 (6-7) years
To fit bust
53 (54.5) 58 (63) cm
21 (21½) 23 (25) inches
Actual bust measurement tunic
54 (56) 60 (65) cm
Yarn A
Madelinetosh Tosh Vintage
100% merino wool, 200 yards / 182 meters per 50 g.
2 (2) 3 (3) x 50 g in Cosmic Wonder Dust
Yarn for the Pocket and teddy
Madelinetosh Tosh Vintage, less than 25 g all together
(Colours T´Challa, Pink Clay and Tern)
Any scrap yarn will do.
Teddy fill
Wool fleece.
Needles
4 mm (US 6) circular needle, 80 cm (32 inches) + dpn or
Magic Loop for sleeves
5 mm (US 8) circular needle, 80 cm (32 inches) + dpn or
Magic Loop for sleeves
3 mm (US 2) (size 86 (98) only) dpn.
Gauge
In stocking stitch on 5 mm (US 8) needles: 18 sts = 10
cm / 4 inches.
For the intarsia in garter stitch for size 86 (98) on 3 mm
24 st x 48 rows = 10 x 10 cm / 4 inches.
For the intarsia In garter stitch for size 110 (122) on 4
mm 22 st x 44 rows = 10 x 10 cm / 4 inches.

Shown in size 98
Tip
This jumper is worked top down. The front pocket in
graphical intarsia is worked in one piece and sewed on.
If you want you can knit the complementary teddy.
Special abbreviations for this pattern.
an. = another

Top down jumper Rib
Using needle 4 mm (US 6) CO 56 (62) 64 (68).
Pm (m1) Gather for working in the round.
Round 1 - 5 Work k1, p1 ribbing.
Change needles to 5mm (US 8) and continue in
stocking st while increasing for the yoke as follows.

Body
From now on we will be working in stocking sts.
Round 1 Change needles to 5 mm (US 8) while
increasing for the yoke as follows.
Size 86 (98) 110: K 2 (5) 6, M1. *K4 (4) 4, M1*. Repeat
to for another 12 times. K 2 (5) 6.
Size 122: K2, M1. * K5, M1*. Repeat *-* for another 12
times. K1. There are now 70 (76) 78 (82) sts.
Round 2-3 K all sts.
Round 4

Size 86 (110): K 3 (7), M1. *K5, M1*. Repeat *-* an. 12
times. K2 (6).
Size 98: K6, M1. *K5, M1*. Repeat *-* an. 13 times.
Size 122: K2, M1. *K6, M1*. Repeat *-* an. 12 times. K2.
There are now 84 (90) 92 (96) sts.
Round 5 - 6 K all.
Round 7
Size 86: K3, M1. * K6, M1*. Repeat *-* an. 12 times. K3.
Size 98: *K6, M1*. Repeat *-* an. 13 times. K6.
Size 110: K1, M1. *K7, M1*. Repeat *-* an. 12 times.
Size 122: K3, M1. *K7, M1*. Repeat *-* an. 12 times. K2.
There are now 98 (104) 106 (110) sts.
Round 8 - 10 K all sts.
Round 11
Size 86: K4, M1. *K7, M1*. Repeat *-* an. 12 times. K3.
Size 98: *K7, M1*. Repeat *-* an. 13 times. K6.
Size 110: K1, M1. *K8, M1*. Repeat *-* an. 12 times. K1.
Size 122: K3, M1. *K8, M1*. Repeat *-* an. 12 times. K3.
There 112 (118) 120 (124) sts.
Round 12 - 14 K all sts.
Round 15
Size 86 K4, M1. *K8, M1*. Repeat *-* an. 12 times. K4.
Size 98 K7, M1. *K8, M1*. Repeat *-* an. 12 times. K7.
Size 110 K2, M1. *K9, M1*. Repeat *-* an. 12 times. K1.
Size 110 K4, M1. *K9, M1*. Repeat *-* an. 12 times. K3.
There are now 126 (132) 134 (138) sts.
Round 16 - 19 K all sts.
Round 20
Size 86 K5, M1. *K9, M1*. Repeat *-* an. 12 times. K4.
Size 98 K8, M1. *K9, M1*. Repeat *-* an. 12 times. K7.
Size 110 K2, M1. *K10, M1*. Repeat *-* an. 12 times. K2.
Size 122 K4, M1. *K10, M1*. Repeat *-* an. 12 times. K4.
There are now 140 (146) 148 (152) sts.
Round 21 - 24 K all sts.
Round 25
Size 86 K5, M1. *K10, M1*. Repeat *-* an. 12 times. K5.
Size 98 k8, M1. *K10, M1*. Repeat *-* an. 12 times. K8.
Size 110 k3, M1. *K11, M1*. Repeat *-* an. 12 times. K2.
Size 110 k5, M1. *K11, M1*. Repeat *-* an. 12 times. K4.
There are now 154 (160) 162 (166) sts.
Round 26 - 30 K all sts.
Round 31
Size 86 K6, M1. *K11, M1*. Repeat *-* an. 12 times. K5.
Size 98 K9, M1. *K11, M1*. Repeat *-* an. 12 times. K8.
Size 110 K3, M1. *K12, M1*. Repeat *-* an. 12 times. K3.
Size 110 K5, M1. *K12, M1*. Repeat *-* an. 12 times. K5.
There are now 168 (174) 176 (180) sts.

Size 86 (98) Work without further shaping until 12 (14)
cm. Then continue from **
Size 110 (112) only
Round 32 - 36 work in stocking st
Round 37
Size 110 K4, M1. *K13, M1*. Repeat *-* an. 12 times. K3.
Size 122 K6, M1. *K8, M1*. Repeat *-* an. 21 times. K6.
There are now --- (---) 190 (202) sts.
Work until 15 (16) cm. Then continue from **

**Work the Short rows after the Yoke shaping
Place a marker mid-front (m2).
Row 1 (RS) K until 3 st before the marker, w&t.
Row 2 (WS) P until 3 st before m2, w&t.
Row 3 (RS) K until 6 st before m2, w&t.

Row 4 (WS) P until 6 st before m2, w&t.

Divide body from sleeve and work the body
Sm. K 24 (25) 27 (29) (½ back). K 35 (36) 40 (42) sts onto spare needle (right sleeve).
CO 2 sts. K 49 (51) 55 (59) sts (front), remove m2 when you meet it. CO 2 sts. K 35 (36) 40 (42) sts onto spare needle (left sleeve). K 25 (26) 28 (30) (½ back). Now the sleeve sts are on hold and the body sts are gathered for working in the round.
There are 102 (106) 114 (122) sts.

Continue knitting in the round until a total measurement of 21 (22) 24 (27) cm / 8¼ (8¾) 9½ (10½) inches.

Bottom edge
Round 1 Change to 4 mm (US 6). Work rib k1, p1 to the end.
Continue to rib measures 2.5 cm / 1 inch.
BO all sts using Italian BO (optional).

Sleeves
Distribute 35 (36) 40 (42) sts of one sleeve onto 5 mm (US 8) dpn.
Pick up and k 2 st under the sleeve, and knit in the round until a total measurement of 14 (17) 19 (20) cm / 5½ (6¾) 7½ (8) inches, measured from sleeve hole.
Change to 4mm (US 6) dpn and work a k1, p1 ribbing for 2.5 cm. BO all sts.
Knit the next sleeve in the same way.

Finish jumper
Weave in all ends.

Pocket
The pocket is worked in Graphical Intarsia (intarsia in garter stitches).
Work from chart.
1 square = 2 st and 4 rows in garter stitch

Place the pocket on the front and seam leaving an opening for the teddy on the top between the mother sloth front and back paws.

Baby sloth teddy
Yarn
Scraps from the jumper
Needles
3 mm (US 2) magic loop or dpn.

Cast on 20 st using a double-sided cast on such as Judy's magic cast on.

Round 1 K all sts.
Round 2 K1, M1, k8, M1, k2, M1, k8, M1, k1. (24 sts).
Round 3 K all sts.
Round 4 K1, M1, k10, M1, k2, M1, k10, M1, k1. (28 sts)
Round 5 K all sts.
Round 6 K1, M1, k12, M1, k2, M1, k12, M1, k1. (32 sts)
Continue until the piece measures 6 cm / 2½ inches.
Decreases for head
K1, K2tog. K10, k2tog tbl. K2, k2tog. K10, k2tog tbl. (28 sts)
Knit another 3 cm from the decrease row.
Full measurement 9 cm / 3½ inches.

Next row
Round 1 K1, K2tog. K8, k2tog tbl. K2, k2tog. K8, k2tog tbl. (24 sts)

Round 2 K all sts.
Round 3 K1, K2tog. K6, k2tog tbl. K2, k2tog. K6, k2tog tbl. (20 sts)
Round 2 K all sts.

Embroidery face of teddy
Using duplicate stitches make the face from the chart. Begin at the top and work your way down. Beginning 4 rows below the finishing round.
Stuff the little guy with teddy filling of your choice - for example, wool fleece.
Seam up using kitchener stitch, 10 stitches on each side.

Legs
With the front facing, pick 4 sts up and knit along the increase / decrease line, turn and pick up 4 sts downwards. 8 sts all together knit in the round until leg measures 7 cm.
Decreases
K2tog, k2, k2tog, k2. (6 sts). Break the yarn.

Toes and fingers
Like a 3 needle BO, using yarn peach colour: Knit a stitch from both front and back needle, wrap the yarn around right needle and make a chain BO. Repeat 4 more times. Break yarn.
Repeat on the last stitches = 3 toes. Make a knot using the CO thread and the BO thread on each toe. Make 2 knots on each then weave in ends.

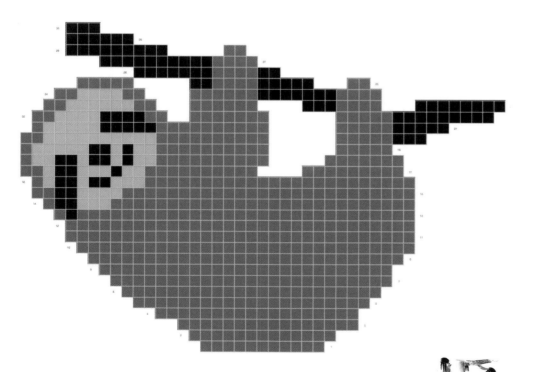

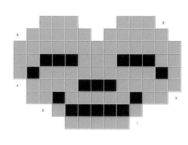

My mum is taking care of me. She carries me around for nearly two years.
In this pocket you can take good care of the little three-toed teddy and be his mum.

Charlotte Kaae

#REDtreetinytoes

Easy Going

Pygmy Three-toed Sloth Teen~Adult
Design Charlotte Kaae
Skill level 5
Photo pg 80 - 81

Designer Charlotte Kaae
- a chick jacket
#REDeasygoing

Skill level 5
Sizes
EU + UK XS (**S**) M (L)
To fit bust
82 (88) 94 (100) cm
32¼ (34½) 37 (39½) inches
Actual bust measurement (jumper)
98 (108) 114 (120) cm
38½ (42½) 44¾ (47¼) inches
Length
58 (**60**) 62 (64) cm
22¾ (23½) 24½ (25¼) inches
Yarn A
Isager Silk Mohair
75% Kid mohair 25% silk 212 m / 231 yards per
25 g.
9 (9) 10 (10) x 25 g col 3S.
Yarn B
Isager Alpaca 1 eco
100% Alpaca 400 m / 437 yards per 50 g.
3 (3) 3 (3) x 50 g col 7S.
Yarn C
Madelinetosh Prairie
100 % merino 768 m / 839 yards per 112 g
1.5 (1.5) 2 (2) x 112 g col First light.
Needles
12 mm (US 17) circular needle, 80 cm / 32
inches.
Hook 10 mm
Gauge
In Brioche on 12 mm (US 17) needles: 9 sts = 10
cm / 4 inches.
Always check your gauge and adjust needle
size accordingly.
Swatch and pattern description
Using three threads held together and 12 mm
(US 17) needle CO 18 sts.
Row 1 (RS) Knit all sts.
Row 2 (WS) K1. Make a loop as follows *Twist
the yarn over and around the left index finger.
Knit the next st by pulling both 2 threads on the
left index finger through the st and leave the
stitch on the left needle.
K1 st in the back of the same st (= 1 twisted st).
There are now 2 loop sts + 1 twisted st on the
right needle. Lift the 2 back sts over the first st
= 1 loop st *, repeat from *-* and end with a K
edge st. Repeat the 2 rows, to a measurement
of 10 cm / 4 inches.
To get the gauge right measure if the center 12

sts = 10 cm / 4 inches.

Shown in size Small.

Special abbreviation
brkRsl dec = brioche 2 st decrease which leans
to the right, worked over three sts. Slip the first
st knitwise, knit into the next st, pass the sl st
over, pass the st back to left needle and sl next
st over, pass st back to right needle.

Patterns used
Loop knitting
Single loops knitted back and forth on needles:
The loops are made on the WS rows and end
up on the RS. see description above.

Tip
This jacket is worked in one piece using three
threads at a time, one of each yarn type
mentioned. This will provide the jacket with the
desired furry texture.

Body Front and Back
Using 12 mm (US 17) circular needle and three
threads of yarn CO 87 (97) 103 (107 st) and
work brioche knit:
Row 1 (RS) K1, *sl1yo, k1*. Repeat *-* to last 2
sts. sl1yo, k1.
Row 2 (WS) Sl1 st purlwise wyif. *Brk1, sl1yo*.
Repeat *-* to last 2 sts. br1, k1.
Row 3 (RS) Sl1 st purlwise wyif. * sl1yo, brk1*.
Repeat *-* to last 2 sts. sl1yo, k1.
Repeat row 2 - 3 to work measures 6 cm / 2½
inches.
Last row must be a RS row where you regulate
the stitches to 88 (98) 104 (108) st (incl 1 edge st
in each side).
Loop knitting
Row 1 (WS) Sl1 purlwise wyif. Change into
loop knitting as described above to last st. K1.
Row 2 (RS) Sl1 purlwise wyif. K all.
Edge stitches are worked Sl1 purlwise wyif in
the beg of each row, k1 in the end of each row,
RS as well as WS. This will not be mentioned
further.
Continue until work measures 41 (42) 43 (45) cm
/ 16¼ (16½) 17 (17¾) inches.

Armhole and Neck Shaping
Row 1 (RS) K 19 (22) 24 (25) sts. BO 4 st. K 41
(45) 47 (51) sts. BO 4st. K 19 (22) 24 (25) sts.
The work is now divided in left front, back and

right front.
There are
19 (22) 24 (25) sts at each front
42 (46) 48 (50) sts at the back.

Left front
Work in loop knitting until work measures 10 (11) 12 (13) cm / 4 (4 ¼) 4 ¾ (5 ¼) inches from armhole, ending with a RS row.
Shaping neck opening left front
Row 1 (WS) BO 4 sts, work patt as set to last st. P1.
Row 2 (RS) and all following RS rows K all sts.
Row 3 (WS) BO 3 sts, work patt as set to last st. P1.
Row 5 and 7 (WS) BO 2 sts, work patt as set to last st. P1.
Row 9 (WS) BO 1 sts, work patt as set to last st. P1.
There are now 7 (10) 12 (13) sts.
Work until work measures 17 (18) 19 (20) cm / 6¾ (7) 7½ (8) inches from armhole.
BO all sts.

Right front
Row 1 (WS) Work in loop knitting until work measures 10 (11) 12 (13) cm / 4 (4 ¼) 4 ¾ (5 ¼) inches from armhole, ending with a RS row.

Shaping neck opening left front
Row 1 (RS) BO 4 sts. K all.
Row 2 (WS) and all following WS rows Sl1 purlwise, work patt as set to last st K1.
Row 3 (RS) BO 3 sts. K all.
Row 5 and 7 (RS) BO 2 sts. K all.
Row 9 (WS) BO 1 sts. K all.
There are now 7 (10) 12 (13) sts.
Work until work measures 17 (18) 19 (20) cm / 6¾ (7) 7½ (8) inches from armhole.
BO all sts.

Back
Work in loop knitting to a measurement of 15 (16) 17 (18) cm / 6 (6¼) 6¾ (7) inches. Ending with a WS row.
Row 1 (RS) K 8 (9) 10 (11) sts.
BO 26 (28) 28 (28) st. K to the end.
Left shoulder
Row 2 (WS) Work in pattern as set.
Row 3 (RS) BO 1 st. K to the end.
There are now 7 (8) 9 (10) sts.
Work without further shaping until work measures 17 (18) 19 (20) cm / 6¾ (7) 7½ (8)

inches from armhole.
BO all sts.
Right shoulder
Row 1 (WS) BO 1 sts. Work in patt as set.
There are now 7 (8) 9 (10) sts.
Work without further shaping until work measures 17 (18) 19 (20) cm / 6¾ (7) 7½ (8) inches from armhole.
BO all sts.

Finish body
Seam shoulders and pick up 26 (30) 34 (38) st and work the sleeves in the round in brioche st patt.
Round 1 (RS) *K1, sl1yo*. Repeat *-* to end.
Round 2 (RS) *Sl1yo, brp1*. Repeat *-* to end.
Round 3 (RS) *Brk1, sl1yo*. Repeat *-* to end.
Repeat rounds 2 and 3.
AT THE SAME TIME work decreases.
Decreases
Make a decrease every 5 cm in a total of 3 times working a brkRsl dec in the beg of the round.
Work without further shaping until work measures 44 (45) 46 (47) cm / 17 ¼ 17 ¾ 18 ¼ 18 ½ inches or to your preferred length. BO.

Work the next sleeve in the same way.

Finishing
Weave in all ends and make chain crochet edge around the front and the neck.

This long and woolly fur is so cool, I simply had to replicate it in knitting.

Charlotte Kaae

#REDeasygoing

Parrot Pocket

Orange Bellied Parrot Child
Design Charlotte Kaae
Skill level 3
Photo pg 170 - 171

Design Charlotte Kaae
-a lovely tunic or vest with a parrot pocket
#REDparrotpocket

Skill level 2
Sizes
EU 86 (98) 110 (122)
UK 12 – 18 month, (2-3) 4-5 (6-7) years
To fit bust
53 (54.5) 58 (63) cm
21 (21½) 23 (25) inches
Actual bust measurement (Vest and Tunic)
54 (56) 60 (65) cm
21¼ (22) 23½ (25½) inches
Length (vest)
35 (38) 41 (45) cm
13¾ (15) 16¼ (17¾)
Length (tunic)
42 (44) 48 (52) cm
16½ (17¼) 19 (20½)
Yarn for the Vest
Main Yarn (MY)
Zealana, Air, Chunky. 40% Brushtail Possum
fiber, 40% Cashmere, 20% Mulberry Silk.
146 meters / 159 yards per 50 g.
Vest colour L04, 3 (3) 4 (4) balls
Yarn for Parrot
Contrast colour (CC)
Zealana, Air 40% Brushtail Possum fiber, 40%
Cashmere, 20% Mulberry Silk.
191 yards / 175 meters per 25 g.
Less than 20 g altogether.
A12 Lime, A 10 Pink, A 02 Red, A 17 Snow
A   Black (any scrap yarn will do).
Yarn for the Tunic
Main yarn (MY)
Manos Del Uruguay Gloria 100% superwash
merino, 200 m / 219 yards per 100 g.
Tunic Pop 2 (2) 3 (3) skeins
Yarn for Parrot
Manos Del Uruguay Gloria. Less than 30 g all
together.
Muro, Vereda, Mariquita, Juanita, Malaquita
and Negro (any scrap yarn will do).
Needles
5.5 mm (US 9) circular needle, 60 cm / 24 inches
+ 80 cm / 32 inches.
4 mm (US 6) 60 cm / 24 inches circular needle +
dpn. 10 stitch markers.
1 buttons.
Gauge
In stockinette st on 5.5 mm (US 9) needles: 17
sts = 10 cm / 4 inches.
For the Intarsia in garter st on 4 mm 18 st x 36

rows = 10 x 10 cm / 4 inches.

Shown in size Vest 86 / 1-2 years, Tunic 98 / 2-3
years.

Tip
This Vest / Tunic is knitted top-down, the front
pocket in Graphical Intarsia is knit in one piece
and sewn on.
Being worked top-down you can decide on
either vest or tunic as you prefer.

For vest and tunic
CO 56 (62) 64 (68) sts using 4 mm (US 6) dpn
and yarn MY.
Row 1 (WS) K all.
Row 2 - 5 As row 1.
Change to 5.5 (US 9) circular needles (still
working back and forth) and continue in
stocking st.
Row 1 (RS) Set up for raglan:
Center back, K 8 (9) 9 (10) (right back), pm (m1),
k2, pm (m2).
K 8 (9) 9 (10) (right sleeve), pm (m3), k2, pm
(m4).
K 8 (9) 9 (10) pm (m5) (mid front),
K 8 (9) 9 (10) pm (m6), k2, pm (m7).
K 8 (9) 9 (10) (left sleeve), pm (m8), k2, pm (m9).
K 8 (9) 9 (10) (left back).

Raglan increases
Row 1 (RS):
K to m1. M1R, sm, k2, sm. M1L.
K to m3. M1R, sm, k2, sm. M1L.
K to m6. M1R, sm, k2, sm. M1L.
K to m8. M1R, sm, k2, sm. M1L.
K to end. There are now 64 (70) 72 (76) sts.
Row 2 (WS):
P to m9. M1p, sm, k2, sm. M1p.
P to m7. M1p, sm, k2, sm. M1p.
P to m4. M1p, sm, k2, sm. M1p.
P to m2. M1p, sm, k2, sm. M1p.
P to end.
Row 3 (RS) Work increases at all markers as
row 1.
Row 4 (VS) P all without increases.
Repeat row 3 - 4 to a total of 166 (174) 182
(196) sts.
There are now worked 14 (15) 15 (16) raglan
increases all together.
AT THE SAME TIME
When work measures 6 cm / 2½ inches, gather
for working in the round. Pm (m10) in mid back,
and now work 5 rows of short rows like this:

Short rows

Row 1 (RS) K to 3 sts before m5 mid front, w&t. Remember increases.

Row 2 (WS) P to m10. P to m9. M1p, sm, p2, sm, M1p. P to m7. M1p, sm, p2, sm, M1p. P to 3 sts before m5 mid front, w&t.

Row 3 (RS) K to m10 mid back (no increases), K (with increases) to 6 sts before m5 mid front, w&t.

Row 4 (WS) P (with increases as on row 2) to 6 sts before m5 mid front, w&t.

Row 5 (RS) K (no increases) to m10 (mid back).

Ending short rows

Round 1 Work as usual with the usual increases at every raglan. When meeting a wrapped st work like this:

On your way you will meet a wrapped st. Work these sts like this:

Go below the wrap and pick up the first "leg" of the st, place it on the left needle and work a k2tog tbl on the st and loop. You will only do this on this every round in order to close a hole in the knitting that appeared from the working in short rows. You can now remove m5.

When front piece measures 12 (14) 15 (16) cm / 4¾ (5½) 6 (6¼) inches,
divide body like this:

Round 1 (RS) Sm (m10). Remove all other markers as you meet them.
K to 1 st after m1. CO 2 (2) 4 (4) new st (for tunic pm after 1 (1) 2 (2) sts).
Slip sleeve sts onto spare needle to 1 st after m3 (for tunic pm after 1 (1) 2 (2) sts).
K to 1 st after m6. CO 2 (2) 4 (4) new sts.
Slip left sleeve sts onto spare needle to 1 st after m8.
K all sts to m10 (mid back).
Body is now gathered and there are 92 (96) 104 (112) sts in body. Sleeves sts are left on hold.

For Vest only

Work until 21 (22) 24 (27) cm / 8¼ (8½) 9½ (10½) inches.

Bottom edge

Change to 4 (US 6) needles and work 5 edge rounds as follows:
Round 1 P all.
Round 2 K all
Round 3 P all.
Round 4 K all.
Round 5 P all.
BO all sts.

For Tunic only

Row 1 - 7 K all sts.
Round 8 Increase 2 st at each side like this. M1R 1 st before marker, M1L 1 st after marker.
Repeat row 1 - 8 for another 7 times.
There are now 124 (128) 142 (152) sts.
Work until 40 (42) 46 (50) cm / 15¾ (16½) 18 (19¾) inches.

Bottom edge

Work bottom edge as for vest.

Sleves vest and tunic

Using 4 mm (US 6) needles, pick up and k 2 (2) 3 (4) sts under the sleeve, and work as bottom edge as described at vest.
Work other sleeve in the same way.

Finish

Weave in all ends and make a sewn buttonhole in the neck.

Parrot diagram

Parrot pocket

The parrot is also a pocket
The pocket is worked in Graphical Intarsia (intarsia in garter sts).
Work form chart Sloth Mum
1 square = 2 sts and 4 rows in garter st.
In every col change make sure to twist yarn in my favorite way: Old yarn over New yarn.

Finish pocket

Place the pocket on the front and seam button and top and the wings to the Vest or Tunic, leaving an opening for pockets for the hands.

Now let us see if the wings can take off for a flight.

_____

The precious few... In the pocket you can hide your precious treasures.
Charlotte Kaae
#REDparrotpocket

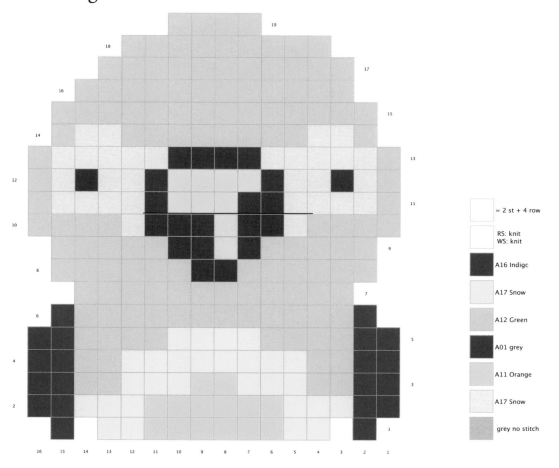

	= 2 st + 4 row
	RS: knit WS: knit
	A16 Indigo
	A17 Snow
	A12 Green
	A01 grey
	A11 Orange
	A17 Snow
	grey no stitch

Hopeful Inflight

Orange Bellied Parrot Teen~Adult
Design Charlotte Kaae
Skill level 3
Photo pg 168 -169

Design Charlotte Kaae
- a cropped jumper
#REDhopefulinflight

Skill level 3
Sizes EU + UK XS (S) M (L)
To fit bust
82 (88) 94 (100) cm / 32 (34½) 37 (39½) inches
Actual bust measurement (cropped hoodie)
88 (94) 100 (106) cm / 34½ (37) 39½ (41¾) inches
Length
25.5 (27) 29 (31) cm / 10 (10½) 11½ (12 ¼) inches.
Yarn
Handspun Hope,
Organic Merino Wool. 100 % organic merino wool.
169 m / 185 yards per 100 grams.
Col A 5 (5) 6 (7) skeins Cosmos
Col B 1 skein all sizes Rich Eucalyptus (for the Embroidery)
Needle
5 mm (US 8) circular needle, 80 cm (32 inches) circular needles + 40 cm / 16 inches or dpn.
Gauge 16 st and 24 rows = 10 x 10 cm / 4 x 4 inches in stockinette on needles 5 mm.

Tip
Front and back (both alike)
Embroidery could be done in lighter wool.

Front rib
CO 71 (75) 81 (85) sts using 5 mm (US 8) circular needle, 80 cm (32 inches) circular needles and col A.
Row 1 (WS) *K1, p1* Repeat to last st. K1.
Row 2 (RS) *P1, k1* Repeat to last st. P1.
Repeat Row 1 and 2 to a total measurement of 4 cm / 1½ inches, ending with a WS row.

Stocking stitch
Row 1 (RS) K all sts.
Row 2 (WS) P all sts.
Repeat row 1 and 2 another 2 (3) 4 (5) times.
Shape armholes
Row 1 (RS) BO 3 (3) 4 (4) sts. K to end.
Row 2 (WS) BO 3 (3) 4 (4) sts. P to end.
Row 3 (RS) BO 2 (3) 3 (3) sts. K to end.
Row 4 (WS) BO 2 (3) 3 (3) sts. P to end.
Row 5 (RS) BO 2 (2) 3 (3) sts. K to end.
Row 6 (WS) BO 2 (2) 3 (3) sts. P to end.
Row 7 (RS) BO 1 (2) 2 (2) sts. K to end.
Row 8 (WS) BO 1 (2) 2 (2) sts. P to end.

Row 9 (RS) BO 0 (0) 0 (2) sts. K to end.
Row 10 (WS) BO 0 (0) 0 (2) sts. P to end.
Row 11 (RS) BO 1 (1) 1 (0) sts. K to end.
Row 12 (WS) BO 1 (1) 1 (0) sts. P to end.
Row 13 (RS) BO 0 (0) 0 (1) sts. K to end.
Row 14 (WS) BO 0 (0) 0 (1) sts. p to end.
There are now 53 (53) 55 (55) sts.

Work straight until armholes measure 15.5 (16.5) 17.5 (18.5) cm / 6 (6 ½) 7 (7 ¼) inches from beginning of shaping. Last row is a WS row.

Shape neck and shoulders
We will now BO for neck opening on both sides at the same time.
Row 1 (RS) K14 (14) 14 (14) sts. Join a second ball of yarn and BO center 25 (25) 27 (27) sts. K to end.
Work both sides at the same time as described below.
Row 2 (WS) RS of front: P to end of RS. Work Left side of front: BO 2 sts. P to end.
Row 3 (RS) Left side of front K to end. RS of front: BO 2 sts. K to end.
Row 4 - 7 Repeat row 2 and 3 twice more. There are now 8 sts on each side all sizes.
Row 8 - 9 Work without shaping.
Row 10 - 11 Work as row 2 and 3, though only BO 1 st each time.
Repeat row 8 - 11. There are now 6 sts left on shoulder, all sizes.
Next row BO all sts both sides.

Back
Work as for front.

Sleeves
CO 55 sts all sizes and work 4 cm / 1½ inches rib edge as for front and back.
Stocking stitch
Row 1 (RS) K all sts.
Row 2 (WS) P all sts.
Work straight until work measures 8 cm / 3 inches, ending with a WS row.
Increases
Increases will be worked in size (M) L (XL). In size S there will be now increases.
Row 1 (RS) K1, M1, k to last st. M1. K1.
Row 2 to -- (20) 20 (16) Work as set without increases.
Repeat row 1 to -- (20) 20 (16) another 0 (1) 3 (5) times.
There are now 55 (59) 63 (67) sts.
Work straight until sleeve measures 42 (43) 44

(45) cm / 16½ (17) 17¼ (17¾) inches from the beginning, ending with a WS row.

Shape sleeve cap
Row 1 (RS) BO 3 sts, k to end.
Row 2 (WS) BO 3 sts, p to end.
Row 3 (RS) BO 2 sts, k to end.
Row 4 (WS) BO 2 sts, p to end.
Row 5 (RS) K1, k2tog, k to 3 last sts. K2tog. K1.
Row 6 (WS) P all sts.
Repeat row 5 - 6 another 13 times.
There are now 17 (21) 25 (29) sts.

Hoodie
Sew together shoulder seams. Pick up and K46 (46) 54 (54) sts around the neck.
Row 1 (WS) K6, P to 6 sts before end, while increasing evenly to 66 (66) 70 (70) sts. K last 6 sts.
Row 2 (RS) K all sts.
Row 3 (WS) K6, P to 6 sts before end. K6.
Continue straight until hoodie measures 36 (37) 38 (39) cm/ 14¼ (14½) 15 (15¼) inches from the base of hoodie.
Finish hoodie
Fold the hoodie and graft the top together.

Finishing
Set in sleeves, sew side seams and the sleeve seams.
Embellishment embroidery is placed from bottom of left sleeve all the way up to top shoulder and further up across the hoodie to the top.
Using col B split two half thickness.
Work embroidery pattern in duplicate stitches or cross stitches.
Now the parrot has got wings. Let it fly.

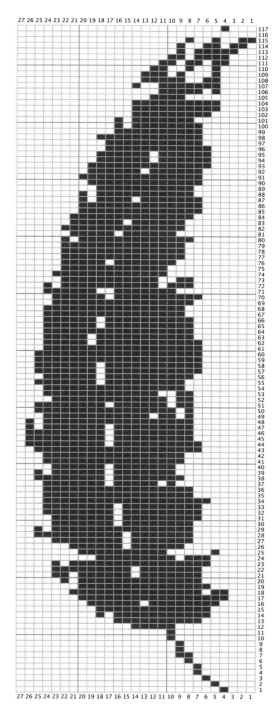

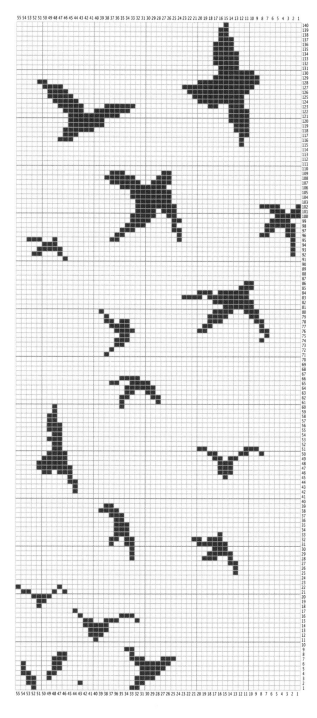

☐ = 1 st and 1 row

■ = embroidery col

☐ = background col

Blow and wish... - if only one feather could become dozens of birds.
Charlotte Kaae

#REDhopefulinflight

R:E:D: 283

On the Edge

Green Turtle Teen~Adult
Design Lisa Renner
Skill level 3
Photo pg 116 - 117 (vest)

Design Lisa Renner
- a jumper or vest to wrap you in softness
#REDontheedge

Skill level 3
Sizes
EU (34) 36 (38) 40 (42)
UK (8) 10 (12) 14 (16)
To fit bust
(82) 86 (90) 94 (100) cm
(32) 34 (35½) 37 (39½) inches
To fit waist
(64) 68 (72) 76 (82) cm
(25) 27 (28½) 30 (32½) cm
Actual bust measurement (jumper) without stretching
(70) 74 (78) 82 (88) cm
(27½) 29 (31) 32½ (35) inches
Please note:
Worn bust measurement (jumper)
(84) 88 (92) 96 (102) cm
(33) 34½ (36½) 38½ (40½) inches
Length
(52) 54 (56) 58 (61) cm
(20½) 21½ (22) 23 (24) inches
Yarn
Isager, Alpaca 1 (two threads)
100 % alpaca, 400 m / 437 yards per 50 g
Col A (1) 1 (1) 1 (1) x 50 g White
Col B (1) 1 (1) 2 (2) x 50 g Col 47
Col C (1) 1 (1) 2 (2) x 50 g Col E4S
Col D (1) 1 (1) 2 (2) x 50 g Col E8S

Needles
4.5 mm (US 7) circular needle, 60 cm / 24 inches
and 80 cm / 32 inches.
4 mm (US 6) circular needle, 60 cm / 24 inches
and 80 cm / 32 inches.
4.5 mm (US 7) and 4 mm (US 6) dpn needles.
4 stitch markers.

Pattern used
Stocking st and
rib patt k3, p3 for neckband and
rib patt k8, p2 for body and sleeve.

Gauge
In stocking sts needle 4.5 mm (US 7): 22 sts
x 30 rows = 10 x 10 cm/4 x 4 inches without
stretching.
To be able to measure accurately, make a
swatch at least 6 sts and 4 rows bigger than the
gauge indicates.

Remember to check your gauge and adjust
needle size accordingly.

Shown in EU size 38 / UK size 12

Tip
For this jumper we are using alpaca 1 held
double, sometimes two strands of the same
colour, sometimes two strands of different
colours.
This jumper is worked top-down. You may
therefore adjust the length to suit your
preferences exactly.
It is meant to have a snug fit. If your
measurements are ½ - 1½ inches larger than a
given size, you may very well knit that size. The
yarn is soft and yielding and willing to wrap
your body, and the jumper looks good with a
tight fit.

Neckband, rib patt
CO 126 (132) 132 (138) 144 sts using 4.5 mm (US
7) circular needle and double yarn Col A. Make
sure the CO is even and not too tight, as it will
make a visible edge later. Join for working in
the round.
Round 1 - 33 is worked in rib patt k3, p3 in
colours as follows:
Rounds 1 *K3, p3*. Repeat from *to* to end.
Rounds 2 - 8 Work in rib patt as established:
K3, p3.
Rounds 9 - 11 Change to Col A + Col B.
Round 12 - 14 Change to 4 mm (US 6) circular
needle, 60 cm and continue Col A + Col B.
Rounds 15 - 19 Change to Col B + Col B.
Rounds 20 - 22 Change to Col A + Col B.
Rounds 23 - 25 Change to 4.5 mm (US 7)
circular needle, 60 cm and continue Col A +
Col B.
Rounds 26 - 33 Change to Col A + Col A.
Round 34 Work w&t on the first st.
The knitting has now been turned and you will
be working the other way around. What was
previously the WS will now become the RS.

Body
We will now place a marker to indicate the
raglan increases.
Round 1 (RS)
Pm (m1) K 32 (34) 34 (36) 38 sts (the back).
Pm (m2). K 23 (24) 24 (25) 26 sts (right sleeve).
Pm (m3) K 48 (50) 50 (52) 54 sts (the front).
Pm (m4). K to last st; that will be the st with the
wrap.

Now work this particular st like this: Stick RH needle through this st right below the wrap and now again stick the RH needle through the same st, but above the wrap, and now continue knitting this st and the loop tog. These 23 (24) 24 (25) 26 sts will be the left sleeve. K to m1.

Short rows and raglan increase
We will now work back and forth to make sure the jumper gets a great fit.
Increases are made in sleeves and body on some rows and only in the body on other rows.
Row 1 (RS) Sm. K2, M1, patt to 2 sts before m2. M1, k2. Sm, k2, M1, k 3 (4) 4 (5) 5 sts, w&t. (3 sts increased.)
Row 2 (WS) P to 2 sts after m1, M1p. P 3 (4) 4 (5) 5 sts. W&t. (1 st increased.) There are now 130 (136) 136 (142) 148 sts.
Row 3 (RS) Work to 2 sts after m1, M1. Work to 2 sts before m2, M1. K2. Sm. Work to 1 st after last wrapped st. W&t. (2 sts increased.) There are now 132 (138) 138 (144) 150 sts.
Row 4 (WS) P to 1 st after last wrapped st. W&t.
Row 5 (RS) Work to 2 sts before m1. M1. K2. Sm. K2, M1. Work to 2 sts before m2, M1, k2. Sm. K2, M1. Work to 1 st after last wrapped st. W&t. (4 sts increased to 136 (142) 142 (148) 154 sts.)
Row 6 (WS) P to 1 st after last wrapped st. W&t.
Row 7 (RS) Work to 2 sts after m1, M1. Work to 2 sts before m2, M1. K2. Sm. Work to 1 st after last wrapped st. W&t. (2 sts increased.)
Row 8 (WS) P to 1 st after last wrapped st. W&t.
Row 9 - 16 Repeat row 5 - 8 **twice more.**
There are now
150 (156) 156 (162)168 sts.
The short rows have now been completed.
There are now
48 (50) 50 (52) 52 sts on the back,
48 (50) 50 (52) 52 sts on the front,
27 (28) 28 (29) 30 sts on each sleeve.
Work to m1.

Body working in the round and Increases type 1
We will now again be working in the round and begin following the Turtle diagram from round 1.From now on, there will be raglan increases in a routine of four rounds like this:

Round 1 in body and sleeves.
Round 2 no increases.
Round 3 increases only in body.
Round 4 no increases.

Round 1 (RS) Sm. K2, M1. K to 2 sts before m2, M1, k2, sm, k2, M1. K to 2 sts before m3. M1, k2, sm. k2, M1. K to 2 sts before m4. M1, k2, sm, k2, M1. K to 2 sts before m1. M1, k2. (8 sts incr.)
Round 2 Sm. K as set to m1.
Round 3 (RS) Sm. K2, M1. K to 2 sts before m2, M1, k2, sm. K to 2 sts after m3. M1. K to 2 sts before m4. M1, k2, sm. K to the end without further increases. (4 sts incr.)
Round 4 Sm. K as set to m1.
Repeat the 4 increasing rounds until you have 45 (46) 48 (51) 52 sts in each sleeve, 84 (86) 90 (96) 98 sts in each front and back.

Increases type 2
From here on work increases in body as well as sleeve on every other round until there will be 53 (56) 60 (67) 70 sts in both sleeves and 92 (96) 102 (112) 116 sts in the front and back.
AT THE SAME TIME Size 34 (36) 38 (--) --, look out for the line in the diagram saying
"Size 34 stop"
"Size 36 stop"
"Size 38 stop"
When you reach that line in the diagram, then go to the line (purple)
"All sizes raglan last 4 rows" and continue diagram from there, still working your increases as planned.
Size 40 - 42 AT THE SAME TIME, look out for the first line in the diagram saying "Size 40 and 42 expansion line".
Size 40 only: work 2 more rounds in Col 47 and then continue diagram.
Size 42 only: work 4 more rounds in Col 47 and then continue diagram.
Both sizes: Still working your increases as planned.
At second Size 40 and 42 expansion line:
Size 40 and 42: Work 4 more rounds in Col E4S and then continue diagram,
still working your increases as planned.

You should now have
53 (56) 60 (67) 70 sts in both sleeves and
92 (96) 102 (112) 116 sts in the front and back

and be ready to begin line 51 in the diagram.

Armhole divide
We will now divide the work to set the sleeve sts aside and work the body part only.
We will also CO sts for the sleeve hole, using the knitted CO method.
Round 1 Using Col D and work line 51 in chart all sizes.
Sl (m1) to right needle. Work back sts to m2. Remove m2. Turn work. CO 2 sts. Pm (m2), CO 2 sts. Turn work back to RS again. Work right sleeve sts onto spare needle. Remove m3. Work front sts to m4. Remove m4. Work left sleeve sts onto spare needle. Turn work. CO 4 sts. Turn work back to RS again.
Now move m1 to stay in the middle of the 4 new sts just made.
Now all body sts are gathered on one needle with a total of 192 (200) 212 (232) 240 sts.
Body from armhole divide
Round 2 Sm. Work line 52 in diagram 1 to m2. Sm. K according to diagram to m1. Continue working in the round, still following diagram 1 for two more rounds.

Decreases and diagram 2
From now on we will follow diagram 2.
PLEASE NOTE: the sts in Col E will not be knitted, but placed afterwards by embroidery, so from now on we will be working in Col D only. We will also begin decreases.
Round 1 Sm. K2, k2tog. Patt to 4 sts before m2. K2tog tbl, k2. Sm. K2, k2tog. Patt to 4 sts before m1. K2tog tbl, k2. (4 sts decreased.)
There are now 188 (196) 208 (228) 236 sts.
Rounds 2 - 5 Patt as set without decreases.
Repeat round 1 - 5 another 5 times.
After that there will be 168 (176) 188 (208) 216 sts in the body.
Continue without shaping until work measures 32 (33) 34 (35) 36 cm / 12½ (13) 13½ (13¾) 14¼ inches from armhole divide.

AT THE SAME TIME
When you reach line 49 in diagram 2, keep repeating line 49 for the rest of the jumper.

Rounding the bottom edge, front
Short rows.
Row 1 (RS) Patt to 4 sts before m2. W&t.
Row 2 (WS) Patt to 4 sts before m1. W&t.

**Row 3 (RS) Patt to 6 sts before last wrapped st. W&t.
Row 4 - 12 Repeat row 3 another 9 times.**

Rounding the bottom edge, back
Row 13 (RS) Patt to 4 sts before m1. When meeting a wrapped st work like this: Pick up the "wrap" and place it on the needle tog with the st. K tog the st and its wrap. W&t.
Row 14 (WS) Patt to 4 sts before m2. W&t.
Row 15 - 24 Repeat from **to**.
Row 25 (RS) Patt to m1. When meeting a wrapped st work like this: Pick up the "wrap" and place it on the needle tog with the st. K tog the st and its wrap.

Ending bottom edge
We will now again be working in the round.
Round 1 (RS) Patt to m2. Patt to m1; When meeting a wrapped st work like on row 25.
Round 2 Patt all sts.
Repeat round 2 for another 2.5 cm / 1 inch.
BO all sts.

Sleeves
Distribute 53 (56) 60 (67) 70 sts of one sleeve onto 4.5 mm (US 7) dpns.
Round 1 (RS) CO 4 sts using the knitted CO method. Work new sts: k2. Pm (m1). K2. K all sts to m1.
Continue straight until sleeve measures 4 cm / 1½ inches from armhole divide all sizes.

Decreases and rib pattern
Round 1 K1, k2tog. K 6 (7) 9 (3) 4 sts. *p2, k18*. Repeat *-* another 1 (1) 1 (2) 2 times. P2, K 3 (5) 7 (1) 2 sts. K2tog. K1. (2 sts decreased.)
Round 2 - 8 Work new patt as set without decreases.
Round 9 K1, k2tog. K 5 (6) 8 (2) 3 sts. *p2, k 8, p2, k8*. Repeat *-* another 1 (1) 1 (2) 2 times. Patt to 3 sts before end. K2tog. K1. (2 sts decreased.)
Round 10 - 16 Work new patt as set without decreases.
Round 17 K1, k2tog. Work patt as set to 3 sts before end. K2tog. K1. (2 sts decreased.)
Round 18 - 24 Work as set without decreases.
Repeat round 17 - 24 until 36 (40) 40 (40) 40 sts remain in sleeve. That will mean the last decrease in size 34 and 40 will only be worked in the beg of the round.
Continue straight until sleeve measures approx 45 (47) 49 (51) 53 cm / 17¾ (18½) 19¼ (20) 20¾

inches from armhole divide.
BO all sts very loosely.

Second sleeve
Work as the first sleeve.

Finishing
Sew any remaining openings at the armholes closed. Weave in all ends.

Finish Bottom bands body and sleeve
For the bottom band, place the jumper WS out on an ironing board. Fold the bottom band WS to WS in a 2.5 cm / 1 inch wide fold.
Pin the folded edge in place. Place a damp tea towel on top and carefully press the band down with the iron.
Now sew the fold to the WS using Col D.
Neckband
Turn the jumper back with "out side" out. Fold the neckband to the RS, folding it to the line where stocking st begins. Pin and press it as described for the bottom bands. Now attach it using Col A, sewing into a loop on the sweater and then into a CO loop on the band, all done from the RS.
WHEN SEWING: Make sure to sew loosely to ensure that the edge remains as stretchy as the knitting. Check from time to time by pulling at the seam.

Embroidery
Using two threads of Col A yarn.
According to diagram work in dublicate sts. See the photos for instruction.
They make out little turtle just hatched hurrying towards the waves to escape from threats.
Steaming
It is not necessary to wash the jumper prior to wearing it. Simply place it on the ironing board and steam it. Hold the iron 2 cm / 1 inch above the knitting, press the steam button and enjoy watching the sts fall into place.

The fragile minuttes where the turtle hatches, the vital crawl towards the waves has inspired me to this jumper. Also the years of the teenagers getting ready to leave home are essential days. So for them I made this new take on the Icelantic jumper.
Lisa Renner
#REDontheedge

Turtle Diagram 2

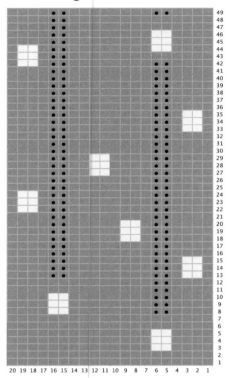

Turtle Diagram 1

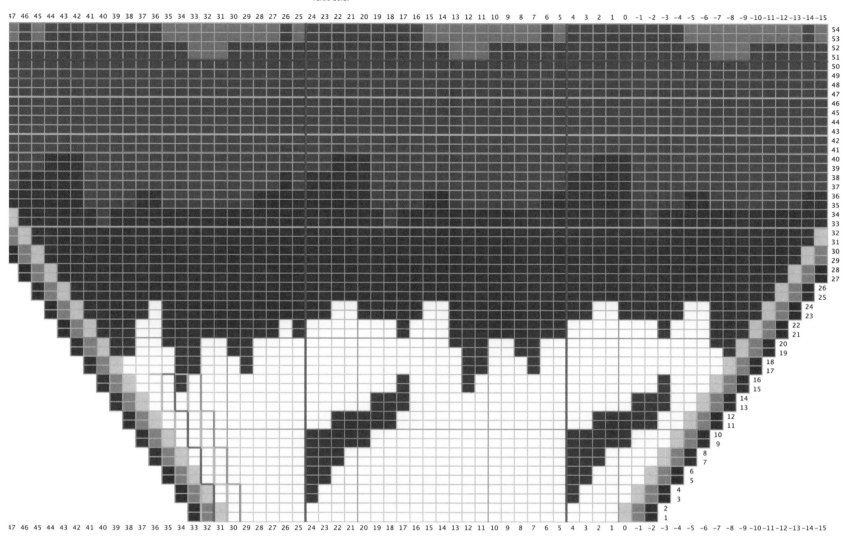

Turtle 16.8.

- □ knit
- ・ purl
- ▨ Size 34 front and back
- ▨ Size 36–38 Front and back
- ■ Size 40–42 Front and black
- □ Col A
- ■ Col B
- ■ Col C
- ▨ Col D
- ▨ Col E
- □ Size 34 sleeve
- □ Size 36–38 sleeve
- ▯ Size 40 sleeve
- □ Size 42 sleeves
- □ Size 34 stop
- □ Size 36 stop
- □ Size 38 stop
- □ Size 40 + 42 expansion line
- ▯ Size 40 stop
- ▯ Repeat all sizes
- ▢ All sizes raglan last 4 rows

Shield of Love

Green Turtle Child
Design Lisa Renner
Skill level 2
Photo pg 288

Design Lisa Renner
-a vest to keep little turtle warm
#REDshieldoflove

Skill level 2
Sizes
EU 82 (86) 98 (110) 122
UK 6 month (12-18 month) 2 (4) 6 years
To fit bust
51 (53) 55 (59) 63 cm
20 (21) 21½ (23) 25 inches
Actual bust measurement (jumper)
56 (61) 63 (67) 71 cm
22 (24) 24¾ (26½) 28 inches
Length
38 (40) 44 (48) 52 cm
15 (17¼) 18 (19) 20½ inches
Yarn Zealana TUI
70% Fine Merino, 15% Cashmere, 15%
Brushtail Possum, 111 m / 121 yards per 100 g.
Col A Rose T07 2 **(3)** 3 (4) 5 x 100 g skeins.
Needles
9 mm circular needles 80 cm / 32 inches.
8 mm (US 11) needle, 40 cm / 16 inches + 60 cm
/ 24 inches + 80 cm / 32 inches.
8 mm (US 11) dpn.
Gauge
In garter st on 8 mm (US11) needles.
10 sts = 10 cm / 4 inches. (Only st are to be
measured now rows)
Remember to check your gauge and adjust
needle size accordingly.

Shown in size 82 / 6 month.

Body, rib pattern
Garter st and stocking st.
Edge
Using 9 mm (US 13) circular needle, 80 cm / 32
inches, CO (144) 160 (176) 192 (208) sts.
Row 1 (WS) K all sts.
Row 2 - 7 Sl1p wyif, k to the end of row.

Body
Gather to work in the round
Round 1 (RS) Change to 8 mm (US 11) circular
needle and gather to work in the round.
Pm (m1). *K (15) 17 (19) 21 (23) sts, p1*.
Pm (m2). Repeat *to*.
Pm (m3). Repeat *to*.
Pm (m4). K (23) 25 (27) 29 (31) sts, p1.
Pm (m5). Repeat *to*.
Pm (m6). Repeat *to*.
Pm (m7). Repeat *to*.

Pm (m8). K (23) 25 (27) 29 (31) sts, p1.

Round 2 (RS) Decreases
Sm. K2tog. *K to 3 sts before next marker, k2tog
tbl, p1. Sm. K2tog*.
Repeat *to* another 6 times (until decrease
worked at m8). K to 3 sts before m1. k2tog tbl.
Decrease 16 sts.
There are now (128) 144 (160) 176 (192) sts.
Round 3 - 4 (RS) Sm. Work as set without
decreases.
Repeat row 2 - 4 until you have 4 sts between
m1 and m2 all sizes.
There are now 48 sts all sizes.
AT THE SAME TIME, change to a 40 cm / 16
inch circular needle, when the working needle
gets too long.

Middle section
Round 1 P all. Remove m2 - m8 as you meet
them.
We will now work back and forth to close the
middle part of the shield.
Row 1 (RS) Using 8 mm (US 11) dpn.
Preparation: Slip last st of round back from right
hand needle to the dpn.
Remove m1. With this st on RH needle: K2.
K2tog tbl, k2tog tbl. Turn (no wrap).
You now have 5 sts on the dpn. The remaining
sts are still on the circular needle. We will
gradually decrease and work the sts from the
circular needle.
Row 2 (WS) Using a second dpn, sl1 st purlwise
wyif, p2. P2tog. P2tog from the circular needle.
Turn (no wrap).
Row 3 (RS) Sl1 st knitwise wyib. K2. K2tog tbl.
K2tog tbl from the circular needle. Turn (no
wrap).
Row 4 (WS) Sl1 st purlwise wyif, p2. P2tog.
P2tog from the circular needle. Turn (no wrap).
Repeat row 3 - 4 to 8 sts remain, that is 5 sts
on the dpn and 3 sts on the circular needle.
Finishing row (RS) Sl 4 sts without working
them. Slip last st from dpn to the circular
needle. Take both needles through the hole, to
the WS of the work.
Now BO the sts from the WS like this: hold the
two needles together,
k1 st from front needle tog with 1 st from back
needle.
*k1 st from front needle tog with 1 st from back
needle, slip first st over second st for BO*.
Repeat *to* twice more. Break yarn.
Drag the thread through last st.

Tommy

CO (26) 30 (34) 38 (42) sts.
Row 1 (WS) P to last st. K1.

Increases

Row 2 (RS) Sl 1 st purlwise wyif. K1 M1. K to 2 last sts. M1. K2. (2 sts increase.)
Row 3 (WS) Sl 1 st purlwise wyif. P to last st. K1.
Row 4 (RS) Sl 1 st purlwise wyif. K to the end.
Row 5 (WS) Sl 1 st purlwise wyif. P to last st. K1.
Row 6 - 13 Repeat row 2 - 5. (2 sts increase.)
There are now (32) 36 (40) 44 (48) sts.

Tommy pattern

Row 1 (RS) Sl 1 st purlwise wyif. K to the end.
Row 2 (WS) Sl 1 st purlwise wyif. **K** to the end.
Row 3 - (10) 12 (14) 16 (18):
(RS) Sl 1 st purlwise wyif. K to the end.
(WS) Sl 1 st purlwise wyif. P to last st. K1.
Repeat rows 1 - (10) 12 (14) 16 (18) twice more.
There are now three P lines on the RS.

Last purl line

Row 1 (RS) Sl 1 st purlwise wyif. K to the end.
Row 2 (WS) Sl 1 st purlwise wyif. **K** to last st. K1.

Armhole decreases

Row 1 (RS) Sl 1 st purlwise wyif. K1 K2tog tbl. K to 4 sts before end. K2tog. K to the end. (decrease 2 sts.)
Row 2 (WS) Sl 1 st purlwise wyif. P to last st. K1.
Repeat row 1 - 2 another (3) 4 (5) 6 (7) times.
There are now (24) 26 (28) 30 (32) sts.

Neck opening front

Row 1 (RS) Sl 1 st purlwise wyif. K1 K2tog tbl. K (5) 6 (7) 7 (8) sts. K (6) 6 (6) 8 (8) sts onto spare needle. K to 4 sts before end. K2tog. K2.
The work has now been divided into left and right front with each (8) 9 (10) 10 (11) sts.

Right front

Row 2 (WS) Sl 1 st purlwise wyif. P to the end.
Row 3 (RS) Sl 1 st to spare needle. K to 4 sts before end. K2tog. K2. There are now (6) 7 (8) 8 (9) sts.
Row 4 (WS) As row 2.
Row 5 (RS) K to 4 sts before end. K2tog. K2.
There are now (5) 6 (7) 7 (8) sts.
Row 6 (WS) As row 2.
Row 7 (RS) K to 4 sts before end. K2tog. K2.
There are now (4) 5 (6) 6 (7) sts.

Row 8 (WS) BO all sts working p.

Left front

Row 1 (WS) P to last st. K1.
Row 2 (RS) Sl 1 st purlwise wyif. K1 K2tog tbl. K to last st. Sl 1 st to spare needle.
There are now (6) 7 (8) 8 (9) sts.
Row 3 (WS) As row 1.
Row 4 (RS) Sl 1 st purlwise wyif. K1 K2tog tbl. K to end.
There are now (5) 6 (7) 7 (8) sts.
Row 5 (WS) As row 1.
Row 6 (RS) Sl 1 st purlwise wyif. K1 K2tog tbl. K to end.
There are now (4) 5 (6) 6 (7) sts.
BO all sts working P.

Neckline

Row 1 (RS) Begin at left shoulder. Pick up and k (6) 6 (6) 7 (7) st . K (8) 8 (8) 10 (10) sts from spare needle. Pick up and k (6) 6 (6) 7 (7) sts before right shoulder. Pick up and k (16) 18 (20) 21 (22) sts along the back neckline - not in the top of the back, but in the 3rd ridge (see photo).
Row 2 (WS) BO all sts very loosely.
Weave in ends.
The shield is now ready to protect your little ones going out in the world...

The turtle was my first pet, a birthday present when I turned two years old. We did not know much about how to treat a turtle correctly. We made so many mistakes. I must send my apologies to "Skille" who has moved onto Turtle Heaven many years ago. I hope you have your beloved showers many times a day and plenty of warm sunshine to enjoy.
The turtle amazes me with beautiful colours and patterns. On dry land a big and clumsy and vulnerable animal; in the sea however swimming with the elegancy of a ballet dancer. I could create an entire book on only turtle inspiration.

But here you go: a top easy knitted vest. Make one, make two, inhabit the whole neighbourhood with little turtles. For the children to wear and feel like a turtle, feeling warm and comfortable like my childhood "Skille" when she was dazing in the sun after a warm shower.
Lisa Renner

#REDshieldsoflove

Sunset Getaway

Polar Bear Teen~Adult
Design Lisa Renner
Skill level 3
Photo pg 70 - 71 - 72

Designer Lisa Renner
- a hoodie to get away.
#REDsunsetgetaway

Sizes
EU and UK XS (S) M (L)
To fit bust
79 (85) 91 (97) cm
32 (34) 36 (38) inches
Actual bust measurement (jumper)
106 (111) 118 (126) cm
42 (44) 46½ (49½) inches
Length
68 (71) 74 (76) cm
27 (28) 29 (30) inches
Yarn
Önling No 2. 100% superfine wool, 120 m / 131
yards per skein, 25 g.
10 (12) 14 (16) in col A, light grey
1 (1) 1 (1) in col B, dark grey
1 (1) 1 (1) in col C, mustard
1 (1) 1 (1) in col D, celery
2 (2) 3 (3) in col E, white
Needles
4 mm (US 6) circular needle, 80 cm (32 inches).
3.5 mm (US 4) and 4 mm (US 6) dpns.
3 mm circular needle, 80 cm (32 inches).
3 mm circular needle, 60 cm (24 inches).
4 st markers.
1 dpn needle 2.5 mm
Gauge
In stocking st on 4 mm (US 6) needles 21 sts x
28 rows = 10 x 10 cm / 4 x 4 inches.
Remember to check your gauge and adjust
needle size accordingly.
Stitch patterns
The st patterns for this pattern are stocking st,
garter st and ribbing.

Shown in EU size L / UK size L, with base col A:
light grey, B: dark grey, C: mustard, D: celery, E:
white.

Body, rib pattern
CO 224 (232) 248 (264) sts using 4 mm (US 6)
circular needle and yarn in col A.
*****Round 1 (RS)** Pm (m1) *P4, k4*. Rep *to* to
the end.
Round 2 - 10 (RS) *K4, p4*. Rep *to* to the
end.
Round 11 - 16 (RS) Change to Col B. *K4, p4*.
Rep *to* to the end.
Round 17 - 18 (RS) Change to Col C. *K4, p4*.
Rep *to* to the end.

Round 19 (RS) Change to Col D. *K4, p4*. Rep
to to the end.
Round 20 (RS) Change to Col E. *K4, p4*. Rep
to to the end.
Round 21 - 28 (RS) Change to Col A. *K4, p4*.
Rep *to* to the end.
Round 29 - 34 (RS). *K5, p3*. Rep *to* to the
end.
Round 35 - 40 (RS). *K6, p2*. Rep *to* to the
end.
Round 41 - 46 (RS). *K7, p1*. Rep *to* to the
end.
Round 47 (RS). K all sts.***
Continue in the round until a work
measurement of 43 (45) 47 (49) cm / 17 (18) 18½
(19¼) inches.

Dividing into front and back
Row 1 (RS) K 110 (114) 122 (130) sts. BO 4 sts
loosly. K to 2 sts before m1. BO 4 sts loosly.
Move the last st back to LH needle.
The work is now divided into front and back
with each 108 (112) 120 (128) sts.

Diagram, back
Work the back in stocking sts. That is knit on RS
and purl on the WS.
Work first and last st as a dbe1. This will not be
mentioned further.
Follow the diagram for knitting the sleeping
bears.
In order to keep the bear beautiful white we
will not let the black yarn "travel" on the WS.
Instead we will make little mini skeins of yarn
approx. 3 m / 3 yards, for each spot of black
and yellow at the diagram and leave each skein
to hang on the WS to be used on this particular
spot, once you return from the other side. (This
is Intarsia knitting.)
For the white yarn use only 1 skein. So, the
white yarn will be worked in fair isle (twist the
yarn in every col change, and drag the white
yarn to the place where it is to be used next
time).
Row 1 (RS) K 4 (6) 10 (14) sts. Begin working the
diagram row 1. Work to the end of diagram. K
to the end.
Continue working all lines of the diagram. Then
continue straight until work measures 24 (25)
26 (27) cm / 9 ½ (10) 10¼ (10½) inches from the
beginning of sleeve hole.

Neck opening, back
Row 1 (RS) K 42 (43) 46 (49) sts. K 24 (26) 28 (30)

sts onto spare needle. K to end.

Left back
Row 2 (WS) Dbe1. P to last st. K1.
Row 3 (RS) K 3 sts onto the same spare needle. K to end.
Row 4 (WS) Work as row 2.
There are now 39 (40) 43 (46) sts.

Short rows, left shoulder shaping back
Row 1 (RS) K to 10 (12) 14 (16) sts before end, w&t.
Row 2 (WS) Dbe1. P to last st. Dbe1.
Row 3 (RS) K to 8 sts before last turn, w&t.
Row 4 (WS) As row 2.
Row 5 (RS) K to 8 sts before last turn, w&t.
Row 6 (WS) As row 2.
Row 7 (RS) K all sts.
Row 8 (WS) BO all sts in purl.

Neck opening, right back
Row 1 (WS) K 3 sts onto spare needle. P to last st. Dbe1.
Row 2 (RS) Dbe1. K to last st. Dbe1.
There are now 39 (40) 43 (46) sts.

Shortrows, right shoulder shaping back
Row 1 (WS) Dbe1. P to 10 (12) 14 (16) sts before end, w&t.
Row 2 (RS) K to last st. Dbe1.
Row 3 (WS) P to 8 sts before last turn, w&t
Row 4 (RS) As row 2.
Row 5 (WS) P to 8 sts before last turn, w&t
Row 6 (RS) As row 2.
Row 7 (WS) P all sts.
Row 8 (RS) As row 2.
Row 9 (WS) BO all sts in purl.

Front
Row 1 (RS) Unravel first st so that you get a st and a yo. Work dbe1 on these two. K to last st. Dbe1.
Row 2 (WS) Dbe1. P to last st. Dbe1.
Continue straight until work measures 21 (22) 23 (24) cm / 8 (8.5) 9 (9.5) inches.

Neck opening front
Row 1. (RS) K 45 (46) 49 (52) sts. K 18 (20) 22 (24) sts onto spare needle. K to end.

Right shoulder
Row 2 (WS) Dbe1. P to last st. K1.
Row 3 (RS) BO 1 st. K to end.
Row 4 - 13 Repeat row 2 - 3 another 5 times.

There are now 39 (40) 43 (46) sts.
Continue straight until work measures 25 (26) 27 (28) cm / 10 (10¼) 10½ (11) inches from beginning of sleeve hole.

Short rows, right shoulder shaping front
Row 1 (RS) K to 10 (12) 14 (16) sts before end, w&t.
Row 2 (WS) Dbe1. P to last st. Dbe1.
Row 3 (RS) K to 8 sts before last turn, w&t.
Row 4 (WS) As row 2.
Row 5 (RS) K to 8 sts before last turn, w&t.
Row 6 (WS) As row 2.
Row 7 (RS) K all sts.
Row 8 (WS) BO all sts.

Left front
Row 1 (WS) BO 1 st. P to last st. Dbe1.
Row 2 (RS) Dbe1. K to last st. k last st.
Row 3 - 12 Rep row 1 - 2 another 5 times.
There are now 39 (40) 43 (46) sts.

Short rows, left shoulder shaping front
Row 1 (WS) Dbe1. P to 10 (12) 14 (16) sts before end, w&t.
Row 2 (RS) K to last st. Dbe1.
Row 3 (WS) P to 8 sts before last turn, w&t
Row 4 (RS) As row 2.
Row 5 (WS) P to 8 sts before last turn, w&t
Row 6 (RS) As row 2.
Row 7 (WS) P all sts.
Row 8 (RS) BO all sts.

Sleeves
CO 40 (48) 48 (48) sts
Work rib as front work from ***-***.
Increases
Set-up round Sm. *K 6, M1*. Repeat *to* 4 (0) 0 (0) sts before m1.
There are now 46 (56) 56 (56) sts.
Round 1 - 3 K all sts without increase.
Round 4 Sm, k1, M1. K to 1 st before m1. M1, k1. There are now 48 (58) 58 (58) sts.
Repeat round 1 - 4 another 22 (21) 24 (27) times. There are now 92 (102) 106 (112) sts.
Continue straight to a total measurement of 45 (47) 49 (52) cm / 17¾ (18½) 19¼ (20½) inches.
BO all sts.
Make the other sleeve in the same way.

Hoodie
Row 1 (RS) Begin at the front sts on the spare needle. Using 3.0 mm circular needle. Pm (m1).

K all 18 (20) 22 (24) sts.
Pm (m2). Pick up and k 19 (20) 21 (22) sts on the way to the shoulder seam.
Pick up and k 16 (16) 16 (16) sts on the way to the sts on the spare needle back side. K 12 (13) 14 (15) sts from the spare needle.
Pm (m3). K the remaining 12 (13) 14 (15) sts from the spare needle. Pick up and k 16 (16) 16 (16) sts on the way to the left shoulder seam.
Pick up and k 19 (20) 21 (22) sts on the way to m1. Do not turn work.

The overlap of the hoodie
Pm (m4). Using a dpn needle 2.5 mm pick up the loops on the WS behind the 18 (20) 22 (24) sts between m1 and m2. Now continue again using the 3.0 mm circular needle and k the picked up sts.
These 130 (138) 146 (154) sts will become the hoodie.
The marker m1 indicates the opening of the hoodie. You can remove this marker when you do not need to indicate the opening anymore. The marker m3 indicates mid-back of hoodie and that one stays in place. The markers 2 and 4 will also be needed later.

Row 2 (WS) Knit all sts to the end. Turn work.
Row 3 (RS) Slip first st purlwise wyif. K all sts to the end. Turn work.
Row 4 (WS) Slip first st purl wise wyif. P to 1 st before end. K1.
Row 5 - 6 Repeat row 3 and 4.

Neck detail WS
(Optional)
Row 1 (RS) At the base of the hood (row 1) we will now pick up and k sts from the WS.
This will perform a little detail on the WS and provide the hood with a firm edge to keep it in space and simply look lovely. This is a little tricky and optional.
We use a contrast col yarn.
Using col D and 3mm circular needle 60 cm / 24 inches, pick up sts on the WS of the hood, beginning at the left opening. Pick up and k 1 st at each st from the WS of the hood behind row 1. Continue until you have picked up 130 (138) 146 (154) sts.
Row 2 (WS of neckband Col D) Sl1 purlwise wyif. P to last st. K1.
Row 3 (RS) Sl1 purlwise wyif. K to end.
Row 4 (WS) Sl1 purlwise wyif. P to last st. K1.

Finish neckband

Beginning at the RS opening of the hood RS. Using Col A and needle from the RS. Hold the two needles with the RS and the WS neckband tog (WS to WS).
K2tog, that is 1 st from the front side needle and 1st from the back side needle. Repeat *to* to the end.
Next row (WS) Change to 4.5 mm circular needle. Sl1 purlwise wyif. P to last st. Dbe1.

Shaping the hood incr/dec

Row 1 (RS) Dbe1. K1, k2tog. K to 1 sts before m1. M1, k1, sm, k1, M1. K to 4 sts before end. K2tog tbl, k1, dbe1. There are still 130 (138) 146 (154) sts.
Row 2 (WS) Dbe1. P to last st. Dbe1.
Row 3 (RS) Dbe1. K1, k2tog. K to 4 sts before end. K2tog tbl, k1, dbe1.
There are now 128 (136) 144 (152) sts.
Row 4 (WS) Dbe1. P to last st. Dbe1.
Repeat row 1 - 4 another 8 times.
There are now 112 (120) 128 (136) sts.
Now repeat row 3 - 4 another 0 (1) 2 (3) times.
There are now 112 (118) 124 (130) sts.
Continue straight until the hood measures 17 (18) 19 (20) cm/ 6¾ (7) 7½ (8) inches, measured from the purl row at the base of the hood.

Decrease 1, hood

Row 1 (RS) Dbe1. K to 3 sts before m1. K2tog tbl, k1, sm, k1, k2tog. K to last st. Dbe1.
Row 2 - 4 Work as set without shaping.
Repeat row 1 - 4 another 3 times.
There are now 104 (110) 116 (122) sts.

Decrease 2 hood

Row 1 (RS) Dbe1. K to 3 sts before m1. K2tog tbl, k1, sm, k1, k2tog. K to last st. Dbe1.
Row 2 (WS) Work as set without shaping.
Repeat row 1 and 2 another 7 times.
There are now 88 (94) 100 (106) sts.

Short rows

Row 1 (RS) Dbe1. K to 3 sts before m1. K2tog tbl, k1, sm, k1, k2tog. K to 8 (9) 10 (11) sts before end, w&t.
Row 2 (WS) Work as set without shaping to 8 (9) 10 (11) sts before end, w&t
Row 3 (RS) Dbe1. K to 3 sts before m1. K2tog tbl, k1, sm, k1, k2tog. K to 6 sts before last wrapped st, w&t.
Row 4 (WS) Work as set without shaping to 6 sts before last wrapped st. w&t.

Row 5 - 6 Repeat row 3 and 4.
There are now 82 (88) 94 (100) sts.

Ending the hood, top "seam"

Row 7 (RS) Dbe1. K to 3 sts before m1. K2tog tbl, k1, sm, k1, k2tog. K1, w&t
Row 8 (WS) P 7 sts. w&t.
Row 9 (RS) K1, k2tog, k1, sm, k1, k2tog tbl, k1, w&t.
Row 10 (WS) P 7 sts.
Repeat row 9 and 10 until 12 sts remain.
Last row (RS) K1, k2tog, k1, sm, k1, k2tog tbl, k1. There are now 10 sts.
BO sts and let the edge "roll".

Finish

Weave in ends.
Fasten sleeves to sleeve hole.

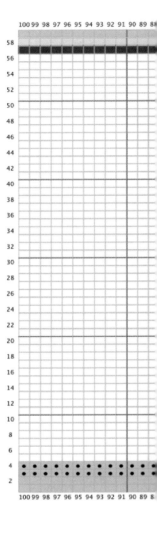

For the teenager: A hoodie to get away to somewhere cool if things get heated around you. Just as the polar bear would love to get away to somewhere colder.
Lisa Renner

#REDsunsetgetaway

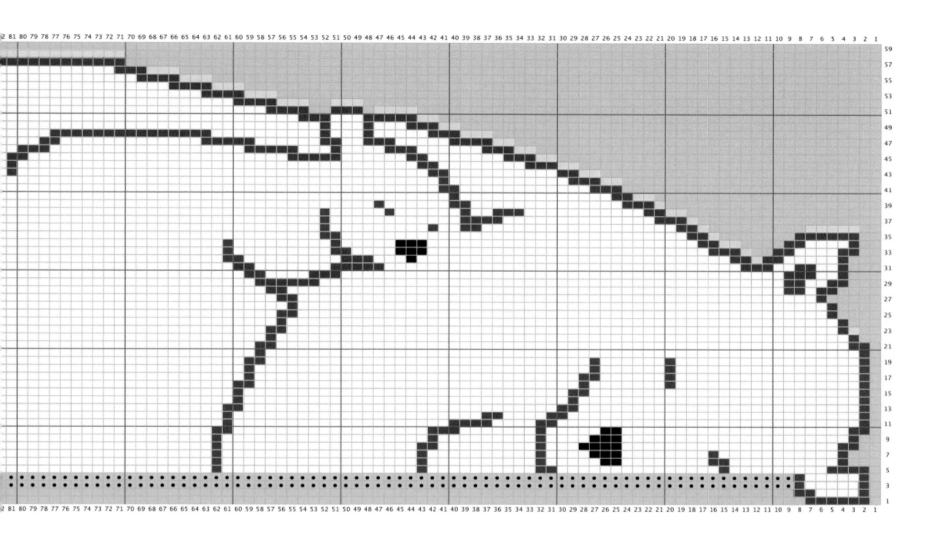

Global Sunrise

Polar Bear Child
Design Lisa Renner
Skill level 3
Photo pg 68 - 69 - 70

Design Lisa Renner
-one jumper, two sides…
#REDglobalsunrise

Skill level 5
Sizes
EU 86 (98) 110 (122)
UK 12 – 18 month (2-3) 4-5 (6-7) years
To fit bust
53 (54.5) 58 (63) cm
21 (21½) 23 (25) inches
12 – 18 month, (2-3) 4-5 (6-7) years
Actual bust measurement (jumper)
60 (64) 70 (74) cm
23½ (25¼) 27½ (29½) inches
Length
34 (40) 46 (52) cm
13½ (15¾) 18 (20½) inches
Yarn
Madelinetosh Light 100 % Merino wool, 384 m
/ 420 yards per 112 g
Col A 1 **(2) 2** (2) skeins Antler
Col B Light across grasses 35 (40) 45 (50) g
Of each col C - Col F 25 (30) 35 (40) g
Col C Translation
Col D Mythical Beast
Col E Sycamore
Col F Nassau blue

Needles
3.5 mm (US 4) and 4.5 mm (US 7) circular
needle, 60 cm / 24 inches.
3.5 mm (US 4) and 4.5 mm (US 7) dpn 5 stitch
markers.
Gauge
In double knitting on 4.5 mm (US 7) needles
and col A and B: 20 dbsts x 31 rows = 10 x 10
cm / 4 x 4 inches
Remember to check your gauge and adjust
needle size accordingly.
Special abbreviations
See all Special abbreviations on page 264 at
the Chimpanzee: David Greybeard.

Stitch patterns
Rib pattern k2, p2
Double knitting

Shown in size 86 / 12-18 month
Tip
This Jumper is worked in double knitting. That
means it can be worn with either side out.
Double knitting is simply working k1, p1 all the
way through the project. Holding the yarn in a
specific way turns your efforts into the magical
double knitting.
Tip
When working double knitting in the round we
recommend that you make a check on your
pattern at the end of every round. This way you
can ensure you have made no mistakes in the
pattern.
We still use the description RS and WS, all
though the WS is now a wearable side, that
can be worn inside out just as well.

Body, rib
Using 3.5 (US 4) circular needle and double
yarn Col B CO 120 (128) 140 (148) sts.
Gather for working in the round.
Round 1 Work rib patt k2, p2 to the end.
Round 2 - 4 (5) 6 (6) Repeat round 1.

Body, establish double knitting
Round 1 Change to needle 4.5 mm (US 7) mm.
Using Col A for front side yarn and Col C for
backside yarn.
As the rib was worked in double yarn, we will
now establish the double knitting from 1 st,
working the frontside of the jumper on the
first of the two loops and the backside of the
jumper from the second loop of the st like this:

Pick up both threads with LH: col A is held to
the right and over as well index finger as long
finger. Col B is held to the left as usual (only
over the index finger, see photo.)
*Using Col **A**, work a k1 on one loop of the st.
Moving working yarn to the back, using RH
needle, go behind **both** threads and work a p1
with Col C on the second loop of the st.
Recap
So this does the trick: *K1 col A, go behind
both threads, p1 col C*. Repeat from *to*.
The "go **behind** both threads" when working
the p1, is the trick and turns the knitting into
double knitting. Repeat *-* on all sts to the
end.
We have now turned the work into double
knitting.
**(This will not be the case if you knit English
or Continental style.)**
Round 2 - 12 (14) 16 (18) Repeat round 1.
Next round change frontside yarn to col D,
change backside yarn to col A.
K1 col D, go behind both threads, p1 col A.
Repeat *-* to the end of the round.

Diagram Polar Bear
From now on we will work the polar bear

diagram on the front of the jumper. Eyes and nose will be added afterwards by embroidery. Pm (m1) dbs 15 **(17) 20** (22) dbs. Pm (m2). Work Polar Bear diagram (for 30 dbs). Continue in bdk to end of round.

Continue working the diagram changing colours on the RS according to diagram. The WS main colour will stay white all the way up, as shown in WS diagram.

When the jumper reaches a measurement of 21 (24) 30 (36) cm / 8¼ (9½) 11¾ (14½) inches, leave the body on hold while working the sleeves.

Sleeves, rib
Using 3.5 (US 4) dpn and double yarn Col B CO 32 (36) 40 (40) dbs.
Gather for working in the round.
Round 1 Work rib patt k2, p2 to the end.
Round 2 - 4 (5) 6 (6) Repeat round 1.

Establish double knitting as for body
Round 1 Change to needle 4.5 mm (US 7) mm. Using Col A for RS yarn and Col D for WS yarn. *K1 col A, go behind both threads, p1 col D*. Repeat from *-* to the end.
Rounds 2 - 12 (16) 21 (26) Repeat round 1.
Next round change frontside yarn to col D, change backside yarn to col A.
K1 col D, go behind both threads, p1 col A. Repeat *-* to the end of round.
AT THE SAME TIME work increases.
Increases
Round 3 Bdk1, M1dbk, work to 1 dbs before end. M1, dbk1.
There are now 34 (38) 42 (42) dbs.
Rounds 4 - 10 Work as set without increases.
Repeat rounds 3 - 10 for another 4 (5) 5 (6) times.
There are now 42 (48) 52 (54) dbs. Continue without increases to a total measurement of 19 (23) 28 (32) cm / 7½ (9) 11 (12½) inches.
Set the sleeve aside while working the other sleeve the same way.

Joining body and sleeves
We will now join all pieces for working raglan decreases. Old markers will be removed. New markers will be placed.
Using the circular needle on which the body sts are placed on hold, begin at the end of the back sts (where work was left on hold before knitting the sleeves). Continue as follows:

Round 1 Sm (this will continue m1). Work 42 (48) 52 (54) dbs of one sleeve onto the needle (left sleeve).
Pm (m2). Work the 60 (64) 70 (74) front dbs as set. The former m2 is now named m3 and remains the marker of where the polar patt begins.
Pm (m4). Work the 42 (48) 52 (54) dbs of the other sleeve onto the needle (right sleeve).
Pm (m5). Work the 60 (64) 70 (74) back dbs, all the way to m1.
All 204 (224) 244 (256) dbs are now joined on one needle.
PLEASE NOTE: As we have not made decreases for armhole, the knitting gets very tight, while working the sleeves. To ease your way simply drag the needle with some of the wire ahead of the work as in photo and continue working with the loop of wire sticking out. Make sure it is done at a different place every round. Then it will not create holes in the knitting.
Round 2 Work all sts according to diagram.
Round 3 As round 2.

Raglan decreases
Round 1 Bdk2, k2tog-db, work to 4 dbs before m2. K2tog-db tbl, bdk2. Sm. Bdk2, k2tog-db. Work to 4 dbs before m4. K2tog-db tbl, bdk2. Sm. Dbk2, k2tog-db. Work to 4 dbs before m5. k2tog-db tbl, dbk2. Sm. Dbk2, k2tog-db. Work to last 4 dbs. k2tog-db tbl, dbk2. (8 dbs decreased)
Round 2 Work as set without any shaping.
Repeat raglan dec row 1 - 2 for another 14 (17) 18 (19) times.
There are now 12 (12) 14 (14) dbs in each sleeve.(between m 1 and 2 and also between m4 and 5).

Short rows
You will now work a few short rows back and forth to raise the neckline in the back.
Continue working the raglan decreases as before (on every RS row).
Row 1 (RS) Work as set to 4 sts before m2, w&t.
Row 2 (WS) Work as set to 4 sts before m4, w&t
Row 3 (RS) Work as set with the usual decreases to 2 dbs before last wrapped sdb, w&t.
Row 4 (WS) Work as set without decreases to 2

dbs before last wrapped sdb, w&t.
Row 5 - 6 Repeat row 3-4.
Row 7 (RS) Work without decreases to m1.

Finish neckline
We will now again work in the round.
Round 1 (RS) Work dbk without decreases. The small holes on the left sleeve that appeared in the knitting from turning will close as you work them. The holes from turning on the right sleeve you can work in this way:
Go below the wrap and pick up the first "leg" of the RS part of st, place it on the left needle and work a k2tog tbl on the st and loop.
On the WS part of st, go below the wrap and pick up the first "leg" of the RS part of st, place it on the left needle and work a p2tog tbl on the st and loop.
Repeat when meeting the next two wraps.

Neckband
The neckband is worked in double yarn B.
We will now again turn the knitting from double knitting into traditional knitting.
Round 1 Change to 3.5 mm (US 4) 40 cm / 16 inches circular needle or dpn and col B double thread.
Work a k2, p2 rib establish like this: *On 1 dbs ktog the two sts of the dbs*. Repeat *-* once more. **On next dbs ptog the two sts of the dbs**. Repeat once more. Continue in this way k2, p2 to the end of the round.
Decrease evenly on next round if st number is not divisible by 4
Round 2 *K2, p2*. Repeat *-* to end.
Round 3 -5 (6) 7 (7) Repeat *-* to end.
BO all sts in rib.

Finishing
Weave in all ends. Make sure to weave in ends in the layer between the two visible sides.
Steam your new sweater.

A polar bear enjoying the sunrise in his favorite surroundings. On the other side a fantasy bear in the colours of the rainbow. Perhaps you can find a name for each of them.
Lisa Renner

#REDglobalsunrise

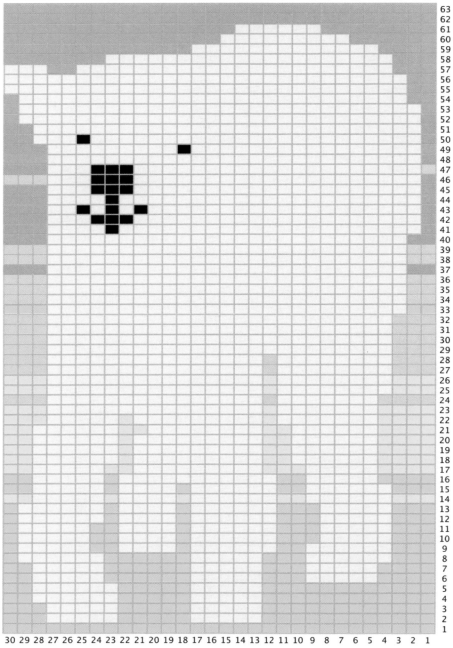

| 30 | 29 | 28 | 27 | 26 | 25 | 24 | 23 | 22 | 21 | 20 | 19 | 18 | 17 | 16 | 15 | 14 | 13 | 12 | 11 | 10 | 9 | 8 | 7 | 6 | 5 | 4 | 3 | 2 | 1 |

☐ 1 dbs, 1 row

▨ Col D

☐ Col E

■ black

▨ grey

☐ Col B

▨ Col F

▨ Col C

☐ Col A

R:E:D: 296

Shy Exhibitionist

Iguana Teen~Adult
Design Lisa Renner
Skill level 2 - 3
Photo pg 160 -161

Designer Lisa Renner
- a jumper worked top-down...
#REDshyexhibionist

Designer Lisa Renner

- a jumper to be seen and to hide away in...

Sizes
EU and UK Sizes S (M) L (XL)
To fit bust
86 (92) 98 (104) cm
34 (36) 38½ (41) inches
Actual bust measurement jumper
114 (120) 126 (132) cm
45 (47) 49½ (51) inches
Actual upper arm measurement
28 (30) 32 (34) cm
11 (12) 12½ (13½) inches
Yarn A
Isager Silk mohair
75 % kid mohair, 25 % silk, 212 m / 231 yards
per 25 g
Col A 4 (4) 5 (5) x 25 g
Col 47 Thunderblue.
Col B 4 (4) 5 (5) x 25 g
Col 66 Iceblue.
Col C 4 (4) 5 (5) x 25 g
Col 0 White.
Needles
8 mm (US 11) and 7 mm (US 10 ¾) circular
needle, 80 cm /32 inches.
7 mm (US 10 ¾) and 8 mm (US 11) dpn or
circular needle and 40 cm / 16 inches. 6 stitch
markers.
Gauge
In stocking stitch on 8 mm (US 11) needles:
12 sts x 17 rows = 10 x 10 cm/ 4 x 4 inches.
To be able to measure accurately, make a
swatch with at least 18 sts and 20 rows and
measure over the centre 18 sts x 21 rows.

Always check your gauge and adjust needle
size accordingly.

Shown in size M

TIPS
This Jumper is worked top-down using 4
threads held together. In the beginning 4
threads of same color. Later on we graduate
the colours, one thread at a time.

By knitting top down you can adjust the
length of the jumper and the sleeves as you
go. You can try the jumper on as often as you
fancy and find your favorite length. Advice:
Be careful not to knit the jumper too long; it
might then appear heavy.

Stitch markers
Using stitch markers is essential for
separating the different sections when
working this design.
We have used numbered stitch markers –
markers with numbers printed on them.
If you don't have numbered markers, use
different coloured markers and make a list of
the position of each marker:
purple marker = m1
blue marker = m2 ... etc.
This will help you to stay on track.

Tip
The CO will become the neck opening. Make
sure to work this CO fairly tight.

Neckband
Using shorter 7 mm (US 10 ¾) circular needle
40 cm / 16 inches and 4 threads of yarn A,
CO 84 (84) 84 (90) sts. Gather for working in
the round.
Round 1 (RS) *K3, p3*. Repeat *to* to the
end.
Round 2 - 7 Repeat round 1.

Body Stocking stitches
Set-up round (RS) Change to needle 8 mm
(US 11) 40 cm / 16 inches.
Pm (m1) (left front). K3.
Pm (m2) (left shoulder seam). K6 (6) 6 (8).
Pm (m3) (LS of back).
K 21 (21) 21 (23) sts.
Pm (m4) (RS of back). K 6 (6) 6 (8).
Pm (m5) (right shoulder seam). K3.
Pm (m6) (right front). K to the end.

Shaping shoulder by increases
Row 1 (RS) M1L. Sm. K3. Sm. M1R. K to m3.
M1L. Sm. K to m4. Sm. M1R. K to m5. M1L.
Sm. K3. Sm. M1R. K 2, w&t. (6 sts increased)
Row 2 (WS) P to m6. M1pR. Sm. P3. Sm.
M1pL. P all the way to m2. M1pR. Sm. P3.
Sm. M1pL. K2, w&t. (4 sts increased)
Row 3 (RS) K to m1. M1L. Sm. K3. Sm. M1R.

K to m3. M1L. Sm. K to m4. Sm. M1R. K to m5. M1L. Sm. K3. Sm. M1R. K to 2 sts after last wrapped sts, w&t. (6 sts increased)
Row 4 (WS) P to m6. M1pR. Sm. P3. Sm. M1pL. P all the way to m2. M1pR. Sm. P3. Sm. M1pL. K to 2 sts after last wrapped sts, w&t. (4 sts increased)
Repeat row 3 and 4 another 4 times. In Size L: Only work increases at m3 and m4 a total of three times.
There are now
69 sts in Front and Back (all sizes)
3 sts on each shoulder (all sizes).

Working in the round again
On this row, m3 and m4 will be removed.
Round 1 (RS) K to m1. This is now beg of row. M1L. Sm. K3. Sm. M1R. K to m3. Remove m3. K to m4. Remove m4. K to m5. M1L. Sm. K3. Sm. M1R. K to m1. (4 sts increased)
Repeat round 1 another 3 (4) 6 (8) times.
There are now
77 (79) 83 (87) sts on back & front,
3 sts on each shoulder seam (all sizes).

Shoulder caps Increase/ decrease
The markers now have to be moved in order to shape the shoulder caps.
Preparation: Remove m1. Unravel the last two sts.
Round 1 (RS) Pm (the new m1). Sm. M1R. K to m2. Remove m2. K2. M1L. Pm (the new m2). K1, k2tog. K to 5 sts before m5. K2tog tbl. K1. Pm (the new m3). Sm. M1R. K to m5. Remove m5. K to m6. Remove m6. K2. M1L. Pm (the new m4). K1. K2tog. K to 3 sts before m1. K2tog tbl. K1. Sm.
There are now
71 (73) 77 (81) sts on each front and back.
9 sts between markers on each shoulder.
Colour gradient begins
Here you start taking in new colours. In this row it will be
3 threads of col A + 1 thread of col B.
From there on follow the list of gradient colours at the end of the patt.
AT THE SAME TIME: Continue patt below.
Round 2 (RS) Sm. M1R. K to m2. M1L. Sm. K to m3. Sm. M1R. K to m4. M1L. Sm. K to m1. (4 sts increased)
There are now 11 sts between markers on

each shoulder.
Round 3 (RS) Change to 4 threads of col A. The colour changes will not be mentioned further. This was just to get you started in the right way.
Work as round 2. (4 sts increased)
There are now 13 sts between markers on each shoulder.
Round 4 Sm. M1R. K to m2. M1L. Sm. K1 k2tog. K to 3 sts before m3. k2tog. K1. Sm. M1R. K to m4. M1L. Sm. K1. K2tog. K to 3 sts before m1. K2tog. K1. Sm.
15 sts between markers on each shoulder.
69 (71) 75 (79) sts on each front and back.
Round 5 - 6 Repeat round 2. (8 sts increased).
There are now
69 (71) 75 (79) sts on each front and back.
19 sts between markers on each shoulder.
Round 7 - 9 Repeat the increase/decrease from round 4 - 6.
There are now
67 (69) 73 (77) sts on each front and back.
25 sts between markers on each shoulder.

Sleeve shaping 2
Round 10 Sm. M1R. K to m2. M1L. Sm. K1 k2tog. K to 3 sts before m3. k2tog. K1. Sm. M1R. K to m4. M1L. Sm. K1. K2tog. K to 3 sts before m1. K2tog. K1. Sm.
Round 11 K all sts without shaping.
Round 12 Sm. M1R. K to m2. M1L. Sm. K to m3. Sm. M1R. K to m4. M1L. Sm. K to m1.
Round 13 K all sts without shaping.
There are now
65 (67) 71 (75) sts on each front and back.
29 sts between markers on each shoulder.
Round 14 - 17 Repeat round 10 - 13.
There are now
63 (65) 69 (73) sts on each front and back.
33 sts between markers on each shoulder.

Round 18 - 19 K all sts without shaping.
Size S Continue from ***
Size (M) Work round 20 - 22 and continue from ***.
Size L Work round 20 - 25 and continue from ***.
Size (XL) Work round 20 - 29 and continue from ***.
Round 20 Sm. M1R. K to m2. M1L. Sm. K to m3. Sm. M1R. K to m4. M1L. Sm. K to m1.

Round 21 - 23 K all sts without shaping.
Round 24 Work as round 20.
Round 25 - 27 K all sts without shaping.
Round 28 Work as round 20.
Round 29 Work as round 20.
***There are now
63 (65) 69 (73) sts on each front and back.
33 (35) 37 (41) sts for sleeves, that is between markers on each shoulder.

Divide for body and sleeves
Round 1 Leave m1 on left needle. Turn work and use the knitted CO, CO 2 (2) 2 (2) new sts on (what is now) left needle. Sm to left needle. CO another 2 (2) 2 (2) new sts on left needle. Turn work back again.
Slip left sleeve sts onto spare needle. Leave sleeve sts on hold for working later. Remove m2.
Work back side sts to m3.
Turn work and use the knitted CO, CO 2 (2) 2 (2) new sts on left needle. Sm to left needle (this is now m2). CO another 2 (2) 2 (2) new sts on left needle. Turn work back again.
Slip right sleeve sts onto a spare needle all the way to m4. Remove m4.
Work front side sts to m1. This is now beg of row.
There are now
134 (138) 146 (154) sts on the body.
33 (35) 37 (41) sts for each sleeve on hold.
Now body and sleeves are separated. We will work the body.

Body
Rounds 2 - 8 K all sts.

Decreases
Round 1 Sm. K2, k2tog. K to 4 sts before m2. K2tog, k2. Sm. K2, k2tog. K to 4 sts before m1. K2tog, k2.
There are now 130 (134) 142 (150) sts.
Round 2 - 8 K all sts in the round without shaping.
Repeat round 1 - 8 another 2 (1) 1 (1) times.
There are now 122 (130) 138 (146) sts.
Continue straight without shaping until work measures 28 (29) 30 (31) cm / 11 (11½) 11¾ (12¼) inches from armhole divide.
Change to needle 7 mm (US 10 ¾) circular needle.

Rib

Work rib pattern *k3, p3*, repeat to end, though decrease 2 (4) 0 (2) sts evenly to make the number fit for the rib pattern.
There are now 120 (126) 138 (144) sts.

Sleeves

Round 1 Using 8 mm (US 11) short circular needle, 40 cm / 16 inches or dpn. Beg at RS at the centre of the armhole.
CO on 2 sts, using the knitted CO method.
Pm (m1). This is beg of row. CO 2 sts. There are now 37 (39) 41 (45) sts.
Round 2 K to m1. Sm. K all sts to m1.

Decrease

Round 1 Sm. K1. K2tog. K to 3 sts before m1. K2tog. K1. There are now 35 (37) 39 (43) sts.
Round 2 - 8 K all st without further shaping.
Repeat round 1 - (8) Another 6 (6) 6 (7) times.
There are now 23 (25) 27 (29) sts.
Continue without decreases to a total measurement of sleeve 40 (41) 42 (43) cm / 17¾ (16) 16½ (17) inches, measured from armhole of sleeve. We like a long sleeve to "rest" on the back of the hand. Feel free to shorten the sleeves. Try on the jumper to find your preferences.

Bottom rib

Round 1 Change to dpn 7 mm (US 10¾) and work rib patt *K3, p3* to 5 (2) 3 5 sts before end.
Size XS K3, p2.
Size S P2tog.
Size M P2tog, k1.
Size L K3, p2.
There are now 23 (24) 26 (29) sts.
Round 2 Work rib part as the sts appear: K where you meet a knitted st, P where you meet a purled st.
Continue straight to a measurement of sleeve rib of 4 cm / 1½ inches.
BO not too tight. The BO edge should allow you to push your sleeve up a bit if you like to do so.

Finish

Weave in all ends.
Get your favorite jeans out of the wardrobe and get yourself out in the streets flashing your new jumper, telling the story about the Iguana.

List of gradient colours

1 round 3 of col A + 1 col B
1 round 4 threads of col A
6 rounds 3 of col A + 1 col B
8 rounds 2 of col A + 2 col B
8 rounds 1 of col A + 3 col B
8 rounds 3 col B + 1 col C
8 rounds 2 of col B + 2 col C
8 rounds 1 of col B + 3 col C
3 round 4 threads of col C
1 rounds 1 of col B + 3 col C

The colours of this animal are so striking, I had to focus on them. In one way they are very visible on the other hand they are meant to camouflage. In the same way the teenager likes to stand out and to hide away, all in due time.

Lisa Renner

#REDshyexibitionist

My Iguana Friend

Pangolin Child
Design Lisa Renner
Skill level 3
Photo pg 158 - 159

Designer Lisa Renner
- an Iguana to make friends
#REDmyiguanafriend

Sizes
EU 86 (98) 110 (122)
UK 12 – 18 month (2-3) 4-5 (6-7) years
To fit bust
53 (55) 59 (63) cm
21 (21.5) 23 (25) inches
Actual bust measurement (jumper)
64 (66) 70 (76) cm
25 (26) 27½ (30) inches
Length
38 (40) 44 (48) cm
13½ (15¾) 18 (20½) inches
Yarn A
Purl Soho Understory Wool Silk Yak
50% Baby alpaca, 25% Baby Yak, 25% Silk 228
m / 250 yards per 100 gram
4 (4) 5 (6) x 100 gram
Yarn for Iguana
This Yarn can be different yardage, structure
thickness, in fact the higher variety, the better.
Gather approx.
5 shades of indigo (less will do)
5 shades of petrol (less will do)
5 shades of turquoise (less will do)
2 shades of white
2 shades of pink
1 shade of pitch black

Needles
4.5 (UK 7) (US 7) and 5.5 mm (UK 5) (US 9)
circular needle, 60 cm (24 inches).
4.5 (UK 7) (US 7) and 5.5 mm (UK 5) (US 9) dpn.
4 stitch markers.
Gauge
In stocking stitch on 5.5 mm (UK 5) (US 9)
needles and yarn A:
18 sts x 23 rows = 10 x 10 cm / 4 x 4 inches.
Remember to check your gauge and adjust
needle size accordingly.

Shown in size 122 / 6 - 7 years. (Boy 8 years).

Col base Heirloom White.

Body, rib pattern Front
CO 59 (65) 71 (77) sts using 4.5 mm (UK 7) (US 7)
circular needle and yarn A.

Rib pattern, front
Row 1 (WS) K4. *p3, k3*. Repeat *-* to last st.

Dbe1.
Get familiar with the Dbe1 = 1 double edge
stitch in the chapter of abbreviations. It is a
lovely stitch that can provide great finish to all
your future knitting.
Row 2 (RS) Dbe1, p3. *k3, p3*. Repeat *-* to
last st, dbe1.
Row 3 (WS) Dbe1, k3. *p3, k3*. Repeat *-* to
last st, dbe1.
Row 4 - 7 Repeat row 2 - 3.
Row 8 (RS) Dbe1. K to last st. Dbe1.
Row 9 (WS) Dbe1. P to last st. Dbe1.
Row 10 (RS) Dbe1. K to last st. Dbe1.
Row 11 (WS) as row 3.
Row 12 (RS) as row 2.
Continue in rib patt as set for another 3 rows.

Change to needle 5.5mm (UK 5) (US 9)
Row 1 (RS) Dbe1. K to last st. Dbe1.
Leave this part on hold while working the back.
Break the yarn.

Rib pattern Back
CO 59 (65) 71 (77) sts using 4.5 mm (UK 7) (US 7)
circular needle and yarn A.
Row 1 (WS) K4. *p3, k3*. Repeat *-* to last st.
Dbe1.
Row 2 (RS) Dbe1, p3. *k3, p3*. Repeat *-* to
last st, dbe1.
Row 3 (WS) Dbe1, k3. *p3, k3*. Repeat *-* to
last st, dbe1.
Row 4 - 15 Repeat row 2 - 3.
Row 16 (RS) Dbe1. K to last st. Dbe1.
Row 17 (WS) Dbe1. P to last st. Dbe1.
Row 18 (RS) Dbe1. K to last st. Dbe1.
Row 19 (WS) as row 3.
Row 20 (RS) as row 2.
Continue in rib patt as set for another 3 rows.
Do not break yarn.

Gather front and back for working in the round
Using the 5.5mm (UK 5) (US 9)
needles the front part is already on.
Please note: the last st on the front part should
be the prepared Dbe1 (consisting of one loop
and one st).
AND the last st worked on the back part is the
Dbe1 (consisting of one loop and one st).
Now slip the last st and loop from the front
onto the 4.5mm (UK7) (US7) back needle. Pm
(m2), using the front needle and knit all four
loops together tbl using the yarn from the
back. Now k all sts on the back to last st. Dbe1.

Now look at the double edge stitch on the front part (RS of front). It has already been worked. But now lift up the two loops from below this st and place them on the needle in front of the worked st. Place the two loops from the back side dbe1 on the LH needle. Pm (m1) and knit tog tbl all 5 loops. Tighten up the strand. Now all 116 (128) 140 (152) sts are gathered on one needle.

Round 1 K1, *p1, k5*. Repeat to 2 sts before m2. P1, k1. Sm.
 K2, *p1, k5*. Repeat *-* to 2 sts before m1. P1, k1. Sm.
Round 2 K all sts all the way to m1. Sm.
Round 3 K2, *p1, k5*. Repeat to 2 sts before m2. P1, k1. Sm.
 K2, *p1, k5*. Repeat *-* to 2 sts before m1. P1, k1. Sm.
Repeat round 2 and 3 until work measures 25 (26) 29 (32) cm / 10 (10¼) 11½ (12½) inches. Make sure the last round is a round where all sts are worked in knit.

Armhole
Work in patt to 1 st before m2. BO 3 sts loosely. K to 1 st before m1. BO 3 sts loosely. Remove m2. The work has now been divided into front and back with
55 (61) 67 (73) sts on each side. Remove m1. Leave sts on hold while working the sleeves.

Sleeve, rib
CO 24 (30) 30 (36) sts using 4.5 mm (UK 7) (US 7) dpn and yarn A. Join for working in the round.

Rib pattern
Round 1 (RS) *P3, k3*. Repeat *-* to last st.
Round 2 - 7 Repeat round 1.

Pattern and increases
Change to needle 5.5mm (UK 5) (US 9).
Setting up round (RS) Pm (m1). K all sts.
Round 1 K1, M1. *p1, k5*. Repeat *-* to 5 sts before end. P1, k3, M1, k1. There are now 26 (32) 32 (38) sts.
Round 2 K all sts.
Round 3 K2. *p1, k5*. Repeat *-* to the end.
Round 4 K all sts.
Round 5 K1, M1. Work in part as set to last st. M1, k1. There are now 28 (34) 34 (40) sts.
Round 6 - 8 Work as round 2 - 4.
Repeat Round 5 - 8 another 2 (2) 4 (4) times.

32 (38) 42 (48) sts.
Continue straight without further increases to a total measurement of 21 (23) 27 (31) cm / 8 (9) 10½ (12) inches. Make sure the last round is a round where all sts are worked in knit.

Armhole
BO 3 sts loosely and work patt as set to the end.
There are now 29 (35) 39 (45) sts. Leave sts on hold while working the other sleeve the same way.

Joining all pieces
Now all pieces will be worked onto the same circular needle.
Joining round (RS) Use the circular needle the body parts are resting on. Work front sts like this:
Pm (m1). Work patt to end of front sts. Pm (m2). Work the sts of one sleeve onto the same needle.
Pm (m3). Work back sts onto same needle: K to end of back sts.
Pm (m4). Knit the sts of the other sleeve onto the same needle to end. All sts are now joined on the same needle and joined for working in the round.
There are now 168 (192) 212 (236) sts.
Here we begin the raglan decreases. There will be worked decreases on every second round.

Round 1 (RS) Sm. P1. K2tog. Work front sts in patt as set to 3 sts before m2. K2tog tbl. P1. Sm. K2tog. Work sleeve sts in patt as set to 2 sts before m3. K2tog tbl. Sm. P1. K2tog. Work back sts in patt as set to 3 sts before m4. K2tog tbl. P1. Sm. K2tog. Work sleeve sts in patt as set to 2 sts before m1. K2tog tbl.
Round 2 (RS) Sm. K all sts.
Repeat round 1 and 2 until there are
11 (11) 13 (13) sts left in each sleeve. Make sure to end on a round 2, where all sts are worked in knit.

Shaping neckline
We will now be working back and forth in order to shape the neckline to become higher at the back than at the front.
Row 1 (RS) Sm. P1. K2tog. Work front sts in patt as set to 3 sts before m2. K2tog tbl. P1. Sm. K2tog. Work sleeve sts in patt as set to 2 sts before m3. K2tog tbl. Sm. P1. K2tog. Work

back sts in patt as set to 3 sts before m4. K2tog tbl. P1. Sm. K2tog. Work sleeve sts in patt as set to 2 sts before m1. K2tog tbl. Sm. W&t.
Row 2 (WS) Sm. P to 2 sts before m2. W&t.
Row 3 (RS) Work sts in patt as set with the usual decreases to 2 sts before m1. W&t.
Row 4 (WS) Sm. P to 1 st before last wrapped st. W&t.
Row 5 (RS) Work sts in patt as set with the usual decreases to 1 st before last wrapped st. W&t.
Row 6 (WS) Sm. P to 1 st before last wrapped st. W&t.
Row 7 (RS) Work sts in patt as set with the usual decreases to 1 st before last wrapped st. W&t.
Row 8 (WS) Sm. P to 1 st before last wrapped st. W&t.
Row 9 (RS) Work sts in patt as set with the usual decreases all the way to m1. No decrease is made here at m1. Sm. W&t.
There are now 74 (74) 86 (86) sts.

Ending shaping of neckline
In this row:
On your way, you will meet wrapped sts. Just purl them and the little hole that appeared while working the w&t will now be closed.
Row 10 (WS) Sm. P2tog. P to 2 sts before m2. P2tog. Sm. P all the way to m1. Sm (m1). W&t.
There are now 72 (72) 84 (84) sts.

Underlay neck band
The neck opening of this jumper is now done. From now on we are working the underlay that will be folded to the WS of the jumper.
We are now working again in the round.
Round 1 (RS) Patt as set without decreases all the way to m1.
AT THE SAME TIME: when you meet wrapped st: *Notice the wrap of yarn around the st; go below the wrap, pick up the loop of this st and place it on the left needle in front of the st. K loop and st tog tbl. The hole that appeared in the knitting is now closed*. **Repeat *to***
Round 2 (RS) K all sts to m1. This is now BOR.

Neckband underlay decreases.
Round 1 (RS) Sm, p1, k1, M1. Patt as set to 2 sts before m2. M1, k1, p1. Sm. K1, M1. Patt as set to 1 st before m3. M1, k1. Sm, p1, k1, M1. Patt as set to 2 sts before m4. M1, k1, p1. Sm, k1, M1. Patt as set to 1 st before m1. M1, k1.

Round 2 (RS) Patt as set without increases all the way to m1.
Repeat round 1 - 2 until underlay measures 3 (3) 4 (4) cm / 1¼ (1¼) 1½ (1½) inches. BO all very loosely.

Weave in ends. Fold the neck underlay to the WS and sew it, but be very sure to sew with as much elasticity as the knitted material. Steam the jumper.

Iguana
For the Iguana find your lovely leftovers. We have used
20 grams A Dark blue, four or five shades
20 grams B White, four or five shades (some perhaps with speckles)
20 grams C Petrol, four or five shades.
5 grams D Ice blue
And a few meters of contrast colors in
Col E Pink
Col F Yellow.

Feel free to choose your own favorites but make sure to have at least 10 different shades.

TIP: If you choose your own colours, there should be a very light colour i.e. white and a very dark colour i.e. dark blue and some medium light/dark i.e. petrol turquoise, and finally some cool contrast colours i.e. pink and yellow.

Yarn used
Col A Dark blue1 Thunderstorm MT Light + MT silk
Col B White 1 MT Light col Stormborn + Isager alpaca eco 01
Col B White 2 threads of MT Light Fragile + BC Jaipur Silk.
Col C Petrol 1 Manos del Uruguay
Col C Petrol 2 MT Light col Nassau bleu (2 threads)
Col D Ice blue MT Light col Hydroponic + white silk.
Col F col 1 Mt Light + Mt Silk, yellow
Col E col 1 MT Light + Mt Silk, pink
In the pattern we mention where to use col A, B, C or D. It is up to you which one of the shades you choose each time.

The Iguana
Using dpn 5.0 mm and col A, CO 9 sts (all sizes).
Row 1 (WS) P6 sts. Sl 3 sts. These three sts will never be worked on the WS. They will become the icord edge. Turn work.
Row 2 (RS) K9 (even though the yarn is in the wrong place).
Row 3 (WS) Sl1 purlwise wyif. P5, sl 3 sts.
Row 4 - 7 (RS) Repeat row 2 and 3.

Stripes type A
Row 8 (RS) K3. Change to col B. Twy. K to the end.
Row 9 (WS) Sl1 purlwise wyif. P to 3 sts before end. Sl 3 sts.
Row 10 - 13 Repeat row 2 - 3.

Row 14 (RS) K3. Change to Col A. Twist Col A and make sure Col A yarn has a suitable length to not drag the work together but suits the length the yarn is crossing. K to the end. Now pull the two twisted yarns tight to make sure the sts at the twist are firm and fine, though not too tight.
Make this check every time you change from one col to another.
Row 15 (WS) Sl1 purlwise wyif. P to 3 sts before end. Sl 3 sts.
Row 16 - 23 Repeat row 2 - 3.

Repeat stripes type A (that is row 8 - 23) another 1 (1) 2 (2) times.
Stripes type B
Row 1 (RS) Change to col B. Twy. K to the end.
Row 2 (WS) Sl1 purlwise wyif. P to 3 sts before end. Sl 3 sts.
Row 3 (RS) K8, M1, k1.
There are now 10 sts.
Row 4 (WS) Sl1 purlwise wyif. P to 3 sts before end. Sl 3 sts.
Row 5 (RS) Change to col A. Twy. K6. Change to col B. K to the end.
Row 6 (WS) Sl1 purlwise wyif. P3, change to Col A. P to 3 sts before end. Sl 3 sts.
Row 7 (RS) K 10.
Row 8 (WS) Sl1 purlwise wyif. P to 3 sts before end. Sl 3 sts.
Row 9 (RS) Change to col C. Twy. K4, Twy. Still using Col C: k3. Change to col A. K to the end.
Row 10 (WS) Sl1 purlwise wyif. P1, change to col C. P3, Twy. Still using Col C: p2. Sl 3 sts.
Row 11 (RS) Change to Col A. K10.
Row 12 (WS) Sl1 purlwise wyif. P to 3 sts before end. Sl 3 sts.
Row 13 (RS) K6. Change to col B. K to the end.
Row 14 (WS) Sl1 purlwise wyif. P3, change to Col A. P2, Twy. Still using Col A: p1. Sl 3 sts.

Repeat Stripes type B another 1 (2) 2 (2) times, without the increase on row 3.
Stripes type C
Row 1 (RS) Change to col B. Twy. K to last st, M1. K1. There are now 11 sts.
Row 2 (WS) Sl1 purlwise wyif. P to 3 sts before end. Sl 3 sts.
Row 3 (RS) Change to col A. Twy. K to 3 sts before end. Change to col B. K to the end.
Row 4 (WS) Sl1 purlwise wyif. P2, change to Col A. P to 3 sts before end. Sl 3 sts.
Row 5 (RS) K all sts.
Row 6 (WS) Sl1 purlwise wyif. P to 3 sts before end. Sl 3 sts.
Row 7 (RS) Change to col C. Twy. K all sts.
Row 8 (WS) Sl1 purlwise wyif. P to 3 sts before end. Sl 3 sts.
Row 9 (RS) Change to col D. Twy. K4, Twy. Still using Col D: k to 3 sts before end. Change to col C. K to the end.
Row 10 (WS) Sl1 purlwise wyif. P2, change to col D. P to 3 sts before end. Sl 3 sts.
Row 11 (RS) K all sts.
Row 12 (WS) Sl1 purlwise wyif. P to 3 sts before end. Sl 3 sts.
Row 13 (RS) K to 3 sts before end. Change to col C. K to the end.
Row 14 (WS) Sl1 purlwise wyif. P2, change to Col D. P2, Twy. Still using Col C: p to 3 sts before end. Sl 3 sts.
Row 15 (RS) Change to col C. Twy. K all sts.
Row 16 (WS) Sl1 purlwise wyif. P to 3 sts before end. Sl 3 sts.
Row 17 (RS) Change to Col A. K all.
Row 18 (WS) Sl1 purlwise wyif. P to 3 sts before end. Sl 3 sts.
Row 19 (RS) K to 3 before end. Change to col B. K to the end.
Row 20 (WS) Sl1 purlwise wyif. P2, change to Col A. P3, Twy. Still using Col A: P to 3 sts before end. Sl 3 sts.

Repeat Stripes type C twice more, this time include the increase in row 1. After these two repeats there are now 13 sts.
Follow from now on The Iguana diagram from row 1.

Please Note
From row 100 (WS) Reduce sts by BO sts in beg of row.
Row 109 (RS) BO 3 sts in beg of row.
Row 111 (RS) BO 2 sts in beg of row.
Row 118 (WS) BO all sts.

Finish
Place the iguana on the jumper as shown in photo page 300.

Fasten the jumper with your preferred embroidery sts. We have used seam st and blanket st.
Make an additional row of blanket sts to become the crest.

Leg
CO 7 sts, using dpn 5mm (UK 6) (US 8) and col C.

Row 1 (WS) P to last st. Dbe1.
Row 2 (RS) Dbe1. K to last st. Dbe1.
Row 3 (WS) Dbe1. P to last st. Dbe1.
Repeat row 2 and 3 until work measures 7 cm / 2¾ inches.

Knee
Row 1 (WS) Dbe1. P to 2 last sts. W&t.
Row 2 (RS) K to last st. Dbe1.
Row 3 (WS) Dbe1. P to 1 st before last wrapped st. W&t.
Row 4 (RS) K to last st. Dbe1.
Row 5 - 10 Repeat row 3 and 4 another 3 times.
Row 11 (WS) Row 1 (WS) Dbe1. P5. Dbe1.
Row 12 (RS) Dbe1. K to last st. Dbe1.
Row 13 (WS) Dbe1. P3, p2tog. Dbe1. (6 sts)
Row 14 (RS) Dbe1. K to last st. Dbe1.
Row 15 (WS) Row 1 (WS) Dbe1. P5. Dbe1.
Row 16 (RS) Dbe1. K2, k2tog. Dbe1. (5 st)
Work 5 rows without further shaping.

Toes
Row 1 toe 1 (RS) On the two loops of the dbe st K2. *Do not turn. Slide the st back to right end of dpn. K2* Repeat another 5 times. Ending: K2tog. Break yarn, drag yarn through loop.
Toe 2
Row 1 (RS) K the st in the "front leg" of st. Do not slip st. Work k1 on the "back leg" of the st. *Do not turn. Slide. K2*. Repeat another 7 - 8 times.
Toe 3 - 4
As row 2.
Toe 5
As toe 2, though only repeat 5 times.
Make another leg in the same way.
Sew on legs for the iguana.

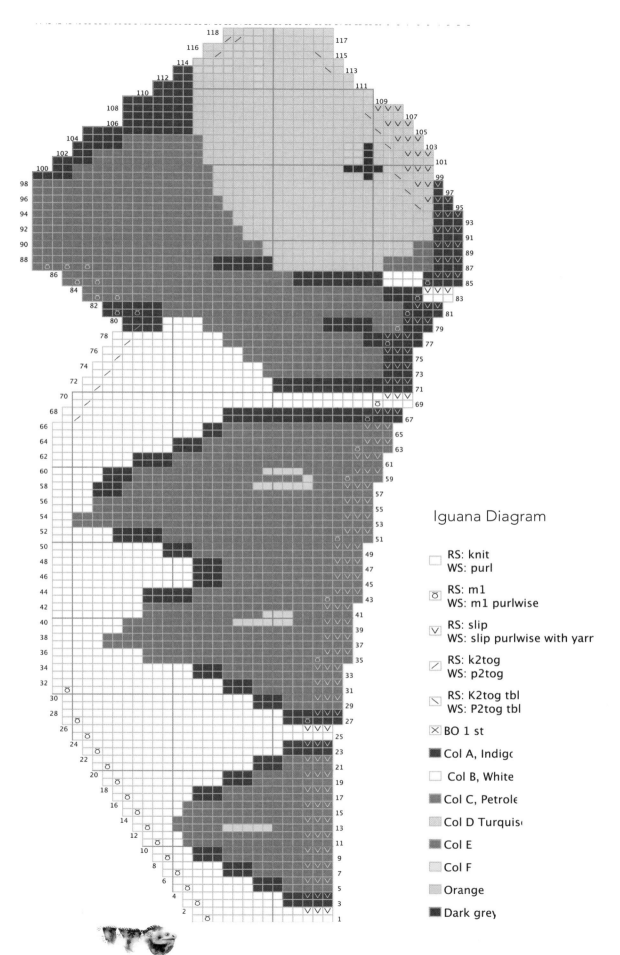

Iguana Diagram

□	RS: knit / WS: purl
⌾	RS: m1 / WS: m1 purlwise
⋁	RS: slip / WS: slip purlwise with yarn
╱	RS: k2tog / WS: p2tog
╲	RS: K2tog tbl / WS: P2tog tbl
⊠	BO 1 st
■	Col A, Indigo
□	Col B, White
■	Col C, Petrole
▨	Col D Turquise
■	Col E
▨	Col F
■	Orange
■	Dark grey

All about the scales

Pangolin Teen ~ Adult
Design Lisa Renner
Skill level 3 - 4
Photo pg 46 - 47 - 189

Design Lisa Renner
- a jumper to look good for any occasion...
#REDallaboutthescales

Sizes
S M L XL
To fit bust
82 (88) 94 (100) cm
32¼ (34½) 37 (39½) inches
Actual bust measurement (jumper)
98 (104) 110 (116) cm
38½ (41) 43 (45½) inches
Length
63 (65) 67 (69) cm
25 (25½) 26½ (27¼) inches
Yarn Madelinetosh Tosh Merino Light
100 % Merino wool 384 m / yards per 112 gram
Col A, Dark Colour (DC)
2 (2) 3 (3) skeins
Col B, Light Colour (LC)
2 (2) 2 (2) skeins
Col C, Light Colour (LC.2) Optional
1 skein
Contrast A
3 m / 3 yards
Needles
3.5 mm (US 4) circular needle 80 cm / 32 inches
+ 40 cm / 16 inches + dpn.
4.5 mm (US 7) circular needle 80 cm / 32 inches
+ dpn + 40 cm / 16 inches + 60 cm / 24 inches.
4 stitch markers
Gauge
Brioche Purl pattern on needle 4.5 mm.:
17st x 44 rows = 10 x 10 cm / 4 x 4 inches
Brioche Rib pattern on needle 3.5 mm.:
18 st x 40 rows

Special abbreviations used for this pattern
sl1yo2 = slip 1 st with a yarn over needle. This
st already had a yarn over from previous row.
So now there is 2 yarn over this st.

Patterns used
There are two patterns used.
We have named them:
Brioche Rib pattern and
Brioche Purl pattern.
They are mostly worked in the round and are
easy to learn.
For the knitting sample see below:
"Purl brioche pattern, worked back and forth".
We recommend to do test knitting only in Bri-
oche purl pattern.

Shown in Size M. Col A Dubrovnik. Col B Kitten. Col C Berlin.

Tip
Whenever we write: "slide" it means slide the
work back to the right end of needle.
Brioche Rib pattern, worked back and forth.
Row 1 (RS) DC K1. *K1, sl1yo*. Repeat *to* to
last stitch. K1. Turn work.
Row 2 (WS) DC K1. *s1yo2, p1*. Repeat *to* to
last stitch. K1. Turn work.
Row 3 (RS) LC K1. *K1, brk1*. Repeat *to* to
last stitch. K1. Slide.
Row 4 (RS) DC K1. *K1, sl1yo*. Repeat *to* to
last stitch. K1. Turn work.
Row 5 (WS) DC K1. *s1yo2, p1*. Repeat *to* to
last stitch. K1. Slide.
Row 6 (WS) LC K1. *brp1, p1*. Repeat *to* to
last stitch. K1.

Brioche rib pattern, worked in the round
Round 1 (RS) DC *K1, sl1yo* Rep *to* to end.
Round 2 (RS) DC *K1, sl1yo2* Rep *to* to end.
Round 3 (RS) LC *K1, brk1* Rep *to* to end.

Brioche Purl pattern, worked back and forth.
This is how you do your test knitting:
CO 24 sts.
Row 1 (WS) LC K1. *k1, sl1yo*. Repeat *to* to
last stitch. K1. Slide.
Row 2 (WS) DC K1. *k1, brp1*. Repeat *to* to
last stitch. K1. Turn work.
Row 3 (RS) LC K1. *p1, sl1yo*. Repeat *to* to
last stitch. K1. Slide.
Row 4 (RS) DC K1. *p1, brk1*. Repeat *to* to
last stitch. K1. Turn work.
Repeat row 1 - 4 until a total measurement of
111 cm / 4.25 inches.

Purl brioche pattern, worked in the round, as it is used in the pattern
Round 1 (RS) LC *Sl1yo, p1*. Rep *to* to the
end.
Round 2 (RS) DC *Brk1, p1*. Rep *to* to the
end.
Round 3 (RS) LC *P1, sl1yo*. Rep *to* to end.
Round 2 (RS) DC *P1, brk1*. Rep *to* to the
end.

Rib body
Using DC and needle 3.5 mm (US 4) circular
needle 80 cm / 32 inches.CO 168 (176) 188 (200)
sts. Gather for working in the round.
Set up round
K all sts. Pm (m1).

Round 1 (RS) DC *K1, sl1yo* Rep *to* to end.
Round 2 (RS) DC *K1, sl1yo2* Rep *to* to end.
Round 3 (RS) LC *K1, brk1* Rep *to* to end.
Repeat round 1 - 3 another 3 times.
Round 13 - 14 (RS) Repeat round 1 - 2.
Round 15 (RS) DC *K1, brk1,* Rep *to* to end.

Establish Brioche Purl pattern
Round 1 (RS) LC
Change to 4.5 mm (US 7) circular needle 80 cm / 32 inches.
Sl1yo, p1. Rep *to* to the end. Sm.
Round 2 (RS) DC
Brk1, p1. Rep *to* to the end. Sm.
Round 3 (RS) LC
P1, sl1yo. Rep *to* to end. Sm.
Round 4 (RS) DC
P1, brk1. Rep *to* to the end. Sm.
PLEASE NOTE
After each DC round there are no yarn overs on the needle. Only DC yarn.
Use this as a check point.
These four rounds make up the pattern.
Continue straight until work measures 34 (36) 38 (40) cm / 13 ½ (14 ¼) 15 (15¾) inch.

Placing of marker no 2
Work 84 (88) 94 (100) sts. Pm (m2).
Patt to the end.
Increases
Round 1 Work 2 sts in patt. M2. Work in patt as set until 2 sts before m2. M2. Work 2 sts in patt. Sm. Patt 2 sts. M2. Work in patt to 2 sts before m1. M2. Patt to end. Sm.
There are now 176 (184) 196 (208) sts.
Round 2 - 8 Work in patt as set without increases. Work the increased sts into the established pattern.
Repeat round 1. There are now 184 (192) 204 (216) sts.
Continue straight without further shaping until work measures 40 (42) 44 (45.5) cm 15¾) (16½) 17¼ (18) inches.
Make sure that you end up working a LC round.

Armhole
DC Work to 2 sts before m2. BO 4 sts. Work to 2 sts before m1. BO 4 sts.
The work is now divided into front and back with each 88 (92) 98 (104) sts.
Leave sts on a holder while working the sleeves.

Rib sleeves
Using DC and 3.5 mm (US 4) dpn needle, CO 36 (40) 40 (44) sts.
Gather for working in the round.
Round 1 - 15 Work rib as for body.

Establish Brioche Purl pattern
Round 1 (RS) LC
Change to 4.5 mm (US 7) dpn.
Sl1yo, p1. Rep *to* to the end. Sm.
Round 2 (RS) DC
Brk1, p1. Rep *to* to the end. Sm.
Round 3 (RS) LC
P1, sl1yo. Rep *to* to end. Sm.
Round 4 (RS) DC
P1, brk1. Rep *to* to the end. Sm.

Increases
Round 1 Work 2 sts in patt. M2. Work in patt as set until 2 sts before m1. M2. Work 2 sts in patt. Sm.
There are now 40 (44) 44 (48) sts.
Round 2 - 22 Work in patt as set without increases.
Work the increased sts into the established pattern.
Rep round 1 - 22 another 5 (5) 7 (7) times.
There are now 60 (64) 72 (76) sts.
Continue straight without further shaping until work measures 46 (48) 50 (52) cm/ 18 (19) 20 (20½) inches.
Make sure that you end up working a LC round.

Armhole
Next row DC Work to 2 sts before m1. BO 4 sts.
There are now 56 (60) 68 (72) sts.
Leave sts on a holder and work another sleeve in the same way.

Joining all pieces for working in the round
Using the circular needle from the body part.

Round 1 (RS) LC Beg at left sleeve. Pm (m1).
P1, k1 (regardless of how these sts were previously worked). Patt across the sleeve to 2 last st. K1, p1 (regardless of how these sts were previously worked). Pm (m2). Work front sts onto the same needle as follows: K1, p1, k1 (regardless of how these sts were previously worked). Patt across the front to last 3 sts. K1, p1, k1 (regardless of how these sts were previously worked). Pm (m3). Work right sleeve sts onto

the same needle as follows: P1, k1 (regardless of howthese sts were previously worked). Patt across the right sleeve to 2 last st. K1, p1 (regardless of how this st were previously worked). Pm (m4). Work back sts onto the same needle as follows: K1, p1, k1 (regardless of how these sts were previously worked). Patt across the back to last 3 sts before m1. K1, p1, k1(regardless of how these sts were previously worked). Now all sts are gathered on the same needle and you can continue working in the round.
There are now 288 (304) 332 (352) sts.
PLEASE NOTE. Remember to twist the yarn around each other at each colour change at the beginning of a new round.
Round 2 (RS) DC Sm. P1, k1, patt to 2 sts before m2, k1, p1. Sm. K1, p1, k1. Patt to 3 sts before m3. K1, p1, k1. Sm. P1, k1, patt to 2 sts before m4. K1, p1. Sm, k1, p1, k1, patt to 3 sts before m1, k1, p1, k1.
Round 3 (RS) LC Sm P1, k1, patt to 2 sts before m2, k1, p1. Sm. Sl1yo, p1, k1. Patt to 3 sts before m3. K1, p1, sl1yo. Sm. P1, k1, patt to 2 st before m4. K1, p1. Sm, sl1yo, p1, k1, patt to 3 sts before m1, k1, p1, sl1yo.
Round 4 (RS) DC Sm. P1, k1, patt to 2 st before m2, k1, p1. Sm. Brk1, p1, k1, patt to 3 sts before m3. K1, p1, brk1. Sm. P1, k1, patt to 2 st before m4, k1, p1. Sm, brk1, p1, k1, patt to 3 sts before m1, k1, p1, brk1.
Round 5 (RS) LC As round 3.

Decreasing rounds, raglan decreases 1
We will now do raglan decreases at all four markers.
Round 1 (RS) DC Sm. P1, sks. Patt to 3 st before m2, k2tog, p1. Sm. brk1, p1, sks. Patt to 4 sts before m3. K2tog, p1, brk1. Sm. P1, sks. Patt to 3 sts before m4. K2tog, p1. Sm, brk1, p1, sks. Patt to 4 sts before m1, k2tog, p1, brk1. Red with 8 sts.
There are now
86 (90) 96 (102) sts in front and back
54 (58) 66 (70) sts in both sleeves.
Round 2 (RS) LC Sm. P1, k1, patt to 2 sts before m2, k1, p1. Sm. Sl1yo, p1, k1. Patt to 3 sts before m3. K1, p1, sl1yo. Sm. P1, k1. Patt to 2 sts before m4, k1, p1. Sm. Sl1yo, p1, k1. Patt to 3 sts before m1, k1 p1, sl1yo.
Round 3 -20 Repeat round 1 and 2 another 9 times, so that the decrease round has been worked a total of 10 times.
There are now

68 (72) 78 (84) sts in front and back.
36 (40) 48 (52) sts in both sleeves.
AT THE SAME TIME
Round 6 There will now be a colour change only in LC.
DC stays the same all way through.
Round 6 LC2
Round 8 LC
Round 10 LC
Round 12 LC2
Round 14 LC2
Round 16 LC
Round 18 LC2
Round 20 LC2
Round 22 LC2
Round 24 LC
Round 26 LC2 From here on only use LC2 it will now be mentioned as LC.

Decreasing rounds, raglan decreases 2
We will now work raglan decreases only in the sleeve.
Round 1 (RS) DC Sm P1, sks. Patt to 3 st before m2, k2tog, p1. Sm. brk1, p1, k1. Patt to 3 sts before m3. K1, p1, brk1. Sm. P1, sks. Patt to 3 sts before m4. K2tog, p1, Sm, brk1, p1, k1. Patt to 3 sts before m1, k1, p1, brk1. Red with 4 sts.
There are now still
68 (72) 78 (84) sts in front and back,
34 (38) 46 (50) sts in both sleeves.
Round 2 (RS) LC Sm. P1, k1, patt to 2 sts before m2, k1, p1. Sm. Sl1yo, p1, k1. Patt to 3 sts before m3. K1, p1, sl1yo. Sm. P1, k1. Patt to 2 sts before m4. K1, p1. Sm. Sl1yo, p1, k1. Patt to 3 sts before m1, k1 p1, sl1yo.
Rep Round 1 and 2 until 34 (38) 38 (38) sts remain in the sleeves.
That is another 0 (0) 4 (6) times.

Decreasing rounds, raglan decreases 3
We will now work raglan decreases only in the sleeve and on each 4th row.
Round 1 (RS) DC Sm P1, sks. Patt to 3 st before m2, k2tog, p1. Sm. brk1, p1, k1. Patt to 3 sts before m3. K1, p1, brk1. Sm. P1, sks. Patt to 3 sts before m4. K2tog, p1, Sm, brk1, p1, k1. Patt to 3 sts before m1, k1, p1, brk1. Red with 4 sts.
Round 2 (RS) LC Sm. P1, k1, patt to 2 sts before m2, k1, p1. Sm. Sl1yo, p1, k1. Patt to 3 sts before m3. K1, p1, sl1yo. Sm. P1, k1. Patt to 2 sts before m4. K1, p1. Sm. Sl1yo, p1, k1. Patt to 3 sts before m1, k1 p1, sl1yo.
Round 3 (RS) DC Sm P1, k1. Patt to 2 sts before m2, k1, p1. Sm. brk1, p1, k1. Patt to 3 sts before m3. K1, p1, brk1. Sm. P1, k1. Patt to 2 sts before

m4, k1, p1. Sm, brk1, p1, k1. Patt to 3 sts before m1, k1, p1, brk1.
Round 4 (RS) LC As round 2.
There are now
still 68 (72) 78 (84) sts in front and back,
32 (36) 36 (36) sts in both sleeves.
Round 5 - 28 (36) 36 (36) Repeat round 1 - 4
Another 6 (8) 8 (8) times.
There are now
still 68 (72) 78 (84) sts in front and back
20 sts in both sleeves all sizes.
Round 29 (37) 37 (37) (RS) DC Sm P1, k1. Patt to 2 sts before m2, k1, p1. Sm. brk1, p1, k1. Patt to 3 sts before m3. K1, p1, brk1. Sm. P1, k1. Patt to 2 sts before m4, k1, p1. Sm, brk1, p1, k1. Patt to 3 sts before m1, k1, p1, brk1.
Round 30 (38) 38 (38) (RS) LC As round 2 (in decreases3).

Neck opening
Next Round (RS) DC Sm. Patt as round 3 to 20 (22) 24 (26) sts after m2. Patt next 28 (28) 30 (32) sts onto a spare needle for neck opening. Patt remaining 20 (22) 24 (26) sts to m3. Continue in patt without shaping to m1.
Break yarn. Sl remaining sts from m1 to neck opening left side onto right needle without working the sts.
The sts on the spare needle constitute the centre front neck opening sts. They are for the moment left on hold. Now patt back and forth over remaining sts as follows:

Neck opening back and forth
Beg at left front of neck opening to work a WS row.
Row 1 (WS) LC BO 2 sts pwise.
Now we will work the Bp patt fort and back for the next 4 rows like this:
If you now meet a purl st: Work *k1, sl1yo*.
If you now meet a knit st: Work *sl1yo, k1*.
Repeat *to* to 3 sts before m2 (the first marker, you will meet). P1, k1, Sl1yo. Sm, k1, p1.
Work again either *k1, sl1yo* or *sl1yo, k1* to 2 st before m1 (next marker you meet). P1, k1. Sm, sl1yo, k1, p1.
Work again either *k1, sl1yo* or *sl1yo, k1* to 3 sts before m4 (next marker on your way). P1, k1, sl1yo. Sm, k1, P1.
Work again either *k1, sl1yo* or *sl1yo, k1* to 2 st before m3. P1, k1. Sm, sl1yo, k1, p1.
Work again either *k1, sl1yo* or *sl1yo, k1* to last st. K1. Do not turn work: Slide work and work the WS once more from the beginning of

left neck opening. Now using the dark colour.
Row 2 (WS) DC K1.
If you meet a st without yarn over: *k1, brp1*.
If you meet a st with a yarn over: *brp1, k1*.
Repeat *to* to 3 sts before m 2 (the first marker, you will meet). P1, k1, brp1. Sm, k1, p1.
Work again either *k1, brp1* or *brp, k1* to 2 st before m1 (next marker you meet). P1, k1. Sm, brp1, k1, p1.
Work again either *k1, brp1* or *brp1, k1* to 3 sts before m4 (next marker on your way). P1, k1, brp1. Sm, k1, p1.
Work again in either *k1, brp1* or *brp1, k1* to 2 sts before m3. P1, k1. Sm, brp1, k1 p1.
Work again either *k1, brp1* or *brp1, k1* to 1 st before end. K1. Turn work.
Rows 3 (RS) LC BO 2 sts.
If you meet a knit st: Work *p1, sl1yo*.
If you meet a purl st: Work *sl1yo, p1*.
Repeat *to* to 3 sts before m 3 (the first marker, you will meet). K1, p1, Sl1yo. Sm, p1, k1.
Work again either *p1, sl1yo* or *sl1yo, p1* to 2 st before m4 (next marker you meet). K1, p1. Sm, sl1yo, p1, k1.
Work again either *p1, sl1yo* or *sl1yo, p1* to 3 sts before m1 (next marker on your way) K1, p1, sl1yo. Sm, p1, k1.
Work again either *p1, sl1yo* or *sl1yo, p1* to 2 sts before m2. K1, p1. Sm, sl1yo, p1, k1.
Work again either *p1, sl1yo* or *sl1yo, p1* to last st. K1.
Do not turn work. Slide work and work the RS once more, now with the dark colour.
Row 4 (RS) DC
If you meet a yarn over st: *brk1, p1*
If you meet a purl st: *p1, brk1*
Repeat *to* to 3 sts before m 3 (the first marker, you will meet). K1, p1, brk1. Sm, p1, k1.
Work again either *p1, brk1* or *brk1, p1* to 2 st before m4 (next marker you meet). K1, p1. Sm. brk1, p1, k1.
Work again either *p1, brk1* or *brk1, p1* to 3 sts before m1 (next marker on your way). K1, p1, brk1. Sm, p1, k1.
Work again either *p1, brk1* or *brk1, p1* 2 sts before m2. K1, p1. Sm, brk1, p1, k1.
Work again either *p1, brk1* or *brk1, p1* to last st. K1. Turn work.

Left shoulder shaping, short rows
We will now be working back and forth over the sleeve sts and step by step create a shoulder yoke.
In order to be able to work the bp patt forth an

back in short rows use a separate 4.5 mm (US 7) circular needle 40 cm / 16 inches or two dpn. Begin where the yarn is ready at left shoulder.
Row 1 (WS) LC using a separate 4.5 mm (US 7) circular needle or a dpn.
K1.
If you now meet a purl st: Work *k1, sl1yo*.
If you now meet a knit st: Work *sl1yo, k1*.
Repeat *to* to 3 sts before m 2. P1, k1, Sl1yo. Sm, k1, p1.
Work again either *k1, sl1yo* or *sl1yo, k1* to 2 st before m1. P1, k1. Sm. P3tog. WNt (WNt = Wrap No turn: Move yarn to front, slip 1 st , move yarn to back, slip st back to left needle). Do not turn. Slide.
Row 2 (WS) DC K1.
If you meet a st without yarn over: *k1, brp1*.
If you meet a st with a yarn over: *brp1, k1*.
Repeat *to* to 3 sts before m 2. P1, k1, brp1. Sm, k1, p1.
Work again either *k1, brp1* or *brp, k1* to 2 st before m1. P1, k1. Sm, sl1yo. W&t.

Rows 3 (RS) LC Brk1. Sm, p1, k1.
If you meet a knit st: Work *p1, sl1yo*.
If you meet a purl st: Work *sl1yo, p1*.
Repeat *to* to 2 sts before m2. K1, p1. Sm, K3tog. WNt. Do not turn. Slide work.

Row 4 (RS) DC Sl 1 st pwise. Sm, p1, k1.
If you meet a yarn over st: *brk1, p1*
If you meet a purl st: *p1, brk1*
Repeat *to* to 2 sts before m2. K1, p1. Sm, Sl1yo. W&t.
Turn work.
Row 5 (WS) LC Brk1. Sm, k1, p1.
If you meet a purl st: Work *k1, sl1yo*.
If you meet a knit st: Work *sl1yo, k1*.
Repeat *to* to 2 st before m1. P1, k1. Sm. P3tog. WNt. Do not turn. Slide.
Row 6 (WS) DC Sl1 st pwise. Sm, k1, p1.
If you meet a st without yarn over: *k1, brp1*.
If you meet a st with a yarn over: *brp1, k1*.
Repeat *to* to 2 st before m1. P1, k1. Sm, sl1yo. W&t.
Repeat row 3 - 6 until a w&t has been worked on last st at left front opening, or until last k3tog has been worked. PLEASE NOTE: The DC row is also to be worked before continuing to next chapter, but this time work last st on the row: k1....Turn.
Right shoulder shaping, short rows

Beginning where the yarn is, at left neck opening.
Row 1 (WS) LC K1. Sm. k1, p1.
If you now meet a purl st: Work *k1, sl1yo*.
If you are meet a knit st: Work *sl1yo, k1*.
Repeat *to* to 2 sts before m1. P1, k1. Sm, p1.
Repeat *to* to 3 sts before m4. P1, k1, sl1yo. Sm, k1, p1.
Repeat *to* to 2 sts before m3. P1, k1. Sm. P3tog. WNt. Do not turn. Slide work back and work the DC row from left neck opening.
Row 2 (WS) DC Sl1 pwise. Sm, k1, p1.
If you now meet a st without yarn over: *k1, brp1*.
If you now meet a st with a yarn over: *brp1, k1*.
Repeat *to* to 2 st before m1. P1, k1. Sm, p1.
Repeat *to* to 3 sts before m4. P1, k1, brp1. Sm, k1, p1. Repeat *to* to 2 sts before m3. P1, k1.
sl1yo. W&t.
Rows 3 (RS) LC
Brk1. Sm, p1, k1.
If you meet a knit st: Work *p1, sl1yo*.
If you meet a purl st: Work *sl1yo, p1*.
Repeat *to* to 2 sts before m4. K1, p1. Sm, K3tog. WNt. Do not turn. Slide work.
Row 4 (RS) DC Sl 1 st pwise. Sm, p1, k1.
If you meet a yarn over st: *brk1, p1*
If you meet a purl st: *p1, brk1*
Repeat *to* to 2 sts before m4. K1, p1. Sm, Sl1yo. W&t.
Row 5 (WS) LC Brk1. Sm, k1, p1.
If you now meet a purl st: Work *k1, sl1yo*.
If now meet a knit st: Work *sl1yo, k1*.
Repeat *to* to 2 st before m3. P1, k1. Sm. P3tog. WNt. Do not turn. Slide.
Row 6 (WS) DC Sl1 st pwise. Sm, k1, p1.
If you meet a st without yarn over: *k1, brp1*.
If you meet a st with a yarn over: *brp1, k1*.
Repeat *to* to 2 st before m3. P1, k1. Sm, sl1yo. W&t.
Repeat row 3 - 6 until a w&t has been worked on last st at right front opening, or until last p3tog has been worked. PLEASE NOTE: The DC row is also to be worked before continuing to next chapter, but this time work last st on the row: k1. Turn.
Last row (RS) Break yarn both colors. Slip sts to right hand needle without knitting until you reach m1.
Neckband

Change to needle 3.5 mm (US 4) circular needle 40 cm / 16 inches.
Setting up round (RS) DC Knit to end of row of left front. Remove m2. Pick up and knit 6 (7) 7 (7) sts before you reach front sts on spare needle. K sts from spare needle. Pick up and knit 6 (7) 7 (7) sts before you reach right front opening.
K all sts to m1. Remove m3 and 4 as you meet them. Now m1 is BOR (Beginning Of Round). If you have an uneven number of sts work a k2tog on last two sts.
Round 1 (RS) DC *K1, sl1yo* Rep *to* to end.
Round 2 (RS) DC *K1, sl1yo2* Rep *to* to end.
Round 3 (RS) LC (The LC from the beginning of the work, the lightest) *K1, brk1* Rep *to* to end.
Rep round 1 - 3 another 3 times.
Round 13 - 14 (RS) Repeat round 1 - 2.
Round 15 (RS) CC1 *K1, brk1,* Rep *to* to end.
Round 16 - 17 (RS) Repeat round 1 - 2.
Round 18 (RS) LC2 (The darker LC2 used in top of work) *K1, brk1,* Rep *to* to end.
Round 19 - 24 (RS) Repeat round 1 - 3 twice. Change to DC BO all sts.

Weave in all ends.
Close the little hole under the armhole.
Now the jumper is ready to show how handsome and wide shouldered the wearer is.

Human passion and desire are what threatens the pangolin of extinction. In our desire to ~~look good and perform well~~, we buy (useless) trad Chinese medicine. With this jumper I simply want the man to look strong and handsome on his own grounds.
Lisa Renner

#REDallaboutthescales

Scale up

Pangolin Child
Design Lisa Renner
Skill level 3
Photo pg 44 - 45

Design Lisa Renner
a- jumper with opening left raglan line...
#REDscaleup

Sizes
EU 86 (98) 110 (122)
UK 12-18 month (2-3) 4-5 (6-7) years

To fit bust
53 (55) 59 (63) cm
21 (21½) 23 (25) inches

Actual bust measurement (jumper)
64 (66) 70 (74) cm
25 (26) 27½ (29) inches

Length
38 (40) 44 (48) cm
13½ (15¾) 18 (20½) inches

Yarn A
Alpaca pure
100 % Finest Alpaca, 100 m / 109 yards per 100 gram
4 (5) 6 (7) x 100 g in Helix 3003 Salt & Pepper

Yarn B
Madelinetosh, Prairie
768 m / Yards 112 gram. 10 gram in 7 colours.

Needles
5 mm (US 8) and 6 mm (US 10) circular needle, 60 cm (24 inches).
5 mm (US 8) and 6 mm (US 10) dpn 5 stitch markers.

Gauge
In stocking stitch on 6 mm (US 10) needles and yarn A:
14 sts x 20 rows = 10 x 10 cm / 4 x 4 inches
Remember to check your gauge and adjust needle size accordingly.

Stitch patterns
Rib patt k1, p1.
Stocking stitches.

Special abbreviation
sk2p = slip one st, k2tog, pass slipped st over the knit tog. (2 sts dec)

Shown in size 86 / 12-18 month

Body, rib pattern
Work Italian cast on (optional) CO 90 (94) 102 (106) sts using 5 mm (US 8) circular needle and yarn A.
If Italian CO: Make a loop. *CO 1 st purlwise, CO 1 st k-wise* Repeat *-* till the total number of sts is 90 (94) 102 (106), do not count the first loop made. Make a loop to "lock" the sts.
Row 1 *K1, s1 purlwise wyif*. Repeat *-* till 2 sts before end (1 st and the loop from the beginning) K2tog.

Row 2 *S1 purlwise wyif, k1* Repeat *-* till 2 sts before end, k2tog tbl. If you prefer traditional cast on, just CO as usual, join for working in the round and work one more round than mentioned below.
Join for working in the round.
Round 1 - 7 (8) 9 10 Join the work for working in the round. Work p1, k1, rib patt. Make sure the work does not twist by gathering.

Body, stocking stitch
Round 1 Change to 6 mm (US 10) circular needle. Pm (m1). K 20 (21) 23 (24) sts.
Pm (m2). P1, k1, p1, k1, p1. These 5 sts will perform the tree trunk in which the pangolin is climbing.
K 20 (21) 23 (24) sts. Pm (m3). K 22 (23) 25 (26). Pm (m4). K the 23 (24) 26 (27) sts to the end.
Round 2 Sm. K to m2. Work 5 sts in moss st patt (that is k where there is p and p where there is k). K to end of round.

Shortrows
Row 1 Patt as set to 6 (7) 9 (10) sts after m4. W&t.
Row 2 P to 5 (6) 8 (9) sts after m4. W&t.
Row 3 K to 4 sts after the wrapped st. W&t.
Row 4 P to 4 sts after the wrapped st. W&t.
Row 5 - 8 Repeat row 3 and 4.
Row 9 K to the end of the row.

Continue in the round
Round 1 The holes that appear in the knitting from the w&t are now all disappeared except for the last w&t made. This one we are now closing.
K to m2. Work 5 sts moss st part. K to 1 st after m 3. Here you have the w&t that is still "open". Place RH needle in the loop below the wrap and then also in the st itself and knit st and loop tog. K to m4. Remove m4. K to end of round.
Continue in the round in patt as set. Work straight till work measures 25 (26) 29 (32) cm / 10 (10¼) 11 ½ (12 ½) inches measured from mid front. Whenever m2 is unnecessary it can be removed.

Armhole
Patt to 1 st before m 3. BO 2 sts loosely. K to 1 st before m1. BO 2 sts loosely.
The work has now been divided into front and back with 43 (47) 49 (51) sts on each side. Remove m1 and m3.
Leave sts on hold while working the sleeves.

Sleeve, rib
Work in Italian cast on (optional) CO 24 (26) 30 (34) sts using 5 mm (US 8) dpn and yarn A. Work sleeve rib as for the body.

Stoking stitch and increases
Round 1 Change to 6 mm (US 10) dpn. Pm (m1). K1, M1. K to last st. M1. K1. There are now 26 (28) 32 (36) sts.
Round 2 - 6 Knit.
Repeat round 1 - 6 another 5 (5) 6 (7) times. There are now 36 (38) 44 (50) sts. Continue straight without further increases to a total measurement of 21 (23) 27 (31) cm / 8 (9) 10½ (12) inches.

Armhole
Work to 1 st before m1. BO 2 sts loosely. There are now 34 (36) 42 (48) sts. Leave sts on hold while working the other sleeve the same way.

Joining all pieces
We will be working back and forth on circular needle in order to establish the opening in the left raglan line.
Row 1 (RS) Work front sts like this: Unravel the first stitch on the needle, so that you have a stitch and a loop. Work dbe1 over these two (2tog tbl). P1, M1 (for button band). Pm (m1). Patt to last front sts. P1. Pm (m2). Knit the sts of one sleeve onto the same needle. Pm (m3). Work back sts onto same needle: P1, k to last st, p1. Pm (m4). Knit the sts of the other sleeve onto the needle till 2 sts before end. Pm (m5). M1 (for button band), p1. Dbe1. All sts are now joined on the same needle. (increase 2 sts) There are now 156 (168) 184 (200) sts.
Row 2 (WS) Dbe1, p1, k1. Sm. P to 1 st before m4. K1, sm. P to m 3. Sm. K1. P to last st before m2. K1, sm. P1. Patt the remaining front sts to m1. Sm, k1, p1. Dbe1.
Now you have established a pattern where the st on each side of m2, m3 and m4 are worked in moss sts patt. The three sts in the beginning of each row are worked in dbe1, 2 moss sts.

Raglan decreases
Row 3 (RS) Dbe1, 2 moss sts. Sm. K2tog. Patt to 3 sts before m2. K2tog tbl. 1 moss st. Sm. 1 moss st, k2tog, k to 3 sts before m3. K2tog tbl, 1 moss st, sm, 1 moss st, k2tog. K to 3 sts before m4. K2tog tbl, 1 moss st, sm, 1 moss st,

k2tog. K to 2 sts before m5. K2tog tbl, sm, 2 moss st. Dbe1. (reduce 8 sts)
Row 4 (WS) Dbe1, 2 moss sts. Sm. P2tog. Patt to 3 sts before m4. P2tog. 1 moss st, sm, 1 moss st. P2tog. Patt to 3 sts before m3. P2tog.1 moss st, sm, 1 moss st. P2tog. Patt to 3 sts before m2. P2tog. 1 moss st, sm, 1 moss st. P2tog. Patt as set to 2 sts before m1. P2tog. Sm, 2 moss sts. Dbe1. (reduce 8 sts)

Row 5 - 6 Repeat rows 3 - 4
Row 7 (RS) Dbe1, work 2 moss sts. Sm. K2tog. Patt to 3 sts before m2. K2tog tbl. Work 1 moss st. Sm. Work 1 moss st, k2tog, k to 3 sts before m3. K2tog tbl, work 1 moss st, sm, work 1 moss st, k2tog. K to 3 sts before m4. K2tog tbl, 1 moss st, sm, 1 moss st, k2tog. K to 2 sts before m5. K2tog tbl, sm, 2 moss st. Dbe1. (reduce 8 sts)
Row 8 (WS) Dbe1, 2 moss sts. Patt as set to last 3 sts. Sm, 2 moss sts, Dbe1.
Repeat row 7 and 8 until you reach a number of 10 (10) 12 (14) sts in the sleeve. That is between m2 and m3 and between m4 and m5.
AT THE SAME TIME
Buttonholes
Row 9 (RS) Patt with the usual shaping to m5. 1 moss st, yo, 1 moss st. Dbe1.
Row 10 (WS) Dbe1, 1 moss st, k1, 1 moss st. Patt to end.
Row 11 (RS) Patt with the usual shaping to m5. 1 moss, p2tog. Dbe1.
Row 12 -16 Patt as set without buttonholes.
Row 17 Repeat Row 9 for buttonholes, but make sure there will be room for a buttonhole in the neckline as well (as mentioned in chapter "neckline row 3)
Shortrows
Row 1 (RS) Dbe1, 2 moss sts. Sm. K2tog. Patt to 3 sts before m2. K2tog tbl. 1 moss st. Sm. 1 moss st, k2tog, k to 3 sts before m3. K2tog tbl, 1 moss st, sm, 1 moss st, k2tog. K to 3 sts before m4. K2tog tbl, 1 moss st, sm, 1 moss st, k2tog. K 4 (4) 6 (8) sts. W&t.
Row 2 (WS) Dbe1, 2 moss sts. Patt as set to 5 (5) 7 (9) sts after m 3. W&t.
Row 3 (RS) Patt to 3 sts before m3. K2tog tbl, 1 moss st, sm, 1 moss st, k2tog. K to 3 sts before m4. K2tog tbl, 1 moss st, sm, 1 moss st, k2tog. K 2 (2) 4 (6) sts. W&t.
Row 4 (WS) Dbe1, 2 moss sts. Patt as set to 3 (3) (5) 7 sts after m 3. W&t.
Row 5 (RS) Patt to 3 sts before m3. K2tog tbl, 1

moss st, sm, 1 moss st, k2tog. K to 3 sts before m4. K2tog tbl, 1 moss st, sm, 1 moss st, k2tog. K to 2 sts before m5. K2tog tbl, sm, 2 moss sts. Dbe1. (reduce 5 sts).
Row 6 (WS) Dbe1, 2 moss sts. Patt as set to last 3 sts. Sm, 2 moss sts. Dbe1.

Neckband and last button hole
Row 1 (RS) In this row adjust if necessary by decreasing 1 st, to ensure you have an uneven number of sts.1 dbe. Work in rib patt: p1, k1 to m5. K1, yo, p1. Dbe1.
Row 2 (WS) 1dbe, k1, k1. Work rib patt as set to end. Dbe1.
Row 3 (RS) Dbe1. Work rib patt to m5. K1, p2tog. Dbe1.
Row 4 (WS) Dbe1. Work in rib patt to 2 sts before end. K1, dbe1, do turn, slip the dbe loop and stitch back to RH needle, 2tog tbl. Row 5 BO all sts Italian BO (optional)
https://youtu.be/-ORLkP5JTo0

Scales
Using 2.5mm (US 1) dpn Yarn B, col A
CO 13 sts. Leave an end of 25 cm / 10 inches for sewing.
Row 1 (WS) K all sts.
Row 2 (RS) Sl 1 st purlwise wyif, pull yarn tight. K4, sk2p, k5. (11 sts).
Row 3 (WS) and all following WS rows Sl 1 st purlwise wyif, pull yarn tight. K all sts.
Row 4 (RS) Sl 1 st purlwise wyif, pull yarn tight. K3, sk2p, k4. (9 sts).
Row 6 (RS) Sl 1 st purlwise wyif, pull yarn tight. K2, sk2p, k3. (7 sts).
Row 8 (RS) Sl 1 st purlwise wyif, pull yarn tight. K1, sk2p, k2. (5 sts).
Row 10 (RS) Sl 1 st purlwise wyif, pull yarn tight. Sk2p, k1. (3 sts).
Row 12 (RS) Sk2p. (1 sts). Pull thread through loop.
Work scales in approx. colours and numbers shown in diagram.
Additionally make three small scales in col 7.

Small scales
CO 11 sts.
and work as for Scales.

Pangolin face
CO 5 sts
Row 1 (WS) P4, k1.
Row 2 (RS) Sl 1 purlwise. K1, m1, k1, m1, k2.

(7sts).

Row 3 (WS) Sl 1 purlwise wyif. P to last st. K1

Row 4 (RS) Sl 1 purlwise wyif. K to end.

Row 5 - 9 Repeat row 3 - 4

Row 10 (RS) Sl 1 purlwise wyif. K1, m1. K to end. (8 sts) .

Row 11 (WS) Sl 1 purlwise wyif. P to last st. K1.

to a total of 10 (10) 12 (12) sts.

Continue in st st until face piece measures 5 cm / 1½ inches.

Increases

Row 1 (RS) Sl 1 purlwise. *M2* Repeat till last st. K1.

There are now 18 (18) 22 (22) sts.

Row 2 (WS) Sl 1 purlwise wyif. Now k to end.

Row 3 - 7 Repeat row 2.

Row 8 (WS) P2tog. BO till 2 sts before end. K2tog. BO.

Weaving in ends

Do not weave in the CO thread as we are using that for sewing the scales onto the jumper. Weaving in ends. Using the BO end, working from the WS:

Sew the thread down the center of the scale. Then sew back up again to where you began, as seen in photo 2.

Pangolin

Now comes the fun with sewing on the scales as shown in diagram. Sew the two sides. Leave

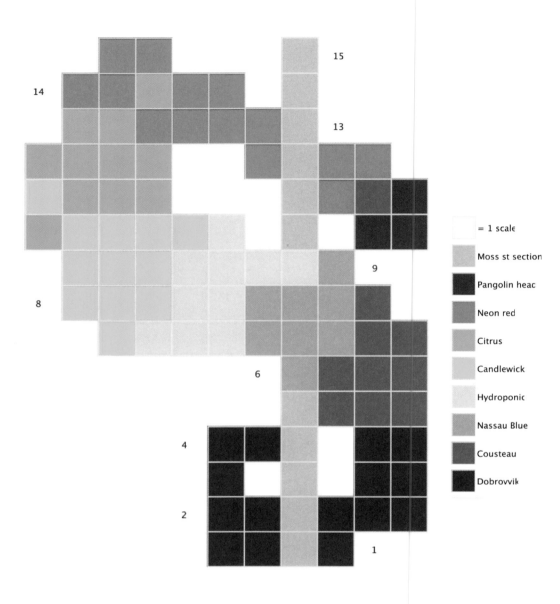

15

14

13

= 1 scale

Moss st section

Pangolin head

Neon red

Citrus

Candlewick

Hydroponic

Nassau Blue

Cousteau

Dobrovvik

9

8

6

4

2

1

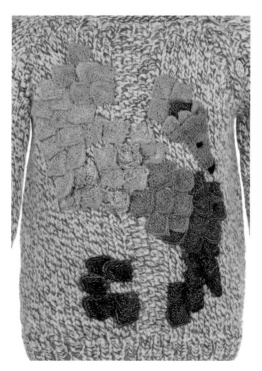

Great passion for investigating exciting textures with the finger is a favorite occupation of the little child. Here I want to give the child something that tickles as well the eye as the fingers when scouting for new adventures.

Lisa Renner

#REDscaleup

Ocean Footprint

———————

Coral Teen ~Adult
Design Lisa Renner
Skill level 3
photo pg 202 - 203 - 204 -205

Designer Lisa Renner
- a jumper with tattoo-inspired embroidery
In size 36 - 48
#REDoceanforest

Skill level 3
EU 36 (38) **40 (42) 44** (46) 48
UK 10 (12) **14 (16) 18** (20) (22)
To fit bust
86 (91) **96 (101) 106** (111) 116 cm
34 (36) **38 (40) 41½** (43½) 45½ inches
To fit waist
68 (73) **78 (83) 88** (93) 98 cm
27 (29) **30½ (32½) 34½** (36½) 38½ inches
Actual bust measurement (jumper) without stretching
74 (79) **84 (89) 94** (99) 104 cm
29 (31) **33 (35) 37** (39) 41 inches

Please note: The rib pattern has a lot of give. When wearing, the unstretched measurements (without overstretching the knitting) equal a "worn measurement":
Worn bust measurement (jumper)
88 (93) **98 (103) 108** (113) 118 cm
34½ (36½) **38½ (40½) 42½** (44½) 46½ inches
Length
54 (56) **59 (62) 65** (68) 71 cm
21½ (22) **23 (24) 25½** (27) 28 inches
Yarn
Kettle Yarn, Islington
Bluefaced Leicester wool and Silk, 400 m / 437 yds per 100 g
Col A 3 (3) **3 (4) 4** (4) 5 x 100 g
Col B 1 x 100 g (all sizes) Actually used
20 (20) **25 (25) 30** (30) 35 g
Needles
3.5 mm (US 4) circular needle, 60 cm / 24 inches.
3 mm (US 2) and 4 mm (US 6) circular needle, 80 cm / 32 inches.
3 mm (US 2) and 4 mm (US 6) doublepointed needles.
4 stitch markers.

Pattern 1:
Moss st rib pattern, for short: moss-st-rib.
RS: K8, work moss st 2.
WS: P8, work moss st 2.
(Moss stitch pattern:
Row 1 k1, p1.
Row 2 p1, k1.
Moss st pattern in general:
P1 over the k1 st. K1 over the p1 st.)
Pattern 2

Stocking sts

Gauge
In moss-st-rib on 4 mm (US 6) needle: 25 sts x 32 rows = 10 x 10 cm/4 x 4 inches without stretching.
To be able to measure accurately, make a swatch at least 6 sts and 4 rows bigger than the gauge indicates.

Swatch
CO 30
Row 1 (WS) P4, *k1, p1, p 8*. Rep *to* 6 sts before end, k1, p1, p4.
Row 2 (RS) K4, *p1, k1, k 8*. Rep *to* 6 sts before end, p1, k1, k4.
Repeat row 1 and 2 to a total measurement of 11 cm 4½. Measure centre 10 x10 cm.

Remember to check your gauge and adjust needle size accordingly.

Shown EU size 36 / UK size 10 in colours siren call (A), Sacred saffron (B).

Tip
This jumper is worked top-down. You may therefore adjust the length to suit your preferences exactly.
It is meant to have a snug fit. If your measurements are ½-1½ inches larger than a given size, you may very well knit that size. The yarn is soft and yielding and willing to wrap your body, and the jumper looks good with a tight fit.

Neckband
CO 156 (156) **160 (168) 168** (172) 176 sts using 3 mm (US 2) circular needle and col A. Make sure the CO is even and not too tight, as it will make a visible edge later. Join for working in the round.
Rounds 1 - 5 Knit. Although the CO is loose, the knitting should be firm.
Round 6 Purl.
Change to col B.
Rounds 7 - 10 Knit.
Round 11 K to last st, k1, work a w&t on the 1st st of the round. Break col B.

Body
The knitting has now been turned and you will be working the other way around. What was previously the RS will now be the WS.
We will now establish the moss-st-rib and place markers to indicate to raglan inrease.

Row 1 (RS) Change to 4 mm (US 6) circular needle and col A.
Pm (m1).
K4 (4) **5 (5) 5** (6) 7, *p1, k1, k8*. Repeat *-* 3 times (all sizes). P1, k1, k4 (4) **5 (5) 5** (6) 7. (These 40 (40) **42 (42) 42** (44) 46 sts make up the back of the jumper).
Pm (m2).
K 34 (34) **34 (38) 38** (38) 38 sts (This is the right shoulder).
Pm (m3).
K 42 (42) **43 (43) 43** (44) 45, p1, k1.
K 4 (4) **5 (5) 5** (6) 7. (This is the front, a total of 48 (48) **50 (50) 50** (52) 54 sts).
Pm (m4).
K 6 (6) **6 (8) 8** (8) 8, *p1, k1, k8*. Repeat *to* another 1 (1) **1 (2) 2** (2) 2 times.
Size 36 (38) 40: P1, k1, k6. (This is left shoulder, a total of 34 (34) **34 (38) 38** (38) 38 sts).

Round 2 (RS)
Back
K4 (4) **5 (5) 5** (6) 7, *k1, p1, k8*. Repeat *-* 3 times (all sizes).
K1, p1, k4 (4) **5 (5) 5** (6) 7.
Sm (m2).
Right sleeve
K 34 (34) **34 (38) 38** (38) 38 sts
Sm (m3).
Front
K 42 (42) **43 (43) 43** (44) 45, k1, p1.
K 4 (4) **5 (5) 5** (6) 7.
Sm (m4).
Left sleeve
K 6 (6) **6 (8) 8** (8) 8, *k1, p1, k8*. Repeat *to* another 1 (1) **1 (2) 2** (2) 2 times.
Size 36 (38) 40: K1, p1, k6.
The pattern has now been established.
PLEASE NOTE: There are areas of stocking sts, that is right sleeve and right part of front. And there are areas of moss-st-rib, that is back, left sleeve and left part of the front. Remember to work the two sts that perform the moss-st-rib in moss sts, that is always work purl over knit and knit over purl.

Shortrows and raglan increases
Row 1 (RS) Sm. K2, M1, work moss-st-rib as set to 2 sts before m2. M1, k2. Sm. K2, M1, k 4 (4) **5 (5) 5** (6) 6 sts, w&t. (3 sts increased)
Row 2 (WS) Work as set (purl and moss-st-rib) to 2 sts after m1, M1. Moss-st-rib 4 sts. W&t.

There are now 160 (160) **164 (172) 172** (176) 180 sts)
Row 3 (RS) Work to 2 sts after m1, M1. Work to 2 sts before m2, M1. K2. Sm. Work to 4 (4) **5 (5) 5** (6) 6 sts after last wrapped st. W&t. (2 sts increased to 162 (162) **166 (174) 174** (178) 182 sts).
Row 4 (WS) Work to 4 (4) **5 (5) 5** (6) 6 sts after last wrapped st. W&t.
Row 5 (RS) Work to 2 sts before m1. M1. K2. Sm. K2, M1. Work to 2 sts before m2, M1, k2. Sm. K2, M1. Work to 4 (4) **5 (5) 5** (6) 6 sts after last wrapped st. W&t. (4 sts increased to 166 (166) **170 (178) 178** (182) 186 sts)
Row 6 (WS) Work to 4 (4) **5 (5) 5** (6) 6 sts after last wrapped st. W&t.
Row 7 (RS) Work to 2 sts after m1. M1. Work to 2 sts before m2. M1. K2. Sm. Work to 4 (4) **5 (5) 5** (6) 6 sts after last wrapped st. W&t. (2 sts increased to 168 (168) **172 (180) 180** (184) 188 sts)
Row 8 (WS) Work to m1. Sl m1, W&t Turn.
The shortrows have now been completed.
There are
48 (48) **50 (50) 50** (52) 54 sts on the back
48 (48) **50 (50) 50** (52) 54 sts on the front
36 (36) **36 (40) 40** (40) 40 sts on each sleeve.

Body, working in the round
From now on, there will be raglan increases on every RS row.
On every other RS row there will be increases in both body and sleeves.
On the other RS rows there will be increases in the body only.
Round 1 (RS) K2, M1. Patt to 2 sts before m2, M1, k2. Sm. K2, M1. Patt to 2 sts before m3, M1, k2. Sm. K2, M1. Patt to 2 sts before m4, M1, k2. Sm. K2, M1. On your way to m1 you will meet a wraped st. Work these st like this:
Go below the wrap and pick up the first "leg" of the st, place it on the left needle and work a k2tog tbl on the st and loop. You will only do this on this very round in order to close a hole in the knitting that appeared from the working in short rows.
Patt to 2 sts before m1 M1, k1. This last st on the round is also a wraped st. Work it as the wrapped st before.
(8 sts increased to 176 (176) **180 (188) 188** (192) 196 sts)
Round 2 (RS) Work as set without increases

Round 3 (RS) Sm. K2, M1. Patt to 2 sts before m2, M1, k2. Patt to 2 sts after m3, M1. Patt to 2 sts before m4, M1, k2. Patt to m1. (4 sts increased to 180 (180) **184 (192) 192** (196) 200 sts)
Round 4 (RS) Work as set to m1.

Recap
These 4 rounds make up the raglan increases.
Round 1 has increases on both body and sleeves.
Round 3 has increases on the body only. Incorporate the increased sts into the patterns as establishes.
Please note: Always work the 2 sts closest to the markers in stocking st.

Repeat these 4 rounds a total of 14 (15) **16 (17) 18** (19) 20 times (168 (180) **192 (204) 216** (228) 240 sts increased)
There are 104 (108) **114 (118) 122** (128) 134 sts each on front and back - and 64 (66) **68 (74) 76** (78) 80 sts on each sleeve.
AT THE SAME TIME
The moss-st-rib on the body part will expand to left when the increased sts allows it. Expassion to the right: after 20 rounds working in the round establish a new moss st row to the right, in picture opposite. Continue to establish new moss rib columns after another 20 rounds throughout the body front.

Armhole divide
Round 1 Sm. Work back sts as follows:
Patt to m2.
Sl m2 to right needle. Work right sleeve sts up to m3 onto spare needle. Remove m3.
Work front sts in patt to m4.
Remove m4.
Work left sleeve sts up to m1 onto spare needle.

Body from armhole divide
Round 2 Sm. Patt to m2. Sm. Patt to m1.
Rounds 3 - 6 As round 2.

Decreases
Round 1 Sm. K1, k2tog tbl. Patt to 4 sts before m2. K2tog, k2. Sm. K2, k2tog tbl. Patt to 4 sts before m1. K2tog, k2. (4 sts decreased to 204 (212) **224 (232) 240** (252) 264 sts)
Rounds 2 - 5 Patt as set without decreases.

Repeat Rounds 1 - 5 a total of 6 times (24 sts decreased to 184 (192) **204 (212) 220** (232) 244 sts in the body)
Continue without shaping until work measures 21 (22) **23 (24) 25** (26) 27 cm / 8 (8½) **9 (9½) 10** (10) 10½ inches from armhole divide.

Increases

Round 1 Sm. Patt 2 sts, M1. Patt to 2 sts before m2. M1, patt 2 sts. Sm. Patt 2 sts, M1. Patt to 2 st before m1. M1, patt 2 sts. (4 sts increased to 188 (196) **208 (216) 224** (236) 248 sts)
Rounds 2 - 5 Patt as set without increases.
Repeat rounds 1 - 5 a total of 1 (2) **3 (4) 5** (6) 7 times. (4 (8) **12 (16) 20** (24) 28 sts increased to 188 (200) **216 (228) 240** (256) 272 sts).
PLEASE NOTE: The jumper may be lengthened at this point by working 1 - 3 cm / **½ - 1 inch** longer.
Note that this jumper is a light garment worked in fine silk/wool. It is not meant to be long and slouchy and cover your bottom like an Icelandic sweater.

Bottom edge

When body reaches a measurement from sleeve hole at 33 (34) **35 (36) 37** (38) 39 cm /13 (13½) 13¾ (14¼)14½(15) 15½ inches, work bottom edge.
Round 1 (RS) We will now be working another moss st rib pattern.
k3, work 2 sts moss st rib patt (k1, p1). Repeat *to* to m2. HOWEVER PLEASE NOTE: Make sure to begin the two sts in moss st rib patt right over the column of already established moss st rib patt as shown in diagram. It is illustrated by the turquoise part.
After m2 establish the new moss st patt over already established as shown in diagram. You might have a number of sts in the end that does not fit the end to get the patt to the end in your size. That is totally all right.

Right sleeve

Distribute 64 (66) **68 (74) 76** (78) 80 sts of one sleeve onto 4 mm dpns. Pm (m1) and work in the round in patt as set. Continue straight until sleeve measures 13 (14) **15 (16) 17** (18) 19 cm / 5 (5½) **6 (6½) 7** (7) 7½ inches from armhole divide.

Decreases

Round 1 P1, k2tog. Patt to last 3 sts. K2tog, p1. (2 sts decreased)
Work these decreases on every 8th (8th) **8th (7th) 8th** (8th) 8th round a total of 9 (8) **9 (12)**

11 (12) 13 times.
There are 46 (50) **50 (50) 54** (54) 54 sts.
Continue straight until sleeve measures approx 40 (42) **44 (46) 48** (50) 50 cm / 15¾ (16½) 17¼ (18) 19 (19¾) 19 ¾ inches from armhole divide.
PLEASE NOTE: If you plan to make many embroideries on right sleeve, it will will "take up" some of the length so you can work it 1 - 3 cm / ½ - 1 inch longer than what you want to end up with and longer that the left sleeve.

Bottom band

Rounds 1 - 6 (6 rounds) Change to 3 mm (US 2.5) dpns. K all sts.
Round 7 P all sts.
Rounds 8 - 12 (5 rounds) Change to col B. K all sts. BO all sts very loosely.

Left sleeve

Work as the first sleeve though this one has the moss st rib patt to be continued.

Finishing

Sew any remaining openings at the armholes closed. Weave in all ends.

Bottom bands, sleeves

For the bottom band, place the jumper, WS out, on an ironing board. Fold the bottom band WS to WS along the purl ridge. Pin the folded edge in place. Place a damp tea towel on top and carefully press the band down with the iron. Now sew the band to the WS using col A. Beginning at the last BO loop and the last st on the body, sew into a loop on the jumper and then into the corresponding BO loop on the edge. Make sure the edge remains straight all around and does not twist.

Neckband

NOTE: the neckband is folded towards the RS of jumper and sewed on from the RS.
Fold the neckband WS to WS to the front, folding it along the purl ridge. Pin and press it as described for the bottom bands. Now attach it using col A, sewing into a loop on the sweater and then into a BO loop on the band.
WHEN SEWING: Make sure to sew loosely to ensure that the edge remains as stretchy as the knitting. Check from time to time by pulling at the seam.

Steaming

It is not necessary to wash the jumper prior to wearing it. Simply place it on the ironing board and steam it. Hold the iron 2 cm / 1 inch above the knitting, press the steam button and enjoy watching the sts fall into place.

Embroidery

We have been inspired by our illustrator, Lea Hoffmanns, aquarelles for the staghorn coral (see below) as well as the Instagram site from Sina_Luxor.
Sina is the model wearing the jumper. She is a surfer and her life in the water shows beautifully in her instagram profile.
We have been working embroideries in chain sts and steam sts. The web is very inspiring. Find motives that make sense for you and work embroideries. I recommend they are a bit messy and not too neat and tidy, just like tatoos made over time.

Diagram body bottom edge

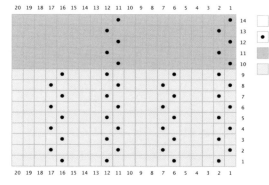

To show the bottom edge.

☐ knit
● purl
▨ Body pattern as worked from top
☐ Bottom edge moss st rib patt

Yarn shops to buy the R:E:D: book

iSologRegn~Garnbutikken i Middelfart~Algade 44~5500 Middelfart~Denmark
www.isologregn.dk
Kunstladen~Postvejen 29~6720 Fanø~Denmark
www.kunstladen.dk
Önling~Rosenkæret 14 2~2860 Søborg~Denmark~
www.oenling.com
Christel Seyfarth Art Knits ~ Hovedgaden 76-6720 Fanø, Nordby~Denmark
www.christel-seyfarth.dk
August & Minona~ Nansensgade 8~3740~Svaneke~Denmark
www.augustminona.dk
Cashmere Company~Skovløkkevej 11~6000 Kolding~Denmark
www.cashmerecompany.dk

Yarn Sponsors

Thank you to all our sponsors for believing in the idea and for your support in so many ways.

Madelinetosh~www.madelinetosh.com
Donation: Tosh merino Light | Prairie | Vintage yarn.
Isager~www.isagerstrik.dk
Donation: Alpaca 1 | Highland Wool | Alpaca 2 | Silkmohair
Zealana~www.zealana.com
Donation: Tui | Air | Kauri | Rimu
Önling~www.oenling.com
Donation: önling n. 1 | önling no 2
ITO~www.ito-yarn.com/en
Donation: Sesai |Rokku Tennen | Shio | Sherishin
Kettle Yarn Co.~www.kettleyarnco.co.uk
Donation: Islington
B C Garn~www.bcgarn.dk
Donation: Jaipur Silk Fino

Also Cooperation with
Manos del Uruguay
Yarn used: Silk Blend | Gloria
Handspund Hope
Yarn used: Handspun Hope
Purl Soho
Yarn used: Alpaca Pure | Understory | Shepherdess Alpaca | Season Alpaca

Abbreviations

beg = begin / beginning
BO = bind off
Brk1 = Knit together the st and its yarn over.
Brp1 = Purl together the st and its yarn over.

brk1^2 = knit together the stitch with its 2 yarn overs.
brp1^2 = purl together the stitch with its 2 yarn overs.
CO = cast on
col = Colour
dpn = double pointed needle
k = knit
kfb = knit into front and back, creating an extra knit st: K1 into front "leg" of the stitch, leaving the st on the needle; then k1 through the back "leg" of that same stitch. (1 st incr)
k2tog = knit 2 stitches together
K2tog tbl = knit 2 stitches together through the back loop
k3tog = knit 3 stitches together
k3tog tbl = knit 3 stitches together through the back loop
LH = Left hand
m = marker
m1 / m2 / m3 = marker 1 / marker 2 / marker 3
p = purl
p2tog = purl 2 stitches together
p2tog tbl = purl 2 stitches together through the back loop
p3tog = purl 3 stitches together
patt = pattern / work in pattern
pm = place a marker on the right needle
sl = slip 1 st from one needle to the other
sl1yo = with the yarn in front, slip the stitch purlwise and give it a yarn over.So the st becomes a st+a yarn over the needle.
sl1yo2 = with the yarn in front, slip the stitch with its yarn overs purlwise and give it a second yarn over.

sks = slip, knit, slip. Slip 1 st to RH needle, knit 1 st, pass sliped st over knitted st. (1 st dec)
sk2p = slip one st, k2tog, pass slipped st over the knit tog. (2 sts dec)
kss = Knit, slip, slip. Knit 1 st, slip knitted st back to LH needle, pass number two st over just knitted st. Slip st back to RH needle.
red = reduced
RH = Right hand
RS = Right side

M1 = make 1 (knit) stitch. With left needle, pick up the strand of yarn before next st from the front and knit it through the back of the loop. (1 st increased)
M1L = Make 1 (knit) stitch, Left leaning. Work as M1.
M1R = make 1 (knit) stitch Right leaning. With left needle, pick up the strand of yarn before next st from the back and knit the loop (1 st increased)
M1p = make 1 purl stitch. With left needle, pick up the strand of yarn before next stitch from the front and purl it through the back loop. (1 st increased)
M1pR = make 1 (purl) stitch, Right leaning. With left needle, pick up the strand of yarn before next st from the back and purl the loop on the "front leg"(1 st increased)
M1pL = make 1 (purl) stitch, Left leaning. Work as M1.
M2 = make 2 (knit) stitches. With left needle, pick up the strand of yarn between the stitches from the front and work (k1, k1 tbl) into that strand. (2 stitches increased)
M2p = make 2 purl stitches. With left needle, pick up the strand of yarn between the stitches from the front and work (p1, p1 tbl) into that strand. (2 stitches increased)
patt = Work in pattern as set.
pfb = purl into front and back, creating an extra purl st: P1 into front "leg" of the stitch, leaving the st on the needle; then p1 through the back "leg" of that same stitch. (1 st incr)
RH = Right Hand
sm = slip marker from left to right needle
st/sts = stitch / stitches
tbl = through the back loop
tog = together
Twy = Twist yarn.
WS = Wrong side
wyif = with the yarn held in front of the work
wyib = with the yarn held at the back of the work

2-dec-L = left leaning 2-stitch decrease: Sl1 kwise, k2tog, pass slipped st over. (2 sts decreased)

2-dec-R = right leaning 2-stitch decrease: K2tog, slip this st back to the left needle and pass 2nd st on left needle over the 1st one, slip the st back to the right needle. (2 sts decreased)

1 dbe = 1 double edge stitch
1 dbe at the end of a row: Using the left needle, pick up the strand of yarn just before the last st from the front and slip it to the right needle with yarn in front (without working it as a stitch). Slip the last stitch purlwise with the yarn still in front, turn.

1 dbe at the beginning of a row: Knit together the first stitch and the picked up strand through the back loop with yarn in back. Please note: Work the dbe very loosely.

w&t wyif = wrap and turn with yarn in front: Holding the yarn at the front of the work, slip the next stitch from the left to the right needle as if to purl. Bring the yarn to the back and slip that same stitch back onto the left needle, still without working the stitch. Turn work. The yarn will now be wrapped around the slipped stitch. A small hole will develop at the turning point, but this will close again after working over that spot.

w&t wyib = wrap and turn with yarn in back: Holding the yarn at the back of the work, slip the next stitch from the left to the right needle as if to purl. Bring the yarn to the front and slip that same stitch back onto the left needle, still without working the stitch. Turn work. The yarn will now be wrapped around the slipped stitch. A small hole will develop at the turning point, but this will close again after working over that spot.

db-dec-L = Left leaning double decrease: Sl1 kwise, sl1 kwise, k1, pass both slipped sts over the knitted one. (2 sts decreased)

db-dec-R = Right leaning double decrease: K1, slip this st back to the left needle and pass 2nd and 3rd st on left needle over the 1st one, slip the st back to the right needle. (2 sts decreased)

brk1 = Brioche knit. That is knit the stitch and its yarn over together.
brp1 = Brioche purl. That is purl the stitch and its yarn over together.

WNt (WNt = Wrap No turn: Move yarn to front, slip 1 st , move yarn to back, slip st back to left needle). Do not turn. Slide.

References ~ Sources Used for R:E:D:

General Information acquired and
Conservation organisations working with a variety of species.

These include:
African Wildlife Foundation, Animal Welfare Institute, ARC Centre for Excellence for Coaral Reef Studies, Amphibian Rescue and Conservation Project, Australian Wildlife Conservancy, ARCUS, Ape Alliance, Amphibia Web, Australian Marine CS, Animal Diversity Web, Animal Fact Guide
Born Free, Birdlife International
Critical Ecosystems partnership Fund, CITES, Conservation International, Critical Ecosystems Partnership Fund, Carnivore and Pangolin Conservation Program

Defenders of Wildlife
Encyclopedia of Life, Earth, Education for Nature, Edge of Existence, Education for Nature Vietnam, Europe Environment Agency
Flora and Fauna International, Facts about animals
Greenpeace, Great Barrier Reef Foundation, Great Bear Foundation, Good Company, Global Shapers Community
Humane Society International

IUCN, International Animal Rescue, International Fund for Animal Welfare, International Anti Poaching Foundation, International Reptile Conservation Foundation, International Rhino Foundation,
International Iguana Foundation,
Iguana Specialist Group IUCN

Jane Goodall's Roots & Shoots, Live Science, Lincoln Park Zoo
Minnesota Zoo, Marine Conservation Society, National Geographic, NOAA, Nature Australia, National Trust of Fiji, Oceana, One Kind Planet, Oceanic Society, Ocean Conservation

Save our Marine Life, San Diego Zoo, Sea Shepherd, Sea Turtle Conservancy, People for Ethical Treatment of Animals, Pew Charitable Trust, Perth Zoo, Sea Turtles 911, Save Vietnam's Wildlife, Smithsonian Institute, PASA, People for Pangolins, Pangolin Conservation, Panthera, Sea Turtle Conservancy, Save Pangolins, Sailors of the Sea, Save the Rhino, Save Vietnams Wildlife, Project Aware Foundation, Stanford University, Rainforest Alliance

The Conversation, The Guardian, The Hebridean Whale and Dolphin Trust, The Nature Conservancy, TRAFFIC, Tusk Trust, the Jane Goodall Institute, Taronga Conservation Society, the National Wildlife Federation, World Animal Foundation, Whale and Dolphin Conservation, World Animal Foundation, Wildlife Conservation Network
World Society for the Protection of Animals,
Young People's Trust for the Environment
World Association of Zoo's and Aquaria, WildAid, World Animal Protection, Zoological Society of London
World Conservation Society,
Sea Turtle Foundation
World Wildlife Fund,
Save the Whales,
SWIFFT,
SeaLife,
4Ocean
UNEP

African Wild Dog
IUCN SSC Canid Specialist Group
Claudio Sillero, Chair

Blue Whale
IUCN SSC Whale Specialist Group
Randall Reeves, Chair

Chimpanzee
The Jane Goodall Institute Global
Patrick Van Veen, Chair

Chinese Pangolin
IUCN SSC Pangolin Specialist Group

Green Turtle
IUCN SSC Marine Turtle Specialist Group
Dr Paolo Casale and Rod Mast, Co-Chairs
Morrison Mast

Numbat
IUCN SSC Australasian Marsupial and Monotreme Specialist Group
John Zichy-Woinarski, Chair
Charles Darwin University

Orange-Bellied Parrot
IUCN SSC Parrot Specialist Group
BirdLife International - Hannah Wheatley and Ian Burford
Stephen Garnett, Charles Darwin University

Greek Meadow Viper
IUCN SSC Viper Group
Jesus Sigala & Chris Jenkins, Co-Chairs
Edvard Mizsei, Jelka, and Ivan

Polar Bear
IUCN SSC Polar Bear Specialist Group
Dr Andrew Derocher
Professor University of Atlanta

Pygmy Three-Toed Sloth
IUCN SSC Anteater, Sloth and Armadillo Specialist Group
Mariella Superina, Chair
Diorene J. Smith

Staghorn Coral
IUCN SSC Coral Specialist Group
David Obura, Chair

The Goldsteiger Beetle
IUCN SSC Invertebrate Ladybird Specialist Group
Professor John Losey, Chair
Cornell University

Atlantic Bluefin Tuna
IUCN SSC Tuna and Billfish Specialist Group
Bruce Collette, Chair

Variable Harlequin Frog
IUCN SSC Amphibian Specialist Group
Phil Bishop, Chair
University of Otago

Fijian Crested Iguana
IUCN SSC Iguana Specialist Group
Tandora Grant, San Diego Zoo
Joseph Brown

Erect Crested Penguin
IUCN SSC Penguin Specialist Group
Paolo Garcia Borboroglu, Chair
Global Penguin Society (GPS)
Thomas Mattern NZ Penguin Research & Conservation, University of Otago

Javan Rhino
IUCN SSC Asian Rhino Specialist Group
International Rhino Foundation, Suzie Ellis

Thank you all

This book represents hundreds of people, websites and organizations working in design and conservation. It is through a collaborative effort from all over the world that we have been able to write this book.

We are honored and sincerely thank Dr Jane Goodall for her foreword.

IUCN Species Survival committees for each animal – as they verified facts for every animal.

Our friends and family, especially Mads, Steen and Mark, who have supported us in the process.

Director General of IUCN Grethel Aguilar Rojas, for writing the IUCN foreword.
Jens Christian R. Olsen, article.
Roberta Fairbairn, editing.
Christel Seyfarth Arts and Knitting.
Website - Birgitte Othel.

The Knitters:
Bente Grønfelt, Trine Dam,
Susan von Magius,
Susanne Ollendorf,
Pia Knudsen, Marianne Sundgaard Schultz, Aase Damhøj, Jytte Bestle,
Karen Antonsen, Inge R Husted,
Jette Sørensen, Gitte Agersbæk,
Silje Jordalen,
Annie Møller Hansen

The models:
Celina L. Kilar-Hamidi
Anushka M. Kilar-Hamidi,
Vigga Mørch Olesen
Karl Henrik Enderlein
Elva Luz Andresen
Angelina

Benyamin Høier
Ayan Nuur
Freja Isolde Darville
Anna K. Borg
Stig Kjartansson
Vivi Lu
Hannah Kloppenborg Jeppesen
Viggo Brodersen
Sina Lyxor

IFA Paris. International Fashion Academy.
DK Designskolen Kolding.

Kickstarter help
Lars von Magius, edit
Søren Andresen, music
Soleil Alien, campaign consulting
Angela Lutrel, Madelinetosh
Christel Seyfarth, Seyfarth art knits

Thanks to all the supporters from the Kickstarter campaign from
Chile, Belgium, Norway, France,
Switzerland, Sweden, United Kingdom,
Australia, United States and Denmark.

Unknown photographers...
And all animal photographers especially
Daisy Gilardini
Nikola Rahme
Johan van Zyl
www.wild-eye.co.za
Edvárd Mizsei
Chris Morecroft
Paul Rushworth
Phil Bishop
All worth following on Instagram for great photos

**R:E:D: authors decided that $10 from each book sold would be shared between
~Oceana~
~WildAid~
~the Jane Goodall Institute~
to assist them further in their conservation work for our Planet's species and the threats they face.**